SELECTED LETTERS OF
DAWN POWELL
1913–1965

SELECTED LETTERS OF

DAWN POWELL

1913–1965

Edited and
with an introduction by

TIM PAGE

HENRY HOLT·AND COMPANY   NEW YORK

Henry Holt and Company, LLC
Publishers since 1866
115 West 18th Street
New York, New York 10011

Henry Holt® is a registered trademark of
Henry Holt and Company, LLC.

Library of Congress Cataloging-in-Publication Data
Powell, Dawn.
[Correspondence. Selections]
Selected letters of Dawn Powell / edited and with an introduction
by Tim Page.—1st ed.
p.   cm.
Includes index.
ISBN 0-8050-5364-6 (hardcover: alk. paper)
1. Powell, Dawn, Correspondence.   2. Women authors, American—20th
century Correspondence.   I. Page, Tim, date.   II. Title.
PS3531.0936Z48   1999
813'.52—dc21   99-20423
[B]   CIP

First Edition 1999

Designed by Kate Nichols

Printed in the United States of America

1   3   5   7   9   10   8   6   4   2

IN MEMORIAM

Joseph Roebuck Gousha, Jr.
August 22, 1921–December 25, 1998

CONTENTS

INTRODUCTION

In addition to her novels, plays, diaries, short stories, and miscellaneous articles, Dawn Powell wrote hundreds—probably thousands—of letters. This volume contains only a small fraction of the correspondence that has been gathered to date; there is undoubtedly more yet to be found.

It is fitting that Powell's earliest surviving letter, from 1913, should have been written to her beloved aunt Orpha May Sherman Steinbrueck, who raised the young girl from her late childhood and was the first person to encourage her authorial ambitions. Powell's last letter, written as she lay dying more than fifty-two years later, was addressed to another cherished family member—her cousin John Franklin Sherman, known as Jack, who had himself been raised by "Auntie May" and who would soon become the guardian of Powell's only child, Joseph Roebuck Gousha, Jr.

In between these appropriately familial bookends, we find the record of a courageous, dramatic, and productive life. Here are letters from a jubilant small-town girl newly arrived in New York and letters from an exhausted sophisticate who could no longer afford her Manhattan apartment. Here are riotously witty send-ups of human frailties set back to back with humble and desperate pleas to anybody who might be able to help her disturbed son. Here are letters to eminent literary figures such as John Dos Passos and Edmund Wilson as well as postcards to a favored great-niece, a small child brokenhearted over the loss of her pet cat.

If Powell's diaries reflect the emotional turmoil that was such a large part of her psychological makeup, her letters tend to show off the witty persona she constructed as a shield. In theory, at least, Powell was confiding private thoughts when she wrote in her diary, but many of these letters were written specifically to *entertain*, in the manner of her best satires. And while she never compromised her distinct sensibility, Powell assumed different voices with different correspondents. With Dos Passos and Wilson, she was wry, analytical, and intellectually allusive. With Margaret De Silver, she was raucous and Petronian. With Jack Sherman, she was warmly supportive. With her sister Phyllis, she was practical, nostalgic, and tender.

In making my selection for this book, I have once again fallen back on the criterion I used to edit Powell's diaries: A letter had to have some sort of lasting interest—as autobiography, as social history, as literature, or as something uniquely other—to qualify for inclusion. Otherwise, this collection would have run to several volumes. While I have tried to represent each period of Powell's life as fully as possible, the fact remains that a great deal of material is available from the 1950s and 1960s, while very little survives from the late 1920s and 1930s, and this disparity is necessarily reflected within these pages.

Unfortunately, many of Powell's letters no longer exist. Carl Brandt, Jr., who now directs Powell's longtime literary agency, Brandt & Brandt, informed me that all confidential correspondence from authors is routinely destroyed, as a matter of professional courtesy. I respect and admire this policy, but only with some natural reservations; fortunately, Powell kept carbon copies of most of her later business letters.

Handwritten and purely personal letters have undoubtedly been tossed out blithely over the years, as homes have been broken up and old papers discarded. Until recently, Powell was hardly a celebrated figure, and her letters were unlikely to have been preserved as keepsakes. (How many grandchildren of Lake Erie College graduates would have recognized the name Dawn Powell twenty-five years ago?) One cannot escape the horrific vision of a line of plastic garbage bags, with some precious and incongruous literary cargo buried amid the debris, waiting to be taken to the dump. It is the stuff of nightmares.

We have yet, for example, to find a single letter from Powell to Esther Andrews, one of her closest friends, with whom she kept in touch mostly by mail for more than thirty years. And where are the letters Powell undoubtedly wrote to John Latouche, Ann Honeycutt, and other friends? During my research for *Dawn Powell: A Biography*, various people, the late Loren MacIver and the late Charles Norman among them, showed me carefully preserved collections of Powelliana. How I wish I had photocopied those documents then and there, for they have proved impossible to track down since.

One especially painful memory is of the day I spent talking vaguely with Eleanor Farnham, Powell's closest friend from Lake Erie College, who was then living in a nursing home in East Cleveland. Farnham had recently suffered a debilitating stroke, and her memory was impaired, but she grew delightfully animated as she told me of the boxes of Powell letters that she kept in her apartment. She knew just where to find them, she said, and they were wonderful. A social worker watched us sympathetically and sadly shook her head. It turned out that Farnham no longer had an apartment, only a tiny room down the hall. When she died, in 1995, Farnham left no papers.

Some other disappointments: A scant four letters to Coburn Gilman seem to have survived, though he was one of Powell's closest confidants for many years. Powell wrote almost every day to her son, Jojo, during his many years of medical confinement, but only a single letter has been preserved. And I continue to suspect that Powell and the playwright John Howard Lawson, who probably had an affair in the late 1920s, reached some mutual agreement to destroy any and all evidence of their friendship. No correspondence whatsoever has turned up on either side, even though we know they wrote to each other regularly for several years, and both of them habitually saved their letters.

Still, nearly a thousand letters have come down to us, and for that we must be grateful. Far and away the largest repository of correspondence is to be found in the Dawn Powell Collection in the Rare Books and Manuscripts Library at Columbia University. Here are the exuberant early letters to Charlotte Johnson, a Lake Erie friend, that were returned to Powell shortly before Johnson's death; dozens of carbon copies of her communications with publishers and agents; letters to family members such as Orpha May Steinbrueck and Mabel Powell Pocock, who predeceased the author; and more than a hundred letters to Joseph Gousha, Sr., Powell's husband. Most recently, Carol Cook Warstler, Powell's niece, has donated the letters addressed to her mother, Phyllis Powell Cook.

Other substantial holdings may be found in the Dos Passos Collection at the University of Virginia; in the Yale Collection of American Literature, Beinecke Rare Books and Manuscripts Library, Yale University; in the Scribner's Archive at Princeton University Library; in the Newberry Library in Chicago; in the Boston Public Library; and in the private collections of Jack Sherman, Michael Stearns, Honoria Murphy Donnelly, Bryan Robertson, and Jacqueline Miller Rice, among others. It seems likely that Rice, who was Powell's original executor, still possesses a good deal of material that should rightly be at Columbia.

Selected Letters of Dawn Powell is unapologetically a reading edition. As was the case with the diaries, I decided early on that some careful editing was both prudent and necessary. Powell wrote her letters very quickly, and I don't believe she would have wanted her occasional redundancies, grammatical lapses, and misspellings published to the world. And so, without adding my own sense to the text or changing any of Powell's meanings, I have gently tightened and corrected some of these letters. (Obvious and intentional mis-spellings such as "yestiddy" and "biyes and goils" have, of course, been retained.)

I have placed the undated letters as closely as I can, through postmarks or context. And I have attempted to identify most of the figures in this book, with the exception of those who are truly well known (Dwight D. Eisenhower, say, or Ernest Hemingway) and those many people who are simply mentioned in passing. Still, Powell's life was unusually well populated, and some of her many friends and acquaintances have proved impossible to track down; I would be grateful to hear from anyone with information about people I have been forced to pass over. On rare occasions, I have obscured names and circumstances as a courtesy to persons still living. I hope the reader will take my word for it that nothing essential has been eliminated.

Although this collection is not intended as a biography, I have fashioned an extended time line that may prove useful to those unfamiliar with the basic facts of the author's life. And then it will be time, once again, to let Dawn Powell speak for herself.

Tim Page
April 11, 1999
Washington, D.C.

DAWN POWELL:

A TIME LINE

1896   Born in family home at 53 West North Street, Mount Gilead, Ohio, on November 28, the second of three daughters of Roy King Powell and Hattie Sherman Powell. (In later life, Dawn Powell will usually give her birth year as 1897, but primary sources support the earlier date.)

1899   A sister, Phyllis Powell, later Cook, born on December 19, 1899. (Older sister Mabel Powell, later Pocock, was born on July 11, 1895.)

1903   Death in December of Hattie Sherman Powell, Dawn's mother, after complications from an abortion. The three daughters will be passed from relative to relative throughout central Ohio for the next several years.

1907   Roy Powell marries his second wife, Sabra Stearns, who proves an abusive stepmother. The family moves to North Olmsted, Ohio.

1910   After Sabra Powell burns some of Dawn Powell's early stories and drawings, the thirteen-year-old runs away to stay with her aunt Orpha May Sherman Steinbrueck in Shelby, Ohio. Steinbrueck lives opposite the Shelby Junction train station and serves meals to hungry travelers. Over the next four years, Powell will hear hundreds of train whistles every day; they will later become an important and recurring motif in her fiction.

1914   Powell graduates from Shelby High School, where she has distinguished herself with high marks and served as editor of the yearbook. In the fall, she matriculates at Lake Erie College in Painesville, Ohio, as a member of the class of 1918.

1915   Powell publishes her first stories in the *Lake Erie Record*. In the
        summer, she works at the Shore Club, a resort near the college, where
        she keeps her first surviving diary.

1916   Powell and a classmate, Charlotte Johnson, write a short play, *I Am
        Looking For a Lady,* and perform it at Lake Erie College. Powell
        spends the summer as a counselor at Camp Caho in Michigan.

1917   Appointed editor of *Lake Erie Record*.

1918   Powell graduates from Lake Erie College and spends the summer in
        Pomfret, Connecticut, writing and farming. On September 2, she
        moves to New York City, where she will live for the rest of her life. Her
        first address is 353 West Eighty-fifth Street.

1919   Powell is a prolific freelance writer for a wide variety of magazines and
        newspapers, all the while holding a succession of day jobs on the side.
        She appears as an extra in a silent film entitled *Footlights and Shadows*,
        starring Olive Thomas.

1920   Meets Joseph Roebuck Gousha, a poet and music critic from Pitts-
        burgh, while working for Near East Relief. The two are married on
        November 20 at Manhattan's Church of the Transfiguration, better
        known as the Little Church Around the Corner.

1921   A mentally impaired son, Joseph Roebuck, Jr., known as Jojo, is born
        to the Goushas on August 21.

1922   Powell begins her first novel, *Whither,* a thinly disguised autobio-
        graphical work about her early days in New York. *Whither* is written
        mostly in Central Park and in the Children's Room of the New York
        Public Library. Joseph Gousha enters advertising, a field in which he
        will become highly successful.

1923   Louise Lee begins her long association with the Gousha family, serving
        as Jojo's caretaker and general housekeeper. A family tradition of rent-
        ing a summer beach cottage in Mount Sinai, Long Island, is established.

1924   In the fall, the Gousha family moves from the Upper West Side to 46
        West Ninth Street in Greenwich Village. Powell will live in this neigh-
        borhood for the next forty-one years. *Whither* is finished and accepted
        by the Boston firm of Small, Maynard.

1925   *Whither* is published and almost immediately disavowed by its author,
        who will always insist that *She Walks in Beauty* (written this year but
        published in 1928) was her first novel. She begins work on *The Bride's
        House.* Jojo's disturbances are increasingly blatant and alarming. Dis-
        agreements with Joseph Gousha spark a temporary separation in July,
        when Powell spends several weeks in Ohio. She likely begins a clan-
        destine affair with playwright John Howard Lawson sometime late in
        the year.

1926   *The Bride's House* completed, leaving Powell with two novels in search
        of a publisher. Roy King Powell dies of a stroke in July. Powell's social
        circle now includes, among others, Charles Norman, Eugene Jolas,
        Jacques LeClercq, Esther Andrews, Canby Chambers, and—more
        tangentially—Ernest Hemingway and Theodore Dreiser. Powell begins
        writing book reviews for the *New York Evening Post*, to which news-
        paper she will continue to contribute occasional pieces for more than
        three decades to come.

1927   Powell spends most of the year working on plays and short stories and
        trying to find a publisher for *She Walks in Beauty* and *The Bride's
        House*. Both books are finally accepted by Brentano's. The peak of her
        involvement with John Howard Lawson probably occurs during this
        period.

1928   The family now lives at 106 Perry Street in Greenwich Village. *She
        Walks in Beauty* is published, generating mostly favorable reviews and
        decent sales. In the fall, Powell writes her first version of her play *The
        Party*, which will eventually be produced by the Group Theatre as *Big
        Night*. She begins work on *Dance Night*. Close friendships with John
        Dos Passos and Coburn Gilman have been established by this time.

1929   Publication of *The Bride's House*. Jojo is now confined in hospitals
        or special schools most of the time. Powell becomes friends with
        Margaret Burnham De Silver, a wealthy woman whose own daughter is
        schizophrenic and housed in the same New Jersey institution as Jojo.
        Late in the year, Powell has what is diagnosed as a "heart attack"; it is
        in fact more probably the first blatant symptom of a mysterious tumor
        that will torment her for the next twenty years.

1930   Completion and publication, by Farrar & Rinehart, of *Dance Night*.
        Poor sales and uncomprehending reviews send Powell into a depres-
        sion. She visits Bermuda with Margaret De Silver, and her friend-
        ship with Coburn Gilman deepens. Powell earns some of her living
        collaborating with the nightclub comedian Dwight Fiske on bawdy
        song-stories.

1931   Powell begins work on two of her finest books, *Come Back to Sorrento*
        and what she calls the "Lila" novel, which will ultimately evolve into
        Turn, Magic Wheel. She also begins keeping a detailed diary, a habit
        she will observe until her death. An early play, *Walking down Broad-
        way,* is transformed, almost unrecognizably, into the film *Hello, Sister!*,
        directed by Erich von Stroheim. In October, the family moves to 9 East
        Tenth Street, which will be home for eleven years.

1932   *Come Back to Sorrento* is published by Farrar & Rinehart, which insists
        upon bringing it out under the name *The Tenth Moon*, much to the

author's disgust. Powell spends the beginning of the year in California, working as a scriptwriter. *Big Night* is selected for production by the Group Theatre. Work is begun on *The Story of a Country Boy*.

1933   The Group Theatre production of *Big Night* opens in January to savage reviews, and closes four days after its premiere. Powell immediately sets to work on another play, *Jig-Saw*. Completion of *The Story of a Country Boy*. Friendship with Edmund Wilson begins; friendship with John Dos Passos deepens. Final break with John Howard Lawson.

1934   Powell "changes her style" and sets to work in earnest on *Turn, Magic Wheel*, her first great satire. *Jig-Saw* is produced by the Theatre Guild, enjoys a modest success, and is published in book form by Farrar & Rinehart. Publication of *The Story of a Country Boy*, which is immediately sold to Warner Brothers and First National Pictures for $12,500—far and away the largest single sum Powell ever earned during her lifetime. (A poor film, *Men of Iron*, released in 1935, was the eventual result.)

1935   Powell continues work on *Turn, Magic Wheel*, to the confusion of her editors at Farrar & Rinehart. She travels to Havana and Key West with Joseph Gousha and their old friend Harry Lissfelt.

1936   Publication of *Turn, Magic Wheel* to excellent reviews. In the fall, Powell heads west once again to Hollywood, where she earns a huge salary and is promised more. Nevertheless, she detests writing for the movies and returns to New York.

1937   At work on *The Happy Island*.

1938   Publication of *The Happy Island*, which is deemed a critical and financial failure, leading to a break with Farrar & Rinehart.

1939   Powell signs with the publishing house of Charles Scribner's Sons, where her new editor is Max Perkins. She works on a radio program for WOR—*Music and Manners*, featuring Ann Honeycutt—and briefly and unhappily serves as book critic for *Mademoiselle*. She draws increasingly close to longtime acquaintances Gerald and Sara Murphy.

1940   Publication of *Angels on Toast* (Scribner's). Early sketches are laid out for *A Time to Be Born*.

1941   America enters World War II. Powell begins making notes for *My Home Is Far Away* and suffers a disastrous involvement with a revue entitled *The Lady Comes Across*.

1942   *The Lady Comes Across* closes in January after two New York performances. Publication of *A Time to Be Born* (Scribner's), which becomes one of Powell's biggest-selling books. The Goushas move to 35 East Ninth Street.

1943 Powell progresses slowly on *My Home Is Far Away* and begins work on *The Locusts Have No King*, originally envisioned as "The Destroyers." She spends a great deal of time at the Hotel Lafayette, her favorite hangout.

1944 Publication of *My Home Is Far Away*, the most directly autobiographical of Powell's novels. She immediately begins a sequel, to be called *Marcia*, but never gets beyond 100 draft pages.

1945 End of World War II and beginning of the Atomic Age. Powell will incorporate her horrified fascination with the Bikini Atoll bomb tests into the final scene of *The Locusts Have No King*, now planned as a deliberately "postwar" novel.

1946 Powell drives to Florida with Margaret De Silver. In the fall, she undergoes a hysterectomy.

1947 Max Perkins dies suddenly in June. Powell attends to Dos Passos after his disastrous automobile accident in September. In November, she is attacked and badly beaten by Jojo and must be hospitalized for four weeks as a result.

1948 Publication of *The Locusts Have No King*. Visit to Haiti and Key West in March.

1949 Powell's long-mysterious teratoma is diagnosed and removed in April. During a monthlong residency at the MacDowell Colony in June, she is stymied by her poor progress on *Marcia*. Death of Mabel Powell Pocock in October.

1950 Powell suffers from writer's block. With financial support from Margaret De Silver, she moves in October to Paris, where she lives at the Hôtel Lutetia on the Left Bank.

1951 Powell returns to New York in January after making a brief stop in London. Her writer's block persists. She quarrels with Scribner's over its lack of interest in publishing a collection of her short stories; Rosalind Baker Wilson then brings her to Houghton Mifflin, which promises to rush the anthology into print.

1952 Publication of *Sunday, Monday and Always*, a collection of Powell's short stories, by Houghton Mifflin.

1953 The demolition of Powell's beloved Hotel Lafayette helps provide her with the impetus to complete *The Wicked Pavilion*.

1954 In October, for the first and only time in her life, Powell has a book, *The Wicked Pavilion*, on the *New York Times* best-seller list. It remains there for exactly one week. Jojo is confined more or less permanently to the New York State hospital system after Louise Lee has a stroke and is forced to leave the Gousha household.

1955 Residency at Yaddo and beginning of friendship with Jacqueline Miller

Rice. Much time is spent drinking at the Cedar Bar in the company of Abstract Expressionist painters.

1956   Powell rewrites *Angels on Toast* as a pulp paperback miniature for Fawcett Gold Medal Books, which publishes it as *A Man's Affair*. She writes a television script based on a tiny story of hers called "You Should Have Brought Your Mink."

1957   Powell completes her novel *A Cage for Lovers*, after a long series of rewrites demanded by the publisher. The book published in October with little fanfare or appreciation. Joseph Gousha is informed that he will be "retired" from his advertising job as of January 1958.

1958   Gousha's retirement leads to the complete collapse of the family funds. By October, Gousha and Powell are forced to vacate their apartment at 35 East Ninth Street and commence a series of residencies in hotel rooms and sublets. Powell does a great deal of writing piecework and searches halfheartedly for a day job. At the suggestion of Malcolm Cowley, Viking Press contracts with Powell for a novel that will eventually become *The Golden Spur*.

1959   Margaret De Silver rescues Powell and Gousha from their poverty with a generous trust fund. Powell continues working on *The Golden Spur*.

1960   Powell and Gousha move to 43 Fifth Avenue. Powell spends much of the spring at Yaddo, where she becomes close friends with Hannah Green. Joseph Gousha is diagnosed with rectal cancer in May; his pain subsides after a long and dangerous operation, but he never recovers his health. Powell returns to Lake Erie College to receive an honorary doctorate.

1961   Powell is hospitalized for anemia; the doctors urge the removal of a mysterious growth, but she refuses. Much of Powell's year is spent taking care of her dying husband.

1962   Death of Joseph Gousha, Sr., on February 14. Death of Margaret De Silver on June 1. Serious illness of Powell's sister Phyllis. Powell's last novel, *The Golden Spur,* is published by Viking Press in October. Edmund Wilson's "Dawn Powell: Greenwich Village in the Fifties," published in *The New Yorker*, constitutes far and away the most serious critical study of Powell's work written during her lifetime.

1963   *The Golden Spur* is shortlisted for the National Book Award but ultimately is passed over. Powell works with Lee Adams and Charles Strouse on a prospective musical-comedy version of the same novel. She moves to 95 Christopher Street. *Vogue* publishes "What Are You Doing in My Dreams?" and Powell begins work on *Summer Rose*, a new novel that she will not live to complete.

1964   Powell travels to Lake Erie College to lecture and meet with the students. She receives the Marjorie Peabody Waite Award for lifelong achievement in literature from the American Academy of Arts and Letters. In August, she is diagnosed with cancer. The *Golden Spur* musical project is put on indefinite hold due to Powell's health.

1965 Powell completes "Staten Island, I Love You!," an article for *Esquire* that will be the last piece of hers published during her lifetime. She attempts to work on *Summer Rose*. In and out of hospitals for much of the year, she dies of cancer on November 14 in St. Luke's Hospital, the same week as the first great New York blackout.

SELECTED LETTERS OF
DAWN POWELL
1913–1965

COUNTRY GIRL

1913–1918

TO ORPHA MAY STEINBRUECK*

Shelby [Ohio]
[ca. September 1913]

My dear Mrs. Steinbrueck—

I take my pen in hand to write this letter. Did you arrive safely in Middletown? If you aren't there please let us know.

Saturday a lady came for dinner and I was alone. She remarked that I seemed awfully young to be running a boardinghouse. I told her I *was* awfully young. Sunday we attended Sunday school, as is our custom (since the Sunday before), and there were only 20 there. Children were not allowed at Sunday school or picture shows owing to diphtheria. While some are getting over it, others are getting it. All through Irishtown and down Broadway are several cases. If any more are reported the schools will be closed. We had dinner at Mary's and we had *Some Feed*.

Today we washed. Mrs. Lovett had a bad burn on her wrist and so, recalling my recent lesson in Emergencies, I bathed it in a warm weak solution of alcohol and bandaged it. Tonight I bathed it again and Gretchen† and I put on

---

*Orpha May Sherman Steinbrueck (1869–1959), Powell's beloved "Auntie May," raised her from her early teens. Although family members doubt that she ever actually operated a boardinghouse, she did serve regular hot meals to travelers passing through the Shelby Junction train station, which was right opposite her house at 121 North Broadway in Shelby.

†Gretchen Steinbrueck, later Quiggle (1892–1936), was Orpha May Steinbrueck's only daughter, with whom Powell had a difficult relationship.

a poultice of flour and soda. I felt awfully important and tried to force some confession from her that she had a horrible bruise on her back or a fractured skull and I was real disappointed when she, after careful thought, said that the only thing she could think of just then was a mosquito bite on her leg which didn't trouble her much—in fact she managed to walk without limping. It was discouraging for a willing would-be nurse like myself and put quite a damper on my exuberant spirits. But I soon recovered and attacked my Virgil, mounted on my faithful pony, as it were.

Mr. Vanatta came tonight and I made him an apology of a sausage and a teentsy weentsy bitsy cup of coffee. Gretchen is absorbed in a study of what her father's uncle's brother's wife would be to her.

This noon the doorbell rang and I admitted a fat, red-whiskered, red-haired gentleman with a figure which would make Juno green with envy, who asked if Mrs. May—or *Orphy*—was in. I said no and without a word he marched off the porch and back to the station. I was telling Grandma[*] about it when it occurred to me that it might have been Emmet Singer and Grandma said that was exactly who it was.

Saturday I decided to make a miniature peach meringue pie. When Benjamin[†] caught a glimpse of me, suspiciously decorated with flour, he gave a low cry of pain and staggered away. He didn't return until late that night when I heard him weeping and gnashing his teeth out in the chicken yard. Don't be worried about the chickens. Even if I do forget to feed them, they appreciate it all the more when I *do*. Well may Benjamin have run at the prospect of a peach meringue concoction. When I set it on the table that noon, with a serenely unconscious look, Gretchen looked at it long and tenderly. Then, with a deep, deep sigh and a murmur about life being too sweet, she sorted out the peaches and avoided the crust. Ever tactful, she observed that they were certainly fine peaches. However, I swallowed it, crust and all, without flinching. While I prefer a natural death, still, violent ones are sometimes more satisfactory.

How are Effie and Charlie[‡] and what does Jack do to pass away the time? Study, I suppose. We had a class meeting tonight and I was elected editor in chief of the High School paper, with Bill Hood business manager. I have to appoint my associate editors before tomorrow night. They will be sporting editor, literary editor, society editor, comic editor, junior editor, sophomore editor, freshman editor and assistant editor in chief. I tried to get Cortez Fish for this

---

[*]Julia Miller Sherman, later Hostetter (1844–1922), Powell's maternal grandmother, did in fact run a boardinghouse in downtown Shelby for some years before remarrying at the age of seventy.
[†]Benjamin was the Steinbrueck family dog.
[‡]Charles Miller was a cousin of Powell's on her mother's side and would become a successful businessman in Johnstown, Pennsylvania. His wife was known as Effie, and together they had a son, John. The hero in Powell's 1934 novel, *The Story of a Country Boy,* is modeled in part upon Miller.

last exalted position but he wouldn't do it. However he treated me on it, which was agreeable to all concerned. Our first number will be out October 15. The paper is about half as big as this sheet and has a gray cardboard back with the name and a design by Hobart Winbigler in red on it, since scarlet and gray are the high school colors. I have to write from about 3000 to 5000 words for it, aside from arranging the articles and correcting them. But it will be fun for me and I need the experience if I intend to pursue a journalistic career.

I haven't heard from Phyllis* or Mabel† for a long time. I don't know what has come over Mabel. Well I must get to my agriculture and outline corn. I'll bet that you never knew that corn was endogenous as well as monocotyledon and belonged to the order of Gramineae. I don't know about this last "order," but I think it's some Elks' Lodge or Eagles. Another thing which it is well for one to bear in mind is that the blossoms are *monoecious*. Who would have believed it of a simple-minded, innocent corn blossom! Well I must close. Gretchen and I send our love to the folks. Bring them home with you.

Lovingly,
Dawnie

P.S. I'm sick of sassage, doggone it.

(COLLECTION TIM PAGE)

TO MABEL POWELL

Lake Erie College
Painesville, Ohio
[ca. September 1914]

Dear Mabel—

This isn't going to be a real letter and I thought twice before yielding to the temptation to squander a stamp, finally decided it was worth the expense.‡

I have been to see the superintendant of the Conservatory who says I may use any of the pianos when they're not in use.§ I won't have much time but since practicing is more of a recreation than a burden, I think I'll dock a little time off my outdoor periods. So please send my classical music—those new classic pieces I got—and my exercise book, especially the big gray Czerny

---

*Phyllis Powell, later Cook (1899–1985), was Dawn's beloved younger sister and one of her closest companions throughout her life.
†Mabel Powell, later Pocock (1895–1949), was Dawn's older sister, with whom she had an early rivalry that was eventually patched up.
‡Powell's early letters to her older sister were often somewhat "cheeky," and this one is no exception.
§Powell became an expert amateur pianist and was later especially fond of improvising jazz and ragtime.

book. I think I have a number of classics there, which I just bought recently, if you will remember, and which I would be ever so grateful to have you send.

Congratulations on the diamond! *Good work.* I had a letter from a friend of mine today which verged onto politics. I think I'll use your recipe, though, for obtaining the diamond. How do you work it? Give Edgar my love.*

Wish I could hear the player piano. Was so tickled to see Auntie May. The girls all say she is perfectly fascinating and that I am just like her (ahem!) in acting out all I say with my hands and eyes. Well, well.

Tell her to come again. Oh yes, when she went out past the choir, with those two girls, a huge murmur went down the line—"Who is it? Oh yes, Dawnie's aunt—etc., etc." They gave me the once over with an admiring look, as if *I* were responsible for her.

Auntie May and I went calling across the hall afterward and tell her that that Pittsburgh girl, Cornelia Wolfe,† in the brown dress, when the other girl was sick, said to me afterward, reproachfully, "Why Dawnie, you never told us you had such a wonderful aunt!" And Bea scolded me for the same thing. So you see she made a big hit. You or Gretchen would do the same I'm sure and Phyllis would be "*it*." Little sisters always are. So you must all come up sometime—Sunday or Monday or Saturday afternoon for over Sunday.

Yesterday the Y.W.‡ cabinet and two other freshmen and myself went on a bat,§ and had a lovely time. Everybody is asking me how I happened to be invited, as I was only one not on the Y.W. cabinet or Board. Search me.

I am appointed to get leaders for the freshman prayer meetings and have to start out with leading it myself. *Good-bye!*

Send the music as quick as quick can be. Love to Grandma and Phyllis and everybody—

Yours—
Dawnie

Don't forget now—immediately. I think it's up at Grandma's.

(COLLECTION TIM PAGE)

*Mabel Powell would marry Edgar Pocock (1891–1986), a successful Cleveland businessman, in 1916. They would have three children: Keith Pocock (1917–1980), who would become a cocktail pianist; Dawn Pocock, later Jarvis (1921–1981), a dealer in antiques; and Dorothy Pocock, later Chapman (born 1923), affectionately known as Tootsie, a mother of five children.
†Cornelia Wolfe (1896–1983) was one of Powell's best friends at Lake Erie and in her early New York years. A published poet, she would go on to a successful career at the Walt Disney Studios in Los Angeles.
‡Powell is probably referring here to the YWCA, which was a highly influential entity on the Lake Erie campus.
§The "bat" was a Lake Erie tradition, a sort of longish picnic that sometimes was rather formal and sometimes consisted of nothing more than, in the words of Powell's classmate Eleanor Farnham, "a little frying pan and a little food."

Painesville, Ohio
Dec. 11, 1914

My dear Grandma:

You can imagine how surprised I was just now to learn from Auntie May's letter that I had a Grandpa born all of a sudden.* In fact I had to sit down and be fanned. But of course I am very glad, since my grandparents are rather scarce—your being the only one up till the fatal hour Wednesday.

How and where did you do it? I know the why of it—"Eventually—why not now?" Wasn't that it? Where will you live, and will you have a honeymoon, as you should?

I was so surprised that I had to sit right down and write to you. I knew you'd beat us all to the altar stunt, even though Mabel was pretty close to it, and Gretchen, too.

I can't recall Mr. Hostetter, but I remember hearing you speak of him lots of times. You may tell him that I thoroughly approve of your marriage, and feel sure that you will be very happy, happier than you have ever been—at least I hope so. I expect to find you looking at least twenty years younger than usual when I come home Xmas. I always did think it was a shame for a good-looking Grandma like you to stay single. I have only time for a little note—I wish you both as happy a married life as you deserve and many more years to enjoy it in.

With loads of love to you and "Grandpa,"

As ever,
Dawnie

(COLLECTION TIM PAGE)

Painesville
January 17 [1915]

Dear Auntie May—

I am writing this while drying my hair. Bea† has gone to Sunday school so I felt free to use her fountain pen. You see I lost mine and have advertised extensively but I guess my baby Waterman is gone forever. I certainly miss it because now I have to copy all of my lecture notes.

Did you get my laundry? I sent it Friday night. And do you think you can do the white dress all right? The Painesville alumni give a big dance in town for

---

*Powell's seventy-year-old grandmother had just married Jesse Hostetter in Shelby. She immediately closed her boardinghouse.
†Beatrice Detling (1897–1973) was Powell's first roommate at Lake Erie College.

the benefit of the new gym and we all dare go with our crew from 7:30 till 11 without chaperones. I am going with Alley Rogers.* There will be loads of Reserve men out and it is a formal ball so it will be dress suits. All the girls are rushing into Cleveland for new dresses. However I'm not, having just paid out a couple hundred for a new ball-dress a few days ago. . . .

My little theme on "Phyllis Takes Care of the Children" is in the *Record* this month. I'd send it to you only it's so punk and besides it costs a quarter. . . .

The girls have organized not a fraternity nor a sorority but a frarority with Greek letters. Our main pastime is playing cards and reading the light airy fiction of [R. W.] Chambers and Elinor Glyn (including *Little Comrade* and *The Man and the Moment*).† I wish I had something to read today. Send me some old *Smart Sets*‡ in my laundry sometime. Say, the suitcase didn't cost any more than to send a box and I didn't have to bother about string and wrapping paper, and have such a time lugging it uptown to the post office. It just cost me 16 cents.

We are going to have tea in Betty's room today. Oh yes, speaking of tea, either tea or coffee is very nice to send in one's laundry. Don't you think so? . . .

I think I'll close now as some kids have just come in to talk about the dance. I have my program all made out and have a pretty good one. I learned a new foxtrot and a new lu lu fado which is the only dance now. . . .

> Love to everybody,
> Dawnie

(COLLECTION TIM PAGE)

TO ORPHA MAY STEINBRUECK

> *Painesville*
> *[ca. January 25, 1915]*

Dear Auntie May:

Received the doughnuts today and your letter with the root of evil in it yesterday. . . . I felt a little bit uneasy about keeping the money. I understand that you got it by robbing the city treasury or something like that. (Don't look in the envelope to see if I've sent it back; rest assured that I soon overcame my scruples.) Thanks ever so much for both. As for the doughnuts, we stuck them in the oven all right and found your predictions quite verified. The oven could hold some more right now.

---

*Possibly Rhoda C. Rogers, who attended Lake Erie College from 1914 to 1916.
†Chambers and Glyn, largely forgotten today, were once enormously popular writers; Glyn's novels—especially *Three Weeks*—were considered downright shocking.
‡Orpha May Steinbrueck habitually passed on her copies of this daring and iconoclastic magazine (edited by H. L. Mencken and George Jean Nathan) to her young niece.

I am over in the library now two hours a day and two hours in the office. The change began with the new semester and I am very much pleased as the library work so far hasn't been at all hard. Dorothy McFee (the curly-haired girl who sat at the end of our table the time you were here) had been working four hours a day in the library and had a nervous breakdown so she only does two hours a day now, and since there is so much work Miss Dunlap* asked me how I'd like it and I jumped at the chance. It is a large library, much larger than the Shelby library, and I am rather interested in the work anyhow, especially since I discovered that the two librarians get more than any other faculty here. I am beginning to see that I am learning as much of real value to me out of the outside work I do as I learn from most of my studies. (I have just finished midyear exams you know and am beginning to realize how little I know.)

Ruth Miller, the other girl who works in the office with me, fainted in the bathtub last night and they had to crawl over the top of the partition to get her out. She's been sick ever since. Moral—Never take a bath!

Well I certainly had a fine time in Cleveland. Betty's house and family are all so lovely and showed me such a good time. The beauty of the thing was that it didn't cost me a cent! Betty's father did the kind philanthropist act. I was very stunning (oh yes) in Rhoda's skirt, Hester McLauren's silk waist, Charlotte Johnson's hat and Rhoda's coat. We left Saturday noon on the streetcar and I got seasick on the way in and had a pleasant seance on the back platform where I exposed to the conductor my luncheon—also my breakfast and half of the night before's dinner. . . .

We went to Taylor's† where I looked with much concern at dinner dresses—"a simple dinner gown," I said, with the most harmless intentions in the world as I only had about 75¢. It would have had to be a very, very simple one I'm thinking at that sum, since the ones the lady showed me ranged from the reasonable price of $38.50 on up. One is inclined to be unreasonable even when the price is that reasonable.

Feb. 13 is the freshman Valentine Ball when we give a short little play written by Eleanor Farnham (one of the girls)‡ called *Fresh Girl*. It is the cutest thing. Bea and I are History—it's a sort of morality play, you know, like Every-student—and Bea and I are tied together. She is the Papacy and I'm the Empire. We always have to write papers on those two factions in history.

The Drama Club gives Mice and Men and I was called down for a tryout

---

*Helen Brewer Dunlap was associated with Lake Erie College from 1909 through 1950, serving as secretary to the president, treasurer, and registrar, among other duties.
†William Taylor Son and Company was one of Cleveland's leading department stores from 1870 until it went out of business in 1963.
‡Eleanor Farnham (1896–1995) was a fellow classmate who would remain a friend of Powell's for life. One of the first woman reporters to be hired by the *Cleveland Plain Dealer*, she later ran a successful publicity agency.

tonight. I thought I'd have to be the Angry Mob perhaps and have lines something like this:

Angry Mob (outside)—Kill him! Drown him!
Angry Mob (still outside)—Kill him! Drown him! Murder him!
Angry Mob (still outside)—Kill! Murder! Drown! Behead! Excommunicate!

I was thwarted in my design to be the Angry Mob. I am a foundling instead
and also a chorus. Whenever the play says—*Chorus:* We-like-school!—why,
I'm the chorus. It's a part which some have spurned but I am delighted with it,
and in this way I get in free. Oh yes, you might come up and see it. It will
probably be in two or three weeks. See your little niece featured in this new
sensation which has set all Europe aflame and caused the present war. . . .

Well, I must close now. Tell Mabel I will write her sooner or later—
probably later—and give Phyllis my love and tell her to write. . . .

Love—
Dawnie

(COLLECTION TIM PAGE)

TO ORPHA MAY STEINBRUECK

Lake Erie Female Cemetery
Grave 85
[ca. March 1915]

My dear Auntie May—
[. . .] The sophomore play was a musical comedy—*Follies of 1917*—the
love story of Argentina, the Spanish beauty, and Mr. Will E. Trippett, the dancing master. They brought in several of the new dances, a number of songs from
Chin Chin and also some original choruses. A real musical comedy, don't you
know? Tomorrow is a Colonial Tea and I wish you were here for it. Everyone is
to wear colonial costume—there will be a minuet and more dancing, then a
progressive dinner party and more dancing. It will probably be awfully pretty
and that's why I'd like to have you here. See?
Well, well, methinks it was in our last effusion that we bubbled so joyously
over our labors in the library. Well let me narrate to you that there comes a time
in the career of every library when it has to be cleaned, when each book must
be spanked, brushed, and put back on the shelf which you have just scrubbed
with a damp dirty rag—and woe be unto the youthful assistant when the library
reaches this time! It has fallen to my lot to clean the history shelves and also the
fiction. I started in on the fiction hoping to occasionally take a start into some
of R. W. Chambers's novels or perchance one of Elinor Glyn's.

Not so! The light summer fiction which weighted the shelves of the fiction room began with Ibsen and led right up through Tolstoi, Björnsky, Harriet Beecher Stowe, Ruskin, Scott, etc. etc., with an occasional frivolous little volume by Ben Jonson. I hastened over fiction and started in on history, getting much satisfaction by dropping *Adam's Medieval Civilization* on the floor and kicking it a little, and by using the twelve volumes of Cambridge's Middle Ages as a footstool, as revenge for the many unhappy hours they had caused me in doing history readings. So you see my enthusiasm over the happy, blithesome life of the librarian has waned. I wax exceeding wroth over it in fact. But thank goodness I'm almost through the history shelves now so I won't have to spend much more time cleaning.

Yesterday Ad Wise* and I sallied forth to get some air and exercise so we merrily marched through the Grove clad in disreputable garments, Ad with a sack of Lorna Doones and me with a stale Cosmo.

"We are wandering through rich black loam," I gurgled.

"Mud!" snorted Ad, pulling off considerable mud from her shoe with a hairpin.

"Let's go over to that meadow and gambol on the green," I suggested as we came to a barbed wire fence which separates the Grove from somebody's farm. It really wasn't green—but it would spoil the effect to say gambol on the brown.

Well Ad just naturally laid herself flat down in the mud and rolled under the lowest barbed wire which was about two inches from the ground. Being more majestic as to figure, I hesitated.

"Gwan an' do it!" urged Ad, from the other side of the fence. I still hesitated. Then I remembered that Ad had the Lorna Doones and I was *sehr hungrig*. I fell into the snare. I lay flat and rolled—but not far. Malicious barbs grabbed on to my skirt and middy. The rich clay loam smelt funny when one was close to it. There I was, while Ad chortled in fiendish glee. I wiggled to the left and then to the right but still I was in the clutches of the deadly barbs. Then Ad felt just a little more charitable and extracted me, not without much mirth on her part and indignation on mine. Finally my anger cooled and we wandered on.

"You did it with a better grace but I do it more natural," quoth I, thus explaining the matter to my own satisfaction. We decided to return by another route and came upon seven small boys whom we invited to play with us, with exceeding good humor. Our generous offer met with derisive hoots and also hunks of the rich clay loam aforementioned, which they threw quite freely.

---

*Adelaide Wise (born 1896) spent only one year at Lake Erie College and has proved impossible to track further.

"*Nice* little girls wouldn't do that," we remarked severely as we retreated to the Grove. Here we found the spot where the summer plays are given. We promptly improvised a little tragedy of Shakespearesque properties which we called *The Spaniard What Blighted My Life*. Ad was fearless Ferdinand and I was Carlotti Bologni. My song was "The Curse of an Aching Heart" while Fearless Ferd warbled in a passionate lyric soprano, "I ain't the guy!" We received tremendous applause from each other and kisses from the small boys on the far side of the bridge.

When I reached my room I discovered that my conscientious roomie had cleaned the room and that my muddy boots were making large inroads on the clean floor, much to the indignation of Bea. Here I ditched the garments—which had been somewhat soiled by rolling in the mud—and dressed for dinner in heavy silence. Heavy silence is very becoming to me. You never saw me in it, did you?

We had a fire drill Friday night. Fire drills are funny things. You haven't been sleeping well for several nights—but on this night you feel that you are going to sing a little snoring solo as soon as you hit the pillow. You compose yourself and have just opened your mouth for a preliminary yawn when a hoarse sound grates on your ear.

"Goody! It's a fire drill," rejoices your enthusiastic, ever-joyous roomie, slipping out of bed.

"Blank the fire drill!" you snarl, giving the covers a toss and leaping out.

"Why Dawn Powell, you ought to be ashamed, etc. etc. etc," reproves your roomie, tripping out. You seize your bathrobe—you remember distinctly that you left it on the foot of the bed—but after all it is the couch cover you seize, not the elusive bathrobe. Where in the blank is it? You frantically search through your sanctuary while girlish hooves are pattering down the stairs, and the fire marshal is demanding where Dawn Powell is. In despair, you search on the cot again. You discover that you really did leave your bathrobe there after all, under the couch cover. So you hurry down the steps. Gray-haired faculty is revealed in silk pajamas and curl papers. The girl you thought your Queen of Queens trips down the stairs in a dirty kimono and a promiscuously cold-creamed nose. After you reach the bottom of the stairs you are placidly informed by the fire marshal that you may go back now—that we cleared the building in less than two minutes! Of course that is some consolation, to know that you have got out very quick, and that your fire marshal loves you for it. *But!* Why in the name of common sense can't they have their fire drills in the daytime instead of at night? Why? Why?

Well—I think I am in beyond my depth. I never could get a fountain pen to last out over ten pages.

Four weeks from Wednesday and then it's Good-bye, girls, I'm through! I may not be home then, however, as we have something framed up. But it will be sometime along then.

Can't you come up for the midyear play—Mar. 23—come up Tues. a.m. or maybe Mon. The play is Tuesday night. Oh yes and then you could stay over till Wednesday and I could go right home with you. See? Wish you could bring Phyllis or Mabel. Love to everybody.

Love,

Dawn

(COLLECTION TIM PAGE)

TO ORPHA MAY STEINBRUECK

[The Shore Club,

*Painesville, Ohio]**

August 14 or 15 [1915]

(take your choice)

Dear Auntie May—

The plot thickens. Your baby niece is developing a calloused index finger from pushing No. 30 thread through an eyeless needle, while the finished garments roll off by the hundreds. Well, to be frank, they haven't rolled off yet but they're gathering momentum for the Grand Roll. You see, I'm sewing all my fall duds. I've made—well, I've finished one corset cover and got a blue-flowered organdy dinner or afternoon dress nearly finished. Then I'm going to get some blue denim for a sailor suit and maybe some crepe nightgowns and also send away for a blue serge Lombard suit—an absolute necessity for this winter. I've only made $15 in tips and don't expect to make more than $30 at the most, although last year the girls made $50 and $60. High cost of loving hangs crepe on the tipper's purse. Of course we get our $50 straight. I need a suit as much as I ever needed anything but I thought at first I'd get a suit and nothing else but all these other things I *must* have so I'll have to do without a winter coat and suit another season someway.

But my request is this—Janette is fixing over my white embroidered dress with net, etc.—and we want to know if there isn't a quarter yard or yard or so more that you could send P.D.Q. to fix it over. I can't get a new evening dress so we want this one made over as nice as possible. See? So hunt around and see if you can't find a little speck of it to send—and right away, too. . . .

---

*The Shore Club was a resort on Lake Erie where Powell was employed during the summer of 1915. It was during this summer that she kept her first surviving extended diary.

Business is dull as ever. I can swim just a little bit without wings now.* Just discovered it yesterday. . . .

Love to everybody,

Dawn

(COLLECTION TIM PAGE)

TO ORPHA MAY STEINBRUECK

[Lake Erie College]
Wednesday night
[ca. October 1915]

Dear Auntie May:—

Just a scrawl before I go to bed. I've been so desperately busy I haven't had time to do more than eat. Speaking of eating reminds me to tell you that I now sit at the Dean's table. She is new and awfully nice. The only thing is that we occupy such an exalted position that none of us dares eat half enough for fear of seeming—er—hungry. . . .

I am a literary editor of the *Lake Erie Record* now†—was elected the other night. But that isn't the worst. I—in connection with Eleanor Farnham and Dort Worthington‡—just got out our anonymous paper, "The Sheet." We worked hard on it and it was rare—a scream from start to finish with some real live news mixed in. We printed it at midnight on a Duplicator Eleanor had. No one knew who printed it or where it came from. It was just like throwing a bomb. Everyone's wild over it and we've cleared $5 already and everyone wants extra copies. Dort and I both have been accused of editing it but we absolutely deny it. They say our stuff sticks out like an apple on a pear tree. . . .

I am working on some stunts for our class play—and working like the devil. Zoology is lots of fun (!!!!!)—we cut up snakes and frogs and cats and dogs and examine their innards and dissect tomato worms and cockroaches. . . .

By the way, Dort told Miss Small§ about "The Sheet" and she thinks it is a fine stunt. So we aren't running any risks. Don't expect to be able to write many letters till I get myself straightened out. . . .

Lovingly,

Dawn

(COLLECTION TIM PAGE)

*Powell would always remain an apprehensive swimmer.
†The *Lake Erie Record* was a quarterly literary and political publication sponsored by Lake Erie College. Several of Powell's first surviving stories and articles are preserved in its pages.
‡Dorothy Worthington was one of Powell's classmates at Lake Erie College. She never graduated and has proved impossible to track further.
§Vivian Small (1875–1946) served as the autocratic president of Lake Erie College from 1909 to 1941. It was Small who ensured Powell's presence at the college, even going so far as to lend her some money for tuition.

TO ORPHA MAY STEINBRUECK

[Lake Erie College
November 1, 1915]

Dear Auntie May:

I am desolated when I think of how long I have neglected you. I have started billions of letters to you but somehow never finished them. Was so glad to hear from you and grateful for the stamps. And more than tickled at the idea of your coming out soon because—must I confess it?—I have many a pang of homesickitude these days. Never worked harder in my life. I am carrying eighteen hours a week—including laboratory work—of classes, and doing five hours a day in the office. I am supposed to do most of my studying during office hours. Did I tell you about my office work? In the secretary's office, they have hired a new assistant for the work that I used to do and other things too so that all of us girls have to do office work in the general office, which includes answering doorbell, telephone, putting out mail, ringing bells for class and running a rotten, rheumatic old hydraulic elevator. If you know anything about hydraulic elevators you know it takes some muscle to run them and it nearly kills my back. At least I think that it's from running the elevator because several of the other girls have backaches, too. Or it may be the aftereffects of carrying heavy trays this summer. At any rate the hours I spend yanking that old cable are not hours of unmitigated bliss.

I told you I was literary editor of the *Record*, didn't I? I have a story in this number—"Susie Fails to Flout the Enemy." The Drama Club is going to present Oscar Wilde's play *The Importance of Being Earnest* on December 11th. I hope you can come up to see it as I have one of the main parts. I am Miss Prism—an old-maid character part.

Last night we had our big Halloween masquerade. Miss Heineman dressed as a clown and I was her dog—in pajamas and excelsior for fur, and a whisk-broom tail. We gave a program in which Miss H. made a speech on the intelligence of dogs and I did tricks. Rather strenuous exercise. Afterward everyone went uptown to see the municipal parade and march with the suffragists. The parade was miles long—full of Charlie Chaplins, Gold Dust Twins, witches and ghosts. There were thousands of people out.

Did I tell you that Miss Scranton gave me a really stunning—almost new— white taffeta dress, which a friend of hers had sent to her? It fits perfectly and is stylish, too.

Maude Adams is attracting several of the girls this week and Elsie Cook and I are going to give a show or something and go in to see her in *The Little Minister* Saturday night. . . .*

---

*Powell regularly wrote and performed "shows" with fellow students to earn money for carfare into Cleveland, where she would then attend a concert or play. Maude Adams (1872–1953) was a distinguished, somewhat boyish actress who made a specialty of the plays of J. M. Barrie, especially *Peter Pan*.

How is Phyllis? I wish she could come up and see me? And Mabel, too. We have Wednesday to Friday for Thanksgiving vacation. Wouldn't it be a nice birthday present for you to invite me to Cleveland for dinner?

Have to leave now! Good-bye.

Love to everybody,
Dawn

(COLLECTION TIM PAGE)

TO ORPHA MAY STEINBRUECK AND
GRETCHEN STEINBRUECK

[Painesville, Ohio
November 28, 1915]
Nineteenth year of Our Existence

Dear relations—

Nineteen is an ugly year, isn't it?* Now eighteen was a round, even, complete year. I felt young and debutantish. But nineteen! It's just a sort of gathering up of all the tag-ends of all the teens—a Review of Reviews—nothing new or thrilling about nineteen. You're just a year older, that's all. Now twenty will be different. It will be something new. I will feel that I've begun to grow up—perhaps even to grow old. I will be at the threshold of that tantalizingly elusive age of the "future." So after all nineteen has its compensations in that it anticipates twenty.

This morning Eleanor Farnham and Sara McLoud gave a breakfast for me and we had toast, pecan rolls, cocoa—and Fried Eggs! When I'm twenty years old, I'm going to live on fried eggs—or else omelettes. Or perhaps poached eggs with an occasional coddled one. . . .

I had the best time at Eleanor's. I never imagined one could do so much in 48 hours. We went in Wednesday noon, and at 3 o'clock, six of Eleanor's girlfriends dropped in for tea—which wasn't tea at all, but cocoa. One of them was Nella Masters, whose picture was in the papers a few days ago as having had $1500 worth of jewelry stolen. I felt quite thrilled to have such a celebrity to talk to. . . .

Dort Worthington is living the simple life now, after getting a genuine Italian something-or-other violin made in 1790 for two or three hundred dollars. Imagine!

With love—
Dawn

Will see you all in three weeks from Wednesday.

(COLLECTION TIM PAGE)

*This letter was written on Powell's nineteenth birthday.

TO ORPHA MAY STEINBRUECK

[Painesville, Ohio]
March 19, 1916

Dear Auntie May:—

I'm mad at you. You didn't come up to see your very own niece cover herself with greasepaint and glory—and hear that the play of which she was coauthor was unanimously conceded to be the best ever given here, etc.* Therefore I'm mad. However, I'll send you a program to show that I am amenable to pleas for forgiveness.

I am reading Barrie's little playlet *Rosalind* and it's the cleverest thing. If you have time get it and read it—it's in the book *Half-Hour Plays* by J. M. Barrie. It throws an encouraging light on middle age. In the same book is *The Twelve-Pound Look* which I believe Ethel Barrymore played in.

Please send me my blue straw sailor hat which I bought last year in the thick of a snowstorm, and which now reposes on the shelf in the closet upstairs, so I believe. The reason I ask for it is that I am going to spend a day or so in Cleveland and unless a straw hat is lodged firmly on my raven locks I'm likely to squander all my substance on a feathery creation for which I have no earthly need or wish—only that Cleveland milliner shops in the spring—and in the fall—have an irresistible fascination for my thin little purse and make it much thinner than is necessary. So—to prevent such a sad, sad blow—better send my hat and I shan't be so likely to be led astray.

Howard Tait writes me of attaining much notoriety—but no money—by having a poem or two of his accepted by the *Cleveland Plain Dealer*.

Well—I am too tired after the rather hard strain of writing, directing, coaching—etc.—a play. Charlotte† and I, as soon as the curtain fell on the last act, chased up to her room, hung up a busy sign and, being quite human, crowed and patted ourselves on the backs with what might appear disgusting egotism. But we felt we had a perfect right to crow after working like sin for ages.

Love—
Dawn

(COLLECTION TIM PAGE)

---

*This would have been *I Am Looking For a Lady*, written with classmate Charlotte Johnson and presented in the spring of 1916.
†Charlotte Johnson (1896–1958) was one of Powell's closest friends at Lake Erie. Her fortunate decision, much later, to return some of Powell's old letters to their author allows us a privileged glimpse into Powell's first years in New York. Johnson eventually moved to New York herself, and the letters stopped. Much of Johnson's career would be spent as an editor at *Ladies' Home Journal*.

TO ORPHA MAY STEINBRUECK

[Painesville, Ohio]
April 23, 1917

Dear Auntie May—

Fancy my amazement to draw from my mailbox today a chatty, closely written four-page letter to Dear Dawn from—"Yours until next time, Nochem"! My amazement was the more profound since I didn't know who Nochem was. I did think it was an awfully cute name and have often regretted that Keith* was not named Nochem. But who he was!—I did not know.

I investigated the letter; I even read it. And finally detected on the envelope a name: Nochem Winitsky, Colgate University, Hamilton, N.Y. And, detecting this, I remembered all. He had been my dinner partner the evening we gave a dinner to the Colgate Glee Club and had the exclusive honor of being the only man who has been able to talk to me steadily for two hours. I was too weak to interrupt and suffered everything from chronic boredom. And then he has to pursue me yet with letters.

I knew that his name was Winitsky, but in my wildest imaginings I never dreamed that it was also Nochem. The two combined give the effect of a chop suey supper with a keg of dynamite in the neighborhood. I don't know just what is proper for me to do. I feel decidedly that it would be unmaidenly for me to answer. Do you think I should return his letter unopened?†

Did I write you that?—no, I didn't. After arriving in Cleveland at 9:30, having passed a strenuous time on the journey, I made a peripatetic movement (meaning I walked) up to Lakeside Hospital, found my friend Helen was out district nursing, made another peripatetic movement (walked) down several unventilated, unfumigated and un-Americanized side streets on which I seemed to be the only female, and aimed for the tall buildings and the Hotel Olmsted.

Not that I wanted to go there. I merely recognized it. I forthwith drifted into Burrows' and cheated them out of several dollars by sticking around nearly 1½ hours, reading all their books. I finished two there, and then bought some pencils and paper and went up to Taylor's Rest Room and wrote a novel until 4 o'clock in the afternoon when my train left. I haven't finished the novel yet and may not get round to it. When I do, I'll have it published in serial (or cereal) form in the *American Journal of Feeble Mindedness*. It will be a cold day when I go to see Helen again. In fact I shouldn't be surprised if it would be wintertime.

I went to a Red Cross Benefit dance the other night downtown. Next week

---

*A son, Keith, had recently been born to Mabel and Edgar Pocock.
†Nochem Samuel Winitsky (1898–1990) transferred the following year to Harvard. After graduating from the law school there, he became a distinguished attorney in Philadelphia under the name of N. S. Winnet.

is our Prom and we are going to have simply a dance from 8 to 12 with cheap music instead of the regular dinner dance and Fischer's orchestra, flowers, programs, souvenirs, etc., and by thus economizing we save about $150, which we will give to the Red Cross. Miss Small wants us to give the Prom as usual but the girls don't want to. She's always harping on how selfish we are and then when a chance comes to sacrifice something, she decides it isn't "customary" and would interfere with the college "policy." Don't know how it's going to come out. . . .

Ben's letters now have to be passed by the censor. They aren't nearly so interesting. However, he says he may get a few days' leave sometime soon.*

I'm going into Cleveland Friday night to see the Western Reserve play *Revizor*.

In conclusion may I say that I ate three cucumber, tomato, and mayonnaise sandwiches, three hunks of cheese, and a chocolate dope this evening and feel like the devil now? I really do. I am sure you ought to know about my symptoms so that you can tell Dr. Summer and have him send me some Goo.

I have a feeling of extreme weariness about 10 o'clock every night and often am obliged to take to bed for several hours before feeling rested. In the morning I have the same feeling of weariness. Don't care about getting up, even. I have a sensation of emptiness in the belt several times during the day and at other times I suffer with sensations of heaviness in the same spot, and loss of appetite; the latter-named symptoms are especially marked after mealtimes. Often when standing in my room with nothing on I have peculiar chilly sensations. I could stand that way for hours experiencing the same sensation. At other times, particularly when I have a coat on, I feel very warm and seem to have no chills. I take little interest in work and exhibit a strange, almost uncanny preference for reading cheap fiction and loafing. Some people I have a sensation of pleasure on seeing; others fill me with unaccountable pain.

These strange symptoms will probably bring you up to Painesville at once. I hope they do. I should like to see you before I am operated on. Yes, it has come to that. They tell me an operation is the only thing so I have secured a B&O operator to perform the operation.

Yours,
Dawn

(COLLECTION TIM PAGE)

---

*No further information—not even a last name—has been found for "Ben," who was apparently a boyfriend of some significance to Powell from 1917 to 1918.

TO ORPHA MAY STEINBRUECK

[Painesville, Ohio]
May 15, 1917

Dear Auntie May:

Did you think your pampered pet (meaning myself) had gone to war?* Well she hasn't, but let me whisper something—she has a strong inclination to go to Fort Benjamin Harrison, Indianapolis, Ind., and train to be an ossifer. She thinks she can be as good an ossifer as several of her little friends from Case and Reserve who are learning Tacticks there. The main thing that has kept me from dashing off several letters to you in my usual spirited style has been Stamps. Then I spent Sunday uncovering the bottom of my top dresser drawer and located a stamp in the corner half crushed by the debris. I rescued it with glee and put it into circulation at once, as advertised!

I have a confession to make. I was found drunk on the campus the other night and have been asked to leave Painesville. I feel that I am not altogether to blame as I was not really *very* drunk—just about half under. So I'm coming to live with you and be a social parasite. I see you don't believe me. Well, you wait and see—when I come marching in with two or three trunks and a sack of animal crackers Friday night this week! Will that be all right with you if I weekend with the Steinbruecks over the 20th of this month? You see Saturday, the 19th, is our Field Day so we have no classes. We also have none on Monday and I have only one on Tuesday which I want to get excused from. So I thought it would be nice for me to come home this Friday, getting there at 6:15. Would you mind? Besides, I want to locate a high-salaried position for the summer and I expect to visit places in Cleveland to see about something to do. I have something under consideration but I'm not sure of it yet. By the way, what do you think of law as a profession for me? I mean it and will talk it over when I see you.

I have my course arranged for next year. Spanish, French, the English Drama, History of the United States from 1830 to now (emphasis on growth of political parties), 19th-century English writers, Ethics, and Ornithology, which is bird study. I get a scholarship for $100, the usual $200 loan, and only have to do two hours a day of office work. Since I expect to go into law, I will also take a course in Argumentation and Debate.

Yesterday Charlotte and Cornelia and I went on a bat—three miles out in the country and cooked our dinner and had a fine time. We had eggs, too—and pork chops! And a pie each!

Tonight is initiation night in Philologia. We take in three new members a year and I as executive chairman have charge of the initiation stunts. We are

---

*The United States had recently entered World War I, then known as the Great War.

going to have a hot program. Charlotte is to be taken in and I'm revenging myself on her for all her past misdemeanors.

I wish you would come up. You be planning to come up June 19. We give *Midsummer Night's Dream* then, and I am Puck in it. Expect me to unload Friday night on the 6:15.

Love,
Dawn

(COLLECTION TIM PAGE)

TO MABEL POWELL POCOCK

Fox Hill Farm
Pomfret, Conn.
July 13, 1918

Dearest Mabel—

You asked about my job here. To tell the truth, it isn't a job at all. I thought I had explained it to you. You see it began with Rachel Schwab. Her classmate—Margaret Swain—lives in Painesville, though she herself is in New York most of the time. On her visits home, I became acquainted with her and she became interested in me. She thought I could write things. She has always spent her summers here in Pomfret—although she isn't here now—and she and Rachel thought it would be good for me to have a summer in an *artistic atmosphere* where I could develop my *genius.**

Miss Matthewson has this big farm and estate and people come here for the summer—they also come for the winters because it is such a lovely place. There are usually several rather famous people—artists, writers, etc.—and Miss Matthewson† herself is so clever and interesting. For the privilege of staying here—I might add incidentally—our friends pay $15 per week. Well, since we don't get any of the $15, we won't dwell on that. Margaret, being a friend of Miss Matthewson's—and also a friend of Cinderella Boult's‡—arranged for me to come and stay here and write stories or anything I wanted to, and Cinderella would criticize them, since she is a well-known critic herself. Also, she is an artistic photographer. So between Rachel and Margaret and Cinderella and Miss Matthewson they fixed it all up.

---

*No information has yet been found on either Rachel Schwab or Margaret Swain. They did not attend Lake Erie College.
†It is unclear to which member of the Matthewson family Powell is referring, but descendants of the family still owned the farm in 1999.
‡Ella Boult, whom Powell always referred to as Cinderella, was a writer, photographer, and suffragist who made a home in Pomfret for many years with the painter Beatrice Stevens. The sophisticated Boult seems to have been an important mentor for Powell, who saved her letters until the end of her life.

In the mornings I farm, as I told you before. Everyone else does, too—
hoeing, etc. And afternoons I "write," but don't get worried. I haven't any
intentions of going to New York, renting a garret and starving to death writing
stories. I'm going to New York but I'm going to have a position. Besides, it
costs something to starve in New York.

There aren't many young people around—in fact, just a girl from Washington, D.C., and her companion. They take me driving occasionally and invite me
to teas, etc., but I avoid them—hence have acquired a reputation for an "artistic temperament." If there was anything in it besides a teaspoonful of tea and a
bar cracker, no artistic temperament on earth could keep me away.

To keep myself from getting bored with myself, I've taken up suffrage. Miss
Boult—"Cinderella"—is the head of it here and I go round the country stirring
up my suffering sisters, distributing pamphlets and explaining things to them
and having them sign their name as supporting "The Cause." I've had lots of
fun doing it. Many women didn't know what it meant—some of the most shiftless people live around here on farms. Some of the women don't take the least
care of anything and are fairly intelligent, too. This week, I have the car and
chauffeur of one of the big suffragettes here, at my disposal, and I'm going to
Aberdeen and some little places around here. I've had astonishing success, they
say. The suffragettes here say it's because I'm a stranger. Thus far I haven't broken any windows or beaten up any policemen, nor do I expect to go on any
hunger strike—Lord forbid!

As for Christian Science,* I went to that church all the time I was in
college—not because I wanted to, but because we had to go to some church a
certain number of times and that one had the shortest service and was very
painless. You can think about anything you want while the two readers fight
out the service between them. It's very soothing. There are a lot of good people
interested in it and a number of very intelligent ones so I suppose there must be
something sound about it. I use the creed on my worries and it works very well,
also on nervous conditions—just simply refuse to admit that they exist. I rather
hesitate to believe in it for *everything*. Taken with a grain of salt, it's all a good
thing. Go to it—eat it up! But remember the salt.

I forgot to say that Margaret Swain is companion to Irene Brown, the artist,
who is immensely wealthy. This summer they are taking a lot of poor boys up to
Cape Cod and camping out for the summer. Margaret gave me a $10 gold piece
for Commencement and so did her father and brother—they're awfully nice.
(Wish my father had given me one too!) And Rachel gave me $20. This took
care of my expenses here. And I have enough to pay my carfare down to New

*Mabel had recently converted to the Christian Science faith.

York in August. Which is all that is necessary. After I get there—I'll be a Christian Scientist.

I will write often—you say I should—but I detest it. However, I'm so glad to hear from the folks "out west" (as they call Ohio here) that I suppose I'll have to keep up my part. My love to my love of a nephew and give him a big hug! Also to Edgar and the rest of my family.

Lovingly,
Dawn

P.S. I put a bouquet of black-eyed Susans before your picture on July 11.* Did you like them?

(COLLECTION TIM PAGE)

TO ORPHA MAY STEINBRUECK AND GRETCHEN QUIGGLE

Fox Hill Farm
Pomfret, Conn.
July 16 [1918]

Dear folks:—

How does it feel to be Mrs. Quiggle?† And how does it feel to be Mr. Quiggle's mother-in-law? It makes me so furious to think that I'm never around when my family take it into their heads to get married. Here I am, twenty-one years old, and never saw anyone married yet. I won't know what the proper form is at all on my own happy wedding day (which is some ten or twenty years distant, I trust). But so long as Heinie and Gretchen had the priest—etc.—I suppose it was perfectly regular and legal without my presence. Perhaps, too, I might have given the bride away and Gretchen was afraid of that.

Speaking of the priest—I have been doing a lot of suffrage work lately and a lot of it has been among the Irish and I've had a perfect circus. If they look as though their husbands drank, I tell them they want to vote to get the saloons out and they say, "Sure, then, I'm a suffragette." And if they look as though they liked a nice nip themselves now and then, I use the soft pedal on my prohibition line and say that the pope is all for suffrage and there's some talk of there being a lady pope. So then they say, "Sure, I'm a suffragette!"

I had such good luck with my volunteer work—going around and talking to women—that I'm to get paid for it from now on. I go out every day on my

---

*July 11 was Mabel's twenty-third birthday.
†Gretchen Steinbrueck had recently married Henry Quiggle.

Vice Crusade. This is a hotbed of suffragettes—some of them were the ones who "picketed" the White House. (If there's money in that I'll be in the next lot to go down.) I got my luck by unwittingly going to the priest's house and I'd been told that all the Catholics were rabid Antis and to stay off. But I didn't know who it was and not until someone saw her name on my list did I discover that it was the priest's wife—I mean housekeeper—that I had persuaded (because she knew someone who used to go to Lake Erie). Well when all the Catholics saw her name they thought it was all right and wanted a vote right away. I promise them a district school board if they look as if that is what they want, or a flytrap on the public square, and I've given my personal guarantee— the word of a Powell—that there will be neither brewery, distillery or saloon if they'll join our happy throng of suffragettes.

I reckon I won't be here very long so they can't get me. New York's a big city. . . .

Dawn

(COLLECTION TIM PAGE)

TO CHARLOTTE JOHNSON

Fox Hill Farm
Pomfret, Conn.
July 22 [1918]

Weather today—Hotter'n Hell

Dear Charlotte—

[. . .] There is this about letter-writing, I grant it freely. One can gas on ad infinitum about the eternal ego without receiving any personal violence in return or any interruption. Thus is it superior to conversation. Fwinstunz, I propose to confide in you steadily for the next three hours on the way I *feel* about things and the peculiar way I have of *looking* at things and how *hard* it is to be *different* from other people and how something—I just don't know what—tells me that I'm not going to live an *ordinary* life but am going to *rise* and *rise* and *rise*. And then, mayhap, I'll whisper in pale ink the things women's husbands have said to me—married men, understand, with married wives— and how they somehow *instinctively* turn to me in a crowd. And how at operas they do not turn to their wife on their right, at the emotional passages, but just seem to *feel* for my hand and squeeze it unconsciously and I never realize it— perhaps they give my elbow or knee a slight pinch and if it's *terribly* emotional they push me out of the seat or bite my ear. . . .

Did I tell you that I am a Suffragette and skid around the country urging the women to become one of us? I apply separate tactics to each of them and enjoy myself and them. One woman didn't want to be one because she thought women ought to be supported. I clapped heartily but asked just where we were to get this support and she responded, offhand-like, "Oh, from their men folks." But I can see how that is a good reason: I do not believe in women suffrage because I believe women ought to be supported. Or, for that matter, I do not believe in woman suffrage because I believe in daylight saving. I might add that my zeal in this direction was excited by Miss Boult who is head of it here— and by the knowledge that I was to draw Big Moneys. I'd patrol the White House for fifty cents. For a dollar I'd go on an anti-suffrage beat. That's the way I am, you know—funny, *awfully* funny. In fact, just as odd as I can be. . . .

I'm getting used to being by myself and I like it. I remember I used to be that way until I got to college. Then I got used to crowds. Now I tear off to my lonely hut after every meal. . . .

Miss Coit who is an architect—age 25—from Boston just drew up alongside and said, "Oh—at your *writing*! Now please go on with your work or I shall be perfectly furious for having disturbed you! When you left the house everyone said, 'The little Miss Powell has gone off to write,' and I know I ought not to disturb you but I was lonesome!" See that? Ha ha. Ha ha. Ha ha ha. So every time I vanish it is to *write*. If they but knew! Could they but see the cigarette stubs, the cheap magazines, the *letters* I write and in fact all in the quaint little ordinary ways I spend my time instead of in soul diggings! Wouldn't that blast you? I wish you were here and we'd go off together to *write*.

As a matter of fact I've only written three stories since I've been here. All of them are stories about the Mushroom and while Miss Boult says they're all right, they aren't as good as my first Mushroom story. But that really isn't bad, is it?—three stories a month when I am working mornings and all of my afternoons on suffrage last week.

Also, I'm reading Dumas from first to last again. I read him when I was about eight or nine and I'm reading all of it again because I have the set in my little house and I always was devoted to him.

I wrote to Frances* today for thoughts on N.Y. I have $10 minus $6 to get me down there and the rest to get me settled until I can locate a job. Don't you want to share my apartment? I think it will be sort of an interesting experiment. Worth the $4. Miss Hutchinson hasn't anything definite for me—just told me to call when I got to New York. I don't suppose I'll go before the middle of September but I'm determined to go.

I'm putting Ben away by the cold-pack method—haven't written him once

---

*Presumably this refers to Frances Johnson, Charlotte's older sister.

since I've been here and though I think more and more of him I hate to have interferences with my schedule for the future.

Write soon.

Lovingly,
Dawn

P.S. I forgot to say that I didn't tell Miss Coit I was writing a letter. I simply smirked as though it were a novel or two.

(COLLECTION TIM PAGE)

TO ORPHA MAY STEINBRUECK

Fox Hill Farm,
Pomfret, Conn.
Aug. 26 [1918]

My dear Auntie May—

Why in the devil doesn't my dear Auntie May write to her languishing niece who is just about to ditch the farm life and go out to battle with the Worruld? I love the farm but there comes a time when the sight of a flock of Jerseys grazing on a patch of poison ivy fails to thrill and one yearns to go someplace where the band plays all the time and life is not so simple. And so, having these sentiments I decided to make Labor Day the date of my departure for New York City. God knows the thought of five feet of me struggling along in the heart of the wicked city occasionally gives me an empty sensation around the lung and just below the stomach but 'tis written that I go to New York—so why try to fool with the gods?

Old ladies with vivacious enthusiasm ask me if I realize what it is for a young girl to go to N.Y. alone. They paint dark pictures of the knocks just coming to me. But even if I believed in their prophesies, I'd go just the same!

I'm going to stay at the Three Arts Club unless they are full. If they are—I will stay at the Downtown or else the Brooklyn Y.W.C.A. until I can get in the Three Arts. It's awfully nice. I have $14 from suffrage work and Cinderella— who is so much like you!—is going to stake me to two weeks' board. I'm not going to worry about anything—just jump right in.

I've tried to get in the canteen service, etc., and go to France but I can't until I'm 25 years old. I may get in the W.A.A.C. in clerical work and go over unless I'm too young for that, too.

Cinderella has been wonderful—writing to different editors who are her friends about me, arranging for interviews for me when I get there, writing reference letters and so forth. I'm going to take any interesting job if it pays enough to live on and any ordinary one if it pays more than enough. Get me?

Mabel says Jack* is with you. I would love to see him. Is he going to spend the winter there? I think it would be great—raising boys for a change. And have you got a piano? It would be fine if he would take to piano. We ought to have some musical genius in the family, don't you think?

Is Grandma still in Cardington? I'm going to write to her there. I want to find out a few peticklers about the Sherman family. Once I wrote a history of 'em and seems to me they came from Connecticut. I met a man the other day who was some remote connection of General Sherman. I confessed modestly that I was too—am I?—that the General was in fact own mother to my grand-dad, if not closer.

Tell Phyllis to write.

Much love,
Dawn

(COLLECTION TIM PAGE)

*John Franklin Sherman (born 1911), the son of Orpha May Steinbrueck's brother Jay Sherman, would become Dawn Powell's favorite cousin, later the guardian of her son, and finally the person who pro-vided the legal authority to free the Powell literary estate from its twenty-nine-year limbo.

NEW YORK YOUTH

1918–1931

TO CHARLOTTE JOHNSON

October 18 [1918]
353 West 85th Street
New York

Dear johnson—

Look at me in my old dirty kimono—with my hectic flush, racking cough and sore back, all run down by demon rum and Spanish flu.*

I admit I rather enjoy having Millie bring my breakfast tray with the morning's mail on it. Of course if there isn't any morning's mail I enjoy it just the same for a fried egg—ah God!—is as beauteous to me in the first flush of morn as a letter.

Still—when there are both—

I am a philosopher. Don't deny it.

I far t'would rather do some Darn Thing and then regret it than not do it and regret *that*. Now that I'm in the Navy for four more years, I have vague apprehensions—reasons why I shouldn't have enlisted. But it does give you a comfortable, settled feeling.

Besides I ought to get in closer touch with the Navy. Don't you think so, too?

---

*Powell had just joined the United States Navy as a "yeomanette," but a routine entrance examination showed that she was suffering from Spanish influenza. This epidemic would kill some twenty million people worldwide in 1918–19.

But sh!—don't breathe a word of all this to a soul till I have been sworn in and received extreme unction. . . .

I must tell you about Katherine.* She went down Monday, enlisted as yeoman—they saw she had a B.S. degree, had done major work in Bacteriology, and accepted her and put her to work immediately as assistant to the examining surgeon. Also she makes cultures of typhoid—etc., etc.—and makes reports of men's bodies—heavings—in the nude. It must be embarassing to them to have a most beautiful young lady of our age give them a physical exam.

There I went and spelled *embarassing* with one *r*. I don't like two *r*'s in that word. It isn't right for one word to have two sets of doubles.

On Monday I went down and enlisted as typist. I talked with one of the petty officers—a woman—who liked me and she talked to the Commander on my behalf. They thought with my college degree—which seems to be rarer in New York than anyplace else according to the experience which I have had!—that I ought to be given some work not strictly routine. So they sent me to the Naval District Communications Superintendent.

I must tell you about this. These headquarters are way down on the riverfront—below Wall Street. As soon as I entered the building one of the guards took my application blank in to the Commander. I waited while nice college-jackies talked to me, wished me luck, etc. The Navy atmosphere is like a coeducational college—in all these places.

The yeoman who took my blank in said, "I don't know what you had on there but the Commander and all seemed to like it awfully well because he said, 'Ah—that's the kind we want!' " I was glad I had been able to admit a B.A. degree. The chief yeoman then interviewed me as no one talks to the Commander directly. The chief talks to you—goes and "translates" what you say to the Commander. Very courtlike.

Here is where certain little features come in which make the Navy so much nicer than the business world. When the chief yeoman called me in, instead of sitting and letting me stand as in all business offices, he rose, gave me his swivel chair, and stood all the time he was interviewing me, begged my pardon every time his telephone rang. Those little things do count a lot. On the space devoted to "Past Experience" I put:

> Assistant to Librarian—etc., etc.
> Reporter—†
> Assistant Efficiency Manager‡—five weeks with all the data.

*Katherine Vedder, later Chapman, and still later known as K. V. Busch, was one of Powell's first friends in New York. They would remain in correspondence until Powell's death.
†In addition to her college activities, Powell had worked for at least one summer at the *Shelby Globe*.
‡Improbably, Powell had briefly held this position with the publishing firm of Butterick and Co. when she first arrived in New York.

The Commander wanted to know the nature of my efficiency work. I elucidated. Ah, johnson, this is where my passion for schedules has led me! For he said they needed someone in the efficiency department they were working up—to see that all departments were doing their work efficiently and on scheduled time. I should report there for duty as soon as I had my medical exam.

But I can't get a medical appointment till next Tuesday so in the meantime I'm luxuriating in ease.

Johnson—don't you think that's funny though that I should draw schedule-making as my life's work—when I used to get so absorbed in my dinky little schedules and make out one for everything—my solitaire statistics, etc.!! It's funny.

There is a chance—they told me—of being sent to Europe on certain duty and I must be willing to take that chance. Was I willing? Well I should guess!

I am glad to do something like this. Should the war end before the four years my work would continue for a year afterward at least.

I draw $93 the first month, $102 the second and third, and $35 a week for six months then. Oh say! Say!

Damnable.

Ben is coming to New York for the weekend! He is an ensign now—got his commission last week.

Darn it all why can't I have any fun—

Don't say anything to a soul about the Navy till I get my final papers. Of course I'm in—but there's always a chance of their discovering that you've been suffering for 40 years with the tuberculosis.

Gee I'm thrilled.

There is also a chance I may get transferred to Washington in a few months. This, however, does not strike my fancy so much.

Is Frances as homesick as she was? It would be fun to be in Honolulu a while, though I prefer to stay in New York just now. If I had the chance to go I would feel as though I ought to go—but I certainly wouldn't be brave enough to go without some congenial friend—all alone as she did. I know—after this summer—what it is to be alone and I have a horror of being alone again. I don't want to do anything alone again.

I don't want to go to Australia or South Africa and be alone. You know I used to. I want someone with me *always*. I don't know what I should have done if I hadn't found Katherine when I came to New York.

I will write and tell you as soon as I'm all sworn in.

Much love,
Dawn

TO CHARLOTTE JOHNSON

[New York
November 12, 1918]

Dear johnson:

I got out of the hospital yestiddy but be dammed if they'll let me go back to work.* I gained five pounds during my suffering and feel like a million ($1,000,000). And what sympathy do I get? None. Me and my lungs were as good as new last Friday but in the Navy it's as hard to get out of a hospital as it is to get into the service. You are well—your doctor admits it—you think there's nothing to do but go back to work. Not so. First the inspecting doctor has to thump you in the ribs and command you to say 99. Then he rolls you over and whacks you on the back and says—say 99. You gasp out "99" with no resistance. That is, the old doctors make you say 99. Those of the new school make you say 1-2-3-4. I fancy it really is far superior as a test to 99.

I came out with flying colors from this ordeal and prepared to face forth. No—not again. My name must be sent to the Navy yard, passed on by somebody (very likely Admiral Usher), gravely considered by other officials, probably the President. . . .

You ought to have seen New York yesterday. It wasn't so wild they say as on last Thursday but gee everyone was happy and they're still celebrating. Dancing in the streets—everybody singing—French sailors carried on the shoulders of American sailors down Fifth Avenue. Today I got in a jam down at Fifth Avenue on 38th Street—the Friars and Lambs, two theatrical clubs, are starting on different sides of the street and racing to see who can get the most money for the war fund, arriving at a certain time at a certain place. A Scotch troop is playing bagpipes and the siren blows all the time.

I will write again soon—and oh johnson it was wonderful of you to think of the money. It means I can get my uniform right away. Incidentally I can return most of it on the 25th—all by December 10th, as I am so deep in I want to get out as quickly as possible.

Tenderly and peacefully,
Dawn

(COLLECTION TIM PAGE)

*The newly appointed naval "yeomanette" had gone directly from her entrance examination into the hospital and happened to be released on Armistice Day, the formal end of World War I.

TO CHARLOTTE JOHNSON

353 West 85th Street
December 6 [1918]

Dearest Charlotte—

I've been waiting till I could say all I felt like saying. I hate to write letters that just say "Am well. Good-bye." But even they are comforts, I admit.

Do you know I've lived about twenty years since Sept. 2—the date of my arrival in New York? Everything whirls around you all the time and you grab what you want and then let it revolve again. It makes me dizzy to think of all the warm friendships and Passionate Affairs I've been through in three months. The funny part of it all is that you have to come to New York to appreciate the virtues of a small town just as you have to go to college to learn how easily you can do without a B.A. And all the men say "I love you" and look at you with long wistful "I-surely-am-hit-now" gaze and you kiss them and say this is the first time I've ever cared like this and then you never see each other again. And on the subway in the mornings you suddenly find yourself talking to a man or girl who is a genuine soul-mate. They get out at Times Square and you see them looking back at you through the windows and both of you know you'll never meet again. Somehow there's nothing tragic in it, though. You recognize and love it all as Life—the World—Humanity—whatever it is.

There was the man—Frederick Schneaburg, Jr., University of California, now in Navy—who asked where we were on the subway and because I smiled back he grabbed my arm and told me he had just inherited half a million dollars from an uncle down in the Honduras and it was his guardian, the vice consul for the Honduras, that he was now on his way to. He was so handsome! And so young! And so—gee! He came to see me twice, then his boat left for the South and I know I'll never see him again. Then a little aviator—Lt. Edwin Foster from Georgia—and now Lt. Wilbur Wright, a trick aviator, six feet tall, blond and an old Michigan friend of Katherine's.

By the way, did I tell you that when the Governor of Michigan—Mr. [Albert E.] Sleeper—was in town, Katherine and I went around with him and his wife and Lt. McKee who put on the Red Cross and Liberty Loan drives in Michigan and who knows the Mt. Clemens girls? And the governor hugged me!—the old rascal—and introduced Katherine and me to Senator [Truman Handy] Newberry and everybody as his two protégées. Katherine's dad is an old friend of his, which was the cause of it all. We were his own guests at a reception given in his honor at the Michigan Soldiers and Sailors Club here. Oh—I tell you! Driving up in his own car and leaving for home with the Royal Party.

I heard from Cornelia Wolfe. I must tell you she asked about you and said she wanted to hear of you. Do you write her at all? I know how you feel and it would be difficult to renew relations, wouldn't it? Awfully awkward? Still, it seems so *unnecessary* to let a friendship of any sort slip out of your life—and the longer one keeps up hostilities the harder it is to come together again. I do long for the old days. It's hard to keep up with the girls I work with—to say as catty things as they do and remember always to look out for yourself and put in a bad word for everybody else whenever you get the opportunity. That is New York and the—what d'ye call it?—the "work-a-day" world! None of this college loyalty stuff.

I've been "doing the Village" quite consistently lately and feel that sooner or later I'll be among 'em. There are three stages you go through in regard to the Village. First and foremost "Oh-so-this-is-Bohemia!! My dear! Don't you just *love* it all? Everything is so—well, so absolutely *spontaneous*, don't you know!!! Bohemia—oh thrills!"

Stage No. II—you realize that all the biyes and goils from back home think Bohemia's great so you begin to see it with jaded eyes. Everyone tries to be a freak—wants to be noticed—does everything for effect and down in his heart is worse than ordinary—is in fact a ten-cent rube like yourself. Bah! Village theatricals! Bah! Bah! Bah!

Stage No. III—you combine and condense and admire and sift—and after all the Village is the Village when all's said and done.

I'm wondering if you're planning to spring into the world in February and draw your degree in absentia or lie low until June then—watch this space! Do you have any idea what you want to do? I don't know whether I want to go to France anymore or not—do you?—but I just *itch* to go on a steamer someplace and the places I lean toward are Honolulu and Australia! I simply have to stick at what I'm doing for six months more because it's too expensive shifting positions always but I would like to plan on going away next summer, along in August or September. By that time probably Frances [Johnson] won't be in Honolulu anymore so it wouldn't be much fun but let's read up on Australia or New Zealand. I adore blazing trails, don't you? And see what we can do to get there.

I want to stay here, though, until I've earned a little money—perhaps made a dollar or two payment on my college debt. It's hard getting adjusted but the uniform solves the clothes problem to a great extent. Of course I can't get any new dinner clothes or fancy shoes but at least I have a complete outfit for work, which is the main thing. I don't get paid for my hospital time after all but I will have loads of money on Dec. 25 and will immediately refund some of your money so you can be swelling your "going-away" fund. You can't imagine how I appreciated that loan. I owe you $40 now.

Say—I wonder if it costs billions to go to Australia. Maybe Rachel [Schwab] would like to go along—the more the merrier, especially when it's a long long way from home and you get homesick. I'll see what I can find out about occupations there. It would be better to start out in September, wouldn't it? That's the best starting-out time. But meantime you can't sit and twiddle your thumbs from February till September. First of course you'll want a rest. You can't go right to work from midyears and just at the time of year when you feel most like the devil. Possibly you might rest in Vincennes and work on a play—a novel—or a book of poems. You know, I believe you ought to collect the best of your poems and have them published. Your uncle would do it—or even if he didn't you could borrow the money—it ought not to cost over $200—and it would be the best possible start because a book of your own gives you moral backing, prestige among publishers whether you make any money on it or not, and there is always that chance in a million that it may make good. With a college degree and a book of your own you could move the world. Perhaps you could have it ready to be published in March—call it some clever name—with all your mystic things in it. *Oh Charlotte!* I know you could do it. Start on it now—find out rates from publishers—collect and produce your gems and in the spring there you will be!

If you do approve of Australia I suppose your mother would like you to be home in the spring. You ought to get a column or two in the Vincennes paper—or perhaps in an Indianapolis one—or a Richmond one—to occupy your spare moments. It's too much of a struggle to get your experience away from the people who make allowances for your mistakes. Do you know I really believe we can work the Australia idea? Providing a study of it makes it appear attractive. The thing to do is to get your hooks in and I'll get mine in so we can make a dollar or two on the side writing for the home papers!

I'm working hard now—have complete charge of all the mail sent out from our headquarters, keep a record and file of everything and sometimes have to stay at work till 7 o'clock at night. Had to work all Thanksgiving morning—all alone.

Much love,
Dawn

(COLLECTION TIM PAGE)

TO CHARLOTTE JOHNSON

[New York]
January 12 [1919]

Dear johnson—

If I have ugly babies I'm going to kill them. Unless they happen to have a rich father. Then I might let them live a few years to see just what sort of numbskulls they developed into. The zeal for experimenting might carry me far. Beauty is after all the only thing in the world that matters—not mental or spiritual beauty or any of that lying rot, but splendid physical beauty—healthy or unhealthy beauty so long as it is beauty. Of course we don't want utter idiots but at least we don't want a supernormal brain—a nuisance to the world at large and a stumbling block to the progress of beauty. Let us not mention money—it is so obvious that it is money that makes beauty possible, so that very likely money is the only thing that matters more than beauty. Isn't it pitiful the number of women who develop their brains because they can't be beautiful? It probably is a tremendous comfort to them but I prefer to live brainless since I can't be beautiful—a display of Intellect simply calls attention to your Lack of Looks. Let us be merry and remember the people in the world who are happy because they are not Educated Up to Their Misery.

For the fourth time I tried to dye that damnable dress. It spotted once more. It is really sort of too bad since that blue beaded dress—you remember it?—is all worn out and the hem unravels—very stupid, isn't it? No, clothes after all are what matters—that is what it all amounts to: money is necessary to buy clothes which make for beauty which is the Supreme Goal. And if we can't attain the Supreme Goal by natural methods we can at least get halfway there by making a good appearance. Exactly. I knew I would arrive eventually.

How many friends one could have, too—with money. I wonder if there is ever anyone who likes money just for money's sake alone. Poor old Money. People just like him to introduce them to nicer things.

And girls! They are all very well when they get used to each other but they don't seem to care about getting used to each other.

I wish I had a raspberry. A red one. I don't like black ones, do you?

I'm tired of hoping for things to come out right. Not that hoping isn't a good thing. It's all right when you haven't anything to do but sit down and hope but when you're busy it's simply wasting mental force. Because nothing ever does come out. People are for the most part liars and four-flushers—men only want one thing and women are a lazy good-for-nothing lot.

Imagine if you had a big warm good-looking coat and a dress that was absolutely your own—even fitted you—one that was altogether and looked nice too. No, I can't imagine it. Besides if you had that you wouldn't ever be invited out. Instead of being invited out and always worrying about how to look decent in what you had to wear, you would take out your big warm coat and your altogether dress, which didn't look as though you'd made it, and say, "Where can I wear them—who can I look nice for?" There, I'm perking up a bit.

I haven't read a thing since I came to New York. Last night I saw *Listen, Lester*—a very clever musical comedy. Two or three successful playwrights live in our apartment house. Come on to N.Y. and write plays with me. This is a very nice place to stay. We could have a big attractive room, lavatory and two closets for $11.50 a week or two small ones and a private bath for the same money. $11.50 apiece, with breakfasts and dinners. Fair enough. Then when Frances comes we might get a bargain in a furnished apartment on the Drive. I don't care for living quarters in the Village—bohemian they may be but they're drafty and dirty and no bathrooms mostly. We could get (see *Times* Jan. 12) a cozy three-room apartment and bath on West 15th, furnished, for $45 a month. Or we could get three rooms and bath on Riverside for $100 a month. When F. comes, we'll take the Drive apartment. $33 apiece. Fair enough. Only $8.50 a week. And we could besides take someone else. And they all have pianos and victrolas in 'em. Bohemian I be but I prefer to boheme in normal surroundings because bohemian atmosphere makes me feel normal. . . .

Only I'd like to travel first. Say, johnson—let's go to Paris and live. Let's get together *determined* to be successes and make money and then meander over the globe. Leave here 'long about July—maybe October—and go to Paris to live a year. Then go and live a few months in London—in Petrograd—in Italy and maybe skid over to Cairo for a weekend. Then come back after about three years and stay here a spell—get a gorgeous apartment on Fifth Avenue, overlooking Central Park, and have a little Group. And entertain! O! Um! Eh?

When do you get out? On the 23rd, I am sending you $25 and will you still be in Painesville? It's nice to know that I can start in paying off some of my debts now. I'm starting with you and Cinderella and will eventually work up to college, I trust.*

Damn! I spent $10.50—honest!—on a hat I only wore once and can't wear again. And I need a hat! Isn't that the limit! Tell me should I pay Rachel—or try to, soon—or do you think I'd better start in on college first?

I feel like one of those cherubims—wings but no sense of direction and no legs and no nothing.

Much love and write me quick to tell me if I should engage the apartment.

Dawn

P.S. Of course I do want you to come here and New York with me. The only thing is I'm afraid you'll get here and—and—'n' everything and then You'll Blame *ME*!

(COLLECTION TIM PAGE)

---

*In fact, Powell would pay off very few of her college loans, and Lake Erie would still be billing her for past tuition in 1952.

TO CHARLOTTE JOHNSON

> *[New York]*
> *Easter Sunday*
> *after a hard day's wash*
> *and no dinner yet, uther*
> *[April 20, 1919]*

Dear ole hoss johnson—

I did a funny thing. Just wrote you a hull page and tore it up. Never take back a thing but I just wrote a few jesting words which were not truly felt within this beating bosom and before I knew it—zip!—in the wastebasket they goes.

Just back from 13 days home. Do you know I learned more in those 13 days? I feel all tender and lovely toward all my relations and I love all my friends bitterly and would die for any of 'em providing it were painless and free. Funny. My sisters, aunt, cousins, nephews, and practically all my fathers and mothers are enveloped in this vast, all-embracing affection of mine. I wants to buy them all gumdrops and teething rings and canned fruit. I want to do little acts of love and kindness for everybody. Funny. . . .

Sister Mabel fixed all my clothes for me—bragged and bragged about me fore my face too. I love my sister Mabel. Friend Bill Bowers—late of A.E.F. and Amherst College—was home (Mansfield) and we declared our boundless love for each other and here it is a week later and not a word from him yet!!!! My aunt was still 'ansome and a beautiful little blond cousin, Adelaide Sherman, age 4, is living with her.* Sister Phyllis was proud of me and also bragged. I bragged too. I told of my successes and bragged all over everything. I became quite a braggart, in short.

Then I went up to Cleveland and busted in on the Farnham who introduced me to all the *Plain Dealer* and they took my picture in the little union suit—called it "When Donnie comes marching home in her Union Suit, Mother Machree." Little did I reck. Also they wrote a story of me but I scorned all interest in this. Ha! The P.D. with the Farnham and me then sojourned—the ten of us—to the Rathskellar for a snack before I sailed for P'ville. And so help me bob I never was so thrilled for ten years as I was anticipating on that streetcar. . . . Much welcome and I brag two, three hours. Everybody help me brag. No johnson there to sneer and puncture bragging tho e'en so I longed for her.

I see Miss [Helen] Dunlap at sunup regarding debits. Owe college $800— Miss Small $55. Fair enough. Miss Dunlap was so interested in me. It certainly does your heart good to have someone so interested. Wanted to know:

---

*Adelaide Sherman (1915–1989) was one of Jack Sherman's younger sisters.

1. How much salary?
2. How much for board?
3. How much for uniform?
4. How much carfare?
5. And always glad to hear about you. Come again.

But glad as I was to see everyone, I had not the slightest desire to be always among 'em. No. My happiness was highlighted by the consciousness of being able to fly out into the World again at once. Pleased to discover that interesting fact. By the way thanks for working over all my junk. Did you know anything about my Gorky book—and any other fiction book I may have had and forgotten about? . . .

Went back to Cleveland, saw my picture in paper with interesting story in which I reveal a few casual Navy secrets. That little item has kept me in a state of nervous postponement ever since. " 'Yes,' said Miss Powell, 'they won't send us to sea but I have plenty of thrills because I handle all confidential matters such as the news of troopships and how *much grain we sell to Sweden!*' "*

Isn't that enough to give anybody the willies? I wait for the courtmartial sentence—certain to fall if the Navy discovers aforesaid innocent little remark. . . .

Talk about ambition, story ideas, etc.—you do a lot better when you're among people you know. People you don't have to study and get acquainted with. I came back all charged up with new ideas, ambition, and could have written I'm sure if I'd stayed there another week. Get back here and feel it all oozing away again because I can never get into that complete detachment necessary for creation. If I have a free evening I think, "Ah, I will write." I sit down. I listen for a telephone call. I yearn for somebody exciting to call up. I meditate. I decide I need new toothpaste—also that I'm hungry. I buy food. I see it is 10 o'clock. No one has called me up. I'm mad. I go to bed huffy. Such is genius midst the thrills of the city. . . .

Lots of love,
Dawn

(COLLECTION TIM PAGE)

---

*This article has yet to be found in the unindexed Cleveland newspapers of the period.

TO ORPHA MAY STEINBRUECK

411 West End Avenue
November 23, 1919

Dear Auntie May—

Been waiting till I had some exciting news to tell you but as nothing is settled yet I can't tell you. See the story—"Impressions of a First Voter"—which I
got in the *New York Sun.** I sent it in the day after I voted—and never heard till
the other day when they sent me a check for $4.25. Then I got the old copies it
was in. As it only took me fifteen minutes to write the thing—it was just what
had happened so all I needed to do was exaggerate it a little—I think it was
easy money and I intend to do a lot of it. Ain't you proud?

I have two fiction stories in *American Agriculture* and *Southern Ruralist*—
Red Cross publicity but written up like straight fiction. Also I have a 2000-
word woman-stuff story in *Fashion Art* either for December or January, unless
the printers' strike affects that, too.

Also I have left the Red Cross.† There is no chance for advancement and as
long as everyone else in my line of work gets $50 and $65 a week I see no reason why I should be working along on $35—particularly when that's the high-
est salary they can pay. They want me back but I shan't go back for less than
forty, much as I like the work. It costs too much to live to turn out original copy
every day for practically nothing.

So all this week I've been doing extra work in the movies—a new Selznick
picture of Olive Thomas—I guess the name is *Out of the Night.*‡ I worked all
day Monday over at the Universal Studio at Fort Lee, all day Tuesday, and
Wednesday from 8:30 in the morning till 7 o'clock Thursday morning! Four
hundred extras—all of us—in evening dress supposed to be at a cabaret and
we didn't dare leave the set from Wednesday morning till Thursday morning,
except to go down and eat. Along about 3 a.m. we all lined up for coffee and
sandwiches and staggered home Thursday morning—simply dead. It's supposed to be a big cabaret fire—there's a panic scene in which one of the poor
extras got her nose smashed and another got her dress torn off. Believe me, this
movie life is no cinch.

Olive Thomas is awfully attractive—has a very coarse voice, though. You
know she is Jack Pickford's wife. Her brother, Bill Duffy, is her director and he
is quite nice—we had a nice talk. The regular Selznick director is Jack Noble—

---

*"Impressions of a First Voter" ran in the November 8, 1919, edition of the *New York Evening Sun*.
†Powell worked briefly in the public relations department of the Red Cross.
‡The film was eventually released as *Footlights and Shadows*. No print of it seems to have survived. Olive
Thomas (1898–1920) is probably best remembered for her suicide (or accidental overdose) in Paris the
following year, which has sometimes been described as the first great Hollywood scandal.

poor man, he had a job managing all that mob. I met Miss Thomas's leading man and talked with him behind scenes for a while. Darcy is his name, or D'orsay. He is English—6 ft. 5 and awfully handsome. Served in the British army and she just got hold of him about three weeks ago. Of course he is conceited though. I saw Eugene O'Brien down in the restaurant where they all eat. He is beginning to have a few gray hairs but is as handsome as ever, otherwise.

We had to dance—and we had cabaret from the Follies. They have people to put on their regular act you know. And that wonderful orchestra. We would be just dead and then Mr. Noble would have the orchestra jazz a little and we'd get up and shimmy as lively as the rest of them.

But believe me, I'm through. I never saw such a group of absolute moral degenerates in my life as those movie extras—all the old ham actors that failed on the regular stage hang around the picture studios. The women are awfully bad and the men—some of them are stunning-looking but you wouldn't want them to touch you. They put their hands all over you—I was so furious the other day I could have cried. I may get a story out of the thing yet for the *Sunday Morning Telegraph*. I will try to discourage these would-be movie stars.

I've seen so many people from college lately.

Phyllis said Gretchen was sick. Is she any better now? I do hope so. And how is James[*]? Are you going to California? Please go. I did think of going out but now I am planning to take an apartment with a girl here. We can get a good two room and bath furnished for $85 a month and on figuring things up it's almost cheaper than boarding. Then you can come and live with us if you won't interfere with our wild parties—as we're sort of counting on something like that once in a while.

Is Mabel still in Mansfield? I will write you as soon as I get definitely settled. Much much love to everybody.

Dawn

Saw the Prince of Wales[†]—about a yard away. He is the cutest thing you ever saw. New York went simply crazy over him everywhere he went. He is blond and rosy faced—

(COLLECTION TIM PAGE)

[*]James Quiggle was the only child of Henry and Gretchen Steinbrueck Quiggle.
[†]This would have been the future Edward VIII, who abdicated the throne to marry Wallis Warfield Simpson.

569 West End Avenue
[ca. January 1920]

Dearest Auntie May—

This certainly has been a big month for me. I bought some oil stock ($200, got rid of it before I had even paid for it so did not lose or gain on it), worked harder on my new job than I ever did in my life, got two people good jobs— and leased an apartment at $165 a month!

Helen Kessel* (an Iowa girl studying piano with Leginska) and I saw the apartment, leased it till Oct. 1 and moved in yesterday. It is living room, bed-room, kitchenette and beautiful bath—all new and furnished exquisitely by an interior decorator . . . except silver and bedding and until we raise more money we use ten-cent silver and sleep in my Navy cape and Helen's Y.M.C.A. cape. The living room is done in blue and brown. There are cretonne window blinds and bronze-colored hangings—blue tiling on our fireplace—a tall blue and bronze floor lamp, two other unusual-looking side lights—a mahogany gate-leg table, blue Wilton velvet rug—china cabinet full of white china with blue borders—bathtub of that kind that grows right out of the floor. Bedroom has twin beds—a night table with telephone (not in yet) and electric light on it— white dressing table with those movable mirrors—you know what I mean.

Also, Helen has her own Steinway here. Of course $165—$82.50 apiece— is an awful rent to pay for two rooms and bath & pantry, even when you are used to New York prices, but everything is brand new here and of course it is on West End Avenue in the 80s. I would rather live here, though, than in a $7 or $8 a week lousy room on the East Side someplace and since I expect to stay in N.Y. I think I might as well have a home of my own and Helen feels the same way. It is just six blocks from 411 W. End so you have an idea where it is, don't you? Right near 353 [West 85th Street]—you remember!

I have been working like mad, writing stories on Baku and Mesopotamian oil wells for the *Oil and Gas Journal*, on Boy Scouts in China for *Boy's Life* Mag. (April—it's called "East Is West in Boy Scoutdom"), on Burmese music for *Musical Monitor*, Pekinese poodles for *Dogdom*, and Japanese labor unions for the *American Federationist*. (That's Samuel Gompers's own labor paper and he wrote personally to my director saying my article was one of the most interest-ing he had read on that subject and he would use any further articles sent him.) Also I sold some more stuff to the *Evening Sun*—as a little sideline.

My job keeps me busy.† I have to keep up on all export and international

---

*Helen Kessel, later Lissfelt (1894–1970), would be the bridesmaid at Powell's wedding. She studied with the self-styled Mme Leginska (1886–1970), born Ethel Liggins in England, a distinguished pianist and teacher who would later become a conductor.
†Powell was then working for a relief organization the Interchurch Center.

trade news so I get *Commerce Reports* and sometimes some Spanish and French papers with trade news in them. I got Charlotte Johnson a job with me. She was only getting $25 a week where she was and I got her $40 with me. They took her without a murmur on my recommendation, which flattered me highly. . . .

Now, Auntie May, there is no excuse for your not coming to see me this spring. Unless we take another girl you can sleep in our living room or if Helen's father comes to see us you can sleep with him. He is a widower—a doctor—and has oil wells in Texas so you could do worse. I'll see what I can do about it!

Seems funny to get domestic again. We're not going to eat much as eating is too expensive. Helen has written home for some jelly so we'll live on that for a while. Meantime, if you see any of my ex-towels or sheets floating around your commodious lavatory send 'em on—as we don't care what we use. . . .

Much—much love to you all. Is Gretchen all right now and J.F.* and Phyllis?

Dawn

TO ORPHA MAY STEINBRUECK

569 West End Ave.
[May 1920]

Dearest Auntie May—

I know I'm a lemon on correspondence but I've thought about you so much it seemed sort of unnecessary to write. Besides, I've been working harder than I ever did before in my life. I left the Interchurch on April 1st when all publicity staff was dismissed and for three weeks I jazzed around without a job in the world. Then I went to the Near East Relief—the "Hunger Knows No Armistice" concern for Armenians—and they had a week's work—$50 a week—which I took, and they kept on needing me so I've been there three weeks now but don't know how much longer. Last week I did three stories on the side for that sixteen-volume series, "Boys and Girls Bookshelf." It took me four of my evenings and all day Sunday to do it and I got $66 for it. So last week I made $116—biggest week's salary I've ever made.

However it's a darned uncertain business getting rich in the writing game. When you start rolling you go big for a week or two, and then the next week there's nothing doing.

---

*I.e., cousin Jack Sherman.

Tonight I had to interview a man who has just returned from Armenia, and he asked me to dinner as that was the only time he had. He's a professor at Columbia University so we dined with all the dignitaries at the Faculty Club. Besides he was handsome and funny so we had a lot of fun.

The other Saturday my very Most Adorable* and I took the train to Tarry-town and walked through Sleepy Hollow Cemetery. You should have seen those old Dutch epitaphs on cracked old tombstones of 1690 and the early 1700s. I am sure you would love Joe, Auntie May. I do.

I have met some interesting people lately. Condé Nast—the publisher of *Vogue* and *Vanity Fair*, you know—and Bruce Barton,[†] who writes for *Women's Home Companion, Ladies' Home Journal,* and incidentally conducts one of the big advertising agencies in town. . . .

> Much—much love,
> Dawn

TO ORPHA MAY STEINBRUECK

> *[New York*
> *ca. November 10, 1920]*

Dearest Auntie May—

Please come and give me away next Saturday. We haven't got the license yet but we're going to be married November 20.

Please come. I have to have a relative present to make it respectable.

> Thrillfully yours,
> Dawn

Powell and Gousha were married on November 20, 1920, at the Church of the Transfiguration, also known as the Little Church Around the Corner.

---

*"Most Adorable" was Powell's pet name for Joseph R. Gousha (1890–1962), with whom she was work-ing at Near East Relief and who would become her husband in November 1920.
[†]The highly successful advertising executive Bruce Barton (1886–1967) was later the author of the famous inspirational best-seller *The Man Nobody Knows.* He would remain an occasional acquaintance for the rest of Powell's life.

TO JOSEPH GOUSHA

[New York
Undated; probably early 1920s]
for all morning papers

OPEN LETTER TO MR. D. W. GOUSHA*

My dear Mr. D. W. Gousha—

May I thank you, in the name of the American public, for the joy your beautiful performance of last night gave to me (personally). It was a magnificent piece of work, and one that I fully appreciated. (Fully.)

(for
Yours   by   the people
on)
Dawn Powell (pickfordchaplin)
Hollywood, L.I.

(COLLECTION TIM PAGE)

TO MABEL POWELL POCOCK

[31 Riverside Drive
Late 1920 or early 1921]
Dearest Mabel—

The box came and there was much rejoicing among the Goushas. The luncheon set is a beauty and the two dresser scarfs were at once set into action owing to absence of said articles in my Hope Chest and barrenness of dressing table and chiffonier. The table pads also were in great demand as we have a beautiful mahogany table and need protection for it from my cooking. The Bunwarmer pleased Joe—he having a great eye for the luxuries of life. Also he was highly partial to the little tea-cloth whatchamacallit. And the pillowcases! My word. Such elegance. Thanks so much. . . .

I like married life. It seems queer to feel absolutely happy and contented. We have a lot of financial difficulties to face right now with our own moving and general furniture expenses as well as Joe's family expenses—and I haven't had anything new since I was out to see you. But it's silly to worry yourself unhappy about money when you have everything else—the man you want, first and foremost. Furthermore, after being left to shift for ourselves ever since we were infants, don't you think it's wonderful to have someone finally spoil us— just like we should have been spoiled when we were kids? Somebody that

*An apparent reference to the visionary film director David Wark Griffith (1875–1948).

insists that the thing you want is the thing you're going to have instead of just handing you what there is left with a "Take it and be darned glad you get anything." Independence, too, is all right only I do enjoy having Joe to look after everything for me instead of doing it myself.

I'm making some extra money now by writing little stunts for children to amuse themselves by—like making paper furniture or something. It's for a book, a kindergarten Home Manual, and I'll get about fifty dollars for my work—I hope! At any rate, I have to have it done by Monday—and it's very easy. Then I'm doing seven short biographies for the Boy's Own Bookshelf—a series of boys' books put out by the University Society. Aside from that I'm keeping house, a job and a husband—of the three I like the last one best!

Thanks much for the box—and much love. Tell Phyllis I will write directly. Give Keith [Pocock] a good hug for me.

Dawn

(COLLECTION TIM PAGE)

TO MABEL POWELL POCOCK AND
PHYLLIS POWELL

Saturday, Sept. 3, 1921
St. Luke's Hospital [New York]

Dearest Mabel and Phyllis—

My first pen-and-ink letter. This is my twelfth day and yesterday they let me sit up for half an hour—lifted me out of bed into a chair. Today the doctor said I could take a few steps—not leaving the room—but no written order was left so they are just letting me sit up again. I feel pretty good but won't be able to leave for another week—both on my own account and on the baby's.*

You see, I didn't know till two days afterward that they didn't think the baby was going to live. I had a terrible time and it was just as hard on the baby. He is awfully husky but being born was a tough business for him and just before he came out his heart went bad. Doctor said I should have had my babies five or six years ago. That would have been awkward, as I would have had some difficulty in explaining them about that time. I didn't dilate at all. Poor little lamb had a clot on his brain that caused a sort of convulsive paralysis besides several bad bruises from the forceps. Joe didn't tell me but the doctors let it leak out to me by saying that it looked as if the baby had *a* chance after all.

---

*Joseph Roebuck Gousha, Jr. (1921–1998), Powell's only child, had been born in St. Luke's on August 21. Within a few years it would become clear that the boy was mentally impaired, and he would be institutionalized for much of his life.

We had to have a special nurse for him night and day for a week ($12 a day besides the $6 a day for me) and consulting infant specialists were called in. On Friday he began to perk up and now he is entirely out of danger and is raising the dickens in general although his external bruises haven't quite healed up yet. The clot is all absorbed and he is okay. He was able to recover so quickly I suppose because he had such a swell appetite and general constitution to fall back on. He has coal-black hair and big blue eyes and a tiny little nose and a beautiful mouth and one ear flat and the other sticks out. He is unusually tall. Got that from me. He has a fat little face—looks just like a Chinese mandarin but very very beautiful.

He likes to box with me. They bring him in every three hours to nurse except at night and he always begins proceedings by kicking me thoroughly and then with a loud whoop he punches me one with his right fist, then with his left and after using me as a punching bag for a few minutes to get his appetite up, he gives a grunt and pounces on me with his mouth and makes vulgar smacks and does his best to bite hard enough to make me yell. When he's through he throws his arm over my breast with an air of "I may be through now but it's mine and nobody else can have it when I don't want it." So you see if he was sick to begin with he certainly isn't now. He looks as much like Keith [Pocock] as anybody—his face is shaped like that but his nose and eyes are like his father's. Joe is crazy about him.

I have a lot of trouble with the hospital. After all the money we're spending in this damn place, the second night after the baby was born I was absolutely neglected and the nurses bullied me and wouldn't bring me the bedpan and I cried all night and Joe raised the devil till they fixed things up. Then last night one nurse thought I had reported her. I hadn't but she came in and jumped all over me and when I began to cry she snapped, "Stop that nonsense!" She began all over again and I asked her to please leave the room as I was in no condition to argue. (Nurse put me back in bed here.) I couldn't take a step out of bed and naturally couldn't hold my own with her. Well when Joe came he rushed right out for the head nurse and while he was doing it the other nurse came dashing back in with milk and ice water and magazines and everything to try to fix things up but it was too late. She'd done enough damage already. My temperature was up and my heart was batting around and I was mad and I was hysterical. Finally the head nurse came in and fixed everything up and changed my nurse and was awfully upset and so on. It's perfectly terrible though to know that you've got to stand for it because you're not able to be moved yet and even if I were I wouldn't dare take Jojo away from the doctor's constant supervision for another week. So what can you do?

The doctors—they are all women—are wonderful and were indignant about the first affair but with very few exceptions the nurses are mean as the dickens. I hear them scolding patients almost within a few hours after they've had babies. When I was in labor they wouldn't answer my bell at all—the membrane had ruptured so I had to stay in bed all during my labor. Now once again Joe has fixed things up but when you think that in the two weeks I have been here he has paid them $181 for my room, special nurses and delivery-room fee, in addition to the $75 (it may be $100) for the doctor—well, you'd think I ought to get decent treatment. Well tomorrow I will be able to walk to the bathroom so I won't be dependent on their damn old nurses.

I had some stitches taken out the other day—otherwise I could do a little more, as sitting up today didn't make me sick at all.

I had ten bouquets—all kinds of roses and everything from everybody and it cheered the room up considerable. Your little blue jacket came in awfully handy during the cool days. They say it is frightfully hot now but I don't notice it at all as there seems to be a cool breeze in here all the time.

A woman came in last night from Brooklyn on the streetcar—arrived at 2 a.m. and by 3 her baby and she were resting nicely. Had practically no pain at all. How do they do it?

Scrub girl just came in and we had confidential chat.

I look like the devil, I observe by the mirror—all puffy-eyed from crying and sort of gray-complexioned. Regular vampire. Anyway my husband loves me just the same.

Wish doctor would come and leave order for me to walk as I'd like to start in my recovery. Say, in one of the new shows—*Getting Gertie's Garter,* I think—Hazel Dawn is starred and there is an Eleanor Dawn in it, too. Here's hoping I don't have any Phyllis Dawn or even another Jojo for some time to come. Too strenuous a life for me.

I would enjoy a good bath but I guess they think baths are pretty dangerous—even sponge baths. A nice woodsy or gamy smell about a patient is a sign they're getting along nicely and the nurses hate to sponge you off more than twice a week for fear the fragrance will go away.

They say there isn't a free bed in this hospital but they treat everyone as if it were a charity affair.

Husband's coming up soon. And lunch coming in—blah! Hospital food!

Merrily yours,
Dawn

P.S. Will write more gaily when I get over these hospital blues.

TO ORPHA MAY STEINBRUECK

[31 Riverside Drive
ca. January 1922]

Dearest Auntie May—

Didn't you get my last letter—telling you how much I liked the corset? I haven't written since because Baby has been so sick. He wasn't gaining weight and my regular doctor was reducing his food all the time on account of his suddenly getting eczema. Then, two weeks ago Sunday, he had a convulsion. Joe took care of him and our doctor turned the case over to the specialist we had when he was little. On Tuesday he had three convulsions and I took care all alone of two but the specialist was here when he had the next. She examined him and found it was due to nothing serious like brain trouble or that sort of thing, but simply because he wasn't getting enough food. The eczema was due to that too. She told me what to do but he didn't gain any weight so last Saturday I asked her if I could try Imperial Granum and she said all right. He also gets a little bit of yeast cake in hot water and the white of an egg beaten up in his bottle. Well he seems to be doing fine on the Granum. He is more lively than ever, tears everything to pieces around him and raises the dickens in general. So I feel much better. I think he'll get along all right now. He had some onion soup yesterday and thought it was pretty good. . . .

Sat. Never do finish things anymore. Raining all the time. Teeney Weeny looks fatter today and I hope he is. 12 lbs., 14 oz. is such a little bit for a 5 mo. baby. He ought to weigh 17 lbs. How much did Jimmy [Quiggle] weigh when he was 6 months? He must be a pretty big boy.

Most of my experience in taking care of babies I got from your methods with Jack [Sherman]. He was such a cute baby, wasn't he? Jojo has the same shy, wistful little smile.

I am still writing when I can wedge in a few moments and had a very encouraging letter from *Munsey's* asking for some more stuff (I guess I told you), also from *Hearst's*. Will mail you next thing that comes out.

Much love,
Dawn

(COLLECTION TIM PAGE)

TO ORPHA MAY STEINBRUECK

[31 Riverside Drive
New York City
ca. February 15, 1923]

Auntie May you old rascal—

What do you mean sending such a handsome Christmas box? We used the lunch cloth and napkins right away—needed them, of course, as you knew—and I have worn the slippers and corset regularly. I'm crazy about the corset. I never had any so absolutely satisfactory. Of course I spent half an hour trying to squeeze into it (you flattered me about two inches) but once in I stayed in. But even though it was hard to get on I think it's just right for me because I don't feel squeezed at all. Just comfortably snug. And by the time I work off five more pounds—!

I'm dancing now to reduce. I can kick way over my head—sideways and everything.

Baby went to the doctor's for an examination Thursday and tickled him to death. He weighs 24 pounds—and the correct weight is 23 and 1/4, so he's more than made up for his early backwardness. His flesh is firm and perfect and no sign of eczema any more. He creeps but I keep him in his bed. He walks around and jumps up and down in his acrobatic style.

The little chickens you sent him were all broken, sad to say, but everything else was all right. Did the little cold cream jar stand the travel all right? I sent two of those pure wool satin-covered crib comforts to the girls—you remember that shop on Broadway—but I guess they didn't like them or didn't get them or something because I haven't heard a word. Jojo needed one himself and I guess I might as well have kept them for him if they didn't want them.

I had a box of canned fruit and cake and jelly and wonderful bacon from Papa and some writing paper and rompers for Jojo. An electric curling iron and a big bottle of Houbigant's Ideal perfume and a Kodak and a beautiful new coat all from Joe. Our roof is leaking during this thaw.

When you heard the Hotel Belleclaire orchestra by radio, did you remember it was just two blocks away from us, up Broadway?*

You remember Lenore Ulric† in *Kiki*. We saw her in a limousine with old David Belasco‡ one midnight, getting out of a house on 75th Street here—just at the corner of West End. He had his arms around her, but don't you tell. . . .

Love to all,
Dawn

(COLLECTION TIM PAGE)

---

*The Hotel Belleclaire still stands at the corner of West Seventy-seventh Street and Broadway in Manhattan.
†Ulric (1894–1970) was an actress and beauty.
‡Belasco (1854–1931) was perhaps the most celebrated theatrical producer of his day.

TO ORPHA MAY STEINBRUECK

[333 West 86th Street
November 21, 1923]

Dearest Auntie May—

This is the first letter I've written in ages. Cal and the cherries and peaches did arrive and they were all wonderful except Cal—and I was so sorry to miss him. Did you say our janitor was impudent? It looked like that in your fine Italian hand, but anyway he is. He thinks he owns the house and has to be given the devil every so often. I expected Cal Monday but no one told me he had come and I was only out a few minutes. I am glad you have help. My nurse is wonderful* and the maid is good, too, although not too good.

We're not settled even yet. We like the place very much though.†

Three years ago yesterday we were married and you were in New York. We celebrated with a dinner and the opening of a new play called *Failures* and a new hat for Mrs. Me.

You should hear Jojo—he's grown up into "Junior" now. He shouts "Kick the Ball!" when he goes out and sees the big boys playing. He wears three-year-old clothes. He dances and sings to the Victrola and reads "Cinderella" and calls me "Mother, dear!"

We have a new Chinese rug much larger than the one we had when you were here. We use both in our large living room.

I thought of Uncle Stein‡ Saturday. We went to the opera to hear [Maria] Jeritza§ in *Der Rosenkavalier.* It is a comedy and filled with lovely German waltz music. Jeritza is beautiful and has a gorgeous voice and is the first Metropolitan prima donna I ever saw who was able to be really funny.

We saw Ethel Barrymore¶ in her new play *The Royal Foundlings.* It is a poor play but Ethel is beautiful and doesn't look over 30. . . .

Joe is fine and business has been prospering. Loads of love and I'm sure I had more to tell but forget. Calm your anxieties about the Gousha stork at least for a year. Plumbing is too convenient.

[Unsigned and possibly incomplete]

(COLLECTION TIM PAGE)

---

*The reference was most likely to Louise Lee (c. 1880–1960), who would serve as Jojo's nurse and companion for the next three decades.
†Dawn, Joe, and Jojo had recently moved to 333 West Eighty-sixth Street, after 31 Riverside Drive was set to be demolished.
‡Uncle Stein was Orpha May's ex-husband, Otto K. Steinbrueck, a pharmacist in Archbold, Ohio.
§Maria Jeritza (1887–1982) was a beautiful Austrian soprano, known for her lively acting.
¶Ethel Barrymore (1879–1959) enjoyed a career of more than half a century as a leading actress of both stage and screen.

TO HELEN KESSEL LISSFELT

TO HELEN KESSEL LISSFELT

Gifford House
Provincetown, Mass.
September 12, 1924

Dear Helen:

Actually we're on our vacation! We're 100 miles east of Boston on the tip of Cape Cod. The place is full of sand dunes, ocean, fish, painters and Greenwich Villagers. We feel right at home. I miss Jojo, but I call him up and Louise [Lee] assures me he's having a very good time. Next time I'll bring him, though, because he'd have fun sliding down the dunes. How is Claire [Lissfelt's daughter]—now in her first winter underwear, I suppose?

I sold my novel—or rather my agent did—to Small, Maynard and Co. and they are to have option on my next three.* The terms are very good, the agent says, except they want fifty percent [of the] movie rights and she's haggling with them over that, as they ought not to get more than 25%. When I get back we'll have a celebration unless we're so broke we can't buy the necessary Fig Newtons. Joe is all sunburned and frightens the native children. They think he's Othello. . . .

Affectionately,

Dawn

(COLLECTION CLAIRE LISSFELT MYERS)

TO JOSEPH GOUSHA

[Undated; probably early 1920s]

Dearest dearest darling,

Can you ever forgive me, sweetheart? I can't believe that I could be so cruel and I will never forget how terribly I hurt you. I despise myself for letting things like that happen between *us* and I am always the one to blame. Dear I will try to be good but I know these things leave scars. I do love you so much and I respect you more than anyone in the world because you are the only really noble person I ever knew. I love you.

(COLLECTION TIM PAGE)

Exactly what provoked the preceding letter remains unexplained. However, Gousha and Powell were deeply at odds with each other for much of the mid- to late 1920s and had many drunken battles. In 1925, the couple decided to

---

*In fact, Small, Maynard, which issued her novel *Whither*, would soon be acquired by Dodd, Mead, and Powell's next two books would be published by Brentano's.

separate—perhaps temporarily, perhaps for good. Dawn went with Jojo to Ohio to see her sisters (both of whom were now married with children), her father, Roy Powell, and Orpha May Steinbrueck.

TO JOSEPH GOUSHA

3427 Clarendon Road
Cleveland Heights*
[ca. June 21, 1925]

My sweet—

I do hope you are having a rest, dear, and that it is a blessed relief to wake up without our usual morning turmoil. Please tell me if it is and I shall feel repaid. I know it will be hard to come home at night to an empty house but I'm sure your nerves must bask in privacy. I'm not being sarcastic, dearest, only I've just realized what you must have gone through all these years with no place or no time to be alone and I think of myself as a hero to give it to you. Do let me swell my chest. I haven't had a minute to even *think* of you because—well, picture me that weekend at Brett's and you have it all over again: no housework, merely kids and perpetual motion. It took me four hours to compose that telegram, pencil in hand, with all babies in bed!! When Jojo gets more adjusted it will be easier.

He would break your heart. He waked up in the middle of the night to say, "Daddy will come back—he will come back—" and he wandered about desolate and lonely all day yesterday. He smiled tonight for the first time because Uncle Edgar [Pocock] smoked a cigar and played streetcar with him and being with a man settled his nerves.

They have a lovely place and a huge backyard all fenced in so Mabel's children are perfectly safe all alone there. However, it took your little treasure just half an hour to get out of it and land in the street running hell-bent. Dozens of cousins piping up in horror, "Oh Auntie Dawn, Jojo climbed the fence!" The young city slicker! So naturally I don't feel so easy about that backyard. Ten minutes later there was a wail as Tootsie, age two, tried to follow her naughty cousin's example.

This is the most remarkable family I ever saw. Bohemian? Say! Keith, age eight, very devoted to me and a darling boy, has for *years* left his harassed (not a bit) parents sleeping in bed to go down, get himself dressed for school, get his own breakfast and go to school. This morning Jojo woke at 5 and I dressed him and took him downstairs and he had a wonderful time out in the dewy grass until breakfast. About 8, Keith came down, then later Dawnie, age 4, and fat

---

*Edgar and Mabel Pocock were now living at this address in a tony suburb of Cleveland.

little Tootsie made a noise and I went upstairs and here they were chasing around stark naked and whispering softly to avoid waking their parents. Tootsie proudly called my attention to her belly button after first anxiously inquiring what Jojo had done with her potty as she wanted to use it. (She is *two*, my dear.) She dressed herself then and asked me to hand her a safety pin from the top of the dresser. She bosses Jojo and he is very fond of her. They went down and got their own breakfast and presently their mother appeared, beautiful and serene about 9 and played the piano for a while.

No dinner is ever cooked for them. Whenever they feel hungry they come in and cut a piece of watermelon or get some bread and milk—feeding themselves, of course. They laughed themselves sick watching Jojo try to eat. . . .

Today I fared forth to Painesville and never again. I took Jojo and in the taxi with Eleanor [Farnham] I suddenly glanced at him and saw tears streaming down his face very quietly. It was homesickness of course but he merely sobbed that he wanted to go back to Tootsie. It took two hours to calm him down and by that time I did not look like the rich New York alumna at *all*. He had sat all the pleats out of my dress and left in their place a large wet blue stain. I arrived like that at college, a hat on one ear, my dirty child under one arm, my face gray—sort of a *leberwurst* color—and all my friends telling me how crushed my verve was and how awful I look. It was emphatically not a fanfarade for the successful prodigal's return, with the successful Eleanor all cool and immaculate by way of contrast. Everyone was kind and pitying and I could have shot myself for going back. And my sisters think I look awful and I do, so I shall not go out of the house again. I haven't had a minute to touch the piano or write so be patient with me. I will get into form soon.

Jojo disappeared this morning and I was afraid he had climbed the fence again. Instead I found him upstairs, door shut, sitting in the baby's bed. "I want to be alone," he said. "I want to be in the teeny tiny room *all alone*!" He is sweet and I ache for him, he is so desolate for his daddy.

Let me tell you—the first thing I saw out at Lake Erie was a bottle of Hennafoam Shampoo!* It was sitting on the ledge of the washroom. Little did they reck.

I hope I lose some pounds for you and come back svell and svelte. Today Eleanor told me *Whither* was in the *Plain Dealer* in Ted Robinson's† column of books. Nice?

Darling, I know this letter doesn't sound a bit like me but my brain is so lousy. I guess I'll have to pump it out and fill it up with glue. Then I'd always know where the glue was.

---

*Hennafoam Shampoo was one of Gousha's clients in his increasingly successful advertising career.
†Edwin "Ted" Robinson (1878–1946) was a poet, columnist, and editor in Cleveland, long associated with the *Plain Dealer* and widely read throughout the area.

In a few days we'll both be acclimated and perhaps I can get a little more to myself occasionally. Oh, sweetheart—sweetheart. I need you so always, don't I? But I'm glad you're not here and I'm glad you are having a thought to yourself. Perhaps it's a good thing I left to teach me to be a better sweetheart to you. There's no pen or ink here. Dearest—dearest—do you miss me? I am so bad and I've been so selfish always and you've been so brave and sweet. I love you so and oh never never were you so far away from me. But I must learn to be independent and not lean so hard on my poor dearest when he has so many worries.

Good-bye darling,

Dawn

Sunday—

Jojo was discovered in the garage this morning taking his two younger cousins for a ride in the auto. He was driving and honking. He woke up today at 5 and said he wanted to go to bed and sleep (my wish, too). Then he began to cry and cry. He said he wanted to go back to New York and get in bed with Daddy. There was no consoling him until Uncle Edgar allowed him to get in bed with him and kiss him. I'm afraid he's going to be a little melancholy for a while for his dear "favver."

It's cool and fresh and lovely here and aside from our son's temperamental difficulties everything is fine.

(COLLECTION TIM PAGE)

TO JOSEPH GOUSHA

[Cleveland Heights, Ohio]

June 25, 1925

My sweetheart—

Poor dearest. I didn't want to worry you. We thought it would be such a good plan and I believe it has done us good. Your wife you will find a much more chastened, amenable creature and Jojo in spite of his depressions has preserved his appetite and feeds himself, climbs up and downstairs from cellar to garret, runs small autos, etc., with much zest. I think he has caught the germ of self-reliance.

I could probably stick it out till August easily, with profit to him at least, but it's too much to put on anyone—even relatives. Unlike their children, he has to be watched every second. The few minutes yesterday when I wasn't watching he almost kicked a second-story screen out and was sitting on the sill ready to fall out in another second. And he vaulted the porch railing. So I can't blame my sister for saying he's four times the responsibility her gang is.

He is—as you have suspected before—totally unmanageable. He got into the cold cream and smeared it all over my sister's newly decorated walls, he wet the bed twice in spite of a hearty spanking, he wakes up the whole house (including the three kids) a good three hours before their time, thus endearing himself to exhausted parents. And he has never cried so much or so inopportunely in his life. You know what a strain it is, too, to feel that your child is wrecking the placid family routine, to say nothing of their best bed and furniture. So, in spite of ideal physical conditions—regular country air, cool and fresh, and nice kids to play with—I'm afraid I can't get them to stand for it as long as would be desirable. He has been thoroughly hateful and no one can do a thing with him. I have beat him until I'm weak but really, dear, you wouldn't believe how downright nasty our little treasure is. I am inclined to believe that he needs a few weeks of stern discipline after Louise's babying and in spite of her convenience to me I almost think he needs school. I really daren't visit anyplace else with him and apologize frantically from morning until night. I'm telling you this so that you will understand.

Personally this place is a flawless summer resort and both of us enjoy the automobile. If he were as good as he has been many other times, I could stay here for weeks. But as things stand I rather think we'll be home in another two weeks to avoid an unpleasant rupture with my family.

We may go to Auntie May's over the Fourth but I'll hardly spend more than a day and a night unless my son is rid of his demons through some miracle.

Eleanor gave a studio party for me last night—in a sort of Fine Arts Building where we dropped in on a sculptress (Miriam Cramer), an artist (Belle Humphries), a stunning commercial artist (Alice Mason) and all sorts of newspaper women including Eleanor Clarage (see June *American Mercury*) who interviewed me for the *Cleveland Times*. A few lady fairies to be sure in the lot but I withstood their advances. Friday night, Selma and Louise Lockart are dining me at the Cleveland Athletic Club. Saturday night a party at Nat Howard's. But I assure you I don't vibrate to the social key after 15 hours of chasing my particular little rainbow.

Of course you detect the blow to my vanity. I expected to pose as the calm, self-possessed ideal mother of the little ideal boy. Instead I present the quite customary tableau of Despondent Mommer and Brat. I shan't suggest your joining us.

Tweet, perhaps we can work out some program of self-preservation when we get home so that you will not be so tragically starved for the individual freedom you are enjoying now and which I realize now you must have been pining for. Perhaps we could take alternate weekends. At least we could spend our

Friday nights in some hotel and sleep late Saturday mornings. And our child needs some discussing—whether more Louise-ing, which saves me at the time and we probably will both pay for later, or school, in which case I wouldn't get anything done. He does need school discipline, though. I think I may be able to get him into better shape at home. . . .

Love,
Dawn

(COLLECTION TIM PAGE)

TO JOSEPH GOUSHA

[East Cleveland, Ohio
Late June 1925]

My dearest—

Yesterday we came over to Phyllis's and we are much calmer owing to a Victrola, an old-fashioned music box, a ukelele, a guitar and a banjo—all of which your son plays at will—to say nothing of a marvelous view of a railroad track along which any little boy can see engines and trains and get a real thrill.

Last night he was so tired that when we came in from the auto he disappeared, announcing that he was going to Shut-Eye Town with Uncle Morgan [Cook].* I found him upstairs in bed under the covers, coat and hat and shoes and all on. He slept until nearly eight this morning. I think the confusion of kids over at Mabel's upset him—also the fact that he was considered a queer child. Here the two babies are very quiet and Phyllis thinks he's wonderful, and he is quite ideal. He dreamed about you last night and said he'd hurt Daddy and wanted to go to New York and put witch hazel on it. I'm very fond of him again. . . .

Everyone thinks I am most obnoxiously fat and seeing myself in so many full-length mirrors I realize for the first time what a sight I am—though I am down to 137 lbs. since I left New York. You mustn't be so tactful with me hereafter. The evening at the Howards'† was the first breath of New York life I've had. Eleanor stayed upstairs with Marjorie the wife, who has tonsilitis, and Nat and I stayed downstairs and talked Cabell and "Rhapsody in Blue," he being a passionate Gershwin fan and my having accidentally brought a Gershwin piece along from the *Tell Me More* show. You would like him so much as I do. Being a candid soul, he gave me a bitter blow. "I thought you were a stunning girl

---

*Phyllis Powell had married Morgan Cook in 1922. They had three children: Carol Cook, later Warstler (born 1923); Phyllis Cook, later Poccia (born 1924); and Alice Cook, later Hoover (1930–1987).
†Nathaniel Richardson Howard (1898–1980) was a Cleveland-based journalist and editor and a longtime friend of Powell's.

when I saw you last time you were here," he said. "My, you must have put on a frightful amount of weight since then. Er—er—of course you're still a stunning *woman* but you're not a girl any more. Ravages of childbirth and so forth, I suppose." Hot dam.

The kids at Mabel's got into the ergo-apiol box in my suitcase, each ate one of these delicious bonbons and then threw up heartily. They're always looking for candy and I may as well announce right here that your son has cultivated an all-day-sucker appetite and when such dispensations are made he gobbles up his and then quietly and authoritatively takes all the suckers away from the other kids and gobbles those. What an appetite that child has. After his usual hearty breakfast yesterday he ate Graham Crackers until 11 and then, faint with hunger, snatched a handful of pickled beets from a dish and stuffed those down, too. I'll swear he's gained five pounds. He seems to realize, the little darling, that he's eating off of somebody else and he ought to make the best of it. . . .

I think I will stay perhaps a few days over next Sunday but I'll see how things go. Next door here is a boy with whooping cough and Jojo runs away every few minutes, too, toward the railroad track. One time he ran away up at Mabel's and when captured explained that he was going to get Mother the *Evening Post*. This morning I caught him as he was running lickety split for the railroad and he said he was going to get the milk for breakfast.

We mustn't tear ourselves apart this way, must we, dear? I'm glad in a way that we did this once so that we could see what a fizzle that theory is. And moreover living in Cleveland's Westchester has taught me that that life is emphatically not what we want at all. Two miles from the car line and from groceries—how would I ever remember butter or oranges?

But I must say Jojo has improved. He runs up and downstairs, feeds himself (also his chest and chair and the floor), gets himself a drink (and also wets his own pants, alas). We are used to sleeping with each other now and really it comforts me to come to bed and get squeezed tightly by two little arms and have him breathe into my neck and occasionally drench my nightie with holy water. He is constantly astonished and pleased to wake up and find me there. I don't mind him at all except when people have such swell furniture and things that he is always ruining something and then I have to keep apologizing for him. I would like to come back on a day when I can see you instead of having you rush right off to the office. Perhaps I may come in the daytime after all and arrive in the late afternoon. I'll see.

I love you true and please do you like me as much as before dear? I see you soon. Write what you want me to do, lover.

Dawn

(COLLECTION TIM PAGE)

TO JOSEPH GOUSHA

Wednesday morning at Phyllis's
[East Cleveland, Ohio
ca. July 1, 1925]

Sweetest—

Here I have time to think and what I think about is you and how I miss you and how I love you and how can I bear another day away from you. Whatever made you so sweet, anyway? Maybe eating vinegar and salt and Worcestershire every night. Was that it, mr. fish?

Oh you're going to be so surprised if you take me back. I'm going to sew buttons all over you and have tripe and nasty fish and every morning a stack of oranges and when you say, "My dear—is there any butter, bread, coffee, etc.," I will laugh scornfully and say, "Certainly. I remember everything." And when you read the paper I'll sit quietly sewing on a lot of buttons on your hats and overshoes and never interrupt at all. And I'll sell a lot of stories to *Snappies* and have big fat checks every week and everybody will say what a swell wife you have.

When do you want me, lover? Should I come next Monday or should I wait to arrive on the following Sunday? Should I bring a new baby back for you like the Lissfelts got? What did they name her? Jojo wants you to save lots of money and go to Paris and see Cynthia*—with him as escort of course. He just emerged from the kitchen with a tomato and handful of bran flakes, which were being stuffed into his ever eager mouth. He has just learned the delights of strange food.

I think I'm going back to Mabel's tonight—at least I am if the tea and dinner I have a date for tomorrow still hold. Edgar's car hasn't come yet but in any case we'll drive down I guess. But maybe you'd better send me about $5 Friday or Saturday in case I have to come back on the train and I owed Edgar $5 of your $10 and spent $1.90 already of the other five. Pretty bad?

Won't we be glad to see each other? Have you missed Jojo any or was it a relief to have his confusion out of the way? He's getting entirely too independent. A little self-reliance is a dangerous thing. He opens and shuts windows and doors and helps himself to a number of things he ought not to have. I am not in the same mellow benevolent mood I was yesterday, after being kept awake by him from three to seven last night after he fell out of bed and was waked up enough to appreciate each train that went by the rest of the night. I don't know whether he'll be any easier in New York or not, but at least I'll have a few hours' peace every evening and my dearest to soothe me and remind me

---

*Powell is probably referring here to Cynthia Chapman, the young daughter of her friend Katherine Vedder and a contemporary of Jojo's, then living in France.

that there is something else to life besides chasing kids. Gee, I haven't had one meal without jumping up a million times for my child.

Men are funny, too. Morgan and Edgar yell at me in great disgust when I chase Jojo away from a cellar full of saws, awls, nails, etc., or a garage full of lawnmowers, pitchforks, paint cans, etc., and they say, "For Heaven's sake, leave him alone, Dawnie. He can't hurt a thing in there." And when Morgan insists on taking him under his wing and then Jojo falls all the way down cellar on the top of his head, he smiles indulgently and says, "He isn't hurt. He can't hurt himself."

The preventive philosophy is none of their creed whatsoever. Their idea of watching a kid for you is to tell you what happened to him—how he fell off the clothesline or cut himself with a butcher knife or something. Isn't that funny. . . .

The first part of this letter was typed; the rest was hastily scrawled in pencil.

Afternoon—

I have just spent two hours trying to beat my son into some sense of obedience but I haven't enough brute strength behind me. I have worked up a slow furious hate for him and believe I'd better come home as these dizzy rages are too murderous for either my good or his. I'd like to be his stepmother just for a day. I think I might be gentle with him after that. He has not the faintest idea of ever doing what he's told. Besides I hate *him* for all the inconveniences my relatives have caused me too. I'm afraid this trip has cured me completely of even any liking for him. I'd like to tie him up and beat him to a pulp. I know this sounds terrible but I'm in such a state that writing it to you helps let some of the poison out. It's terrible to be from dawn to dawn with somebody that gets on your nerves so. The only person I've ever hated like this is my cousin Gretchen—the futility of it maddened me so. I'd like to give him a few proper licks to straighten both of us out.

Please let me come home quick—seeing my son in his worst light constantly puts me in a bad light and calls out constant arguments.

(COLLECTION TIM PAGE)

Powell returned to live with Gousha in New York, but the two of them would lead fundamentally separate lives under the same roof for the next three decades. Particularly when she was writing, Powell increasingly insisted upon moving into a friend's vacant apartment or a hotel room to do serious work. One favorite such getaway was Atlantic City.

TO JOSEPH GOUSHA

[Hotel Traymore
Atlantic City
ca. March 9, 1926]

My dearest dearest—

I was so disappointed waking up this morning without you. I am so wound about you, dearest. I want you now so I can tell you the marvelous idea— ministers' old wives sitting on benches talking to each other with their husbands' voices rumbling behind their words ("Believe me, dear brethren, we must learn to love our God boom boom"—waves going out again—and coming in—) and very dimly the auctioneer's voice behind them on the Boardwalk shop ("67—67 and a half—this beautiful sable going at 67 and ¾—show it to 'em Rose, go ahead—that lady over there—67 and ¾—I'll tell you what I'll do—I'll throw in this beaded bag—show it to 'em Rose—let's see now—72 and a half—I thought so—I thought so") and then later on when the husband's voice from the ocean vanishes and the minister's wife hears just the auctioneer's voice and the sable coat—see what I mean? ("I left a dear friend in the hotel— a very dear friend crippled for years—")

I have written a lot on the novel*—mostly at night and a little in the mornings but I don't know whether it's good or not because my writing away from your influence is like a new-baked cake. It is neither good nor bad until it is tasted by the person for whom it was baked. And all my cakes are made for you. It's funny writing away from you—like shouting in a tunnel and getting no echo. I don't think I could do it very long, do you, sweetheart?

Some weekend playwrights or else ministers preparing their speeches are in room 938—typewriting all night! If it's one I am annoyed; if it's the other I am sympathetic. The ocean is so gorgeous. All smooth today. I wish you would ride in on it waving to me with your merman's tail. (Little woman getting feverish.)

We are so tight together. Like two goobers. I love you and want to be as good to you as you are to me. Well so long, dimwit. See you in the terlet.

Your wife,
(signed) Dawn Gousha

(COLLECTION TIM PAGE)

---

*Powell was then in the middle of writing *The Bride's House*, which would be published in 1929 by Brentano's as her third novel.

TO PHYLLIS POWELL COOK

[New York
Undated; probably spring 1926]

Dearest Phyllis,

Just heard how sick you've been and I was so upset. What did you do with the kids and who took care of you? Can you hear the hurdy-gurdy man out here playing the Sextet from *Lucia?* Spring in Greenwich Village. I sent you some books if you feel like reading. I'm sure you'll enjoy having the Balzac *Droll Stories*, guaranteed to cure rheumatism in ladies or gents over a hundred years old.

Jojo is fine. Tell Mabel he started talking the other day about his Uncle Bob out in Cleveland and I had no idea who he meant until he said he had a bicycle. I told him, "Aunt Phyllis is so sick" and he said, "Uncle Morgan's pretty well, I guess." He said, "Jojo got Tootsie a drink" which is a good joke because Tootsie always had to help *him* get one. He writes a good deal and the other day I saw a big page full of writing and saw one word "fommy" and I said, "What's that?" He was very disgusted. "That's *fommy*," he said, "fommy in 'Gunga Din.'" Then next to it was another word "You-ny," and I wanted to know what a youny was. (Youny, he said.) So he read it off: "The yoony fommy wore—was nothin' much before, and rather less than half of it behind. . . ." I just died. Do you remember that part?—"The uniform he wore was nothing much etc."—and he'd spelled it his own way.*

We've been having a great many parties and entertaining a great many celebrated people. Besides I've been doing my best to get my novel finished by June 1st for fall publication. I've been reviewing books every week in the *Evening Post*, too.† Next week, I review Ben Hecht's new book. It's quite funny— *Count Bruga*—and sometimes lewd. I read *Topper* by Thorne Smith and laughed my head off.

We are thinking of spending two weeks out in Montana on a dude ranch this summer. Joe does the advertising for the ranch and they said we could come out free (it's $50 a week a person otherwise). I'd like it for the horseback riding and Jojo could stay in the country with Deesie,‡ in New Jersey, where he has an elegant time. I can Charleston but it doesn't reduce me a goddam. I have a story in the next *Snappy* and will send it if you're interested in belles-lettres.

Tell Mabel to put kerosene on her bald spot if she wants to grow hair. If she wants to grow corn just sprinkle a little manure over it.

---

*At the age of four, Jojo had already memorized Rudyard Kipling's poem "Gunga Din."
†Powell would continue to contribute occasional reviews to the *New York Post* for much of the rest of her life.
‡"Deesie" was Jojo's pet name for his nurse, Louise Lee.

I hope you get well soon and write if you get a chance and let me know your plans, if any. Love to all the babies.

ooоxxx,
Dawn

(COLLECTION TIM PAGE)

TO JOSEPH GOUSHA

[Calling card, 1926]

Mrs. Gousha (nee Dawn Powell) has the honor to tell Mr. Gousha (knee Most Adorable) that on the evening of Monday, June 21, 1926, (1926) promptly at 10:59 Alarm Clock time she loves him very much.

R.S.V.P. (Ring Soon Very Prompt)

(COLLECTION TIM PAGE)

In July 1926, Powell went to Ohio to visit her father, Roy Powell, who had suffered a paralytic stroke that was to prove fatal. While this letter seems to reflect Powell's abiding love for Joseph Gousha, it is also more than likely that by this time she had begun an affair with the radical playwright John Howard Lawson (1894–1977).

TO JOSEPH GOUSHA

*Hotel Cleveland
Cleveland, Ohio
10 a.m.
[ca. July 4, 1926]*

Dearest lover—

I am sitting here trying to finish that book but it's very hard. I have to be near you, dear, to do it. I couldn't do anything on the train. Oh my dear we must go away together, be together, tight again without any other people. Away from you I know I cannot live without you because you are all around me—coloring everything I do or think. We have been too independent of each other this last year and this mustn't be, because we are grown together and I don't want to know how to stand alone. It really is important for us to go away alone together—remote from everyone else—because we are getting slowly more individualistic and I don't like it. I know I would be happy with you anywhere in any little town or field that I passed. More and more people are crowding between us saying—"*He* is my friend" and "*She* is mine—" and this must not be, darling, must it? We must be Mr. and Mrs. Gousha, take it or leave it. I don't know what I mean but the idea of my going alone to Paris should never have occurred to either of us.* It never would have two years ago. I can't bear to sleep away from you, dearest, and my mind is just empty without you. Please fishie let's be tight close again—and never never separate again. It isn't good to learn that we can breathe and eat away from each other. I will be back before Saturday I think, tweetie winker.

love love love love,

Dawn

I may come on day train arriving at 12:45 midnight. Want to see you so much, dearest. This is the train to Elyria. Be good and sleep a lot only better get an alarm clock. Can I come before Friday if I wish, tweetie? Maybe Wednesday or Thursday?

I was just sick as we pulled away from N.Y. I don't see how I could be happy anyplace else.

(COLLECTION TIM PAGE)

The following two letters were written at the deathbed of Roy Powell.

TO JOSEPH GOUSHA

237 E. College Street
Oberlin, Ohio
Monday night
[ca. July 5, 1926]

Dearest lover—

I am so glad I came home because I was really needed. Aunts and uncles were here but no daughter and there was the usual talk. He is a skeleton. I stayed with him a good deal of the day (someone has to be with him and there is no nurse and my stepmother of course is almost a wreck). He is perfectly conscious and that's what makes his struggles to speak so pitiful. He is apt to choke any minute. I stayed up alone with him from 10 to 3 this A.M. and will stay up again tonight. Mabel and Phyllis are here now but they get so excited they can't do anything.

Today I cried thinking that once a dark vivacious woman loved this poor wreck of a man (and she was just my age)† and at midnight I saw her with long

---

*Powell would consider escaping to Europe on several occasions throughout her life, but her only actual visit would take place in the autumn of 1950, when she would settle in Paris for about three months.
†Powell is referring here to her mother, Hattie Sherman Powell (1872–1903), who died at the age of thirty-one. Powell herself was then almost thirty.

brown hair lying beside him on the bed while his second wife* slept in the next room. He was better yesterday than today and the first thing made Sabra show me his whiskey—this is almost the only thing he takes besides hypodermic injections. Phyllis looks marvelous and it's good to see her again. . . .

This morning I took a walk thru some lovely old unpaved section of the town and saw hay scattered on the road and saw bushy tumbledown houses and smelt things fying (not broiling or roasting but *frying*) in kitchens and heard women's voices very soft and rich saying, "Honey get out 'a' thah" and then when I saw lovely little fair children on black or high-brown mothers' laps I remembered I was in the colored section since Oberlin is ⅘ black and those ⅘ are all mixed up. This situation in a beautiful old Methodist northern village is much more curious than in New York. I wished for you because it's all so sedately village with beautiful lawns and enormous trees.

Dearest lover I love you so much and nobody has ever been so good to anyone as you to me. Will you be even gooder when I return because I'll be so tired tweeter—

Dawn

Sitting up tonight.

TO JOSEPH GOUSHA

237 E. College St.
Oberlin
Tuesday evening 6:15
[July 7, 1926]

My most adorable—

Even sitting up with groaning men alone at midnight cannot quite remove the soothingness of wide streets, slowly waving great trees, and air and quiet. My head is a drum all tied up tight and God how tired I am of *sitting*. (I was before I came even and here it's the best thing I do). I sat up from 10 to 3:30 alone last night (it seems much longer since everyone is in bed by nine). I had to work last night with him—rubbing him all over with alcohol, greasing him and feeding him whiskey drop by drop. Reminds me of Jojo's infancy. The money didn't come today but I didn't need it anyway. I may go—if it comes

*The "second wife" was Powell's hated stepmother, Sabra Stearns Powell (1877–1956), from whom she had fled as a young teenager in 1910.

tomorrow and a nurse comes here—down to Shelby on tomorrow night's train and up to Cleveland on Thursday night and back home by Sunday morning.

I am so mad. Both Phyllis and Mabel look young and slim and beautiful and I am the fat ugly one and I hate it. I am so tired sitting sitting sitting in restaurants, trains, and now sickrooms, with an eternal electric fan and nauseating smell of flowers. I hate flowers. All except red roses maybe.* Oh dear tweet, here is a lovely little town and I have to sit in a coop and look out at it. Hundreds of relatives around driving me crazy teetering around. Comfortable bed when I do get there but I can't sleep on a comfortable bed. And family jawings all around.

I am so tired sitting, dearest. Well, I will see you soon.

Call up Louise. Jojo would be a relief after this. I love you. And things aren't half bad if I weren't so on edge about everyone. Papa is sinking but nobody knows what [sic].

> Good-bye tweet,
> Dawn

I have no time really to feel free.
Don't get drunk, lover.

(COLLECTION TIM PAGE)

Roy Powell died on July 8, 1926, and was buried in Butternut Ridge Cemetery in North Olmsted, Ohio. Almost exactly thirty years later, his second wife, Sabra, would be interred next to him.

TO JOSEPH GOUSHA

> [Mount Sinai, Long Island
> ca. October 8, 1928]

Dearest—

Alone out here, I think of all the ways I have failed you and especially in the last few weeks when I have not done one thing to help. It doesn't seem fair or decent when you have had so much to bear that I should go on with my toy balloons and confetti as if life were just a big Mardi Gras. It seems to me I controlled my life until I got too happy—you arranged that—and then I just took a flying leap into the air and stayed there while you waded through the mud. You are the one who was meant for air and sunlight, you are the one whose flame burns always high and blue—true altar fire. I am the big D.S.C. bonfire on a

---

*This is a reference to Dawn and Joe's first formal date, at the Claremont Inn in Manhattan on February 28, 1920, when he brought her a bunch of red roses—a romantic gesture she would never forget.

Bleecker Street curb*—a big blaze but of no quality, only big enough and dangerous enough to overwhelm your precious glow.

Why should you go on forever with debts, work, indignities—not one consolation for the high pride which is you and which I fell in love with—while I am pampered and coddled (always by you with a faint chorus probably arranged by you) until I lose all consciousness of my responsibilities—until in fact I lose sight of my own real happiness which is with you and always will be, no matter how wild I run or how childishly perverse I act?

I want to tell you all these things because even if we live a hundred years life is still too short to say the truth in—that you have always made me happy, that always I find your quality superior to any other man's, that always I know my own bouncing talents are doing their best to crowd out a far rarer gift—yours. I do know all this, dear, but if eight years ago I might have done something about it, now I am softened by your own tenderness so that it is hard to know how to go about a plan of life more to your advantage. I have, loving you, been incredibly selfish and ruthless. I want so much to change and arrange our lives so that you will be the coddled, free, happy one. You were so gay and so arrogant, darling, when I first met you. That is the way you were meant to be—we both know that—not the crushed, hunted, half-defiant, half-cringing person that circumstances try to make you, circumstances that I am going to do my best to change, dear.

Love, always—and what a selfish, dependent, barren sort of love it has been!

D.

(COLLECTION TIM PAGE)

TO ORPHA MAY STEINBRUECK

106 Perry Street
New York
November 26 [1928]

Dear Auntie May—

I have been working hard and finished a play last week which looks pretty good. I have two plays on the market now but outside of nibbles now and then I would be a fool to expect production within the next two years, because it's the toughest game in the world to play—all a question of graft, pull, and mostly sheer luck. My novel *The Bride's House* is already being printed—it's dedicated to "Orpha May" and is scheduled to be out February 18. I'm sure you won't

---

*Bonfires sponsored by the Democratic Party were then a common sight in lower Manhattan, especially around election time, in a holdover from Tammany days.

like it as well as the other book. It's supposed to be about a farm—a big old farm in northern Ohio—about 1898 or before or later—how do I know? I think the characters must have come out of a lot of old family albums I've seen in my day. The book at the end is good and the whole effect is good but the first half is so damned dull you'd never read on to the end if you had any sense.

Joe has shifted jobs from the H. C. Michaels Co., which was getting a little weak on its feet, to the Paul Cornell Agency. It means that we're broke for about three weeks since we never save any money and are, on the whole, pretty shiftless. And I can't let either of the maids go because I'd be insane without Louise [Lee] to look after Jojo and Marie* really saves me money because she does the laundry so much better and cheaper than the laundry does it, as well as doing all my dishes and cleaning every day which God knows would never be done if it depended on Miss Powell. Joe's new job is a swell one—he's secretary of the firm, will be a stockholder, etc.—and the people there think he's so wonderful that they make a great fuss over every word he utters, and if you do have to work it certainly makes it more agreeable when people give you more than credit.

Jojo woke me up the other day. "Mother," he shouted, and when I went into his room he said, "As a matter of fact I can't pull up the shade." I said "What?" and he repeated, "As a matter of fact I can't pull up the shade." I said, "Don't be silly, go on and pull it up." He did and then sat down smiling triumphantly because he'd said "as a matter of fact." It reminded me of the old boyfriend who said "disheveled" and the time Gretchen woke you up to tell of some glorious creature who actually had said, "It's immaterial to me."

I keep learning things. The December issue of some magazine called *College Life* has a story of mine which they paid me nothing for. I investigated it and found out they'd bought rights to it from *Munsey's* and that like a fool I'd been signing something with *Munsey's* from time to time which gave them all rights. I wouldn't even have a word to say if they sold it to the movies. The best magazines don't do that but *Munsey's*, it seems, gets away with whatever it can.

I think I will come out this winter for a few days after my book comes out.

> Love and best wishes—
> Dawn

(COLLECTION TIM PAGE)

---

*Marie Jeffers worked as a maid for the Gousha family for more than twenty years. Powell often made note of Jeffers's sayings and opinions in her diaries.

TO MABEL POWELL POCOCK AND
PHYLLIS POWELL COOK

The Harbor
667 Madison Avenue
[Fall 1929]

Dear Mabel and Phyllis:

I am getting well.* They thought at first my heart was permanently crippled but so far they see no damage. The right lung filled and jammed the heart out of place but they gave me stuff—icebags and morphine—and I was only in real pain about four days and nights, and the X-rays showed it was pleurisy causing the pericarditis and that as soon as it got well the heart would be all right.

Joe was terribly upset—I think it is worse for the one responsible—and he was up with me alone two nights and when I started going out of my head he was simply wild. We were stuck out there in the country—five miles from anywhere.† He had to leave me and canoe across the bay just to phone and then the doctor came and told him I could not possibly be out of bed for a year— and even that with luck. So they taxied me to New York ($30—and me ready to pass out any minute) and I'm here at this marvelous private hospital overlooking Park Avenue with $50-a-day rooms but mine is charming at $11 a day (we'll be in the street when I get out) with nurses $18 a day so if I didn't get well I suppose Joe could sue them.

But everyone is so kind—the place isn't like a hospital—furniture green with Oriental rugs, telephone at bedside, broiled squab, live lobsters, broiled sweetbreads, crabmeat, delicious French soups, orange juice—anything you want at any time. These things do help you to get well.

Debutantes and broken-down brokers are here for "rest," bring their own pink silk sheets and radios and squirt perfume up and down the hall. . . .

Love,
Dawn

(COLLECTION TIM PAGE)

*What was initially called a heart attack, as described here, was more likely an early symptom of Powell's teratoma, a rare type of tumor that would affect her from the mid-1920s until it was finally diagnosed and removed in 1949.
†From the late 1920s through the late 1940s, the Goushas annually took a beach house in the hamlet of Mount Sinai, Long Island, near Port Jefferson.

TO ORPHA MAY STEINBRUECK

106 Perry Street
Feb. 27 [1929]

Dearest Auntie May—

I wrote you telling you how much I liked those swell little pants but I never sent it. My book* doesn't come out till Feb. 28 (tomorrow) but it has already had a big advance sale and gone into a second edition. More exciting than that is my play, which will be produced probably on Labor Day here.† I lunched with the director yesterday and he wants me to write another play with him— we think the same way so I think I will. It has been a winter of work and worry and I'm thinking of getting a house for this damned family business out in the suburbs and then taking a hotel room in town where I can stay and work and Joe too and then go out to our "home" on weekends. Because I'm too fond of Jojo to ignore him and his nurse when they're around so it's very hard to write—I do anyway but I'm a wreck.

Love,
Dawn

P.S. March 11—Forgot to mail this. Book already in second edition and doing well.

(COLLECTION TIM PAGE)

TO PHYLLIS POWELL COOK

106 Perry Street
June Thursday [1929]

Dear Phyllis,

Jojo has a broken leg and I have tonsilitis and he's in Westfield New Jersey and I'm here and that's the trouble.

A month ago he was spending the weekend with his nurse who has a house there in the country and he fell out of a tree—only three or four feet but it was a twist he gave his leg I guess and two bones broke. Deesie (the nurse) set it as best she could and put it in splints and drove him to a very fine hospital in Plainfield, N.J., and then called me up. I was scared of course and went out at once, but it was a clean break. He was at the hospital a week and seemed to think it was all very enjoyable even with one leg in a plaster cast. Then we took

---

*This was *The Bride's House.*
†She may have been referring to *The Party*, eventually staged by the Group Theatre in 1933 as *Big Night*. In any event, nothing would come of this planned production, and *Big Night* would be the first of only two plays by Powell to be staged during her lifetime.

him to Deesie's house in Westfield so he'd be near the Plainfield doctor and when we took him there for a new cast a few days ago and X-ray the leg was going straight but bone very slow in building so he has to take ultraviolet-ray treatments and Armour's Liver Extract while I can't go out as I have fever of 104 one day and 97 the next. All rheumatism and tonsils. Did you have yours out and were you better after you did and was it bad? (Answer no to all these questions.)

Jojo seems very contented and is so patient it breaks your heart. He has a wheelchair and a few little colored friends who bring him flowers. It will take a longer time than usual to heal because of this lack in his system.

Somebody stole that lovely green scarf you gave me. It matched an evening dress of mine and I wore it under my white evening wrap and left both in the dressing room and when I went to get them the scarf was gone and since it was supposed to be such a refined beautiful home I didn't dare say I suspected the hostess of needing a scarf. Joe gets an awful kick out of those liqueur glasses—guest-sized cocktails—and we haven't broken one yet which is a record.

I have almost finished a new play. Somebody wanted one of my plays for summer stock company but there is nothing in it and they might do it so badly it would ruin its chances for Broadway production. I don't expect to have my new novel done before Xmas at the earliest and maybe it won't be out before fall of next year as it's pretty long.* It's dedicated to you for sentimental reasons but don't get scared—it's about a young girl who goes to Oberlin to live and then has a love life. It's about a town I call Lamptown—sort of a combination of all the factory sections of all the factory towns I ever knew and about a dance hall and a milliner and her son and her husband and the dancing teacher and a Quick Lunch like Kayser's and so on.

I owe $1500 for Jojo's school bill and all I seem to be getting is a lot of prestige and damn little money though *Bride's House* did very well and got better reviews than the other book. . . .

Write me what you are doing and if you have any more children. Are you fat? I was so beautiful and thin last year on Basey Bread but it seems it won't work more than once and now I'm fat as a fool though I notice I got thin these last two days. How're Carol and Phyllis?

Love,
Dawn

(COLLECTION TIM PAGE)

---

*A considerably altered version of this novel, *Dance Night*, would be published in the fall of 1930 by Farrar & Rinehart. Powell always considered it her finest work.

TO JOSEPH GOUSHA

The Beaches
Somerset
Bermuda
[ca. March 31, 1930]
Dearest—

This might be a lovely place with you—all this blue water and white-roofed buildings—but after a seasick voyage this whole works is like a big Alice Foote MacDougall tearoom (beginning in this Quainte Olde House), with the same refined spinsters at hand, doctors of philosophy and young British girls squealing and yipping over the new rector and what a puffick deah he is. The cultured middlewestern voice would be such a relief after the nervous shock of all this squealing.*

I am so tired I could die and look back fondly on my seasickness as the brightest spot so far since I sleep with Margaret and her two kids scream all night—"Mama! Mama!"—and get up at 5 a.m. and raise a whining hullabaloo that makes Jojo seem too ideal.

It's exactly like Pomfret—a beautiful countryside, old and quaint, and then these refined tea-room near-Lesbians all over the place making it quainter every minute with olde china and quainty chairs. Four tables in the dining room and guarded conversation except for the English yipping which makes the old walls ring like the tin they are. Next time I go anyplace I go with you, Mr. Gousha. We could stay in Hamilton, the city, which is full of surreys driven by darkies.

I haven't had two seconds to myself as the estates belong to people and can't be sat on by oneself. At least it served a noble purpose in making me forget all other matters but this. It's exactly like Pomfret—refinement rolling you down into a helpless pulp. To write is hopeless as well as impossible. I hate every goddam inch of the place and all brats and all quaint things.

It's poured rain so far. If I could sleep or the sun would shine I might recover.

Don't worry, dearest, because it's all very good for me and makes Perry Street seem ideal but you know how upset I get over those Pomfret types and how affected I am by tea at 4:15 in the drawing room.

Today we go to Sinky Bay to a picnic with the *14* other Burnhams (includ-

---

*Powell had traveled to Bermuda with a new friend, the wealthy and generous Margaret Burnham De Silver (1890–1962), for a Burnham family reunion. It is very likely that this was the first time she had ever left the United States.

ing eight kids) and there will be liquor which was so perfectly delicious on the boat after I finally had it that it should make up for all else. Will write a cheerier letter tomorrow when the sun shines.

Love love love,

Dawn

Sunday afternoon

Dearest—
I am sending you a little pink oleander and a posy. After I took luminol I slept all afternoon with kids all over me and then took a walk in the rain. I wish you were here to make it as beautiful as it is. The rocks on one side with pinky sand and then these palms and pink oleander blossoms and a bay like a made-up Mount Sinai Bay and air and smell very much like it. Not warm enough to want to go naked or even swim though they say these few days are quite cold. Along the road the rather old Spanishy or Mexican-looking houses look very tiny—as if they were one tiny room. Then when you look at them from the bay you see their fannies backing down to the bay in two and three stories until by the time they hits the water wall they're a small castle. Now how do you account for that architecture? . . .

Love,

Dawn

(COLLECTION TIM PAGE)

TO COBURN GILMAN*

Hotel Traymore
Atlantic City
Friday
[Spring 1930]

Dear Coby—
    I have the jitters due to nature and can't think of any cure but to buy a Victrola or a Nero or a Brutus or what the hell. I am reading *Lady Chatterley's Mister* and could weep. It's such a marvelous book (so far). That Clifford is the greatest figure in history (hey hey). And the woods and mines are so real. How much nicer book-woods are than real ones!

---

*Very few of Powell's letters to her great friend the editor Coburn Gilman (1894–1967) have survived. There has been much speculation on the nature of their relationship, which I have examined in *Dawn Powell: A Biography*.

This is extremely unrefreshing—this goddam vacation. I would rather almost go to Bermuda—certainly I would. I wish you could stock this territory with your friends and visit them until they lose consciousness. I shouldn't be surprised to see myself in town next Wednesday or Thursday but I don't know why or how. I miss you.

Love,
Dawn

(COLLECTION TIM PAGE)

TO COBURN GILMAN

Friday
[Bermuda, Spring 1930]

Dear Coby—

Now I'm in a gaga state of British and Boston refinement so don't let me hear you use any foul language or I'll be all a-twitter. The damned wind blows all the time and shutters bang all night so you don't sleep and after only these few days I have finally bowed to fate and must admit that the tearoom people are fine, high-principled Best People, and that it is Miss P. who is in error. I would like to tell them that Monday night I dreamed of an idyllic love life with a Newfoundland dog, and on Tuesday a donkey who played the piano marvelously was my dream hero. (Page Professor Gilman.)

The coy little sun finally came out yesterday for a long time and I swam and burned agonizingly and in the night realized I'd never get home—that I'd just be buried on this terrible place. (Don't tell Jean I think it's terrible, but damn me if it isn't or else I'm no nature lover as you think.)

Nature note 1.—The wind never succeeds in blowing the oleander blossoms off the trees.

N. note 2.—There are a million little blue and red velvet birds flying around trimming the bushes.

N. note 3.—Mr. Rudyard Kipling is at large here and

> *"If he could smile when nobody else is smiling*
> *If he could laugh when tears were in his eye 'n—*
> *If—if—if so, then indeed, indeed."*

I feel very strange and perturbed in making this journey, and I felt from the minute I got on the boat as if I were going *there* only very lonesomely alone. In my ocean-wave delirium I was certain you'd open my stateroom door any minute. When finally a strange man *did* open it I thought I'd better be examined for hallucinations. (He'd made a mistake.)

Life is so confusing. I've really decided down here that I cannot bear the terrible business of writing things that mean so much to me any more, that the only solution to anything is to write things that take up only your time and an ounce of brain—say short stories—so that it means very little if they fall short, and the gain is financial, so that it smoothes out the difficulties of living. It's difficult enough anyway without deliberately selecting work that is more than you can stand. That is, the only way to *bear* living is not to have things mean anything to you.

Is this clear—oh, Cliff? I don't think so.

Do you want me to bring you an octopus, darling? There are several on hand.

Dawn

(COLLECTION TIM PAGE)

TO JOHN F. SHERMAN

106 Perry Street, NY
[June 1931]

Dear Jack*—

Your letter was so swell I was almost tempted to answer it but I've decided not to. I hope you don't mind but you know how busy we artists are.

I wish you could get a couple weeks off and come visit me. There's no room in town but we could swim and canoe and shoot clams out at the cottage on Long Island. I usually work out there so I never ask anybody out because if there's anything I hate it's being social as soon as I wake up. So you'd have to be social with a couple of rats on the porch until noon and then hide somewhere while I get social and tell you about my adventures in the Civil War. Say, doesn't that sound like a great proposition, Jack? Isn't that nothing? Well, maybe I'll sell something before long and can send you the fare. (Since this is just a promise and no cash involved I might as well make it good and say I'll send you not only the fare but a ruby-studded bathing suit and an ermine stomacher—if not ermine, at least Armour, ha ha ha, always kidding!)

As for New York City it's the only place where people with nothing behind

---

*Young Jack Sherman, Powell's cousin, was now living with Orpha May Steinbrueck at 121 North Broadway in Shelby.

them but their wits can be and do everything. A young man, particularly (Baccalaureate Speech), with a tuxedo and decent manners, can go anyplace, be welcomed in the ritziest circles and even fought over by debutantes. All he needs to do is act wise—men are too scarce for girls to care whether they were brought up anywhere.

The chief difference, too, between New York and everyplace else in the world is that here you brag of your early struggles—how you worked on the section or delivered ice and your folks were mountain whites or blacks—and everybody brought up at Harvard or Vassar or in convents abroad is very envious and hates their folks for always coddling them. The place is full of standard young Harvard men, all exactly alike—we make fun of them. Well, every place else but New York you have to hide all your low beginnings and pretend everybody in the family is white and can read and write and play the harp. What I mean, friend, is that you can be yourself here and it's the only place where being genuine will absolutely get you anywhere you want. If it suits you—as it does me—to live in the toughest quarter of downtown, semi-slums, because the houses are old and quaint and have little courts in back and pushcarts and hurdy-gurdies go by your window with fruit and vegetables and straw hats and geraniums—well, that doesn't prevent you from being asked to Park Avenue penthouses or any place. The very *best* people think to be able to do as you damn please, not caring what anyone thinks, is the mark of aristocracy. (When I say the best people I mean me, of course.) That's what makes Auntie May a swell—yes, and practically most of the Shermans, including your Poppa, because they don't give a damn what a lot of average, mediocre people think.

I showed your letter to several friends of mine and they were all so dazzled to think you had the guts to work in a *machine* shop. No matter what you say they always think it's just a hobby. They all think it was a terribly amusing hobby for me to run the elevator at college and all that rather than lower my pride to take money from my family.

The Goushas, Mr. and Mrs. J. R., are very poor this year. I made money last year but had doctor bills. Now I won't get anything till my novel is finished or my play goes into rehearsal, if ever. These are months off. Meantime, Joe's salary has been cut 25 percent, though we feel lucky the firm hasn't gone under completely during this depression.

Louise, the colored maid who looks like Auntie May, has gone away on a month's vacation and it sure is great sitting around in a mess all day—no dishes wanted, no beds made, nobody tiptoeing around dusting my desk as I write. Hurray for dirt! Auntie May will be shocked at this as I was always so fussy about my room and housekeeping in general.

I have some gorgeous clothes I am crazy to send June and Adelaide* unless they'd be too big. Ask Auntie May. Can they cut up and sew? These include many stunning numbers I wore in high school and the girls may look above their station in them, that's the only trouble. Hope they don't mind court trains.

Much love and to Auntie May,
Dawn

(COLLECTION JOHN F. SHERMAN)

*Jack's younger sisters.

9 EAST TENTH STREET
(AND HOLLYWOOD)

1932–1942

[Chateau Elysée, Los Angeles]
New Year's Day, 1932

Dearest—

This is the swellest place and wouldn't you love it?* My hotel lust is at last satisfied. This is the most deluxe hotel apartment in the place—a little like Pierre's, perhaps, but in much better taste, Ann† says. I wired ahead from the train, thinking I'd get more attention, and I did—a place as big as Coby [Gilman's] entire apartment or almost—beautiful Louis blue and gold drawing room, toile de Jouy tapestries and maple beds (2) with taffeta curtains, huge bedroom, pink and blue marble bath, perfectly equipped kitchen with Frigidaire, etc., sun room and breakfast corner, meals sent up all hours, wonderful servants delighted with a ten-cent tip—and all for $4 a day, merely because it's $300 a month and they had no single room for me. Ann's is much smaller and more expensive. Dorothy Speare lives here and Mrs. Eddie Mayer has a duplex and they tell me Lily Damita.

I'm writing a synopsis or so-called original of that Eden story, pretending it's new on Ann's behest, and Monday we have lunch with Junior Laemmle.‡

---

*This was the first of Powell's two ill-fated attempts to adapt to California life as a Hollywood screenwriter.
†Ann Watkins (1885–1967) was Powell's first literary agent.
‡Carl Laemmle, Jr., was then the senior executive of Universal Studios, which had been founded by his father.

Had lunch with Jack [Lawson] at RKO Studios one day. He is, as near as I can figure, the belle of Hollywood and everybody admires him, to say nothing of the ladies' fighting over him. I've only seen them* twice as their friends are different from the few I know but I expect to go out there tomorrow for the weekend.

I loathed the first night I was here down at Mrs. Eddie Mayer's downstairs—with several women and Jack and Paul Gangliene and the way they all talked. But the sheer geographical excitement of being on the edge of the world high up with trees shooting past your windows on the 6th floor and the heavenly June air. You must do this. Curious and strange air but so far have seen nothing any different from an ordinary Park Avenue or Dwight Fiske† party and people much nicer . . . everyone easy and jolly and glad to see you and champagne and old Mrs. Morgan and old Mrs. Hatch, two dowagers if ever there were, very fascinated by *The Bride's House* and so far everyone explaining, "Of course we know no picture people though I understand there are some quite nice ones that one could have in one's home even."

I suppose this isn't the real Hollywood but of their kind they are much jollier and more intelligent than Dwight's stuffies or Coby's stuffies of the New York vintage. Eric [Hatch]‡ used to be at Paramount but is out now, though butlers and chefs and chauffeurs float around his house freely. Ann says his papa was president of the New York Stock Exchange. I think they'll all give me a pain in the neck after a few days and I know the Lawsons are disgusted but I do get more kick out of being around people who know all my works than around all the Lawson pals who never heard of me. (Don't tell anyone this—it's a shocking revelation of egotism, but no shock to you.)

How is Pee Wee? I hope he isn't interfering with your program too much. Say darling, so far this is incredibly cheap—breakfast sent up by jolly English waiters of orange juice, grapefruit, eggs, bacon, toast, marmalade, pot of coffee—80 cents! And I swear if you saw the place you'd say even if they charged $40 a day it would be worth it once in a lifetime. I haven't spent more than $30 (including train meals and tips) since I left New York. It can't be done. Not drinking much as I have a headache constantly anyway—have had since we crossed the Rockies. I imagine it's the altitude if this be altitude but feel grand and conscious of having a swell vacation, which you must have. It's exactly what we both have needed so I want you to plan to go abroad with Fred

---

*Lawson and his wife, Sue, were now living in Hollywood, where he was enjoying enormous success as both a highly paid scriptwriter and a Communist theorist.
†Dwight Fiske (1892–1959) was a successful nightclub entertainer with whom Powell collaborated on a number of risqué song-stories.
‡Powell's friend the American novelist, scenarist, and short-story writer Eric Hatch (1901–1973) is probably best remembered today for *My Man Godfrey*.

[Lissfelt] or Harry [Lissfelt] or Bill* this summer. Okay. Love to Jojo and be sure to eat in, have a rest, don't drink much and I'll be home by Jan. 15 or sooner.

XX,
Dawn

TO BARRETT CLARK[†]

New York
January 5, 1933

Dear Mr. Clark—

I think it is very good of you to write the article and a coincidence, too, considering that you, as the dashing lecturer on the drama (fresh from Reinhardt and Craig and whatever other foreign fields) on a flying visit to Lake Erie College for Women years ago, started me taking all the drama courses and digging into all the drama shelves.

Born in Mt. Gilead, Ohio, 35 years ago—brought up largely in Shelby, Ohio, but lived around with other relatives in various villages and factory towns all over central Ohio. Lived in grandmother's rooming house in Shelby and often called in by transient theatrical troupes to take part in plays. At 7, made debut in *Hearts of Gold*, as regular child for part was sick and I also had curls. Worked on town newspaper after school hours at 15. Never could bear respectability and rules and ran away from whatever relatives imposed it. (All forebears are Ohioans way back to Indians.)

Graduated from Lake Erie 1918. Came to New York fall of 1918—was a yeoman in Navy, later in publicity and advertising, married an ex–dramatic critic from Pittsburgh (Joseph R. Gousha, now in advertising), had son. My novels are *She Walks in Beauty* (1928, a best-seller),[‡] *The Bride's House* (1929), *Dance Night* (1930) and *The Tenth Moon*. All deal with varying phases of village, factory town, farm life in the Middle West.

I wrote my first play *Women at Four O'Clock*,[§] because I'd carried the mss.

---

*William Messerschmidt, an old friend of Joseph Gousha's, from his boyhood in Pittsburgh.

†Barrett Clark (1890–1953) was an American editor and drama critic whose lecture at Lake Erie College had helped convince Powell she wanted to become a playwright. He had been instrumental in setting up the Group Theatre production of *Big Night*, which was to open on Broadway less than two weeks later. It would be a disastrous flop, though Powell would always believe it to be her strongest play.

‡This is an exaggeration. No sales figures for *She Walks in Beauty* have survived, but it was certainly no best-seller, nor did it receive much critical attention. Powell never mentioned *Whither* in lists of her work.

§In fact, Clark had read *Women at Four O'Clock* as early as 1927 and found it wanting. Still, he admired some of the dialogue and met with Powell to offer his advice.

of the first two novels around for three years, unable to sell them, and I thought perhaps the publishers were right—I'd never make a novelist. Later the novels sold and received amazing praise. Since then, I find I need both forms to satisfy me. Ideas which are essentially comment on manners seem to belong in the play form—you need the physical contact with your audience, get them where they can't miss the direct punch, then let them think about it afterward. Like all forms of satire, it is necessarily unfair, yet quite as fair as the Pollyanna treatment. The form which allows me second thoughts as well as first is the novel— here a character may receive more justice; what he intends to do, what he meant to be, what others think of him are as important as what he does and says; the line he would damn himself with on the stage may be explained by a quick trip through his mind, the novelist's privilege.

The drama form—far easier and more agreeable to me—appeals to me as achieving its ends more quickly and powerfully. The writer has only to present his one side, the audience and critics do the novelist's job of filling in, making excuses, seeing the other side, defending whichever characters they feel best equipped to understand. This public willingness to take active part in an artist's creation seems to make the drama a better medium for social satire. God knows that by the time the various producers, readers, agents, actors, directors, critics, technicians, etc., have gotten a play before an audience the thing practically amounts to a mass movement.

You have my plays—*The Party, Women at Four O'Clock*, and *Walking Down Broadway*. I have another one that bores me so to read that I can't fix it up. I worked too long and too hard on it. I have two others on the fire but I don't like to spoil them by fumbling with them, preferring to wait till they're thoroughly set in my mind. Playwriting seems to me like tightrope walking—it won't allow one false step.

I suppose much of this sounds extremely banal but then one's private thoughts usually are.

Sincerely,
Dawn Powell

(BARRETT CLARK COLLECTION, BEINECKE RARE BOOK
AND MANUSCRIPT LIBRARY, YALE UNIVERSITY)

TO JOHN DOS PASSOS*

[May 1933]

Dear Dos—

I can understand a certain amount of admiration for the Johns Hopkins institution† but I don't see why you should make a fool of yourself over it even with our arthiters as an excuse to hang around. Besides I'm afraid you're coming back with a beard full of Mencken and a Southern accent.

Yesterday at 11, the Jews started parading, pouring out of manholes and kiosks and old ladies' bustles and jumping out of muffs and filing cabinets and by eight o'clock the Bronx and several skyscrapers had vacantly collapsed. They bore big signs saying "Down with Baltimore," "Down with Rheumatism" and "Up with Passos," and "Free Silver"—to tell the truth, I hear drums and shouldn't be surprised that they're still marching what with all the new Jewish babies born in the night and rushed into the parade.

I was enthusiastically anti-Hitler for the first four or five hours but by nightfall I was trying to negotiate a pogrom, or at least arrange for some magic pipes to lead them all into the East River to the strains of inordinately beautiful music. It's very odd how contrarily these demonstrations act—welding into solidarity innocent individualistic bystanders who up to this moment never were against anything. On May Day, for instance, as I promenaded across 35th Street with no more revolutionary thought in my foolish little head than a plan to buy Larvax at Macy's (and not even spray it on the customers as I swooped up and down the escalator)—anyway the Fur and Feather workers were demonstrating, chanting "Free Tom Mooney" and again "Down with Hitler." They were such good, honest, innocent-looking people—more like Ohio Methodists and Baptists than anything else in New York and twice as narrow-minded as God knows good people have to be. But all along the sidewalks panhandlers, men hunting for jobs, traveling salesmen, visiting nurses—people who minded their own business as a rule and never talked to strangers—paused to watch the parade forming and say to each other, "Well, it may succeed in the old country but it will never succeed here." And in the bus going home as it stopped for twenty minutes at Madison Square to allow the now-overwhelming parade to pass, lady shoppers who loathed each other were loudly remarking to each other that it might succeed in Russia but never here—

---

*The distinguished modernist novelist John Dos Passos (1896–1970) was Powell's dear and constant friend for many years, despite political disagreements between them that began as early as the time of this letter, in which she teases him for his then-fervent socialist views.
†Dos Passos was then in the Johns Hopkins Hospital for the treatment of rheumatic fever; Powell's later reference to his "cancer" is unexplained.

and moreover why didn't they go back where they came from? Even the Iowa farmers would have said this, I imagine.

Esther [Andrews]* and Griffin [Barry]† got back in a precarious condition from their pilgrimage. Civilization is cracking up all around, and if you wait a week or two all of us will be with you in your cell—Griffin with gizzard trouble, Esther with a sour back (in fact she and Margaret Neuritis De Silver have been laid up with osteopathy for the past fortnight). Joe has something; my Louise [Lee] has gone away for a nervous breakdown originally scheduled for May 1st but effective as of May 9th; the doctor said I had a tumor or cyst over the heart—formerly merely pleural fluid, whatever that is—and not to worry as there was nothing to do but wait till it was definite enough to cut out and fortunately there was one man in America who could do it so I hadn't a care in the world (I suppose that one man is Percy Hammond).‡ Everybody sits around in shawls and complains and says—Lucky Dos, he's only got cancer.

I've found a very fine book at the secondhand store named *Mona MacLean, Medical Student* by a Graham Travers, written in 1890 and really a darn good novel so far. Very Advanced—believing that there should be women doctors largely to keep male doctors away from one's daughters but what if—once women got to be doctors—they were permitted to prescribe for MEN? "By Gad," said Sir Douglas at dinner as he and Lady Munro were keeping the ball rolling, "it makes me pale to think of all that girl [Miss MacLean] must know about men."

We had an average New York Day yesterday, the telephone being cut off at noon due to no pay bill, at night we sailed up in my elegant Hawes dress (she's still suing me for it) to the Mayfair Yacht Club at East 53rd Street and the river where you sit on a terrace *comme* a deck and gaze at Welfare Island and pretend it's a ship and you're an emigrant and Dwight Fiske tells stories at the piano which drunken rich people scream about—realizing they'd betray their mental age if they frankly admitted they didn't think much of them—and Joe's garter fell off, and it turned out we weren't having a bit of fun anyway so we came home and resumed our separate ailments.

Did you see Berenice's poems?§ They are really excellent, I think. I always

---

*Esther Andrews (c. 1890–1962) was an American editor who enjoyed close associations with several well-known writers, including D. H. Lawrence, Dos Passos, Ernest Hemingway, and Powell. She lived with her lover Canby Chambers in Key West, Florida, for many years; their home became a sort of salon for visiting authors.

†Griffin Barry (1885–1957) was an American journalist and writer who covered, among other things, the early years of the Soviet Union and the Spanish Civil War.

‡Percy Hammond was a New York drama critic who had been particularly savage in reviewing Powell's *Big Night.*

§Powell is referring here to a book of poetry published by an acquaintance, Berenice Dewey, who had recently died.

feel so relieved and grateful when lady poets don't write about what vagabond lovers they are—especially when you have generally only to see them to realize they're only old Aunt Minnie who had all she could do to bed Uncle Eph, and any vagabonding they ever did was about as light and charming as Lizzie Borden's coquettishly peeping over the handle of her axe.

> Love to Katy and get well,
> Dawn

P.S. I saw Julie and Y.K.* a couple of times—I like them both so much. Also, Ed Massey† is in town with thoughts of a little theater upstate for the summer to try out rather Harvardy plays. Sue states the Lawsons may not be able to get a job after July 1st but will probably stay there for the September earthquakes, anyway. Literary note—the models at Ten Eyck, Couturier, where Mrs. De Silver and I are being laced into wholesale linen suits, are reading *Ann Vickers* and *My Lover, My Friend* and using Pinaud's Moustache Wax on their eye-winkers instead of mascara.

(DOS PASSOS COLLECTION, THE UNIVERSITY OF VIRGINIA)

TO JOSEPH GOUSHA

> *[121 North Broadway*
> *Shelby, Ohio*
> *ca. June 27, 1933]*

Dearest—

Still in Shelby having tranquil but profitable time and outside of the terrific brain-stunning heat—gasping for air—it's very fine. I am horrified and embarrassed to think how near I came to finishing that book without a checkup on this country. It's so different at first I almost decided to chuck the novel out of sheer ignorance—but now I'm getting my bearings and enjoying Auntie May and my young cousin Jack Sherman (you would like him). Haven't seen anyone much. But it looks as if I would stay till after the 4th as I want to look over Bethel—the old Sherman homestead and graveyard of [my] grandfather Sherman, *his* father Delano Sherman, and *his* father, Asel Sherman—and see my Great Aunt Lib.

---

*Yeremia Kenley Smith, a writer and horticulturalist, was the older brother of Katy Smith Dos Passos, the author's first wife. His wife was known as Julie.
†George Edward Massey (1894–1942) was one of Dos Passos's early friends and a stage director associated with the New Playwrights Theater.

So take Harry [Lissfelt] or Bill out for 4th of July or come out here. Be good, dear, and I'll see you about Wednesday. Too hot to even write.

Love,
Dawn

(COLLECTION TIM PAGE)

TO JOHN DOS PASSOS

9 East 10th Street
[ca. June 1933]

Dear chum Dos—

Clurman and Crawford and Strasberg*—who were much funnier when Jimmy Durante was with them—say your play is a very fine thing and seem unperturbed by individual automobiles for the characters though personally I would feel perturbed over what characters they'd place in the automobiles. They say they're going to repertoire in Boston next year but I doubt if they've gotten enough moratorium money together to buy your play. Why don't you send it to Chester Erskine at the Hotel Ambassador? He wants to do some spectacular thing and has no money too.

Frankly there is money changing hands around here but not mine. A few days ago while banks closed and all Paris laughed, Knopf gave George O'Neil[†] a large advance on a novel to be written soon, M.G.M. or somebody paid thousands to Phil Stong the *State Fair* man, *Harper's* Magazine paid Selma Robinson $250 for an eight-page pastiche, and *The New Yorker* offered me $70 for four pages of suitably pointless dribble which I could wipe off my nose in five minutes. Carol Hill Brandt[‡] even told me she'd gotten a $6000 advance on somebody's novel and worse luck—she wouldn't lie. I hear Macmillan and Knopf are the only publishers blooming in the depresh. . . .

I stopped writing my monumental novel last week and am sitting now on a China play—a gay, charming trifle for Anna Held to star in.

Love to Katy,
Dawn

*Harold Clurman (1901–1980), Cheryl Crawford (1902–1986), and Lee Strasberg (1901–1982) were, among many other distinctions, the three founders of the Group Theatre, which had presented Powell's *Big Night* in early 1933. They never produced any of Dos Passos's plays.
†Powell's longtime friend George O'Neil (1897–1940) was a poet, playwright, scenarist, and biographer of John Keats. O'Neil later died suddenly in Los Angeles.
‡Carol Hill Brandt (1904–1984) and her husband, Carl Brandt (1888–1957), would be Powell's literary agents for most of the rest of her life.

P.S. I hear the earthquake was just a publicity stunt now to be known as [the] Warner Brothers Earthquake. The Santa Monica casualties turned out to be on inspection three killed in a student airplane and two deaths from canned tunafish.

(DOS PASSOS COLLECTION, THE UNIVERSITY OF VIRGINIA)

TO JOHN DOS PASSOS

[9 East Tenth Street
August 14, 1934]

Dear classmate—

Did you know I got my pin too* and now we're as good as two Masons and everywhere we travel we flash it on other passengers so that we can get acquainted with them and make irreparable friendships? I finished my Thing (now that we're in the picture business we might as well get right into technical terms) today and my head is reeling with the effort to keep to the story and at the same time remember that there *Blushing Brides* that put chum Lawson on his map and also *Hat Coat and Sandwich* by Massa [Francis] Faragoh. I think I worked everything in nicely. I fancy I escaped—so far—most of the horrors of Hollywood since I didn't have to confer or snap ideas. A very nice man named Lloyd Sheldon said, "Oh hello, Miss Powell, rewrite this shooting script." So I took it home and did it and he read it and said simply superb, take it right home and do it all over again, so I did. He added that it was so fine that I must foller him at once to the Stratosphere itself. And this is what pizzles me. I am very distrait and I want to go on a choochoo someplace. Would I be sorry should I do so—the immediate thing is a *Wizard of Oz* United Artists thinks would be darling for me to do†—out there and would I be forced to drink as much as the work (even here in the East all done in bed, too) entails? Or should I accept that invitation of yours to study Provincetown and go up there for a weekend next week instead on a Blue Whatchacallit Tour with other teachers? I could hunt for traces of Dos Passos civilization and blow up my findings in a little bottle for mantelpiece use. As I think it over I see I really have no problem at all. P'town is the thing my soul needs.

The real truth is that there is not a soul in N.Y. and hasn't been all summer. By July 26th 2 p.m. you went about peering under people's hats to see if they weren't relatives—in fact all the people you used to feel elated to get past unrecognized, now you snatch at if you see them two blocks away and beg

*Powell had begun working again as a scriptwriter for Paramount. This time, however, she had managed to convince the studio to let her stay in New York.
†Meditate, if you please, on this fascinating idea. As it turned out, Powell would have no connection with the famous Metro-Goldwyn-Mayer film to be released in 1939.

them to come talk to you and be your chum. And now that Vacation Month is here and the ones who have been away now go even further and the two people left in New York go away—well, aside from my Work of fiddling on *Tony's Wife* for Paramount Inc. I haven't been so desolate since—well, let's see—since I was in Hollywood last.

Does this seem a good reason for going to Hollywood? I guess not. . . .

All the stuff I wrote six years ago has suddenly been sold and every magazine shames me with Cinderella stories written to pay Louise then—and naturally not sold for that reason.

I got in town the day after you left and found messages erased and torn up and copied by dumbfounded maid who finally decided it was Deus Paso but you couldn't fool me—I knew it was the God of the mountains.

Will you organize the California comrades to boycott the Brevoort?* Here we have been boycotting them all summer but it is very expensive. It began one day when a few friends on the terrazzo started going to the Gents' room through the window instead of the formal door and the waiter and the papa-waiter refused all drinks so we boycotted it and went to the Lafayette. The next day, as we were sitting on the terrace, boycotting again, a big man wheeled a little baby past and Coby Gilman said, "Why, what a cunning little son of a bitch." So the big man shook his perambulator at us and said, "If you wait till I get this little bastard home I'll settle with you for calling my child a son of a bitch," at which he wheeled it stormily up the street shaking his fist at the same time while the little snort screamed and dangled by its snaps.

So the big man came back and made a scene with the proprietor. By this time we had named him Horace Hornickel and his Test-Tube Baby. Well, Horace then wouldn't let the Brevoort serve any more Pernods at Table 13 so we went and boycotted it from the Lafayette again. Then the next day as we were sitting on the terrasse—Jimmy Putnam, [Jacques] LeClercq, Gilman and Miss P.—the waiter wouldn't give us anything, not even Perrier, so we swooped over to Gilman's house—everybody did—and ate his dinner for one, boycotting steadily, until presently I decided to call up some friends long distance and somebody took the telephone away and I tipped over in the struggle and went through a glass door and at midnight was ushered by my reeling fellow boycotters to some strange midnight doctor who took two stitches in my arm. The next day Jimmy Putnam went to the hospital with ulcers of the stomach. This is all the fault of the Brevoort. So we are organizing boycotters all over the world—we have even a group who are boycotting the Brevoort from the Aus-

*The Hotel Brevoort on Fifth Avenue and Ninth Street was one of Powell's favorite nightspots.

tralian bush. We want some Silver Shirts, too, and when I go to P'town I will get the Spencers to boycott from there. It is a menace.Did Katy get out by plane or dog-sledge and are von Sternberg's legs as beautiful as they say?[*]

As ever,
Dawn

(DOS PASSOS COLLECTION, THE UNIVERSITY OF VIRGINIA)

TO JOHN DOS PASSOS

[9 East Tenth Street
Undated; early April 1935]

Dear Dos—

Your memo arrives at a moment when I feel all my old Elk and Modern Woodmen blood sweeping through me. This came partly from the crack in the Writers' Congress creed—"defend the Soviet of Russia with our bare bodies"—when suddenly five or ten generations of bigoted Republicans popped out of me as well as an old American Legion button and I was raring to defend my own old Steubenville steppes instead of Max Gorelik's.[†] I hesitate to broadcast these sentiments because no one will give me proper credit for them—anything that pigheaded gets a Mencken or Nathan credit line and it's no fair. I went to two or three meetings which sounded very bright but I swear I couldn't figure out what it was all for or who for until it ended with a parade plan and the singing of the "Internationale" with little hot hands up to little hard heads. . . .

The Theatre Collective at Two Washington Square is now reading and rehearsing Tovaritch Ornitz's[‡] opus—In Old Kaintuck. They told me the second act was no good so they do it as a one-acter or prologue. Lester Cohen was about the Writers' Congress. I understand a number of feuds went on—some between [Edward] Dahlberg and [Jack] Conroy[§] and some between Dahlberg and other people. Isn't it true the boys are going to get a ride to Paris free for this work? I thought they'd have to have a war for that but that will come later.

---

[*]Dos Passos was then working in Hollywood with director Josef von Sternberg and actress Marlene Dietrich on the film The Devil Is a Woman.
[†]Mordecai "Max" Gorelick (1899–1990) was a stage designer, director, teacher, and author with left-wing political views whom Powell knew from her days with the Group Theatre. This letter was written just before the American Writers' Congress, which began on April 26, 1935, and launched the Communist-dominated League of American Writers.
[‡]Samuel Ornitz (1890–1957) was an American author of the so-called proletarian school.
[§]Edward Dahlberg (1900–1977) and Jack Conroy (1898–1990), both left-wing American writers, enjoyed a famous feud.

I am on my Own, as Canby says, having fallen between two stools—if you can call Little, Brown one stool and Farrar & Rinehart another and I guess you can.* I can't think of what wonderful revenge to take—whether to stop the novel right now in its middle and take up radio tap dancing, or whether to finish it. I suppose the finest revenge to take on any publisher is to finish it, but there again which would hurt them most—a little Robert Nathan pastiche or a Hervey Allen pistachio? All I have done so far is to jitter and make veal scallopini and Mrs. Caldwell's Applesauce Cake Number 4 (without raisins) and I have run up a little maternity dress in case I think of that happy haven for nervous run-down women.

Bunny† seems to have vanished off to the Kremlin with so much politics keeping him in and pushing him out of Russia that we can look forward to a new national hero and Bun Wilson Clubs all over the world and Bunny's martyred ashes sprinkled over Stalin's borscht. What did he do with Rosamund?‡ Is she on her bicycle by his side?

The Spencers§ marched up to the Cape and it's almost time for Niles to march down again. Did you receive your Pulitzer all right for best-dressed man in the Keys? Sorry about that fool leprosy of yours. I should think you could get away from the colony once in a while come summer just enough to give it to other people around New York. The plays here are dumb as anything and there's nothing to do for the creeps but the Brevoort terrasse which is jammed with the dregs of the St. Nicholas bus and also dregs of everything else and nasty sunshine and fresh air. . . .

Dawn

(DOS PASSOS COLLECTION, THE UNIVERSITY OF VIRGINIA)

*A draft of Powell's latest novel, *Turn, Magic Wheel*—her first great satire—had met with dislike at Farrar & Rinehart, and an effort was made to sell it to Little, Brown, which also turned it down. The following year, Farrar & Rinehart would bring it out, and it would become Powell's fastest-selling book for that company.
†Powell had just begun her long and satisfying friendship with the critic and scholar Edmund Wilson (1895–1972).
‡"Rosamund" is most likely Wilson's eldest daughter, Rosalind Baker Wilson (born 1923), who would later become Powell's editor at Houghton Mifflin.
§Niles Spencer (1893–1952), an American artist associated with the "precisionist" school, was one of Powell's closest friends. His wife, Elizabeth, was known as Betty.

TO MICHAEL SADLEIR*

9 East 10th Street
April 3, 1936

Dear Mr. Sadleir:

I am delighted that you think so well of *Turn, Magic Wheel* and I am tremendously excited over my first publication in England.

The book, as you probably know, was amazingly well reviewed over here, so well received in fact that my friends dropped off like flies and creditors that should have been in their graves years ago storm my door. The story should really have shocked any decent right-thinking woman but by some quirk these respectable elderly women find time to write me dozens of fan letters (or anyway *two* dozen!). Personally, I couldn't bear Effie Callingham and her genteel charm, but this is the natural revulsion of any author whose noble-minded heroine has hung about the typewriter just a few weeks longer than her invitation merited.

When is the book scheduled for publication? I am now working on a play and another novel. I think Farrar and Rinehart sent you my last play— *Jig-Saw*—which was done by the Theatre Guild here, in 1934.

I hope my little brown cousins in England like me.

Thank you again for your letter.

Sincerely yours,
Dawn Powell

(SAMUEL PALEY LIBRARY, TEMPLE UNIVERSITY)

TO MICHAEL SADLEIR

9 East 10th Street
August 10, 1936

Dear Mr. Sadleir:

Thank you for your kindness in sending me the reviews of *Turn, Magic Wheel*. They seemed to me very encouraging, and even the bad ones seemed to me to have a far clearer and more intelligent standard of criticism than we have here. I think you have handled the book better than it was done here in every respect.

Nothing of course gave me more pleasure than Miss Waddell's note.[†] For

---

*Sadleir (1888–1957), an editor for John Constable, Ltd., and an accomplished novelist, was Powell's first champion in England, where he was responsible for bringing out several of her books.
[†]Helen Waddell (1889–1965) was an Irish translator, medievalist, and novelist known for her sensitive English renderings of Latin literature. She had written Sadleir, "I have just finished Dawn Powell's *Turn, Magic Wheel*; it is the same kind of experience as watching Elizabeth Bergner act for the first time. Odd to discover again the Comic Muse in Radio City, sorrowful, impish and wise. I do congratulate you."

years, her *Medieval Latin Lyrics* and *Wandering Scholars* have been my most treasured books. I give them first place on all Favorite Book lists and find new touches to admire every time I glance at them. Will you please tell her as much for me?

I hope people buy the book. I'm sure it would be much better for them than whatever book they did buy.

Sincerely,
Dawn Powell

(SAMUEL PALEY LIBRARY, TEMPLE UNIVERSITY)

TO JOSEPH GOUSHA

[Hollywood
*Fall 1936]**

Dear ex-Husb.—

I have a very beautiful and fantastically fabulous suite here . . . even to a servants' entrance. This is $225 a month. I am waiting now for my agent, Mary Baker, to arrive to take me to the studio. I got in at noon yesterday—very decent trip, slept all the way—then I called up Lynn Riggs, who wasn't in town, and Joe Bromberg, who was and took me to the Brown Derby for a cocktail, then I came back here and saw Spring Byington in the dining room. Had dinner with her and a drink in her room afterward.

It all seems pleasant enough and I'm sure you would have a good time if you came out. Already I am warned of contracts waiting, three-year ones— six months next year at $1500, six months the following year at $1750—and soon, but I quaver at signing away years like that, in spite of the money. It means New York becomes only an interlude between jobs, as it is for our other screenwriting friends, and not one's home at all. This company, however, lets its writers do often as they please—work in New York or at home—giving much more freedom to the chosen writer than other companies.

The great secret of my assignment continues with public announcement that I am working on my own story "Ladies' Entrance" for Miriam Hopkins. It seems that after this announcement the agent, Mary Baker, had all sorts of calls from studios angry with her for not offering it to them.

Bromberg has just called on the Tone-Crawford† household which is now taking opera lessons, Franchot and Joan warbling duets under the instruction

---

*This marked Powell's second, longest, and last visit to California, where she worked for the Samuel Goldwyn Company. J. Edward Bromberg (1904–1951) and Spring Byington (1893–1971), mentioned in the letter, had both appeared in her plays.
†Franchot Tone and Joan Crawford were briefly married to each other.

of a Signor Morini who has a strong Jewish accent. Bromberg was urged to vocalize and the signor felt he too would make a fine pupil, but Bromberg thought for $15 a lesson the Italian music teacher ought to learn Italian. . . .

Last year Mrs. Pat Campbell* was out but vanished to be found weeks later in a ranch up at Arrowhead in a black evening dress in mourning for her king and working on her memoirs for an English publisher. She stated expenses in Amurrica were so high she was going to get a trailer and live in it, and people were horrified thinking of what a trailer would do to the celebrated old bones, but presently she wafted back to England.

I am going to Mary Baker's for dinner tonight. She is a calm, poised, hard, good-looking young woman who leaves me singularly cold though she is highly thought of in all quarters.

I will send you a commission when I get my salary, and be good and go to a concert or two. Sundays are telephone night rates I believe so I may call you in the country—will you be there in the morning? My telephone number is Hollywood 2171, room 212. Chateau Elysée, 5930 Franklin Avenue. . . .

W.†

(COLLECTION TIM PAGE)

TO ORPHA MAY STEINBRUECK AND
JOHN F. SHERMAN

Chateau Elysée
Hollywood
[ca. October 1936]

Dear Auntie May and Jack the House-Builder—

I am out here for a month, scripting a piece for the Samuel Goldwyn Studios at $1000 a week, all expenses back and forth. I have an elaborate apartment here at the Chateau—with twin Mae West ivory and green taffeta beds and dressing rooms and kitchens and dinette and service entrance and trick ironing closet-board and French-windowed, gold-curtained drawing room and God knows what all. I work when and where I please. At the studios I have a suite of offices with my name on them—my own bath and Frigidaire for Christ's sake, and thick carpets. I work here in bed or sleep or go down there. If I feel like looking at some actress's work I buzz a button and say I'd like to see *These Three* or *Dodsworth* or something and they run it off for my private delight in Projection Room B or C or D and I sit before a little thing marked

---

*Mrs. Patrick Campbell (1865–1940) was a leading British actress who was especially close to George Bernard Shaw.
†"W" stands for "Winks," an early nickname that Powell used only with Joe.

Start-Stop-Focus-etc. and work it just for fun. This is all confidential, understand, so don't tell my secret to the local press. They have asked me if I will sign a three-year contract—each year six to eight months out here—next at $1250 a week, next at $1750 and third at $2000. I am going to wangle just a few weeks in N.Y. as this quick money ruins every writer in the business. They're through in three years then they've learned to live high and forgotten how to write plays or stories or the normal writing tasks, and besides it would wreck Joe's life. This is all right for now and fun in its languid strange way but it gets you nuts from all I can see.

The climate here gets you down so all I do is sleep, and how I'm to get this job done I don't know as it's left completely up to me. It's announced in the papers as something or other but it's all a secret.

Spring Byington is in this hotel—I had dinner with her Sunday. She loves it and of course it is an aging actress's paradise. J. Edward Bromberg is here and he is about the only person I've seen so far—had dinner with him a couple of times. He's in a quintuplet picture now called *Reunion*—says the quints are filthy, backward, dumb little things, badly cared for, definitely subnormal, and the doctor is a tobacco-stained old crook who picks his nose then sticks his finger down the kids' throats. Says they have a hell of a time getting a shot where they all five act halfway bright, but they can hardly even say Mama. They—the quints—get $75,000 for the picture.*

I went to a little dinner for twelve Monday night in one of those big houses people get out here for amazingly little—patios, swimming pools, game rooms, five-car garages. Ralph Bellamy, an actor, and Mischa Auer, a Universal actor, were there and their wives and some English writers—the strangest collections of people and I never know who they are so I make faux pas right and left. Tomorrow night I go to a "sneak preview" where they send for me, don't tell where it's to be, show a picture—I imagine this will be *Come and Get It*—then you all write down whatz the matter with it, then they fix it up before its public presentation.

The place is very queer. It's all so big and bare and sunny you have no feeling—as if you were half asleep all the time. People do things that ought to be fun but nobody seems to have it. All I can do is doze and stick pins in myself to try to get this job done so I can go home. I think you ought to come out here,

---

*The Dionne quintuplets, born May 28, 1934, in northern Ontario, were then the focus of mass hysteria. Exploited by the doctor who had delivered them, Dr. Allan Roy Dafoe, and, to a lesser extent, by their parents, Elzire and Oliva Dionne, they were exhibited widely and appeared in the film *The Country Doctor* (originally titled *Reunion*). According to Pierre Berton's *The Dionne Years* (1977), the "quints" were actually paid $100,000, plus a percentage of the profits, for their work on the film.

though, just to look it over. I'm anxious to see the house—tell me when it will be ready for the housewarming for all the relations.

love,
Dawn

(COLLECTION JOHN F. SHERMAN)

TO JOSEPH GOUSHA

[Hollywood
October 1936]

Dearest Joe—

I can work either at my deluxe offices or my deluxe home but since I can do nothing but sleep—that's the way the climate affects you—I work at the office from about 10:30 to 12:30 then stick pins in myself, finally surrender, come home and go to bed at 3 and wake up at 6, ready to get ready for bed. How this opus is to get done by this process I don't know.

Ben Wasson* and Joe Bromberg are my sole connections so far. Joe took me to dinner last night at Sardi's, then we drove to a little theater group called Contemporary Theater where Walter Coy, another Group actor, was teaching "improvisations" to a few left-wing thespians. It was a little house and they were all seated around a table pretending to be having a family dinner and being waited upon. Later, those not acting this out criticized the pretend-diners for drinking their sauterne (imaginary, of course) as if it were a *sweet* wine and for not conveying whether they were drinking bouillon or cognac later. As cockeyed and earnestly arty as the Group. No one seems to sit around the cafés here though there are quite a few.

I don't drink as there is little incentive, though I get tiny sample bottles of orange gin and put it in tea in my room, and sample California brandy for my coffee, hoping it will wake me up enough to do something. Very dispiriting though not active enough to be genuinely depressing atmosphere. Just blah.

Ben Wasson is a little too nosy to be welcome. He wants to find out the little studio secrets at my place so he can tell his girlfriend Miriam Hopkins, and is so insistent on "Where is the secret preview to be held?," etc., that one is forced to tell outright lies. A rather viperish little man who could do one considerable harm, though in other ways easy company when one knows no one.

I do what I like, come and go as I please, stay in bed all day if I like—in fact, the oddest job imaginable. If I could only pull my brain together, I might get it done. . . .

---

*No information has yet been found on Ben Wasson. He seems never to have received any screen credit.

This "sneak preview" tomorrow night is one the studio holds somewhere out of town. No one is told where, they send a car for me, then everyone is given cards and puts down what they think ought to be changed and then it is repaired before its official opening.

Outside of these feeble social steps I sit, eat, etc., all by myself and sometimes speak to not a human soul all day. Anyplace else you would be lonely but here nothing seems to matter much—a vast indifference in the air and sleep is the only pretty thing.

I am 20 minutes' ride to my office. Taxi. I don't get paid till the ensuing Wednesday, so I'm going to try to rustle some dough out of the agent here, as I'm down to my last $5. Send me [Aldous Huxley's novel] *Eyeless in Gaza* when you're through, will you? I may be able to wrestle with it.

I wake up early so call me—I believe Sunday all day is night rates—$5 for three minutes anytime. If you're in the country I can talk to Jojo too, or I guess I save money by calling you—about 9 here or 12 there. . . .

[Bromberg] was going to Pasadena today on location and very pleased to have as his screen sweetie Esther Ralston. He is a very kind and fat Lissfelt-ish jolly figure, very alarmed at his five-year contract and depressed by the annuities thrust upon all actors out here so that insurance agents fatten and the poor victims are so up to their neck in payments they can't have any spending money.

In its blah, dreamlike, afterdeath way, this is rather fun, though I'm still so dazed to find myself here I can't figure it out. Guess I'll go back to bed now. Cars are $2 an hour. Maybe I will give myself an outing Saturday for three hours if I have the energy.

love and don't be lonesome,
W.

[COLLECTION TIM PAGE]

TELEGRAM TO JOSEPH R. GOUSHA

*[Hollywood
October 15, 1936]*

OFFERED TWO-YEAR CONTRACT SIX MONTHS HERE NEXT YEAR AT TWELVE FIFTY SIX MONTHS FOLLOWING AT FIFTEEN HUNDRED DEFINITELY REFUSED ON GROUNDS OF INSANITY BUT NEGOTIATING ON TERMS OF THREE MONTHS A YEAR IN NEW YORK TRANSFERRED FROM ORIGINAL STORY TO BOOK FOR GERSHWIN MUSICAL* VERY BEWILDERING LOVE = DAWN

(COLLECTION TIM PAGE)

---

*The Gershwin musical project, whatever it may have been, was never realized. Indeed, Powell apparently never worked long enough on any film to receive a screenwriting credit.

Powell attended the second conference of the Communist-dominated American Writers' Congress and sent back this lively report.

TO JOHN DOS PASSOS

*Margaret Widdemer**
Nine East 10th Street
[ca. June 8, 1937]

Dear Dos—

I have just had a close escape from the Soviets and now I'm happy to say I'm back with the fairies (Fascists to you). Anyway you missed it so I suppose you're crowing to yourself or what are you doing anyway, bragging about the way you finished the war, you and Martha Gellhorn?

Esther [Andrews] was in town during the week and friends were wilting right and left under the high voltage and then there was the Writers' Congress with Mr. H. [Ernest Hemingway] pumping all the way up from Bimini on water wings. The meeting proper was vast and impressive, delegates walked in from all over, even Newport, and the platform was a sea of so-called faces. Cameramen crept in and out of Don O. Stewart's[†] slacks and microphones were jammed down everybody's throat and lady organizers tiptoed back and forth across the platform with notes and important whispers. The front part of all the speeches was always good but when the brilliant writer minds summed up they all spelled bushwah.

Don Stewart said he had nothing to say about capitalism except it was a monster and then he told about how he used to think sex was more fun than starving but now he thought he'd been in the wrong and he had to laugh thinking about how he'd been fooled about sex all those years. Then Earl Browder[‡] gave a ringing speech telling about the World War (between la belle France and the Trotskyites) and how many the Trotskyites killed in the American Revolution and the Boxer-or-Trotsky Rebellion in China and the Boer-Trotsky War and he sassed back a writer in *Hound and Horn* or someplace that said Browder was a meanie, and he said Waldo Frank[§] was a fink and the sum total of his speech was that a Communist in America today had all he could do watching magazines for cracks about himself and answering back his rivals without talking about work or strikes.

---

*Powell enjoyed making sport of this popular and somewhat conservative American author (ca. 1885–1978).

[†]Powell would become quite fond of Donald Ogden Stewart (1884–1980), a novelist, humorist, and screenwriter who would later be blacklisted for his Communist activities.

[‡]Earl Browder (1887–1973) was then general secretary of the American Communist Party.

[§]Frank (1889–1967), an unaffiliated radical writer and sociologist, was a natural target for the doctrinaire Browder's scorn.

Muriel Draper,* La Passionaria, sat in the middle of everything with a well-bred smile. About 10:30 all the foreign correspondents marched on, each one with his private blonde, led by Ernest and Miss Gellhorn, who had been through hell in Spain and came shivering on in a silver fox cape chin-up. Walter Duranty† had to leave his outside (blonde not cape) and John Gunther could only get his to the corner of the platform and of course Archie [MacLeish's] own blonde was lost somewhere, but those who had none could take potluck on Muriel Draper or go eat a peach-pit. As a matter of fact, with all the telegrams from people who wouldn't speak, Ada MacLeish said she was going to be all in her singing dress ready for her Carnegie Hall debut filling in for Senator Nye with "If" and "Trees." Ernest gave a good speech if that's what you like and his sum total was that war was pretty nice and a lot better than sitting around a hot hall and writers ought to all go to war and get killed and if they didn't they were a big sissy. Then he went over to the Stork Club, followed by a pack of foxes. Joris Ivens's film [The Spanish Earth] was very good, particularly a soldier-going-home-on-leave part if you know what I mean.

After the meeting a vast horde of women collected, which always makes me rage with Fascist fury even though they're all my friends but Margaret [De Silver] counts for two. Next day the real business of the congress began with a very splendid talk by Kenneth Burke on "The Concept of the Conceptual or the Conceptual Hypnosis of the Concept or Anyway That's neither Here nor There but Take like the Boss Being the Father Hypnosis or Anyway It's a Long Story." Like a flash it came over me that here was the crux of everything and nothing could have summed the whole movement up better so I shot out the door as the angry opposition to this thought got under way and I took the train to Port Jefferson and hid under a bar for two days with nothing but a bare Tom Collins between me and Trotsky's guns. Today I am back in town at "21" for lunch thinking what a simple charming place it was for the first time and all the pansies so intellectually sound, and the little flat Rubensteined faces so much more alert than Genevieve Taggard's‡ Cause-lifted face. I think it will be all right for you to come down now, for the Unity Convention. Best to Katy and Comrades Spencers.

Dawn

---

*Muriel Draper, whom Powell here jestingly compares to the notorious Spanish Communist leader Dolores Ibarruri, was described by Leon Edel as a "parlor Bolshevik of the time, who had a literary and musical salon."

†Duranty (1884–1957) was a British-American journalist, long the Moscow correspondent for the New York Times. Celebrated during his lifetime, he is now generally regarded as a shameless apologist for Stalinism.

‡Poet Taggard (1894–1948) had been one of Powell's closest friends in the 1920s, but the two had since had a savage falling-out.

TO COBURN GILMAN

New York
August 14, 1937

Dear ideal:

I came in on an early train to do over my scenario. Esther [Andrews] arrived just in time to save me from myself. I had been sober so long (nearly a week) and working steadily and had to finish the thing and all I needed was a bender to put work in its proper perspective—take it or leave it, see. What Mr. Geddes* and his office do not know about me is that every time I make over a new scenario I introduce a new and startling lead character who switches the whole play in an entirely fresh direction. This has them baffled. I snicker to myself as I think of the surprises they will find in my latest revisions. It is now all laid in the Riviera and Jule is a man, a sort of Jeeter Lester. I have changed men and women into each other so fluently that I hardly dare think what the possibilities in real life for me are. Dwight [Fiske] wires me to come up to Cape Cod, I think it's near Falmouth, next week, and I may do this a few days, just to have a change of work, since my life has simmered down to that, alas, alack.

Will Cuppy† and I had a glass of water at Childs the other day. He asked about my friend Coby and said you were very mean to him and never spoke to him. I fixed it all up, explaining that you were a big shot now and couldn't go around speaking to every tramp you saw on a chance that one might be Cuppy.

I also went to [Charles] Studin's for an Eric Knight party. The Eastmans were there, Max none the worse for his battle with Hemingway.‡ They stated that they were en route to the Vineyard for a week. I met my favorite hero there, a Professor Clarke, dean of City College, the only nice academe I ever met. Walter Duranty was there, but we have finally decided we don't quite get on. A curious man with some kind of unhappiness or inferiority that makes his whole life an effort to leave a group of ladies with everyone thinking, "Isn't he charming! Isn't he a darling!" He thinks up rather risqué problems to present to groups of elderly *Times* ladies and they gasp and gurgle and this mental tickling seems to be his main sport. Seeing the little groups writhing about is very odd. "Tell me frankly, Mrs. Hightits, supposing you were madly attracted to a man you wished to sleep with but circumstances made it impossible for you to do so, what would you do?" Mrs. Hightits is so taken aback that the *Times*'s Mr. Duranty should make such an improper question, but on the other hand so flattered to the core that she should seem so cosmopolitan, that she flutters and

---

*Powell was working on yet another of her many abortive theater projects, *Red Dress*—this time with the designer, director, and producer Norman Bel Geddes (1893–1958).
†Will Cuppy (1884–1949) was an American author and humorist.
‡The author, journalist, and social critic Max Eastman (1883–1969) had enraged Hemingway with a withering review of the novelist's *Death in the Afternoon*. The two men nearly came to blows over it.

gasps and then you have a daring little group discussion, with Mr. Duranty leading them all by the twats. This is the third time I've seen him do this and I think he thinks of his question for hours before he makes any social appearance. Of course I always throw him, which annoys him, as it stops the smooth flow of his conversation-handling. When he propounded his query to me, I said simply, "Why, sleep with him, of course." This was not the right answer, so he laughed falsely and had to think of something else. "Why do men grow beards?" He was sick and had an operation. Oddly enough, speaking of these jaundice coincidences you hear about, it was the same operation Dorothy Farrell* is supposed to need.

Esther probably told you of our Farrell evening. Hortense Farrell (and indeed all actresses and actors nowadays) has always been just crazy about me and therefore would like me to arrange for her to have the leading part.† The papers stated it was for a girl of 17 and it seems she looks on the stage like a girl of 17. I told a director friend of mine, Tony Bundsman, about this and he snorted, having had her once in a play, and said she had such humps on her back that he had to dress her in wings to cover them. I have letters and public approaches from everybody stating their ideal equipment for the lead. No actor apparently has ever played anything but leads. Most of them, although usually cast as old rabbis, look like a 17-year-old girl on the stage. . . .

Next Sunday Jojo will be 16 years old (I was married when I was 14) and I imagine we will spend the day at his school instead of Mount Sinai.‡ Then on Tuesday or Wednesday if I can get enough done on [the play] *Red Dress*, I will go up to Dwight's for three or four days. If it is anywhere near Woods Hole, I may have a proposition to make to you, a positive eyebrow-lifter, crabs and all. You can take it or leave it, that's the way I am.

If I had any confidence in my ability to choose your reading, I would send you a book or pamphlet of some sort, but by this time Esther is up there with Dorothy Speare's novel so you got something you can get your teeth in. The *Fight* issue on Spain was very excellent. I was sorry Josie Herbst's stuff on Spain in *The Nation* was so dull.§ It was admirable in that it wasn't that glorified personal heroic journalese that anybody who walks past a fight usually adopts, but there is a middle ground of making facts interesting or at least alive without throwing yourself in the middle of them. (See my Naval Reports on the Great War.)

Esther seemed in elegant form. Hope you can get a third week as two is

---

*Dorothy and Hortense Farrell were, respectively, the wife and sister of the novelist and independent radical James T. Farrell (1904–1980).
†Whatever play Powell was then working on was never produced.
‡Jojo attended a series of special schools for the emotionally impaired.
§Powell was never an admirer of the radical American novelist Josephine Herbst (1897–1969), though the two women seem to have been fairly close acquaintances in the 1920s, when Herbst and her novelist husband John Herrmann (1900–1959) introduced Powell to Ernest Hemingway.

very little to a big man like Gilman. Don't forget possum in passing around the seafood as there's hardly enough for Quee and me let alone the belles of Menemsha. Stay in the sun as much as possible and if you must drink, something I can't understand, do it in the sun and if you must do it in a dark chamber, rub yourself with Skol thoroughly so the actinic rays can come in and get you.

Love,
Dawn

(COLLECTION TIM PAGE)

TO MARGARET DE SILVER

[9 East Tenth Street
ca. May 1938]

Dear Maggie—

I have achieved the seventh degree of unconsciousness or whatever it was that old boy in *Heartbreak House* had. (He also did not drink to get drunk, he drank "to keep sober," he said.) I had a wonderful inspiration and changed your tickets to the very next night after you left and Coby and I went. It is a great play and I am so glad I saw it again because I forget how good it is, and how that old boy has more in one play than fifty playwrights have in their joint heads in a century. Mady Christians was very good in it. Orson Welles as the old captain had so much putty and beard and padding on to look 88 that he could hardly balance his head. He looked like something out of Max Factor's "Don't" book. He isn't a very good actor, I fear, but he knows how to put on a good show.

What I meant to say is that I drank a lot of planter's punches last night with Coby and passing strangers such as Dahlberg and Ed Lanham and Nora Benjamin and it was wonderful to forget all the promises I had made to have my play completely done over today and my novel finished some other time. The hell with time. It's a mocker.

Yesterday I passed a little beaming man and thought, So he knows me, does he, and who the hell is he? He stopped and said, I met you at El Bolero a long time ago. So I remembered picking up a lot of Spaniards one night there. It seems he'd been in Spain since. It also seems that the night I saw him he was spending his time for the second year as one of Franco's spies in this country (nice guys I pick up?). Then he went to Spain but they owed him money and tried to kill him so with that splendid integrity spies are noted for he switched to the Spanish side. (He called it the Spanish side. He also said, "You know when I was over here they never told me they were Fascists. I never knew it till I went over." Bright fellow.) Then he got put in jail and was going to get killed and finally got deported. He had a load of *Daily Workers* under his arm which told his story in three installments. He was very pleased with himself. He is a rosy, blue-eyed German-looking little fellow, about as innocent-looking as Niles [Spencer] or a Daniel Reeves delivery boy. He was very proud that the Department of Justice was now after him to find out why any foreign government had spies in this country. I suppose he put down all the seditious remarks Miss Powell made in her cups that night I met him.

We have obtained our house again in Mt. Sinai and will go open it up next weekend. Tonight Joe and Harry Lissfelt and Bill are going to an Aphrodite prayer meeting. That Venus worship thing that the white Russian guy started. I am afraid they're hoping to bring home a couple of priestesses alive and naked more than Beauty itself.

I saw the two Clark sisters at Charlie's studio the other day. They are the biggest bores. Eleanor,* looking very handsome, was coyly talking to every man about "the situation among the elevator men at 70 Fifth Avenue" and then, getting particularly coquettish, she would say, "I have organized my entire building and we hope to strike soon."

Don't beautiful women have any fun anymore? Are they organized against it? . . .

I have started taking exercises because you can't voodoo all those pounds you lose on me this time, dearie. I will voodoo them right back. I now have my stomach under control and 4 lbs. off. It will be back with the first sip of water I take.

Love to Carlo.†

love,
Dawn

(COLLECTION JACQUELINE MILLER RICE)

TO MICHAEL SADLEIR

9 East 10th Street
September 23, 1938

Dear Michael Sadleir:

Thank you so much for your letter. Knowing your work as a writer I value your comment much more highly than I do the usual publisher's voice, however intelligent he may be. I am delighted, of course, that you are publish-

---

*Eleanor Clark (1913–1996) was an American writer who won fame for her novel *The Bitter Box* (1946) and certified her gifts with some memorable travel writing. She was married to Robert Penn Warren for many years.
†De Silver was then living with the celebrated anarchist Carlo Tresca (ca. 1875–1943), who would later be assassinated outside his office on West Fifteenth Street.

ing [*The Happy Island*], after the excellent taste with which you presented my last book.

There are no portraits in *The Happy Island*.* Aside from fear of libel suits, I find no profit or pleasure in straight portraiture. There are frequently snatches of this or that person cautiously pinned to other persons' bodies and love-lives, and it is true I have changed one real man into a woman, but as he has done this himself so often I cannot see that he should object, and have furthermore combined him with two other people. I have been criticized for not taking real news figures for the recognition-thrill it gives readers, so that over here I have learned to look sly and mysterious when readers chortle that they know exactly who is who (but of course in England I should look frank and open). One young man called on me, very upset, and said he recognized himself in my book and wondered if everyone did as there were some rather sacred thoughts exposed. As he had been far from my thoughts I was embarrassed, then realized that here was the pallid pansy whose whole career had accidentally fit into the Bert Willy† pattern. I was horrified. But it turned out the figure he recognized as himself was, of course, the splendid hairy-chested young playwright from the West. But I had a bad 20 minutes of apologizing frantically in the dark before I saw . . . [letter incomplete]

(SAMUEL PALEY LIBRARY, TEMPLE UNIVERSITY)

TO PHYLLIS POWELL COOK

[ca. 1938, fragment]

[. . .] I turned down an offer from MGM for $2000 a week for 18 weeks to adapt a story called "Red Shoes Run Faster."‡ I think if they'd offered me fifty cents or something I could have understood I would have snapped it up. As it was it just annoyed me to think of having to lug all that money around. Everyone is sore at me for not taking it so I could loan them all money or at any rate pay my bills. (I guess I wasn't so dumb after all.) The truth was I figured that it meant four or five months' quick money and then the whole family being in a stew with me there and them here and the publisher so sore at me for not getting my new book done for fall publication that he'd cancel me off the list and I wouldn't have anything ready for publication for two years so that I would pay for four months of grandeur with about three years' setback in my regular

---

*The libel laws in Great Britain have always been stricter than those in the United States, and Sadleir had expressed some concern about bringing out a British edition of *The Happy Island*.
†Bert Willy is an effeminate gay character in *The Happy Island*.
‡The chronically impoverished Powell would have occasion to regret her dismissal of such extraordinary fees, but she believed that screenwriting was a fatal pursuit for a creative artist.

business. Nobody but me figures that way but I think I know how I work and how everybody who goes out there works. Most of them don't do any good work anymore and forget how to get along on an ordinary sum which sooner or later they have to come back to. I told them I would come out for a month or maybe six weeks at the most next time. I also figured that if I'm going to stop writing I'd a darn sight better get into the Red Cross or something that was doing some good instead of glamorizing myself. . . .

(COLLECTION TIM PAGE)

TO MAX PERKINS*

9 East 10th Street
March 1 [1939?]

Dear Mr. Perkins:

I have been scurrying in and out of Coney Island under the delusion that the literary influence of the HalfMoon Hotel† would straighten out my little mind, but just as it gets straight and the book looks like a little beauty and I'm rushing in for your martini reward, then it cracks up again. This always upsets me and I would be sniveling around your office with torn pages in my hand except that I remember it always happens up to the last quarter. Once on the 10-yard line I seem all right.

Then I heard that Padraic and possibly Mary Colum‡ were also working in the HalfMoon and it rather influenced my style. It got to be sort of Chicago Irish and everybody was named Studs and was. I think in a week or two some things may unscramble sufficiently to at least discuss literature in the abstract. I still count on the pieces' being collected by sometime in June.

Best,
Dawn Powell

(RARE BOOKS AND MANUSCRIPTS, PRINCETON UNIVERSITY LIBRARY)

---

*Maxwell E. Perkins (1884–1947), legendary for his work with F. Scott Fitzgerald, Ernest Hemingway, and Thomas Wolfe, had just become Powell's editor at Scribner's.
†The HalfMoon had replaced the Traymore Hotel in Atlantic City as Powell's preferred hideaway for intensive work.
‡Padraic Colum (1881–1972) was an Irish-American poet and critic; his wife, Mary Colum (1887–1957), was a well-known journalist and memoirist.

TO COBURN GILMAN

[9 East Tenth Street
Undated; summer 1939]

well babe
dear sonny machree:

I am sending you the latest news outa *Variety*:

> Don E. Gilman, v.p. in charge of Western division
> of NBC, slipped into town and held a closed round-
> table with member stations and advertising agencies.
> H. M. Feltis, commercial manager of KOMO-KJR,
> was chairman of the session.
>
> Gilman planed north to Vancouver after the session
> and returned here for a day en route home. Under-
> stand that Gilman gave the ad boys a Blue plug.

I must tell you [John] Mosher's* Answer to Hitler. "No," he stated, "I
absolutely CANNOT be dragged back and forth through that Atlantic again. Particularly in that awful brown twill."

"As a matter of fact," he added, brushing some mice off his sleeve with a
delicate gesture, "I have gone right ahead and ordered the same fall clothes I
should have ordered under any circumstances."

If I live through another week of radio it will be something.† I did new
script yesterday, conferred on it, then got stinking and I mean *stinking*, ending
up alone with Pernod at Lafayette. Then blur, though Mr. Gousha informs me
that he came into the living room and I introduced him to a Mr. Clark, who
seemed to have been my escort, a princely fellow, and where I got him or when
or who I will never know as this relationship is not clear.

Miss [Virginia] Pfeiffer‡ is all battered up as she jumped off a yacht up
the Hudson Monday night at 3 a.m. and swam to shore, then walked along Palisades trying to get a hitch, but looked so bad only a breadwagon would pick her
up after two hours' walk. Then breadman took her to his girl's for breakfast and
shoes and dry dress and gave her quarter to come home and she is bad way
besides as I poured liquor all over her last night to brace her up. She was all bit
up by yachtsman, and states it was all due to early training a Frenchman gave
her years ago who, on being socked by her, said, "A woman should never use
force on a man or a horse," so she traveled all over the world preventing rape

---

*John Mosher (1892–1942) was an essayist, short-story writer, and the first film critic for *The New Yorker*.
†Powell was then in the midst of working on a short-lived WOR-AM radio program, *Music and Manners*.
‡Virginia Pfeiffer (1902–1973) was then the sister-in-law of Ernest Hemingway; she would become the longtime companion of Laura Archera Huxley.

with a jeer or a jibe and she says she apparently overjibed at yachtsman's advances so he was out for revenge for lost ego.

Honeycutt, Radio Bigshot and generally unreliable efficiency queen,* now is keeping director [William] Bower, actor Hulick and Artist Powell from murdering each other before Labor Day. Hulick could not open his eyes yesterday due to having started to play golf Saturday and coming to on Monday still on the golf links.

I find getting a salary is very expensive as I have to have shoes to wear and haircuts and often trousies and have no means of getting these things as salary check is pounced on by a vast staff of creditors and husbands. Incidentally, this apartment is reduced to $130 a month from a onetime $188.

Where's Augur? I gather at your side or you would have mentioned it. Or who is at your side? Your mother? I am very envious of you myself now, having vacations and getting out of town to far parts no matter how repulsive the parts are, and not having any family to snatch at your salary, and lavishing all on zipper and other personal adornments, and above all I envy you your close-mouse. I am loose-moused or loose-moosed and only close-moused about fundamentals but by the time I have loose-moused about the superficials, Close-mouser Gilman is delighted to have pause in conversation even if it's a close-mousing on basic mischief, yes?

Here is sample Gilman Close-mouse correspondence:

Very little to tell. Am here at a summer resort. Dined with friends a few times, lunched with a neighbor, went to a sort of ball with party of intimates, as ever—

(here touch of indiscretion comes in as you do come out with your real name instead of A FRIEND).

Never mind, fox, I am keeping all these letters and will sue just as you fear.

As ever,
mother machree

(COLLECTION TIM PAGE)

---

*Author and radio producer Ann Honeycutt (1902–1989) was Powell's director on *Music and Manners*. Powell hated working with her, but they would become close friends in the years after the show was canceled.

TO MAX PERKINS

9 East Tenth Street
October 14, 1939

Dear Mr. Perkins:

I had hoped to have finer news for you at this time about the book.* I took a radio job at WOR in August, writing a show and also appearing on it—every Friday night, it's called *Music and Manners*—and this took up more time than I should have thought a mere half-hour radio show would do, so the book got to marking time until the radio job rattled down to normal. However, the damn thing got more and more demanding and now has me completely swamped as it seems about to become a commercial success—very promising financially for me but very discouraging for my other work. My contract goes on till Nov. 13 and of course is extended when the program is bought. I can't say now whether I can sail through the book by December or whether it will be even later, though there is a chance of getting it done quickly due to its being pent up so long. Anyway that is why the manuscript isn't in your hands this minute. If it suddenly gets a spurt in the next week or so I will gladly let you know, so you can plan for it. It is purely a matter of time to do it now. I have never been so rushed in my life by anything as foolish or as engrossing as radio work, and I must say I like it. In one way it has its advantages to my writing as the radio world is so unbelievable and so strange that I will have a book out of it alone.

Another matter—I have been approached about publishing my short stories. These have appeared in *The New Yorker*, *Harper's Bazaar* and *Redbook*. If you would be interested I will send up the batch first to Scribner's.†

Sincerely yours,
Dawn Powell

(COLLECTION TIM PAGE—PHOTOCOPY)

TO JANET COHEN‡

9 East 10th Street
New York City
June 6, 1940

Dear Janet:

I would like to withdraw *Every Other Day* from your hands as of today and would appreciate your withdrawing the copies you now have out since I have

---

*Powell was then in the midst of finishing *Angels on Toast*, her first book for Scribner's.
†The publisher's lack of interest in her short stories would eventually lead Powell to leave Scribner's for Houghton Mifflin.
‡Cohen was Powell's theatrical agent for a time; this seems to have been her letter of dismissal. Every Other Day, written in 1939, has never been produced. *Red Dress,* mentioned in the letter, is another unproduced play.

only one. I am not sure whether I can do anything with it myself but at least I will feel better trying, particularly since the time for comedy is so short right now, and in any case you've worked over a year on it and I know you must have a great many fresher works that will have to take your time. I think I can do better with it with my contacts and my own understanding of the play, and you can understand that I don't like the prospect of having my pet comedy drag along through all the old Red Dress complications, if a little personal work on my part can save it. I will doubtless put this play through the same ups and downs but can assume responsibility for it myself and not blame you—that will be something, won't it? In any case I think it will be mutually advantageous to withdraw it from your agency. It is hard, I know, to present something you are not very enthusiastic about. Anyway I shall take some flying whacks at it during the summer months and see what happens. I have people asking me for a new play and have had to tell them I cannot write anything now after the blind alleys I have chased up in the last two plays, so this is of more psychological importance to my further work than I can explain, and not a criticism of your hard work on it.

Best wishes,
Dawn Powell

(COLLECTION TIM PAGE—CARBON COPY)

TO MAX PERKINS

[9 East Tenth Street
Summer 1940]

Dear Max:

When my proofs arrived and I found that you had taken such great editorial liberties as to insert in my novel a large chapter on the life of William Morris I was a little startled but deferred as usual to your better judgment.* I decided this was the "strong serious undercurrent" referred to in the catalog and probably gave the book the class angle Scribner's has always insisted upon in its fiction. However a boy just arrived and took it away and said it was an error, and now I am beginning to fear that critics will reproach me for not mentioning William Morris, and perhaps I might put a little note about him somewhere or at least mention his life in my bibliography.

I have yet to see anyone around Ernest [Hemingway] even a few minutes who is not violently affected by him, as you say. He probably has more sheer personal power—I doubt if it's "charm"—than anyone I ever met. Maybe

---

*There seems to have been a mixup in the collation of Powell's book proofs at Scribner's.

Hitler is like that. Anyway, around him it is hard to remember there is anyone else you planned to see or ever cared to. I think people will have to get ernest-proofed first, in order to hang on to their own original prejudices when talking to him.

The cat books are wonderful and I see a great future ahead of me as a cat lover, with my own cat graveyard and cats named Tweetie Heart and Lovey Pie and so on, rather than this hard-boiled little beast I have named Perkins. (I named her before I found out her arrogant nature.) Certainly, I see no prospect of following Miss Mellon's suggestion of wheeling her around in a doll buggy with a doll nursing bottle. I'd much rather have her do it for me. It would be safer.

As ever,
Dawn

(RARE BOOKS AND MANUSCRIPTS, PRINCETON UNIVERSITY LIBRARY)

TO TERESA HELBURN*

9 East 10th Street
August 4, 1940

Dear Terry:

I have been frantically finishing and reading proofs on my novel *Angels on Toast* which is coming out next month so my theatrical itch has been under control. I do have a half-idea for a new play but am trying to hold its head under water until I get some short stories done.

Meantime Monica McCall is handling my play *Every Other Day*—you saw it in its first version, and Robert Klein, the Berlin and London director, is keen to do it, if we find the right woman and the producer. Una Merkel is interested and so is Ruth Chatterton, Klein prefers Merkel and he wants a sort of young Roland Young lead. If you have any idea of a loose motion picture actress (or half-loose) who can play comedy without throwing her weight around too much, do let me know. Klein says he'd rather tone down a burlesque comedienne than try to plant comedy in a straight glamour star.

How have you been and wasn't it too bad about George O'Neil's dying?

Love,
Dawn Powell

(THEATRE GUILD COLLECTION, BEINECKE RARE BOOKS AND MANUSCRIPTS LIBRARY, YALE UNIVERSITY)

*Powell remained friendly with Teresa Helburn (1887–1959), a playwright, director, and producer who was the leading figure in the history of the Theatre Guild, despite the fact that the Guild's production of Powell's *Jig-Saw* had been less than fully successful.

TO MAX PERKINS

[9 East Tenth Street]
August 4, 1940

Dear Max:

I should like a dedication page inserted in *Angels on Toast* as follows:
To Max Perkins

Also I will need one of those "None of the characters in this novel are drawn from living persons" or whatever it is. And Carol [Brandt] probably told you about the credit to *Harper's Bazaar* because of previous publication there of one chapter.

I think you know best how this novel should be presented, but it might be of some assistance to you to know what I set out to do, whether I accomplished it or not. I wanted to catch people as I heard them on trains and buses and bars, let them do their own story without any literary frame whatever, without explanations, without author's tricks, in fact without writing. The effect I was after was the aftereffect. You, the reader, say, hear a strange conversation in a bar. You are not particularly interested but you idly note that the girl is fairly hardboiled, dyed blond, maybe a tart; the man has a middlewestern voice, is middle-aged, big, a good-looking man. You think you have dismissed them from your mind but in the back of your mind for weeks you speculate about them—what did she mean when she said that? where were they from? what was their relationship? what a funny crack to make—and suddenly this unknown couple has influenced your own life—their lives flower in your mind, complete people emerge from just a dozen or so words. Good or bad, you don't know, but at least they live. If you saw them again someday you would almost rush up and speak to them.

So these characters are presented by their own bare words and their business front—a jovial, openhanded, wisecracking front that is so seldom let down that they themselves aren't sure what's under it. They are riding high but like good gamblers are under no delusions that their luck will hold.

I expect to be accused of lampooning the American businessman but neither Lou nor Jay* is representative of anything but Americans at high pressure. I could certainly satirize the businessman, the average business success, but such a pompous, Dale Carnegie, the-office-is-a-holy-thing, success-is-holy, etc., type would not interest me.

I wanted to convey the sense of speed, changing geography with no change in the conversation, the sense of pressure behind the ever-evanescent big deal, and behind these adventurers, their women—the first wives scrambling to keep up the pace or else be lost in the scuffle, the occasional pretties that tone up

---

*Lou Donovan and Jay Olliver are the lead characters in *Angels on Toast*.

their ego, and then the women they want. These women are like army followers—they don't know where the army is going or what for, but all they know is they have to keep up with it or lose.

These are normal people saying one thing and doing another, warning a neighbor of danger while stepping into it themselves . . . [letter incomplete—possibly never sent]

(COLLECTION TIM PAGE—CARBON COPY)

TO EDMUND WILSON

9 East Tenth Street
October 31, 1940

Dear pal,

How about a Guggenheim for a cup of coffee? I am applying for one and if you would like to compare my project to the little-known projects of Tamburlaine, I would like it very much, and if you are going to be disagreeable about it go ahead, and I will report you to the draft board.

I thought Otis's review was very fine except that the faults of construction he noticed were not there at all.[*] It was a novel built almost entirely on conversations—an ear novel if you like—with the implications left for the eye of the reader, and the conversation not a means of exchanging ideas or private dreams but a "line," every person having a "line" as his protection against giving away any part of himself. The construction I chose was to select a theme from each man's "line" and follow it crisscrossing others' "lines." If you don't understand this, I will do the book over with a concordat.

Outside of that I was really very pleased with Otis and if he ever wants a home with every modern vice he has only to look me up in the back of the *Saturday Review* and I will be there waiting, dewy-eyed, a plot in every hand.

I am spending the weekend at your good neighbor Libby Holman's,[†] why I will never know, and may have to borrow that stock horseback-riding suit you keep in the cornfield.

Dawn

(YALE COLLECTION OF AMERICAN LITERATURE, BEINECKE RARE BOOK AND MANUSCRIPT LIBRARY, YALE UNIVERSITY)

---

[*]Wilson apparently shared this letter with the film and literary critic Otis Ferguson (1907–1943), who had published a mixed review of *Angels on Toast* in the *New Republic* on October 28, 1940. Ferguson circled the word *concordat* and amended the letter with the sentence "And chooses her words with the utmost care, too. O.F."

[†]Libby Holman (1905–1971) was an American actress and torch singer, accused in 1931 of murdering her husband, tobacco heir Zachary Smith Reynolds. The charges were later dropped.

PROPOSAL FOR A GUGGENHEIM FELLOWSHIP

[Undated; ca. November 1940]

PLANS FOR WORK:*

A long novel dealing with American manners in the shadow of foreign wars. Laid in New York, the novel will pursue threads in the South and Midwest dealing with people not concerned politically or personally with such wars but affected by them willy-nilly.

As a member of a family rooted in Ohio for nearly 150 years my observations have been concentrated on such people's struggle against or in defense of their inherent provincialism. My novels have followed this trail—the provincial in the city eager to trade his naïveté for a sort of Hollywood culture, the other provincial American determined to keep his roots in a rootless environment, then the provincial returning to his roots with cosmopolitan messages. This pattern seems to me to follow the mass life of America as well as the individual life. The late insistence of Europe and Asia in impressing another life on this native pattern gives an opportunity to study the pattern in protest. It is better to record the lives of these people now than to wait till the glacier has destroyed them and left only a statistical clue.

(COLLECTION TIM PAGE—CARBON COPY)

TO THE SCRIBNER'S PUBLICITY DEPARTMENT

[ca. 1941]

SYNOPSIS OF *A TIME TO BE BORN*

AUTHOR: Dawn Powell
NOVEL: About 75,000–80,000 words.
TITLE: *A Time to be Born* (from Ecclesiastes)
        The Almond Tree Shall Blossom (same)
        The Crackling of Thorns (same)
        Amanda

Amanda Keller had this advantage over her rivals: she knew exactly what she wanted and that was Everything. Representative of the new order of career woman, Amanda exploited every detail of her feminine equipment to solidify her position, and armored herself further by a marriage to the powerful newspaper owner Julian Evans. At 30, Amanda had all the wit, fame and beauty that money

---

*Radically amended, this outline would develop into *My Home Is Far Away*. Powell never received a Guggenheim Fellowship.

and publicity could buy; even the coming of the New War could not detrain her, for she adjusted her ambition to the times and rode the world's debacle as if it were her own private yacht. Having written one best-seller, Amanda adjusted her ambition to becoming a public figure and, with her husband's power behind her, manipulated her career as if she were not a person but a government project.

With Amanda's honestly ruthless activities as a center theme, this novel tells of the hectic period just before and during the early stages of the New War. The imminence of world disaster sped the momentum of Manhattan life—individuals, seeing their personal careers about to be scrapped on the war heap, flung themselves as did Amanda into the business of "getting theirs" before the crash.

Into Amanda's perfectly organized success machine comes a younger woman, equally talented, but with no gift for self-exploitation. It suits Amanda's new plans to make Victoria her protégée, and this odd friendship gives opportunity for contrast between the normal, shy, ever-futile young woman concerned largely with her unhappy love affair, and the shrewd, high-handed Amanda. Vicky's only public value is her known connection with Amanda, and this advantage becomes her greatest burden as time goes on. Vicky works on *Peabody's* Magazine, a smart periodical staffed with would-be Amandas—debutantes, heiresses, etc., privileged women who "want to DO something." Almost lost in the competition between these arrogant young women and her benefactor Amanda, Vicky is comforted by falling in love with Amanda's discarded lover, Ken Saunders. Amanda, in the midst of flying inspections of London war-raids, sponsoring titled refugees, adopting orphans, making clarion calls to arms, and wangling literary favors, is so wounded by this personal blow as to endanger recklessly all that she has hitherto built. As soon as she permits herself human weaknesses, her public structure is weakened, and the latter part of the book deals with her frantic efforts to indulge private emotions without surrendering her public position. On the basis of straight female competition with her protégée Vicky, Amanda is no better than her sisters.

The background is New York from 1938 to the present, showing the effect on private lives of the rising war, with the women, as ever, riding ahead to meet it.

TO MAX PERKINS

[9 East Tenth Street]
February 3, 1942

Dear Max:

Thank you for your note about the show's closing.* I must say that I was so numb from the whole experience that it was a great weight off my mind to have it crossed off the record. After I had walked out on it in Boston, I would have been richer, maybe, but pretty mad if it had been a big hit without my stuff. My play agent had recommended taking my name off the week before it opened, but I was afraid this would please Morrie Ryskind and I didn't want to please him. Besides I had some stories in mind with that background, and I felt they might be helped by certified experience.

The novel† has been a great relief but it seems to get longer by the minute or else I'm getting shorter. I am working very rapidly on it, but I wish you would give me a definite last-minute date. With a supply of benzedrine, cocaine, marijuana and black coffee I could probably finish it by the end of the month, but if this speed is not necessary, let me know.

I am following Isabel Patterson as book critic on *Mademoiselle*,‡ appearing first, I believe, in the April issue. Let me know of possible Scribner stuff coming out about then, appealing to a mysterious average *Mademoiselle* reader, aged 25, college-bred, intelligent, practical, fun-loving, serious-purposed, sophisticated and sincere.

As ever,
Dawn

(RARE BOOKS AND MANUSCRIPTS, PRINCETON UNIVERSITY LIBRARY)

TO BRUCE BLIVEN§

9 East 10th Street
New York City
October 6, 1941

Dear Bruce Bliven:

I have your letter inquiring about my name on the Committee of Sponsors for the aid of refugees at the Biltmore dinner October 9th. I believe that as

---

*This would have been *The Lady Comes Across*, a disastrous revue on which Powell had worked as a dramatist. Her collaborators included lyricist John Latouche (who became a close friend), composer Vernon Duke, choreographer George Balanchine, and production supervisor Morris Ryskind. Despite all that talent, the play was a spectacular failure and closed the night after its New York premiere on January 9, 1942.
†I.e., *A Time to be Born*.
‡Powell would hate her duties at Mademoiselle and refer to it as a "kindergarten" job. She would last barely a year in the position.
§Bruce Bliven (1889–1977) had been associated with the *New Republic* from the early 1920s and would become the magazine's editorial director in 1946.

much help as possible should be given to the victims of war and do not see why they should pay for the general intolerance and political confusion in this country. I do not know in detail the members of two of the organizations sponsoring this dinner-forum but I do know that the Exiled Writers' Committee of the League of American Writers functioned more efficiently than any other committee of the organization. I resigned from the League over a year ago, not because some of its members were Communist sympathizers or *New Republic* contributors (exactly the same thing in the eyes of Governor [Herbert] Lehman and the general public) but because I objected to the League's academic pretensions, its school for the wholesale promotion of mediocre writing, its new theory that anybody is a writer who has a pen and one lesson and the address of a pulp magazine.

I am not willing to work as a member with any organization that follows the Communist Party line at present, though I am as likely to change as anyone else. However, I see no reason to damn individual projects such organizations may have when the cause is humanitarian and the auspices financially responsible. Each of us knows that in the present confusion we are called Reds, Red-baiters, Fascists, Reactionaries and Vegetarians all in the same day, and even if we all truthfully declared our politics our own brothers or mothers would call us liars or Republicans.

The virtue of the Hellman-Hemingway dinner is that no speaker or sponsor is Nazi or America First. The vice is the incorrigible one of the church supper—that the starving Chinese, the ragged prisoner of war, the orphan can only be helped by as many people as possible putting on their minks and sables and eating more than they want.

This isn't a political fault.

Sincerely yours,
Dawn Powell

(COLLECTION TIM PAGE—CARBON COPY)

TO MAX PERKINS

[Undated: clearly 1942]

Dear Max:

I decided to send these proofs back before I got out my scissors and cut it all up. I like the end better this way as it is not quite so pat yet covers more. I had only one or two bottles of ink to spill over these proofs but maybe you have some more up there to finish the job right. . . .

I had a friend of Luce's at 20th Century Fox read the galleys and he said it was nothing like Luce but very like Clare B. but he didn't see how a lady who made her living satirizing other living characters could sue for being satirized. He said the character was hers but none of the facts. . . .*

Best,
Dawn

TO MAX PERKINS†

9 East 10th Street
July 6, 1942

Dear Max:

I hope the jacket for my book‡ is a plain lettered one without figures, and I should like to check the copy on it, since the last jacket had characters mixed up in the blurb.

I do not like at all the approach called to my attention recently in *Publishers Weekly*, which refers to the book as "slightly wacky" and uses other deprecatory phrases that would come better from an angry reviewer than from the publisher. There is nothing wacky in the book, nor is there anything to be gained by suggesting it is a jolly little book for the hammock. It is serious satire in the way Dickens or Thackeray built satire—the surface may be entertaining but the content is important comment on contemporary affairs. There are very few American writers today who are writing satire on the present age—or on any age for that matter—and if I did not think such work was important I would not engage in it. I am sure there must be readers for a novel whose mood follows the tempo of the news they are reading, even though, like the news, it does not always take the point of view they would prefer. That is why I think the book's contemporary scene value should be stressed, and if it is "slightly mad," it is merely reflecting the times.

Best wishes—
Dawn

---

*In later years, Powell would never seem to be able to make up her mind just how much of *A Time to Be Born* was actually based on Clare Boothe Luce, and often she denied any such influence at all. This letter is one of several documents that suggest that Powell knew just what she was doing all the time.
†This unusually testy letter may never have been sent. It does not exist in the Scribner's Collection at Princeton; the only known copy is a carbon in the Powell papers at Columbia.
‡I.e., *A Time to Be Born.*

TO MARGARET DE SILVER

[9 East Tenth Street]
Sunday July 11 [1942]

Dear Maggie:

I turned over an ending of this scenario to Alma yesterday although it isn't ended at all but I couldn't bear it any more.* Two months' hackwork is more than I can stand without going nuts so I hope something goes wrong about that new movie deal so I don't have to flashback and fade in any more crapperoo. Alma's husband† said, when I took up the ms. (also Carlo [Tresca]'s), "Did you wind up that story about Ken and Vicky?" I gave a cry of pain and said, "Don't mention those people. I'm so sick of those characters." So he said with that sterling forthrightness of the honest workingman, "You know I thought you were sick of them from what I read."

Touche got back from Africa having zigzagged in a boat for 6 weeks so no one knew what had happened to him.‡ He was welcomed by his draft board, income-tax collectors, process servers, editors who had not received the promised material, and long-faced representatives of his bank. This has left him somewhat crushed, but he exubers up if out of his orbit. He said the customs official skipped through all his sabotage notes on Africa, and other incriminating papers, but suddenly came on my letters and sat down for a thoughtful study of them, tittering appreciatively from time to time, making a little comment when it was about someone he knew. But finally he got very grave, and began looking suspiciously at Touche. Rapped out sharp questions, etc. It seems he had come to a long section about Carlo Tresca, so that for a while Touche had some trouble clearing himself as a dangerous anarchist, just because the letter implied a connection. This shows how dangerous it is to write letters to anybody.

[Ann] Honeycutt, a friend and I spent a pleasant weekend at Gurney's Inn outside Montauk. Herman Shumlin§ was coming out Saturday, if the place was nice, which it was, but they refused Jews. By that time we were crazy for a Jew to come out and bring us enough cash to bail us out, and we decided to ask him to come out with a wad, then we would meet him down the road and tell him no Jews allowed and take his wad away from him, so everyone's feelings would be saved. No bar there—just fabulous food and Christian pleasures.

---

*This project, apparently a film, remains unidentified and almost certainly never came to anything.
†Neither "Alma" nor her husband has proved traceable.
‡The lyricist John Latouche (1917–1956) had become Powell's friend during the disastrous miscreation of *The Lady Comes Across*. He had lately been in the Belgian Congo (now Zaire), working in a leper colony.
§Herman Shumlin (1898–1979) was an American producer and director.

It was interesting to meet Gentiles, who are really no different from anybody else when you get to know them. It is filled with Schrafft hostesses—genteel, middle-aged widows who keep a Christian Science smile fastened on their mugs until you take a poke at them. It was very pleasant although I like a more restricted type of place—one with no rooms for Christians, either, just members of the Friends of Bastards.

Dos has not showed. I had a pleasant dinner with the Murphs the other day. Honoria is over pneumonia and very handsome.* Coby is taking me to an intimate dinner at the Waldorf tomorrow with Elsa Maxwell and Seversky as hosts and movies of Seversky. Touche said his wife looked so beautiful when he got back that he almost had a go at her himself.

If this movie deal or myself falls through I may take on the Cape, but actually I want a cottage around here for two weeks for Jojo.

Best to wilsons, passos and browns, and other codpieces.†

love,
Dawn

(COLLECTION JACQUELINE MILLER RICE)

---

*Powell had become quite close to the wealthy and talented Murphys—Gerald (1888–1964) and Sara (1883–1975)—to whom F. Scott Fitzgerald dedicated *Tender Is the Night*. Honoria was the couple's only daughter.
†Powell's reference here is to Edmund Wilson, John Dos Passos, and Slater Brown, all of whom summered or lived on Cape Cod, where De Silver herself also had a house.

35 EAST NINTH STREET

1943–1950

[1943]

"The Man in the Balloon" is Part One of a three-part book to be called *My Home Is Far Away*.

My last four novels have been satires on contemporary society. The present book seeks to show the basic illusions and innocence that become fruit for future satire. A child and a century grow up together. This is a story of growth, of people, town and knowledge flowering, bad and good together; of simple turning complex, of complex inviting destruction to resolve it once again to simple. Here is the blind quest for home in people and the belief that the return to simplicity solves everything.

60 miles in northern Ohio contain many small worlds—a Dutch town, a rubber town, a Finnish town, a railroad town, farms, resorts, idyllic villages, a great city. There is unusual variety in provincial life in this section, even in the early 1900s. I have made use of many parts of this section in my early novels.

In Part One, this world is seen through the eyes of two small children, Marcia and Lena Willard. The man in the balloon is the first terror they have ever known but they will live to know genuine terror from the skies. The balloon

---

*This detailed memorandum was apparently written for interested parties at Scribner's. When the book finally appeared, in 1944, it was divided into three parts. The characters of Marcia and Lena Willard were based on the early lives of Dawn and Mabel Powell; a third character, Florrie, was added later and represents Powell's younger sister, Phyllis.

seems to them an omen that nothing is safe, no joy is secure; childishly they come to believe like their mother that if they had never left the little house on Peach Street all would have been well, they would not have seen the man in the balloon, and nothing could have happened to them.

Part One is the period of illusion, and Part Two deals with the disruption of the family, the wandering from town to town of Harry Willard and his daughters, the desperate effort to preserve the illusion in the face of cruelty and disappointment. Like the honest Irish lad in the song they sing to their father's guitar, they are far from home but cling to the thought of it.

(COLLECTION TIM PAGE)

TO MAX PERKINS

35 East Ninth Street
February 4, 1944

Dear Max,

Probably Carol [Brandt]'s secretary told you I graduated from a few weeks in and out of bed with bronchitis to pleurisy and general fury. I was familiar with pleurisy but not with sulfa magic which knocked pleurisy seemingly out, reduced temperature from 104 to 98 in 12 hours and reduced me to a quivering pulp. Yesterday, I thought it was going to be worth it maybe but with pleurisy fairly under control bronchitis proudly took charge again, so I not only have the neighbors shouting complaints all night at my coughing but it keeps me too awake. The typist did what she could but I was not able to get any more organized into typing condition. I think this novel is what is making me sick since it's dredging away at things probably better off dead.* It has a horrid fascination for me, however, and I cannot let it go, though as usual I am simultaneously accumulating notes on another (contemporary) straight novel.† I expected to have this ready by now, complete, but continue tearing it up as I go along for better or worse, acting Camille-ish, so I don't see it life-size before the end of April now, and unless there's a cure for the sulfa cures, I don't even see any fragment of brain coming back ever.

Best,
Dawn

---

*Powell was then completing *My Home Is Far Away*.
†This was *The Locusts Have No King*.

P.S. Changes in Part One involve (a) sharpening Marcia's character (to out-and-out nastiness); (b) changing names so they didn't sound all alike; (c) adding final chapter to show reaction to the death.

I wasn't able to get to the part I like best in Part Two. In fact I am not able to do anything but sit here in bed in several bathrobes glowering and cooking up revenges on the maid who was my child's nurse 20 years ago and whose only joy is in sickness so she can boss the little missy around.*

(RARE BOOKS AND MANUSCRIPTS, PRINCETON UNIVERSITY LIBRARY)

TO CAROL BRANDT
35 East Ninth Street
March 30, 1944

Dear Carol:

Here are Part One and Part Two of *My Home Is Far Away* and there will be Part Three in four or five weeks. I will correct the original copy and take it up to Max tomorrow. Part Three completes the first volume of what will be a trilogy, though I have tried to keep this news even from myself. It should be complete in itself, of course. I think it is possible that a magazine interested more in American native roots than in serial plots might be interested in sections of this, but I am as doubtful as you of its general serial chances. I am not up on magazines generally now but would imagine *Atlantic* or *Harper's*, if anybody. It seems a little regional for *The New Yorker*, though they particularly like one much in this vein that they used in that anthology.

The values here do not seem strictly story values, but character and picturesque ways of American life that are usual but to fiction rather unfamiliar; also the innocent beginnings of currents which are now great forces of national good or evil. This is not a Booth Tarkington midwestern family or a wrong-side-of-the-tracks family, but a family of floaters whose philosophy and experience are far different from those of the conventional family at home or at war with a secure environment; the philosophy inevitably becomes unprovincial, cynical, individualistic.

I don't want to frighten you with the trilogy thought, having you worry about Studs Lonigan popping up sooner or later. Besides, I have a short extremely contemporary novel to do directly after this.†

As ever,
Dawn

(COLLECTION TIM PAGE—CARBON COPY)

---

*Louise Lee.
†Powell probably means *Locusts*, which became in fact one of her longest books.

[35 East Ninth Street
Undated; early 1944]

Dear Max:

I think it was mean of you to force little Minelda* to choose between being a flower girl and lolling around in a go-cart, but I suppose it's a decision she'd have to make sooner or later anyway. I threw her out of the wedding party and let her keep her rattle and the go-cart.

I named Part Two "The Shepherdess in the Snowstorm Ball," by which I mean that glass one on Mrs. Jane's mantelpiece. I don't know whether I should specify Glass Snowstorm Ball or not. Part Three is "Home Is Far Away."

I find in reading the proof, which always bores me anyway, that the last part pulls the whole thing up considerably; also, the pure fictional parts are far better than when I was fascinated mistakenly by facts. And incidentally it was more convincing so I am through with main facts. I think there ought to be a note on the jacket that readers should skip to page 299.

I hear the big invasion hunter is due back next month.†

Love,
Dawn

P.S. I don't see that this book can interest anyone unless the Book of the Month took it or Boston banned it. I can't imagine why it was so vital for me to write it and why such a feebleminded result should have taken so much time and work.

(RARE BOOKS AND MANUSCRIPTS, PRINCETON UNIVERSITY LIBRARY)

[35 East Ninth Street
Undated; early 1945]

Dear Max—

I have been working for some time in a room down the street away from telephones, income-tax men, collectors, friends, tourists, agents and editors. I don't know where I went off the track in my book‡ but I think I was hurrying it too fast and at the same time not getting it anywhere and gazing at the typewriter and it filled me with rage that I had of my own accord stuck my head in this noose. So I didn't call you because I had nothing but a blank to report.

I am in need of considerable money so I put the novel aside to accept an offer

---

*Minelda is a rather unattractive child character in *My Home Is Far Away*.
†Most likely this is a reference to Ernest Hemingway, whose passions included hunting and politics.
‡*Marcia* was the working title of this planned sequel to *My Home Is Far Away*. Powell would labor on it off and on for almost twenty years without ever finishing more than a hundred pages.

from George Abbott to write a play I had once described to him for a $1000 advance.* Most novelists can make money on the side by short stories but I had such bad luck with mine I stopped writing them. Two I wrote five years ago just sold a few months ago, but I can't wait five years for this. I have only a month to do the play in, but as it has been in note form for years I expect to have it done in a week or two. It is about a family reunion in Ohio at the present time and could be a short novel. There is also in it the return of Louis Bromfield to the Soil.

I expected to have the novel done by August but I don't expect to work on it for another fortnight now and plan to have it done in November. I don't feel particularly encouraged about my novel-writing anyway. When I'm on Ohio a wave of admiration for my New York novels comes to me and when I'm on New York a wave of applause for Ohio comes to me. This is confusing when I am in a quandary anyway and have set such grim restraints for myself—no satire, no chance for contemporary sophistication or adult observation.

I do not think there is any excuse for not producing, but there is at present a very great reason for my attempt to make money. My son has been at a rest colony for several years, since a birth injury caused a slight spastic condition and, with maturity, spells of violence. As a child he was a mathematical wizard and extremely scholarly. I think the teachers' attempts to break his concentration periods and "level" him was bad for him. He continues to send for Latin books to translate himself, studies subway and telephone systems, keeps an elaborate diary, and in general shows the usual combination of a type of genius and childishness. Last fall he got depressed by the number of older people in the colony who had spent their lives there and ran away two or three times, begged me to send him someplace else where he could have "intelligent conversation." As these places are limited and the field so full of quacks, I have been consulting psychologists here who believe he might be cured by letting his superior gifts have full sway. He is coming to New York the second week in May and I am arranging for a series of specialists in glands, education, neurology, etc., to study him, if possible, in the Neurological Institute, as a last chance to see if he can be completely restored. New treatments have been put in use since I last had this done and I owe it to him to have it done again. I expect it will cost thousands, which I haven't got, but I have gone ahead with the arrangements on a gambling chance of being able to make it.

This is too complicated to discuss conversationally so I am writing it instead of calling you back on the phone. I find the only way I can ever face any human responsibility is by not facing it, but this I have to do now and it scares the wits out of me.

*George Abbott (1887–1994), the actor, author, producer, director, and all-around "grand old man" of the American theater, worked with Powell on at least two prospective plays, neither of which was ever produced.

I think the vacation from that goddam Marcia will do me good and make the book settle itself in the back of my mind. I will get back to it in a couple of weeks unless somebody else waves their wallet at me.

As ever,
Dawn

TO EDMUND WILSON

35 East Ninth Street
April 11, 1945

HEADQUARTERS FOR MOBILIZATION OF THE DEAD PELVIS

Dear Bunny:

I was asked to call on Latouche, who was sick in bed with strep, and there he was reading a large solemn German tome called *The Function of the Orgasm.*[*] I was particularly struck by a chapter heading called the "The Mobilization of the Dead Pelvis." I decided to recruit and do my bit. Imagine my delight when I dined with the Murphys to find your friend Esther Murphy[†] there, heady with statistics and her long unmated legs flung around each other so that the left one was right and no pants on. She fixed me at once with the old beady, puffed at a cigarette butt (she is one of those smokers who are never seen with the whole cigarette but always the last eighth-inch—I believe she buys them that way) and swung right into the flaws of the Second Empire, but my horrified gaze kept being drawn to this vast length of nudity leading to what George O'Neil referred to as the Blue Grotto, where something was winking away like a Buddha's orb. This, I cried, is the Dead Pelvis at last. I am unable to work today for this haunting, grisly image. I decided she doesn't know she is female, and if she should glance down in the shower and see a set of balls she would only think, Dear, dear, how dusty things get in New York.

THIS DOES NOT MEAN I DO NOT ADMIRE HER MIND.

I have heard no hide or hair of your family's doings so have nothing to add to your worries. We hear that Dos is supposedly on his way back and that he had two or three accidents in addition to the one reported before, i.e., the airplane wing clipping him.

Your name has been coming up in reviews, mostly in reference to your

---

[*]*The Function of the Orgasm* (1927) was an unorthodox (and still controversial) psychological study by Wilhelm Reich (1897–1957).
[†]Esther Murphy (1898–1962) was Gerald Murphy's sister; Wilson thought her remarkably brilliant.

detective-story position.* Sterling North puts in an "as Edmund Wilson has said" so your lofty pronouncements on past participles are not forgotten.

I have been whizzing along on my novel but am now in a state because George Abbott asked me if I had any play ideas around that would do for ZaSu Pitts.† I did have one that I had had the good sense to keep from writing but sent him a few notes on it whereupon he signed a contract for it with advance payment and instructions to have it done by June 1. So here I am looking out the window over a stack of notes on a novel and then a sister stack of notes on a play. The best feature of Abbott is that he is the only person I ever met in the theater who leaves me alone and doesn't want to confer. It's the blab blab blab of the stage that I hate. I do not want to chum up with editors, producers, critics, Teacher or Boss in any form. That is the enemy and any pretense of equality, socially or any other way, is poppycock. I admit their right to vote and spawn, however.

Oh yes, I did see the Philip Rahvs one night in a restaurant, soon after you left, and Nathalie said she was very upset over being called to sign or testify something or other for Mary against you, and that she would not have done so if she hadn't been on the spot as she was equally fond of you.‡

The Dwight Macdonalds§ asked Margaret De Silver to share their home in Truro this coming summer as she was lonely, they felt, and it would be nice to have someone they could leave the children with. (She nixed this.)

Other old buddies of yours, the Herbert Solows,¶ are in Cuba for *Fortune*, studying the sugar plants, as only Herbert can.

Today the Drama Critics awarded their solid china plaque to Tennessee Williams's *The Glass Menagerie* in which Laurette Taylor** gave a Duse-like performance of muted emotions and also unmuted ones to be on the safe side. Esther Murphy, my monitor, declares it a fine play and a great performance. It has a chance of getting the Pulitzer, too. As you know—you secretive old gossip, you—Miss Taylor's stage career has been checkered. Opening in plays in the

*Wilson's recent attack in *The New Yorker* on the vogue of the detective story, "Who Cares Who Killed Roger Ackroyd?," had made him a much-talked-about figure.

†ZaSu Pitts (1898–1963) was an American actress best remembered today for her extraordinary performance in Erich von Stroheim's *Greed*. She had also appeared in Stroheim's ill-fated film rendition of Powell's *Walking down Broadway, Hello, Sister!* (1931). Abbott's plans for her to appear in a Powell play never came off.

‡Wilson was then in the midst of a violent divorce from the writer Mary McCarthy (1912–1989). Nathalie Rahv, wife of the author and editor Philip Rahv (1908–1973), had testified that Wilson "appeared to take delight in scolding and upbraiding his wife for petty matters."

§The writer and social critic Dwight Macdonald (1906–1982) and his wife, Nancy, were regular visitors to Cape Cod, where both Wilson and De Silver generally spent their summers.

¶Herbert Solow (1903–1964), an American journalist and editor, was an active member of the fact-finding committee that investigated the Stalinist charges against Trotsky. His wife, Sylvia Salmi, was a photographer for whom Powell sat on several occasions.

**A famous actress as a youth, Laurette Taylor (1887–1946) made a phenomenal comeback in Tennessee Williams's *The Glass Menagerie* in 1945. Williams (1911–1983) would have to wait until 1948 for his first Pulitzer, for *A Streetcar Named Desire*.

past to rave notices in or out of town, then the show closing next day because of star's remaining in alcoholic stupor. Choosing between the two careers she elected alcoholism and has been beavering away at it for many years.

Then Mother Love saved her. Her son Dwight a year ago took her to a doctor in Hollywood because she was disturbed about her great weight. He found the entire trouble was glandular and treated her for this condition. She thinned out, stopped drinking, opened last week to unanimous raves, wins prizes, stands on her head, is interviewed about her abstinence, declares with a *mouchoir* held to her deep tragic eyes that she only drank because her heart broke when Hartley Manners passed away, however she will have a little medicinal triple Scotch if the reporter can get the waiter fast enough because she is so emotionally upset now over the possibility of Hartley's coming to life again. Mr. [Walter] Winchell then writes mysteriously, "What famed star of what new hit has cast trembling for fear said star can't appear?" So it may be too late.

It reminds me of Shaw's sour remarks on the school of acting that based its technique on the inadvertent fumbles of a former generation of drunken actors. That is, in the old days when all actors were drunkards, the choked hoarse voice, the fumbling at the door, the lurch across the sofa, the sudden sinking into a chair were not subtle ways to express terrific emotional conflicts, but the actor's struggle to get through the act without falling down. The new actors studied this and, drinking less or not at all, adopted these drunken manifestations as proper for great emotional acting. (I cannot find this passage now and I want to fling it at Esther Murphy very soon; it is in the *Dramatic Opinions* somewhere and I must memorize it or she won't take it.) Anyway, it may be that all the praise now and in the past flung at Laurette Taylor's emotional acting may be explained this way.

Rosamund Lehmann's book got raves as literature.* It seemed to me an engrossing old-time sort of "Wife in Name Only" kind of novel, about as literarily important as *Rebecca* or *Gone with the Wind*. I reviewed it this way for *PM* and imagine my fury when they cut out all disparaging remarks and in fact all points, but even so leaving it the only feeble dissenting voice. I wrote a letter advising them to pursue their practice of attacking only unsuccessful firms and writers, and buttering the big advertisers, but for God's sake stop pretending they didn't. They are always running a severe boycotting series about a little merchant down on Second Avenue who is a racketeer because he charges eight cents per wooden button when he should give them away, so please all *PM* readers don't patronize this fellow, and see that the bill for bugging your potatoes instead of worming them passes Congress, and buy *PM* tomorrow, the Only Paper That Isn't Afraid to Be Afraid of Saying Anything. I made irreverent ref-

---

The Ballad and the Source (1944) was Rosamond Lehmann's latest novel.

erences in the review to the Book of the Month Club's Cholly Knickerbocker droolings over Miss Lehmann's beauty and financial and social and noble connections and said that surly subscribers would be won over at once on discovering all these points were above reproach. (I think they selected the book to retrieve their prestige after palming off a nigger writer on their club. Goodness knows, the subscribers must have cried, "I don't believe in slavery but imagine having them come into your club!") Mr. Pippett of *PM* has tried to appease me, not for my value to *PM* but for my loud mouth about their queasy practices.

Gerald Murphy said he had a note from Scotty Fitzgerald* saying she had met me and was very disappointed to find my morale sagging. The only time I met her was in your office that day and I am baffled by my morale's being out in those few moments. Or do you think this was Gerald's tactful way of saying something that was on his own mind?

I saw Don Elder† again and he seemed very pleased with your book but anticipated Pa Doubleday and censor trouble, at least in Boston. This may help. Your successors on *The New Yorker* seem spotty and that department seems disorganized so I hope you get it for next year or are you going to settle over there with Martha Gellhorn and the Talented Girls? Everybody over here is going crazy again, following the period when they were all alcoholics. It makes a nice change. Why don't you write a play, too, so as to draw fire away from my Broadway retreat?

love,

Dawn

(YALE COLLECTION OF AMERICAN LITERATURE, BEINECKE RARE BOOK AND MANUSCRIPT LIBRARY, YALE UNIVERSITY)

TO DR. LUDLUM‡

35 East Ninth Street
May 19, 1945

Dear Dr. Ludlum:

Jojo managed to get through his entire week with no letdown or upset. I spent most of the time with him myself, and found him more reasonable and considerate. I believe this is because I expect more from him and am less adequate myself.

---

*Frances Scott Fitzgerald, later Lanahan (1921–1986), known as Scotty or Scottie, was the only daughter of F. Scott and Zelda Fitzgerald.

†Donald Elder was a senior editor at Doubleday who worked with Wilson on the publication (and, later, on the legal defense) of *Memoirs of Hecate County*. The two would fall out for a time in 1947, and Wilson would leave the firm.

‡Ludlum was apparently a doctor at Gladwyne Colony, where Jojo was then confined. Jojo would be in hospitals or institutions much of his life.

The treatments he has had seem definitely to the good. He was less spastic than ever before, more alert and awakened. The greatest change seemed to be an emotional poise and localization. He seemed to be aware of what he was feeling, instead of bewildered and apt to get himself worked up on a totally unrelated matter.

I took the opportunity to consult a psychologist, Portia Hamilton, Ph.D., of 133 East 58th Street, who has suggested places for friends of mine with good results. I have felt that his periods of order might be utilized for his own growth, though I have no delusions as to the length of these periods. The routine tests she gave over a three-day period showed a range of superior adult to seven-year-old and indicated the lesions and cortical injury diagnosed before by medical examinations. She was hopeful of finding farm work under supervision for the summer months, to break up the runaway habit he got into last fall. She felt that the time away from institutions or sanitarium should not be spent at home, where the excessive pampering and usual city handicaps set him back rather than building ahead on constructive sanitarium treatment. This seems logical and I hope some such plan may be followed this summer. If you have any suggestions, let me know. If possible some permanent summer plan might be worked out, to give the sense of security necessary—say, two or three months a year in one place.

With best wishes, I am—

sincerely yours,
Dawn Powell Gousha

P.S. I enclose a check to apply to Joseph's bill.

(COLLECTION TIM PAGE—CARBON COPY)

TO EDMUND WILSON

35 East Ninth Street
June 4, 1945

Dear Wigmore,[*]

[. . .] It was a breath of spring to find you escaped from the bookworming department into the wide wide world in last week's *New Yorker*. Everyone is very pleased, except possibly Mollie Panter-Downes. Philip Barry, viewed at East Hampton at the Murphys' last weekend, spoke highly of your London article—saying it was the first fresh point of view on the Situation—and in town bruised authors can smile again. . . .[†]

---

[*]Powell played an ongoing game with Wilson in which he was "Professor Ernest Wigmore" and she was "Mrs. Humphrey [*sic*] Ward."
[†]Philip Barry (1896–1949) was a highly successful American playwright. Wilson had begun sending back jaundiced and rather pessimistic articles about London at the end of World War II.

Dos and Katy have been on hand, Dos looking not too well after his foreign travels, where, it seems to me, he saw exactly what he intended to see. Katy is all chatter since her book with dear Edie and exposes her hitherto subtle hand openly now.* They were staying at the Murphys' last week and naturally Edie was in town and Gerald said they were phoning each other from 8 a.m. till midnight and the rest of the time locked together in the bathroom to Dos's intense embarrassment. They say the book is doing splendidly, but rumor says the two ladies used up Dos's goodwill at Houghton Mifflin so if he should want to rest up with a little volume of verse he may find stern faces. . . .

I have lost 20 lbs. through strange assortments of pills of such a mysterious nature that they actually changed the nature of my mind, so I was obliged to give up writing. If I don't write for five years I may make quite a name for myself and if I can stop for ten I may give Katherine Anne [Porter] and Dorothy Parker a run for their money. I did a television script for Gilbert Seldes (it was outlined from the current *Mademoiselle* magazine, so you can imagine the deep thoughts involved). The scripting itself for television is 1000 times more limiting than movie-writing since no one can move extensively on the set, and so literal and exacting that it is like a complicated game. To watch is more boring than radio and not to be compared to the old magic lantern. But the shooting is much more fascinating than a movie lot. I think the thing is a big bust—television, I mean—but then I said that about Technicolor, too. (I was right.)

Bomby Hemingway† (Ernest's 21-year-old son by Hadley) was liberated from prison and is here on leave. He had spent the night at the Murphys' on his way to visit Ernest in Cuba. His prison was the height of German efficiency, for the torture devices were very methodically arranged and suited to the Geneva rules superficially. That is, arms and legs of Allied prisoners were inevitably found infected and ordered amputated. Bomby's arm was saved only by a Polish doctor who gave him shots every week when his amputation time was due and these shots made him frightfully sick. Medical rules prohibited any surgery during fever and upchucking so he saved his arm, but is still sizzling with the drugs. Also the prisoners were given elaborate metabolism and allergy tests as soon as they came in and then carefully deprived of whatever the tests said their systems required, or else given whatever they were allergic to. It seemed a splendid example of German efficiency, with the papers all in order. . . .

Downtown New York is as depressing as ever, the only change in the routine being that Coby has been on the wagon for two months due to back pains. As is usually the case, a clear head makes for seeing life in its true grisly

*Katy Dos Passos and her friend Edith Shay had written a novel together, entitled *The Private Adventures of Captain Shaw* (1945).
†John Hadley Nicanor Hemingway (born 1923), Ernest Hemingway's oldest son, was much liked and admired by Powell.

aspect, so he is grim and literary. Also, sobriety makes one an easy prey to catas-trophe. Last night as he gloomily ate a salad at Margaret De Silver's, Canby Chambers's* horrible spaniel modestly chewed up half Coby's jacket. It was a new suit he had been saving up to buy for a year. No, no, it didn't make a bit of difference, he laughingly assured Canby, but suddenly took a mighty swig of whiskey.

I think it must be very confusing to find yourself obliged to wave a flag and defend your native soil, as you found yourself doing in England. Maybe you will sell yourself the idea that all you want in life is a farm out next to Louis Bromfield's† or a big potato ranch in Bucks County next to George and Bea [Kaufman]'s. George Kaufman is in again. The theater is lousy with Pinafores. George Kaufman's *Hollywood Pinafore* is, according to reports, brilliant with the master's wit and genius. Willella Waldorf, in the *Post*, raised a minor voice to say it was not as sidesplitting as it was meant to be. Sally Benson and some-body else did the colored Pinafore *Memphis Blues* with Bill Robinson and this too is Superb. A real *Pinafore* is now hotfooting to town and it looks as if we were going to be hemmed in again by a D'Oyly Carter Nightmare. As an old Gilbert and Sullivan lover-hater, I am not happy. On Spivey's roof, *View* Maga-zine's surrealist puppeteer is presenting skits by Jane Bowles and other self-styled avant-gardists every evening. Archie MacLeish is Not Happy in the State Department and may creep out. Philip Barry is Not Happy with the Theatre Guild, now that the Guild is taking off his play. He is very discouraged about writing, having barely made a quarter of a million this season, and after all there are two mouths to feed.

Alec Brook‡ had a cover on the *SatEvePost*, being paid highly and then sell-ing the original (a child portrait) to the parents. It seems the *Post* is following Lucky Strike and Abbott Chemicals in discovering art....

I see that the *View* puppeteer's name is John Myers, the puppets are designed by Kurt Seligman, the music is by Paul Bowles, a number is by that oaf Charles Henri Ford, and no doubt the check is signed by Peggy Guggenheim....

with fondest regards,
Dawn

(YALE COLLECTION OF AMERICAN LITERATURE, BEINECKE RARE BOOK AND MANUSCRIPT LIBRARY, YALE UNIVERSITY)

---

*Canby Chambers (c.1895–1958) was an early friend of Powell's and the longtime companion of Esther Andrews. He made his living writing for men's magazines.
†A native of Mansfield, Ohio, Bromfield (1896–1956) had been a third-grade classmate of Powell's and to her dismay and disdain had gone on to become a best-selling author.
‡Alexander Brook (1898–1980), an American artist, was married for a time to Powell's on-again/off-again friend Peggy Bacon (1895–1987).

TO MAX PERKINS

35 East Ninth Street
June 20, 1945

Dear Max:

I had a strange time in Ohio, strange because so much of it turned out to be walking into *My Home Is Far Away*. First, both my sisters met me with a car and that unlimited gas that the middlewesterners always seem to wangle, and we rode around all week. In Shelby (the London Junction) we found that the house we had lived in and where our mother had died in 1903 was now an antique store, so we wandered around there, looking out the same little windows, peeking through the register in the room where she had died, and buying odd items. I had the creeps, the more so for having so recently reconstructed the whole place. Then we went to Mt. Gilead, our birthplace, where the very hotel our father once worked in is now run by our cousins. This was all like a dream for nothing had changed in the town, and it was queer sitting in the office he had once sat in and sitting in the spacious old living quarters we had visited as very small children, finding them exactly as we remembered them, even though I was barely four at the time and expected to find everything much smaller in reality.

I asked very cautiously about my stepmother, now still living in Oberlin, and for the first time heard from my sisters a most amazing story that of course I could never use. When I ran away (at the age of 12) I left my younger sister Phyllis there who was thrashed regularly every day, she told me, but was ashamed to ever tell anyone. When she was only 11 she had to stay up all night with a premature baby our stepmother had given birth to. The stepmother (named Sabra, incidentally) had lost it when it was six months developed and it weighed only two pounds and never opened its eyes, was kept in a tiny sewing basket in the kitchen and died after a week. Sabra was sick and never allowed downstairs to see it, so the baby died and was buried without her seeing it.

Then, Phyllis said, a few weeks later she heard a scream and found Papa wresting a gun away from Sabra who was trying to kill herself, with boxes of mementos laid out for all of her own relatives. Later Phyllis was told to stay out of school and drive with Papa and Sabra to the graveyard. (The baby had been dead a month.) Sabra unlocked the cabinet where the doll we were never allowed to play with was kept, and took the pink silk dress off of the doll. Then the grisly three drove to the cemetery, waited till no one was looking, and Sabra made Papa dig up the baby's grave and put the doll dress on it for a shroud. Then Phyllis was driven back to school and dropped at the schoolhouse to go back in the geography class of the fifth grade with the other children. Stepmother was satisfied, for at least the baby she had never seen had a shroud.

Oddly enough, as my sisters and I pieced together a number of theories about her, the baby's death was not really responsible for her curious prim cruelties, for she had been that way from the first. And she continued the secret thrashings of Phyllis daily, knowing Phyllis was afraid to tell the neighbors or Papa, until the neighbors did find out and gave Phyllis carfare to run away when she too was 12.* Phyllis is soft and forgiving and still sees her but always comes away with some fresh evidence of her psychopathic cruelty. Phyllis is an artist, won three first prizes in the north Ohio art show in Canton this year, makes her own bread, and has raised three handsome daughters.

Everybody worked in war plants, everybody knew everything about the war as translated by letters from whatever husband or son they had there, everybody had storerooms filled with flour, sugar, canned goods, etc., and lived in desperate fear of being obliged to do without whatever they were used to—the necessities there being largely hot biscuits, fudge pie, coconut cake, mashed potatoes. In Cleveland, of course, menus were more modern and elastic. There my brother-in-law, who has two Packards and a Chevrolet for his family, and gas for fifty, talked gloomily of being ruined by the government, though twenty years ago he made twenty dollars a week. To mention Roosevelt is to admit colored blood so no one does. I had forgotten how rich Cleveland people are, the miles and miles of private homes as big as our public libraries, the beautiful country clubs, the glorification of material conveniences, the vast invincible Magazine Public that in New York we can thank God forget. I had the impression that at last I had made good by having a story (good or bad didn't matter) printed free of charge in *Collier's*. No wonder they are firm in the belief that Louis Bromfield is America's leading writer, recognized from coast to coast as such, and Dos Passos and Hemingway are some cranks that had pieces in *Esquire* once, and Culture meant traveling first class, cases of Scotch instead of bottles of rye, children (dumb or bright) in private schools, and a Friend who's been Abroad to settle all fine points.

I was glad to get my background into a fluid state again, as the new book had come out in such rigid form that I didn't see how to recast it. I caught the language again quickly and the familiar combination of open hearts and closed minds that represents so much of the country except New York, where we have closed hearts first, and minds so open that carrier pigeons can fly straight through without leaving a message. Having been reminded again that New York is no part of America, I still feel safer here—at least we can write or paint here without the Woman's Home Companion breathing on our necks.

Best,

Dawn

(COLLECTION TIM PAGE—CARBON COPY)

*The chronology is askew here: Emily Helen Powell in fact lived her tiny life in 1914, when Phyllis would have been fourteen years old. Powell herself was all of thirteen, not twelve, when she ran away.

TO JOSEPH GOUSHA

1428 Vernon Avenue
Key West, Florida
November 14, 1945*

Dear Sir—

I enclose blank check good for up to $50 if *PM* $30 arrived as I am sending $150 to Gladwyne. I recommend your calling on Jojo Saturday or Sunday unless following week. I have tentative reservation for Friday, but Pauline [Hemingway] has wired she is returning Thursday so it may be more practical to stay a few days more in her great house and get some work done. The telephone number here is 727. I will leave Thursday night however unless I decide to stay on (or am invited).

The trip was very pleasant though we went 242 miles out of our way (we were within 28 miles of Harrisburg). Expensive due to five overnights, but very instructive since I realized how cheap and well fed the rest of U.S. is and how much better the service and quality and prices. We haven't realized how steep New York has been getting. We visited Alec Brook in Savannah and had a fine time at his lovely studio—four huge rooms (each about half again as big as our living room), back balconies overhanging the beautiful Savannah River with submarines and warships gliding past, near enough to step on the deck. Outside Savannah, we stayed in the same fine place (beautiful sequoia cabins) that Ginny [Pfeiffer] and I had stayed.

Miami was gay and the Miami Colonial jammed with tourists and a Spanish headquarters. Margaret, Esther and I had to sleep three in a room ($10). No hot water. I bought you two shirts . . . as the men's wear there seemed lavish and cheap. Intended to get more if I got more money and had more time.

Key West is lovely and cool summer heat, though Esther arrived to find her house a wreck by general indifference of Canby and her nephew. Bachelor wreck, I mean. Roof leaking so buckets all over living room, lamps broken, etc. . . .

Love,
W

---

*Powell had traveled by car to Florida with Margaret De Silver.

TO MAX PERKINS

[35 East Ninth Street]
June 13, 1946

Dear Max:

That was very kind of you to save my honor with the deposit. I was in Provincetown hiding from the bank and might have had to run wild in the dunes the rest of my life without your assistance.

I don't really know what is the matter with me and my works. Could be that I have just found out that it's more fun to lie in bed all morning than to tinker around a desk? In fact, I am just crazy about not doing anything at all. It's going to be my new hobby. It may be that housecleaning spell I had a few weeks ago, when I was appalled by the mountains of writing I had piled up in closets and file cases and trunks. Tons of rejected works dating back to the Boer War. It struck me with terrific force that I just wrote too goddam much. Worse, I couldn't seem to stop. It had gotten to the point where my morning pilgrimages to the workroom had me bent over with great market bags of notes and data and my twin novels following me by drosky.

I hired a secretary as a solution to straightening out notes and versions and reversions. However the sound of her typewriter gave me delusions of such efficiency that I got in a frightful state of depression. I took to writing secretly and typing it at night so the little snoop wouldn't know what I was doing. Furthermore, she was a literary type and had a scary habit of dreamily quoting from whatever chapter she had typed during the day. I would bumble into a bar and find her holding a group of wastrels sneeringly spellbound by reciting passages from my work-in-progress. She went to a psychoanalyst every day, too, and I gathered was freeing herself of the idea that she was in any way my inferior. I let her go before I committed myself to the analyst's care. Otherwise she was a very good secretary.

I saw Bunny and Dos in Provincetown. The natives refer to his book as "He-Cat Valley."* He has purchased a 1910 Cadillac or Bearcat chauffeur car and has a man whizzing him up and down the Cape. He was very happy over his success, observing wistfully that it was the first time he had ever been translated into anything but Japanese. Ladies of the Cape vie for his favor, I understand, adorably eager to find out if he is the wow he says he is. Certain other ladies wrote him notes on receiving his book, saying that they would try not to let the book break off their friendship with him but please not to ask them to discuss it.

I was discussing a phase of Dickens's writing with an addled publisher recently, who asked me to do a book on that angle. It seemed to me that all I

---

*Wilson's daringly sensual novel *Memories of Hecate County* had just been published.

needed to do was a few more books, so I agreed but discovered to my astonishment that I would need more than four thoughts to fill the book and that was the extent of my knowledge. I thought I might call the work "The Dickens Dawn Powell Doesn't Know, by Dawn Powell." It was a narrow squeak, though.

I think I should have a book out this fall, if it's only a cookbook. How to defrost Birdseye goulash. Somebody told me I was in *Story*'s short-story anthology but they have not mentioned it to me. I would like to earn a lot of money suddenly—no, I wouldn't either. I mean I would like to GET it, why do I lie to myself?

I will report further if conditions here in the hatch change.

As ever,

Dawn

TO MAX PERKINS

35 East Ninth Street
July 10, 1946

Dear Max—

I was waiting for more of this ms. but decided to give you the straightened-out 99 pages, most of which you saw, except for a few revisions.* I gave a copy to Carl [Brandt] for him to get an idea of the general tone. Offhand, I would describe it as a follow-up of *A Time to Be Born*, which dealt with New York in the beginning follies of war. This book deals with the more desperate follies of postwar Manhattan—the exaggerated drive to perdition of a nation now conditioned to destruction. I have a straight middle-aged love story here, since this seems to be the age for middle-aged folly—for both women and men. Certainly the young folks have no chance (as they did in our youth) except to get killed or invited to middle-aged revels.

I can give you a very explicit description of the novel plot except that all plots reduced to articulate propositions sound the same. While the background is as moralistically burlesque as [that in] *Time to Be Born*, the main story is a deep love story. Two people who take each other for granted, in love and assuming they know all about each other because they don't need to tell each other anything; the destruction of their love by misplaced jealousy which turns out to be true; and the re-creation of a new, more profound love based on finally knowing each other. This, too, seems to me peculiarly Manhattan, the

---

*The novel would be published in 1948 as *The Locusts Have No King*. Among the other titles Powell considered were *Prudentius Psychomachia* and *O Strange New War!*

town for middle age. Elsewhere, middle age is surrounded by its grandchildren or young and chaperoned into discretion.

By the way, I was bookworming in an old bookstore on Fourth Avenue and found a lovely 15-cent book of the type I love—*Underwood's Handbook of English Literature,* Lee Shepard and Dillingham, Boston, 1874 (that being the time when anthologists were genuine scholars and critics so that a preface was a dignified exhibition of brains and erudition instead of a boogey-woogey yak yak of some celebrated opportunist). Anyway, I was fascinated by the personal animadversions in the introductions and footnotes, then I wondered about the penciled marginalia and looking in the front saw that the book was the property of Lulu R. Perkins, 1875. Was that your Aunt Lulu, the one who ran the sporting house in Siam?

More mss. soon—

As ever,
Dawn

I am not sure of the title but like it at the moment.

(RARE BOOKS AND MANUSCRIPTS, PRINCETON UNIVERSITY LIBRARY)

TO MAX PERKINS

Doctor's Hospital
East End Avenue
September 29, 1946

Dear Max—

I have been fending off an operation for a long time and admit I was wrong as you don't have energy for anything but fending anyway. So now I am having it the hard way—operation tomorrow and I'm very pleased. I think it's name is Historectomy (Simple Type) and the doctor is Norman Pleshette. Should have done this before instead of bedraggling myself and typewriter to no good end. I believe I'm not supposed to do anything for some time but these instructions always infuriate me—as if doing what you wanted to do were bad for you and "rest" with your household privileged to exhaust you were good for you. Wish I had ms. further typed.

Best wishes (for both of us),
Dawn

P.S. This is a wonderful place and I'm glad I have any excuse to be here.

(RARE BOOKS AND MANUSCRIPTS, PRINCETON UNIVERSITY LIBRARY)

TO MAX PERKINS

[35 East Ninth Street]
November 7, 1946

Dear Max—

This is the corrected draft of the synopsis I gave you. I will send up some more typed pages next week. My new typist took advantage of my sickness in a sneaking way to have twins and it seems my pages no longer come first with her. You can't depend on anybody these days.

Best,
Dawn

P.S. I was interested in finally reading [Isabel Bolton's] *Do I Wake or Sleep?* It seemed a worthwhile gift for writing pitted against the always fatal reverence for the periphery of society. I mean I had a sense that the author herself had never been able to see beyond the immediate chi-chi, and she was not really well enough acquainted with *that* to make it glitter and sing as it can in rare cases.

THE LOCUSTS HAVE NO KING, a novel of contemporary New York by Dawn Powell

In the Hans Christian Andersen tale a banquet guest, nostalgic for the Dark Ages, accidentally puts on a pair of magic galoshes and finds himself catapulted from his own times into the lawlessness and evil hazards of the 15th century. The reverse happens to Frederick Olliver, medieval scholar, recluse and bachelor. Completely immersed for many years in his medieval research, he emerges at last one night in the autumn of 1945 to find New York a strange and terrifying city—the peace, now being celebrated, as sinister as war, as barbaric as the Dark Ages he has just left.

A quiet man, secure in his studious habits, high-minded and incorruptible in his professional and personal standards, deeply in love with one woman, Frederick discovers that there is no insurance against the emotional tornadoes of modern life; even his own carefully protected garden is not safe from the plague of locusts and destroyers now devouring the world. Peace has brought out the destroyers, no dream is left, no banner is sacred. Frederick, at last awake to his own times, finds that he himself is caught in the rush toward destruction and is inevitably helping the very forces he despises. The League for Cultural Foundations,* where Frederick teaches, provides merely a quickly acquired mask for ignorance; his publisher's new ambition is to print nothing but pseudo-historical harlots' progress and cartoon magazines; the artist's dream is to bring not beauty but soft drinks in five-color reproductions to the

---

*This was Powell's parody of the New School for Social Research, where one of her friends, Peter Monro Jack, discussed "various books he hasn't read; class earnestly sops up this bird's-eye culture."

masses; women's romantic dreams these days are of a Cupid that pays high interest on their alimony or fat paychecks.

In this topsy-turvy new world Frederick is not conscious of change in himself but the truth is he is being subtly corrupted on every side; he is armored against known temptation, but his solitary life has left him weaponless against the unknown. A young girl, Dodo Brennan, whom he dislikes and mistrusts, wrecks his serious love affair with Lyle Gaynor; secure in his own impregnable detachment he nevertheless assists his publisher in trashy fly-by-night ventures. His intelligence and the fact that his eyes are wide open do not deter him from courting betrayal from his new love and dishonor from his work. He meets the new peacetime opportunists—women in business, commercial artists, ex-wives, barflies, patient women waiting for the scourge to pass, lady executives. He meets advertising men weeping over old days as star reporters, publishers whose fortunes and claims to literary omniscience are based on their grandfathers' auction of begging letters from now-classic authors. He finds, presently, that although his 15 years of honorable scholarship have brought him merely academic rewards and starvation fees, his year of surrender rewards him with glory and fortune. Frederick, however, derives only ironic pleasure from this, for he is tortured constantly by the waywardness of his hard, mediocre little Dodo.

If Frederick is unconscious of what the year has done to him, his old love, Lyle Gaynor, is not. Hers is the anguish of seeing him betrayed and betraying her even while he continues to depend on their basic need of each other. What eventually restores Frederick to himself and to Lyle is the realization that out of desperation she too is about to give in to the overwhelming forces around them. For the first time he sees that she needs him, and for the first time they realize that, although they had loved each other long, they had never really known each other until their love had been endangered and fragments analyzed and put together into a lasting mosaic.

(RARE BOOKS AND MANUSCRIPTS, PRINCETON UNIVERSITY LIBRARY)

TO IRMA WYCKOFF*

35 East Ninth Street
June 17, 1947

Dear Miss Wyckoff:

I know you must feel as shocked and devastated as anyone by the death of Max.† I received the message from Mr. Scribner this morning just as I was writ-

---

*Irma Wyckoff was Max Perkins's assistant at Scribner's.
†Perkins had died suddenly at five o'clock that morning.

ing Max a note that Patrick H. was better though the new Mrs. Hemingway was seriously ill as of a new note from Key West. It brought home to me the millions of other people's tribulations that Max went through emotionally besides his own—if he ever had time for his own. I do think we all exhausted him— fighting the new kind of publishing exhausted him and the new kind of author exhausted him. But I don't know what we'll do without him and I am particularly sorry for you as someone who will surely miss the radiance of his presence.

Sincerely,
Dawn Powell

P.S. In case there may be confusion, my ms. was returned by Max for new inserts and is in my hands at present in a nearly completed state.

(RARE BOOKS AND MANUSCRIPTS, PRINCETON UNIVERSITY LIBRARY)

TO MALCOLM LOWRY*

35 East Ninth Street
July 1, 1947

Dear Consul Lowry—

I am sitting here in my room on the roof where I have been Working since 9 this morning. It is now 1. I have finished my nap. I have read some odd pages in *Nicholas Nickleby* which seems to be scattered around the room. I have read very carefully the wrapping on some tan shoe polish. I have made a careful list of people to invite to a large extremely de luxe party in Cleveland, Ohio, if I should ever go there. (It wouldn't take the Wises from Canton more than an hour or two to run in to it.) I have taken a ruler and pencil and designed an ideal desk for the creative type who likes to lie down in a state of free association while creating (this and that). I have read the Houses for Rent in Vermont, New Hampshire and Rhode Island in a section of the May 28 *Tribune* and have figured out pretty neatly supplies to order from Macy's and Sears Roebuck to have sent up there should the occasion ever arise at the same time I do. Supposing I got up there miles from anywhere and had no stickums with initials printed on them to stick in the pages of a looseleaf notebook for the alphabetical listing of casserole dishes which no doubt I will be very much interested in by that time?

In short or long I have burnt myself out and it is barely high noon.

I think I will write a short story. I think I will take a dexedrine pill and go out and have my hair dyed yellow with matching accessories. I think I should take care of my health. I can picture the touching tears of gratitude as I press

---

*Powell had met the novelist Malcolm Lowry (1909–1957) during his visit to New York to promote *Under the Volcano*.

the bills into my dying friend's hand. I can't picture myself paying any creditors or the government or the money I borrowed from my college years ago. ("Don't you worry about this money," I said, my honest little freckled face shining away at them, "I'm going to use this education to make something of myself you'll be proud of and I'll pay this back within five years and be grateful to my dying day.")

All right, if I've turned into such a heel then the hell with the whole thing. I don't deserve to be rich and yellow-haired. I don't deserve to do anything but go downstairs and telephone somebody to come out and have a drink at 5 o'clock. I wouldn't say right now because it might interfere with the delicate creative process.

I think I will cry.

I think I will cry about Max Perkins's being dead only I have a hunch he was so fed up with pushing writers' egos around that he didn't care what happened. The last few times I saw him—in fact only a few days before he suddenly died—he talked a great deal about you. I intended to write you at the time that it struck me he was like an old roué who wistfully thinks that if he could find one more mistress really the equal of Ninon or Lillian Russell he wouldn't be through. Most of the time Max and I spent together was devoted to his anecdotes of the fierce and romantic antics of his loves—Scott Fitzgerald, Hemingway and Wolfe, their duels, braggadociosiosis, love life, binges, etc. He wanted writers to be Richard Harding Davies, only naughtier and nobler. What he heard of you—especially when I told him of your Caballalife and the Bucket-of-Blood—made his eyes glisten with the old lust and I thought, He wishes *he* could have gone down the streets with Marjorie* hunting for you and of course finding you. Anyway you exerted a spell over him and perhaps made him all the gloomier that the great writers were gone and moreover he was himself too tired of patching up all their various marriages, troubles, etc., to do a good job on even a Lowry. He was tired of the new publishing and movie rights and MGM, too. He told me several times of meeting you in the Ritz bar and having drinks with you and also your asking him for cigarettes because your doctor advised against your smoking so you dutifully never bought any yourself.

I heard the *Volcano* on the air. Obviously the studio was highly impressed with the importance of the book and also thought the lost-weekend aspect was the popular one (stressing that irritates me mightily). It was funny to hear your descriptive passages ascribed to Laruelle or the doctor—Si, signor, how beautiful it is here in Quaxaheptul with its 54 cantinas and 18 churches and its two mountains rising behind, etc., etc. Curiously enough, in spite of the poor arrangement of a pretty tough book to arrange, the power and tragedy of the

---

*Marjorie Bonner Lowry (1905–1988), Malcolm's wife, had herself just finished writing a mystery entitled *Horse in the Sky*.

book came through the phony and confusing acting with frightening force. The wit and lazy beauty of the written words softened and tranquilized the picture, but the ear has no philosophy and no fizzwater to mix with the straight stuff.

Naturally your reference to a Mr. Smith's jumping into the ocean on the strength of the hot ukelele playing and floating, sound egg that he was, came a few hours after a heady conference with Coby Gilman on what to do with the eggs I sent him weeks ago that he never used. Mill ends of old agricultural lore perplexed us—do the good eggs float or sink? We had barely compromised on hardboiling the lot so that they may blow up in some beautiful girl's face as she creeps out of his bed heavily veiled when your eggy reference arrived to further confuse us. Naturally, also, a letter arrived from Jimmy Stern from Ireland in the same mail. His reviews were fine, also his advertising, and he said, in answer to my complaints about your lack of advertising, that it was doubtless due to your friend's (Reeves) leaving Reynal. Anyway it is (*Volcano,* I mean) much talked of—your picture with six or seven other Talks of the Town was on the front page of the *Times Book Review* last Sunday and it floated on the best-seller list all on its own momentum for weeks and weeks and is read again and again by Mr. Gilman and other admirers. Jimmy marveled at Marjorie's finishing her novel "with Himself in the house" but concluded that women wrought miracles—and high time, too.

I started to read [Scott Graham Williamson's] *Fiesta at Anderson's House*—so full of tropical description, voodoo, drinking, whoring and a certain attempt at the Lowry rhythm that I could swear the author must have read your mss. at one time—though I found this inadequate attempt to imitate an inimitable prose terribly dull and unconvincing and could not get far enough to bring a suit. Scott Williamson maybe is his name.

Somewhere around here a riderless radio is singing (and am I consterned to hear it) an "I HAD TOO MUCH TO DREAM LAST NIGHT." Good God, is there no end to gamut.

Wolcott Gibbs,* the *New Yorker* drama critic who had an abscessed lung while you were here, was crazy about your book and sourly told a friend you were the only writer he cared to meet. He is recuperating from the abs. and the remark now.

Come back soon—maybe *Horse in the Sky* will fetch you both again.

love (also from Coby),
Dawn
Consulibus ad astra

I look much forward to your new lugubre.

(UNIVERSITY OF BRITISH COLUMBIA)

*Wolcott Gibbs, of whom Powell was never particularly fond, was a *New Yorker* writer best remembered for his parody of *Time* magazine.

TO EDMUND WILSON

35 East Ninth Street
July 3, 1947

Dear Wig old boy—

I want you to be the first to know I am having such a strange reaction to dear Mr. Perkins's death that I can only describe it as psychological. In fact that is the very word. I am suddenly career-mad (not in any way overshadowing my soft feminine side), aggressive, odetsish, contacting, bigdealing, memoing, big-shotting, goingoverpeople'sheading, putthatinyourpipeandsmokeiting, as if all that had ever stood in my way before had been Mr. Perkins. I will send a telegram now to Hollywood as follows: I LAUGH UP MY SLEEVE AT WHATEVER SUM YOU MAY OFFER SIGHT UNSEEN FOR MY NEXT TOME HA HA. I jump on the editor's knee and then on his neck. I pull beards or if cleanshaven wattles. I make mountains out of motes. I am working myself up to sending cables. That is why I want you to tell me a name of a Frog publisher for me to send my works to and address if possible. Can this be arranged? Preferably a mythological character.

Everything is pursuing itself here splendidly. I met a strange Gatsby-like character at the Murphys' last week, named Dr. Hinton. He has an orchid house and a pool of tropic lilies and papyrus, a fabulous collection of Americana, he hates women due to having had a wife, and sweeps in and out of the Hamptons with a retinue of strange servants mostly stolen from the older Hampton families. Do you suppose Murphys generate Gatsbys?

I broke olives on the Brevoort terrace with Herbert Solow, now engaged in experimenting with separate life from Sylvia. He was in a dark morose greenish mood. Joie de telaviv. I hope I don't say that. Peggy is coming in this aft and I have a fine Portuguese crackling on the hob.

best to elena and rosalind and Reuel,[*]
Dawn

(YALE COLLECTION OF AMERICAN LITERATURE, BEINECKE RARE BOOK
AND MANUSCRIPT LIBRARY, YALE UNIVERSITY)

TO CHARLES SCRIBNER[†]

35 East Ninth Street
July 23, 1947

Dear Mr. Scribner:

I was very glad to have your letter about our future. I had long harbored a vague suspicion that Charles Scribner was not a person but a synthetic opinion like Uncle Sam or John Bull, in spite of Max's testimony.

---

[*]Wilson's wife, daughter, and son, respectively.
[†]Charles Scribner (1890–1952) was only the latest member of his family to head the house of Charles Scribner's Sons.

Max must have been tired of everything for quite a while to judge from our more recent conversations—the hopeless state of the world, the new zing-zang publishing cropping up, and the end of the romantic era of publishing. I was considerably dashed by his refusal to hurry me on my last section of the book. I usually counted on him to whip me along the last lap and instead he said, "There's no hurry. Brood over it. Take your time."

I had the feeling he didn't see that one author rushing to get a book to the presses was going to help the world one way or the other, even if it was the Word itself. I admit this was true, though naturally I find more inspiration in the belief that I alone can save the dyke with my writing finger.

On the new novel (of which Max had read about 200 pages) I have about 330 pages and will have it in final shape by the latter part of August if not before. It is a New York contemporary novel (postwar) in the *Time to Be Born* manner and setting. Until better inspiration it is called *The Locusts Have No King*. I hope we can get together soon. I know that Max's death leaves our minds scattered. No wonder he caved in with all of us leaning on him.

Best wishes,
Dawn

(RARE BOOKS AND MANUSCRIPTS, PRINCETON UNIVERSITY LIBRARY)

On September 12, 1947, John and Katy Smith Dos Passos had been involved in a terrible automobile accident near Wareham, Massachusetts. Katy was killed; Dos Passos lost his right eye.

TO JOHN DOS PASSOS

[35 East Ninth Street]
September 17, 1947

Dear Dos—

I am thinking about you all the time and I find two things to be glad about. One, that you are a writer so that agony is of service to you, cruel as our work is—and another, that you have physical pain to dull the unbearable other kind. I am glad you aren't rich so you can concentrate on some hardiron thing like making money because physical pain and the need of money have often saved me from going crazy.

What curious small things one remembers. I think again and again of Katy's exclaiming in the middle of our last Lafayette dinner, "Dos! No chicory! No— NO!" The salami I wrapped up in my kerchief to your slight surprise—my grudgingly offering it back to Katy, who said, "No, you know perfectly well who Mr. Passos brought that salami for." I meant to tell her later that the cat did not see a bite of it as I stuffed it down my own gullet late that night—and very good, too. Before that, the way you lingered in the café with Janet Merrell and her family and Katy said to me out in the hall, "I'd better go back and get him—Mr. Passos is awful hungry and he doesn't know how to get away maybe." Her always perceptive remarks about the trip and about people, about the Scotch who were more Scotch than ever—"If you've lost your way then ask a responsible mon—."

The gray-haired telephone operator telephoned me to say how badly everyone felt and she had her own anecdote—that although she had not been there very long she was given to understand that you were prize guests (knowing the joint, I suppose that meant you got the prize clip) and that Mrs. Dos Passos had given her a present as she left the last time and she was so pleased. I daresay Sara [Murphy] told you that Teresa's eyes were swollen from weeping all day.* "I just loved that little lady," she said. "No matter who was here or what was going on she always had a little whisper to me. Like last time when she was going abroad and she said, 'Teresa, I'm afraid we're going to starve over there so we'll be awfully glad to get back to you.' "

Louise [Lee] is very much disturbed. She tells me something that will amuse you—that years ago in Mt. Sinai you came down one day and handed her a little bouquet of the first Lawson garden lettuce. She said she still has it pressed in her Bible! What odd things people do that we, being only dumb writers, never even dream.

This must be what Gerald [Murphy] had on his mind without knowing it. For days and weeks he seemed sunk and it seemed out of all proportion to the mere inconvenience of his trip. The weekend before, out at East Hampton, he was so strangely sorrowful that I felt he must be going to die or that Sara was or something awful was expected. He stayed on the beach for a last swim and at the top of the hill he stopped and looked back and said, "It's like the Mediterranean today, for the first time." He looked out for a long time and then said to Sara, "No, I don't think we want those days again. No, we mustn't think back. There's something different ahead, there must be, something different and better." I said something about a 31-day trip not being really so final and so filled with dark danger but he said, "I have a feeling the whole world is about to blow up." And our supper was like a funeral. Now I think his extraordinary Celtic radar sensed our own smaller world disaster for he did love and appreciate Katy's specialness.

I had planned to go someplace near the ocean to finish my book as the New

*Teresa Morgan was a longtime and much loved member of the Murphy family's household staff.

York autumn is filled more than ever with demands and distractions, and there is a chance of my making it to P'town possibly next week. If you are there and I can help with letters or other things I will be glad. Let me know if there is anything you want done here.

Love,
Dawn

(DOS PASSOS COLLECTION, THE UNIVERSITY OF VIRGINIA)

TO SARA MURPHY

Hotel Lincolnshire
Boston, Mass.
September 22, 1947

Dear Sara,

Dos just called up and is now glad to be at Stewart Mitchell's,* 923 Memorial Drive, [Cambridge,] where I am going for tea. He was doing well both times I saw him, eager for any subject that led away from the immediate one. In fact, he laughed over many sour aspects of civilization and said many good caustic things that showed a fine point of desperation being released. He was reading *Great Expectations*!!! with fierce intentness—showing he could escape, his mind could work, and his eye was OK, willy-nilly. Anyway I was very glad you urged me to come for he seemed glad I was somewhere around. I am still not sure whether he's such a civilized person he has to make you feel that way or whether he does.

I have my work here and my puny translation of Trollope's autobiography on top of that and may sign it by mistake. So Dos knows he is not inconveniencing me at all which, it so happens, is right. I am crazy about Boston at last, though we agreed yesterday that it might be I had merely reached the Boston in my life, a suspicious sign. I feel a large feather hat growing already in my skull and a reticule in my martini hand.

We talk about writing—a taboo among self-respecting writers as a rule but after all it is all that can save him. In fact we talk the bejesus around and around and around It. I am boring the pants off him and it's good for him. He even spoke of going to Maurice Evans and is anxious for me to stay on, I think, because he would like to set up his usual pattern of someone on this corner for an hour, someone there for lunch, someone over there for dinner. Like Wocky faithfully tending to every weed and bush but not to be detained.

*Stewart Mitchell (1892–1957) had been one of Dos Passos's best friends from their Harvard days.

We each protect him from the last one or the one after, I guess. (I should know since I do the same thing myself.) I saw some of the hospital dishes and saw why he didn't eat, though I think he looked forward today to Stewart Mitchell's and he was drinking Ada [MacLeish]'s salad dressing by itself as the tastiest thing on his menu and still eating some fruit and cheese you had left him. He talked about the article Katy was writing and things they had done in Ecuador and we agreed that it was a fine thing when people did not let you know them too well or refused to know you too well, that human relationships were better on a tantalizing scale—(you can see we were getting too close)— and then he was very pleased to remember the time you said someone had been his old self last night and Gerald had said, "People should never be themselves, least of all their old selves." (Or was that you or was it a collaboration of Mur-phys?) Anyway he is fastening on the thought of you and the Lowndes and Virginia to pull him over the P'town ordeal. He says his eye is much better than the doctor hoped. He is still shaky and said, "I'm so glad you came—I was just going down for the third time" (the only cry he permitted himself).

My room here expires Wednesday but he wants to try the Vendome though I have to be back Friday. If this works I add an ear trumpet and jaegers to my agenda. Maybe this work will turn out to be *Lady Apley's Lover.*[*]

This charming room looks out over dear little shady restful lanes and roars with bedlam so the sandman never comes by. If he isn't here by midnight tonight I'll run him down thru every tavern if it takes till daybreak.

I hope I haven't missed school yet. Home probably by Friday afternoon— before perhaps.

Love,
Dawn

I think he will be all right.

(COLLECTION HONORIA MURPHY DONNELLY)

Two months later, Dos Passos came to his friend's aid when, on November 28, 1947, Powell was badly beaten by Jojo and hospitalized for four weeks. Little is known about this event—Powell was deeply reluctant to discuss it—but she rarely stayed with Jojo alone thereafter.

---

[*]A reference to J. P. Marquand's once-popular satire of Bostonian customs and pretenses, *The Late George Apley.*

TO EDMUND WILSON

[35 East Ninth Street]
Jan. 27, 1948

Dear Wig:

Good God what a shocking nest of really confusing nifties you uncovered. I am extremely grateful and all the madder at Scribner's for rushing me through the proofs saying publication date was February—then when I whizzed your memo up yesterday they said it was not too late, since the book was not due till the latter part of March anyway. Why didn't they tell me I could have more time? The jacket is monstrous, filled with illustrations of gay sophisticates drinking clover club cocktails at fashionable speakeasies or making up their lips like those Follies girls are always doing, so after my first screams I am now sinking into the resignation and lethargy that publishers pray for in their writers. Brandt and Brandt say Scribner's wants a new contract but lesser royalty terms and less advance due to hard times so I am not settling with them till I see what they do next.

Life is very gay here in the metropolis and money grows on bushes as we Freudians say. Eugene Jolas* came in and addressed me bitterly as You Americans with your Malcolm Cowleys and Matthew Josephsons. Can he mean that these idols of our culture are not so to other nations? Later I ran into him unprepared and he was very fine—spoke highly of you, for instance, and angrily of Katherine Anne Porter for insulting him in her Gertrude Stein article in *Harper's*. His *transition* anthology is coming out with Vanguard and he has an autobiography which should be interesting if done at all realistically since he has lived enough lives.

I dined with Glenway Wescott† the other night who spoke a great deal on his theory of the Journal (this being the age of, he says). I daresay it is the age of the journal for anyone who prefers luxurious living and the frightfully amusing bohemian members of royalty (the anecdote and charm thereof depending on contrast of raffish simplicity with purple blood) to the equal luxury of wasting time writing and being divinely late everyplace. I admire his work but he typifies the danger of the young person beguiled by older groups with completed life stories which save the writer any trouble of predicting, speculating and otherwise imagining. Now Mr. W. seems a well-preserved interesting old codger chockful of Crowninshieldish and Maughamish memoirs instead of being actively on the prowl himself.

*The journalist and editor Eugene Jolas (1894–1952) had been one of Powell's closest friends during the 1920s before moving to Paris, where he founded the literary magazine *transition*. The two would again spend a good deal of time together during Powell's months in Paris in 1950.
†The American author Glenway Wescott (1901–1987) was, like Powell herself, a small-town Midwesterner gone cosmopolitan. He admired Powell's work and once told her she was doing for New York what Balzac had done for Paris.

Friday—Dos and I had lunch yesterday and went to the French film *Volpone*, which was a tasty dullish parcel of French ham at its most enthusiastic hamminess. He expects to leave at the end of next week for the Marquands' in Nassau and may go to Havana to visit the Bard himself. Today I had lunch with Niles [Spencer] at the Lafayette. He just sold another picture yesterday which makes his show a big success. I believe he has a *Fortune* commission, too— practically an invitation to court. . . .

The unsatisfactory feature of finishing this particular novel* is that each angle of it lends itself to so much enlargement, and while it might be a sign of the vitality of the characters that they can be treated from so many sides and extended indefinitely, it is disturbing for the author to have none of the plea- sure of *completing* something. This is probably due to the method, a bastardiza- tion of something you said when you were first having your own journal typed with its record of a long relationship. You said the heroine was never *stated* finally, that she appeared in a different light with each meeting—the only vivid method for exposing character in all its fluidity with the observer's own changes taken into account besides. The difficulty is that there is always more change to be recorded, particularly in complicated personalities. . . .

My best to Elena and happy *accouchements* all around.

Resp.,

Humph

(YALE COLLECTION OF AMERICAN LITERATURE, BEINECKE RARE BOOK
AND MANUSCRIPT LIBRARY, YALE UNIVERSITY)

TO MICHAEL SADLEIR

35 East Ninth Street
December 30, 1947

Dear Mr. Sadleir:

Very likely my new novel will be out here by the time page proofs have reached you. Scribners's—(I'm getting proofreading jitters as you see so I put apostrophes everywhere just to be sure and are there two *b*'s in my pub- lisher?)—is slating it for February. The name is *The Locusts Have No King* and it deals with postwar New York in the satirical vein of *A Time to Be Born* and *The Happy Island*. New York is not the same city it was, being overrun now with Americans. From all I hear the West and Midwest holes they left vacant are being filled with New York aesthetes lapping up water and oxygen and Nature's well-turned ankles with an explorer's glee, pumping away at briar

---

***The Locusts Have No King.*

pipes and bedirndled third wives and persisting in trying to crack the native soul by being folksy instead of decently snobbish.

This, of course, has nothing to do with my novel, which I think you will like. I have a perfectly wonderful young lady in it who supplies the love interest and supplies and supplies. She is not the heroine. She is that young, resolutely gay girl who appears to most sedately scholarly men in their early middle age and batters away at them with public jeers at their work and jubilantly pursues a course of humiliating and teasing them that invigorates, debilitates and some-how appeals to their sense of the preposterous so that they feel oddly protec-tive and sorry for her. Eventually my Frederick—(you see I have named him after the hero of *Sentimental Education*, but don't tell Flaubert)—finds she is the one who needs pity.

How did I come to mention a minor figure first? Or the love interest? Probably due to the six or seven generations of patent medicine flowing through my veins that makes me point out the chocolate flavor instead of the tonic itself.

The theme, as you so perspicaciously gathered from the biblical title, deals with the disease of destruction sweeping through our times—no leader is needed, each person is out to destroy whatever valuable or beautiful thing life has. The moral is that in an age of destruction one must cling to what-ever remnants of love, friendship, or hope above and beyond reason one has, for the enemy is all around, ready to snatch it. You will see that I refer to the enemy not as Fascism, Communism, Mammon or anything but the plague of destructivism—inherent in human nature but released in magnified potency since the war.

This solemn message is "packaged," as we say in our advertising, in a possi-bly exaggerated comedy form—no more exaggerated than Hogarth's pictures of similar days. There are a splendid pair of high-salaried hard-drinking lady Babbitts with artistic yens, a quartette of midnight friends (male) who would not know each other by day but who view everybody's business (particularly their catastrophes) with a philosophic pleasure. The weighing of disaster and heartbreak is their nightly chore, harmless and gratifying. The reader can view my noble hero and heroine (Frederick and Lyle) not only through their ideas of themselves and each other but through the mocking laughter of people who do not even know them, other people who knew them "when"—in fact, these two poor nice creatures are given to the reader in the same impartial way all of us are given to our friends: through their own eyes, through their enemies' eyes, through talk behind their backs since they are more or less public figures. . . .

You may be surprised—and I expect severe censure from my own countrymen—that in this period of 1945–1946 these articulates (new word) do not refer to the war. Too realistic, perhaps, but their eyes are on the future and the main chance. Gourmets about to sit down to a superb dinner already steaming up their nostrils do not waste time talking of lunch.

Edmund Wilson, the critic, insists I have been writing "existential" novels for years, before Sartre. I object, for my novels are based on the fantastic designs made by real human beings earnestly laboring to maladjust themselves to fate. There is no principle for them to prove—they may disobey the law of gravity as they please. My characters are not slaves to an author's propaganda. I give them their heads. They furnish their own nooses.* [remainder of letter illegible]

(THE SAMUEL PALEY LIBRARY, TEMPLE UNIVERSITY)

TO MARGARET DE SILVER

[Port-au-Prince, Haiti]
Thursday, March 1, 1948

Dearest Maggie:

This is a very easy place to feel at home in immediately—largely because it simply has no connection with anything or anyplace else in the world. Even Traveler Passos says so. It is easy for a lone person, male or female, particularly here at the Oloffson, which is a huge rococo rambling palace with barely a dozen people wandering around very chummily. Dos got me the prize suite— too luxurious for description—for $9 a day, fine meals, unlimited service. It is the corner suite—vast porch on both sides overlooking the entire city and bay and mountains so at last I am in the sunlight.

The permanents here are very fine—the customary Somerset Maugham cast: retired General Bradford's wife of Washington; a Navy widow of 50; a handsome Mrs. Ford here on Haitian art affairs from a Chicago museum and given to vanishing with suave young Haitians; a ship's doctor who settled here 20 years ago; the proprietor and owner of many Port-au-Prince businesses, young Maurice De Young, handsome, age 29, of Dutch descent (and a baron, I believe), and his black partner Maurice Morency—and this week the Fleet, so there is much drinking of rum, riding in jeeps through the bazaars and other warlike activities.

The Eben Givenses† have a suite that is really a separate house—two bedrooms, living room, bath and porch and meals for all three and service for $16 a day. Rum is better than Cuban—at 90 cents a quart. There is no way of buy

---

*In the end, Sadleir did not like *The Locusts Have No King* and turned it down. It would finally be brought out in England by W. H. Allen in 1953.
†Eben Givens and his writer wife, Phyllis Duganne, were neighbors of De Silver's on Cape Cod. They were also friends of Edmund Wilson's.

ing anything you forgot—such as a bathing cap, a safety pin, etc. My laundry just arrived from the native laundress—negligees, all sorts of fancy stuff—80 cents. When you go downtown two or three young Haitians usually attach themselves and courteously lead you wherever you like to go, intercede for you with shopkeepers, and oddly enough this is sheer friendship. It is really warm but delightful breezes—I sleep like dead. Dos has a huge room—in fact a complete house over by the Givenses'. He is staying till Friday. We went to dinner at a Haitian restaurant—wonderful conch stew, etc. Mr. William Bullitt is at the Embassy, which is lavishly entertaining for the Fleet. Of all things, Maurice De Young here was Malcolm Lowry's boon companion during their trip here (same hotel). And little Truman Capote had this suite when he was here. Esther [Andrews] and party are due today after several false starts.

This is a wonderful place for a frustrated frogophile, because these people are delighted with your French efforts and you find yourself carrying on without the slightest uneasiness, reading your French newspaper and making up words and skipping tenses like a real Creole. I have bought Coby some French books—Sartre's plays and the Lettres de Mlle. de Sospinasse for no reason except Dos recommended them. We swim at the pool (the only one around) at 12 with rum punches and visiting firemen. It is a fine place and atmosphere for work and shakes all of your ideas upside down. The Fleet had been in just 30 minutes when an army group landed in our bar and one colonel turned out to be Dos's cousin-in-law, Col. Shuler, married to a Katherine Dos Passos in Honolulu who had met Dos on his way to the Pacific for *Life*. Also Eben says on their rugged eight-hour expedition to the Citadel two young ladies coming down the mountain on muleback cried out, "Why, you are John Dos Passos!" and it seems they were on some New York magazine.

There is a fascinating little hotel in the town—Hotel Excelsior, rather New Orleans–looking—that I would like someone to try out for me. I'm told it has the only hot water in town and the only good plumbing—room and meals $18 a week. It is down in the town center and probably very hot and maybe for men only but it looks very clean and attractive. Dos and I lavishly entertained his cousin and troops on my balcony and next day Dos and General Bradford and some marines who have attached themselves all went fishing (got nothing). Dos is working hard. So is Phyllis [Duganne] and so am I. The marines plaintively declared they were all going to be writers because wherever they landed they saw the writers lounging around with rum punches and swimming pools. When do they write?, they cried—let us in on this racket. They had spent a drunken evening with Dorothy Parker and her beau in St. Thomas en route here—said she looked older than God and was a mess but not as much a mess as her boyfriend whom they finished off. Their story on Miss Powell in Port-au-Prince will probably be the same.

My, this is a wonderful place and I am almost sure you would like it. I doubt if Coby would for some reason. I haven't seen any beaches.

Love,
Dawn

The General calls me "Water Baby" because he claims I look like the illustrations in his Kingsley book. I better look into this. I may get sore.

(COLLECTION TIM PAGE)

TO JOSEPH GOUSHA

[Haiti]
Thursday, March 11, 1948

Dear Joe—

How's the Snug Harbor and are you treating Fagin* right? . . . The Marines here yesterday. The fleet is in. There is nothing to buy here—no ten-cent stores—and though rum is only 90 cents a bottle and taxis only 20 cents for $1.50 ride (exchange is five cents to our penny) little things like Kleenex or paper like this are very high. The general atmosphere is fine for work and the writers here seem to thrive. If I could lick the ink, pen and drooling ballpoint business I would get more done. . . .

Meals here are fine—in the American style with some native variants. We all (the Givenses, Dos, some writer named Bill Krauss and some embassy employees) went to a native taxi drivers' restaurant the other night— bambooish hut with a fine soup with a crab and other matter in it, a "conk" (conch-meat) stew, rice and beans, marvelous cauliflower, and sugared limes, accompanied by rum and a carafe of a vermouth nature. I daresay that is now working around my innards happily. The routine here is of rounds of drinks being automatically ordered and you're in, whether or not it is your desire (of course it is). This is what may mount up (twenty-five cents a drink). Beer bad and very high—fifty cents a bottle—and in the clip house the girls are told to order it for their sailors as they are told to order champagne other places. The leading whorehouse is called the Square Deal Joint. . . .

Love,
Dawn

(COLLECTION TIM PAGE)

---

*Fagin was Powell's second cat, replacing her beloved Perkins. Fagin would live for another fifteen years.

TO ORPHA MAY STEINBRUECK

[35 East Ninth Street]
May 14, 1948

Dearest Auntie May—

Here are more clippings—or did I send them? Meanwhile English publishers are bidding for it* which pleases me as my regular publisher there turned it down as "too American." More reviews were very good here from a sales point of view but particularly for prestige. Scribner's has a window devoted to me for a week (May 16)—5th Avenue and 48th Street store. St. Paul newspaper says "Miss Powell was commissioned by the Furies to write this. In Greek days Furies lashed out at sins against society and were called the Gracious Goddesses. Miss Powell is our contemporary Gracious Goddess." Charlotte Johnson writes that she would have liked it but for the first time didn't know the people!! (Usually I only write of Lake Erie girls do you know!) Today I am driving up for weekend party at Wellfleet, Cape Cod, at Edmund Wilson's (Margaret De Silver's car). It is cold and rainy.

I have decided not to try for Paris unless I get a pack of money as I would not like to be away from my own base here except with big-splurge dough. At first I wanted to go as a preference to the unbelievable high costs here (combined with large back debts for doctors and low income while back taxes clutched every cent I made) but I want to be there as a vulgarly rich American tourist with a fistful of gold eagles instead of as a simple French peasant carrying my own laundry (and a goddam mean disposition) on my head. . . .

Love,
Dawn

(COLLECTION TIM PAGE)

TO EDMUND WILSON

The Cherries, N.Y.†
June 22, 1948

Dear Wig:

Why don't you write your foreign-correspon-despondent nose-for-news piece on the strange life in New York as gleaned by the ads in our newspapers, such as Dr. Murray Banks and Dr. Sperling, the Sex Psychologists with dancing, coffee, Freud, Marx and bebop. The contours of these gala but dialectical sexical balls must be blueprinted in Moscow. In fact there is no iron curtain as

*I.e., *The Locusts Have No King.*
†This address remains unidentified.

iron as the one between the American Way of today and the accepted American idea of the American way. I am already laughing ha-ha.

I see Evelyn Waugh has done the glamour mortician* after Huxley but I did him first in *The Happy Island* with the concert pianist (broke) getting his free sleeping quarters in a Bronx funeral parlor where he practiced the organ nightly and guarded the stiffs from his own marble slab and painted the corpses with his nice artist's touch until the bereaved husbands were so seduced (what with the special temptation perfume) that they flung themselves on the coffin shrieking, "Becky, come back, I want you, do you hear, want you want you want you."

I was terribly flattered to find on my first visit to Eddie Condon's jazz house that the drummer, no less than the famed George Wettling, had a copy of my book under his arm.† I do enjoy the intelligentsia's pretending they know a horn from a harp while the musicians pretend they know a book from a bookie. This is a very interesting place, much to my embarrassment, and the improvisations have the classic pattern of a basic creative formula. Goddam it I think I'll out–clement greenberg with my aesthetic nifties.

Spivey‡ would like a profile of self for *New Yorker* and no reason why not except she is better and better known than their usual subjects, and her background and observations are more interesting. Why don't you do that? My brilliant agents asked if I would do a biography of Fannie Brice. Signed, they cried proudly. I couldn't have been more excited if it had been George Jessel or Westbrook Pegler. Shall I suggest you for this? All you do is keep out anything that might be interesting and state that she is a good wife and mother.

Dos appeared briefly and disappeared faster.

Others besides you have spoken of the publishing family in my book being Scribner's so there may be some reason for their restraint in advertising it. That's what comes of my foxily disguising a wholesale-druggist dynasty and newspaper-publisher family into a book family. It comes out my own publishers.

This pretty paper (called "Temptation Notes") is all there is left for me to charge at Scribner's Book Store. I've got about all the leather-edged blotters, quill pens, calling and playing cards that I can bear.

I have been asked to write "What's Wrong with the Younger Generation?" for *Harper's Bazaar.* I must find one and see what's wrong—I mean, outside of their being younger. So far this is the only future I see leering ahead. The Fight is off tonight so I don't have to go to the television party and look at it. I hate having my sport ignorance sullied. Do you think these poems are translatable?

---

*Evelyn Waugh's *The Loved One* had just been published.
†Jazz drummer George Wettling (1907–1968) was one of Powell's admirers, and she recorded some funny stories about him in her diaries. He played regularly at Eddie Condon's jazz club.
‡Pianist and singer Victoria Spivey (1906–1976) was then at the peak of her career.

Or good? Marcelin* is the Canapés Verts Man and I am now so involved in my gracious offer to find him publishers that my phone rings with threats from his other friends. I see what you mean. I mean I see what [writer] Slater Brown meant with his homely motto, "Never lend a man an axe after sundown."

best to the eggnog set,
Humph

TO CARL BRANDT

35 East Ninth Street
October 1, 1948

Dear Carl:

Can we get a Hollywood divorce and still be frightfully, frightfully good friends? I mean, hold hands in nightclubs and gaze deep into each other's pocketbooks for the photographers?

Anyway, a lot of miscellaneous things have been bobbing up (including a low state of mind) and it seems a change would be very salutary. New hands, new eyes, new faces, new pocketbooks, new photographers. So, with quivering lip but chin up, I would like to pack up my pretties from all departments, including the best pieces of furniture from your offices (you must admit they were Mother's) and leave your bed and board and dear Freda.

At the moment I don't believe you have any mss. of mine, except possibly plays in the play department (*Made in Heaven* or *Rosy Future*). I should, however, like to know any news of the foreign activity on *The Locusts Have No King*.

I do appreciate your labors on my behalf and it would grieve me if the withdrawal of my business forced you to close the offices. Tell me this isn't so.

I expect to be at MCA for a number of personal and complicated reasons. Much gratitude for the past and fond wishes for your future.†

Shall I burn your letters or will you wait for the blackmail?

Sincerely,
Dawn Powell

---

*The Haitian poet and novelist Philippe Thoby-Marcelin (1904–1975), whom Powell had met during her stay in Port-au-Prince, was also a great friend of Malcolm Lowry's.

†Powell's severance from the Brandt agency, where she had been a client for some fifteen years, would prove only temporary. She was to rejoin the agency in 1951 and would remain there for the rest of her life.

TO EDMUND WILSON

PROFESSOR ERNEST WIGMORE'S TRIUMPHAL TOUR
OF ALL THE AMERICAS AND MORE*

September 16 [year uncertain]

Not having visited the Americas (New York, Oak Bluffs and Fourth Street) since my lecture tour with Mrs. Trollop [*sic*] in 1814, I was prepared for certain changes but hardly for those which greeted me on my arrival. The change, I find, lies mostly in the women, who are older than they were (mostly dark-haired though different-colored at the roots), extremely bossy though abysmally subservient to the ideas of other men. The women (contrary to the men, who dine in a body at Longchamps) eat at Luchow's, which they pronounce through the sphenoid bone so that it comes out on your cheek instead, and spend their time "hammering their noddles for a jeste" as they call it. They are all five feet three ranging up to 140 lbs. when they begin to be five feet one and a quarter. They are found in the quarters of an invisible little people they call "husbands," who are also different-colored at the roots, laughing a good deal at the waggery of visiting lecturers found in their women's beds. This tendency to excessive merriment results frequently in what they call "dropping their choppers." I found, on questioning a Mrs. Z, that this was a complement to their national profession which is dentistry. All American men are dentists and are paid for their work by oil paintings, gouaches, drypoints of large dogs and pastels of little girls with poor "bites." While being measured for a nightcap in a leading hattery called "Wiggins Grotto" I met what I was told was the "top drawers" of the profession. Their attitude toward the prevailing political leaders or "orthodontists" as they call them and toward artists or "plastic denturists" was characteristic of the men in all the countries I visited.

"As you say, Prof. Wigmore," was the general complaint in so many (three) words.

Streets and homes are completely emptied by nightfall which in some cases occurs as early as 11 a.m. On questioning a Mrs. Z, a woman of large "proportions" as they call them in America, I found that at this time the radicals take to the bars, where in periods of unrest they plot subversive activities such as musical comedies, little magazines, Gilbert and Sullivan revivals, as well as making arrangements with each other for cornucopias (a small present given by females of any age on feast days or in moments of lethargy). These, of course, are kept in an excellent state of preservation by applications of vulcanite, novocaine and

*The circumstances behind this parody remain unclear; nor can it be given an exact date. The references to Mrs. Trollope would seem to indicate, however, that it was written in the late 1940s, when Powell's passion for *Domestic Manners of the Americans* was at its peak.

regular drilling. At national orgies or trade routs the men in full regalia present a typically primitive picture as they lock cornucopias in ceremonial dances.

I made a special point of mingling with two prominent women who, for purposes of confusion, I will call Mustard Seed and Podsnapper, to find secret customs of the sex as it exists in the Americas since Mrs. Trollop's time. These women at the time of my mingling were on what they termed the "wagon" or "merry-go-round" or "bandstand." (Ed. note: "to be on the wagon": that is, to drink in the kitchen, in the dark, behind the rose, as we put it.) It was their practice to put cheerful records on the phonograph and take turns engaging in good-natured solo dancing during my talk. Everyplace I went I found people in tremendous unrest lulled only by opportunities to soliloquize aloud. For the most part I mingled with one person at a time, since in groups of two or more I found a careless tendency to interrupt or disagree with me, which would give my readers a wrong impression of the country.

I had the foresight to purchase a basket of the native bridgework to take home to Mrs. Trollop (who, by the way, has lived to a ripe old insolvency). She was as delighted as an old woman and donned them at once.

"Oh, Urnith," thee whitthled. "Itthent America thwell?"

It was so like her.

ERNEST WIGMORE, FELLOW AM. GEOG. SOC.
Brown University Club

(YALE COLLECTION OF AMERICAN LITERATURE, BEINECKE RARE BOOK AND MANUSCRIPT LIBRARY, YALE UNIVERSITY)

TO BROOKS ATKINSON*

[Draft fragment, probably never sent ca. November 22, 1948]

Dear Mr. Atkinson:

Your review of [M. Richard Nash's] *The Young and the Fair* (a play I have not seen) reminded me once again of the shocking position the writer now occupies in the theater. You say, "On its own terms as a minor school drama the play could hardly be better." But, you add, let us not give any credit to any unknown writer for this miracle. No, it is good because "it has been extremely well directed by Harold Clurman." Because of the acting. Because of its "adroitness, fervor and youthful vitality," which, you say, mysteriously "over-shadow Mr. Nash's *neat* little play." The implication is that director and actors could have reached celestial perfection were they not handicapped by the play they are performing [letter breaks off]

(COLLECTION TIM PAGE)

---

*Atkinson (1894–1990) was for many years the magisterial chief theater critic of the *New York Times*.

TO SARA MURPHY

[35 East Ninth Street]
March 8, 1949

Dearest Sara—

I feel as if I had been commuting to Nassau several weekends and there is still one spot on my torso that isn't brown enough to pass.* Evidently my doctors need me more than the British colonials do but I'm sure they will drop me cold as soon as they find they're not obstructing my pleasure plans. I am still so jaundiced regarding the human race that you are well free of my company. I wish I had a horse or a family of goats—Fagin is really horse and goats so why am I kicking?

I have read sections of Marquand's new book† in *Ladies' Home J.* and it is very smooth though George Apley, H. M. Pulham and all his heroes are the same man—that quietly decent, stupid chap with only $37,000 in a group where everybody else has $50,000. I often wonder if he wouldn't be happier (and Marquand have a new plot) if Decent Chappie would only move into a group where the others had only $30,000. I think it would keep his pecker up more and bring out the bully underneath his modest [illegible] self. Yes, that does seem a curious martyrdom—hating fuss and shallow, insecure society life but knocking themselves out to thrash around in it. If that is the life they know they are going to lead, willy nilly, why don't they *pretend* to enjoy it? Or stay home and put up fruit for their old-fashioneds? Who asks anybody to "keep up" anyway? A writing lady said to me wistfully, "How I envy you, being able to go anywhere or see anyone you like at the drop of a hat! My book is always so full I can never do anything I want to." What a nest of psychoanalysts has sprung out of the problems of these compulsive diners.

Every day the papers have more mention of Latouche's signing new contracts for new ballets, pictures, musicals, et al. I still don't know whether this means he's hit his stride or hired a busy press agent. When I saw him last, about two months ago, he said he'd had a very low and rather broke period and had observed a rush of friendly rats leaving his ship. It made me reflect at the time rather sentimentally that all the finest things happened to you when people thought you had money and all the terrible things when they found out you didn't. With these shining words I took the horses out of my carriage and drove myself home cheering.

Jinny Pfeiffer came back from Haiti (where the natives really didn't know their place and she couldn't make a thing on the black market) and is staying

---

*Powell was then undergoing radiation therapy in an effort to reduce the size of a tumor in her chest (see next letter).

†J. P. Marquand's *Point of No Return* had just been published by Little, Brown.

with Helen Culbertson and her Italian friends. They are busy with Pyramid Clubs. I found her rude, crass and glitteringly ignorant.

Throw out a name, will you? Just see what I can do with the little ink that's left in this double-edged pen.

I am really sore at the medical and witches' conspiracy to make me miss sunny Nassau. I wanted to help you with your pyramid and meet the bishop as well as see the duke's very own footprint in the sands of time. Give my love to Archie and Ada [MacLeish] and I will arrange New York for your return.

Love,
Dawn

(COLLECTION HONORIA MURPHY DONNELLY)

TO MABEL POWELL POCOCK AND
PHYLLIS POWELL COOK

[St. Luke's Hospital]
Good Friday [April 15], 1949

Dear Phyllis and Mabel:

Here I am—dismissed private nurses, washed my own hair and had my ass out for iron shots like a little beaver by 7 a.m. I could go home but Dr. [Robert] Solley thinks I should have my blood count up with some iron and sleep.

Here is the family scandal I must now reveal. This here cyst (dermoid) or terra toma is a *twin.** That is, it is my own frustrated twin, a type of cyst that occurs (not very often) in the chest or other sections—even the head of a man or woman. It is made up of parts of various things—hair, teeth, sometimes an eye or a jawbone. It lives off your heart and lung and is "benign"—unless it gets overgrown and shoves out the organs you need which mine started to do. It was as large as a grapefruit and had cut off all but 1/3 of my lung space so it was about ready to shove me out. These twin cysts run in the family. (I shouldn't be surprised but what Grandma's choking spells, etc., indicated one.) They are simply parasites. Well, I was so pleased to hear about my twin Terry Toma that it kept me fascinated right along. It had the staff here fascinated too, so the operation—a five-hour job with three transfusions (3 pts. R.H. negative blood @ $105!)—had quite a gallery of chest experts. The surgeon is one of the best thoracic surgeons—Alexander Ada, a fine-looking,

---

*Powell had suffered for years from mysterious health problems; in 1929, symptoms related to this teratoma had sent her to the hospital, where she was diagnosed with a heart attack. Teratomas (the term comes from the Greek word for "monster") are now identified simply as large tumors, generally associated with the heart; they have nothing to do with failed twins. But Powell would always prefer this more melodramatic and sensational explanation.

keen, very distinguished man about 45. The nurses who were witnesses said he lost six pounds, also that he was in my chest up to his shoulders. Collapsed a lung, removed a rib, then found cyst glued to heart so it took 45 minutes to slice it off there, then it was glued to lung. I was put on oxygen tank and had a tube draining my chest off and a needle infusing glucose in my arm and a behind full of penicillin jabs. In fact, it was something but I was not at all nervous because (a) I was in the best possible hands and (b) I didn't think I'd come out of it anyway so what could I do . . . ?

Dr. Solley, the gay, sweet doctor in charge, is a best friend of my best friends the Murphys and Dr. Passos, so they were busy cabling him about me and it's nice to know the doctor is more than medically involved. I no longer need special nurses and today my entire bandage is removed. (The incision was made sort of below the right armpit toward the back—26 stitches.) Anyway, if it hadn't been for all they learned about chest surgery in the war, I would not be in this fine shape. If I had had it done before they wouldn't have known a lot of fancy precautionary touches. Anyway it just started growing and shoving this year, although Dr. [Nathan] Witt told me all about it 20 years ago with my first attack. I don't even need to be careful, Dr. Ada says. My twin thrives on whiskey, but all I'm giving him is steak and ice cream. Anyway I get all bandages off today. I had nine broken ribs before and probably Terry would keep cracking them if I let him. I was very glad on hearing of my twin that he hadn't popped out of my chest during a formal dinner party, me in my strapless and him grabbing my martini. I rather thought he'd come out saying, "Okay Louis, drop the gun."

Anyway, I breathe wonderfully as if I'd never breathed before. I didn't write Auntie May as I thought you'd tell her what was suitable for a growing girl. By the way Dr. Passos has been in several times after a trip he made for *Life* Magazine to Atlanta, Ga., also Johnson City, Tenn. He said the hills around J.C. were the most beautiful he'd ever seen. Is that your stomping ground? . . .*

I wish Dr. Ada could yank out Mabel's pyloris. I really am tired of pain and think Mabel should be promoted past it. I had my share of gas and rhubarb and soda (shades of Grandma), also peppermint and soda. Anyway, you two ladies start looking in your chests for further twins. I was hoping Terry Toma had saved up a fortune for me. He's still being analyzed in the pathology dept., so I'm not sure what all he had in him but you'll both get your share, fair and square.

Much love,
Dawn

P.S. Joe is spending Easter with Jojo. I will go home Tuesday, I guess.

(COLLECTION TIM PAGE)

---

*Over the years, several members of the Powell/Sherman family had lived in Johnson City.

TO JOSEPH GOUSHA

[MacDowell Colony*
Peterborough, N.H.
ca. June 10, 1949]

Dear—

I am playing hooky to no purpose. The breakfast rush from 7:30 pancakes to studio—over a mile—leaves me dazed for the day and not at all sure of the walk back, let alone thinking. However the sheer shock of three or four miles' walk every day will doubtless wear off and leave my mind a poetic blank suitable for composition. . . .

I have a nice room with fireplace and three windows in a cottage called Pan and my studio (one of 28) is the Helen Wood studio—each of these are endowed like hospital beds. I saw a strange blond dog with a huge bushy tail by my cabin yesterday. It was a red fox. There are deer also but my surprise is that these woodland cabins are so tightly knit and floored that there are no ants or spiders or mold or damp. In fact the woods—600 acres or so—seems to have no bugs in it, it is so well kept.

Lunch—a thermos of coffee and sandwiches—is brought at 12 by truck and we trudge back whenever we please for 6 p.m. dinner. There is no social demand at all nor any cultural enforcements which I feared. The town is all right—about 2500—no pubs except very dreary beer places and the New England rule is no hard liquor without food (dinner complete) and no bar-sitting for anyone. In fact the country—outside New York and Cape Cod and Florida—is singularly graceless, foodless and cheerless as Margaret and I found. I am tireder and tireder every day as my annual Port Jefferson jaunts were enough for me, let alone doing it every day. However, it's marvelous air and if I could ever catch up on rest I might even read a book. The walking is okay but always the same and frankly my head stays in a daze of trying to make it. It will make me whoop with glee to merely take an elevator to my studio back in the naughty city.

There was a cocktail party but the eager inmates had drunk it all up in 25 minutes. However, everyone patronizes the local package store and it's glug-glug-glug in the privacy of the studios and it's glug-glug-glug in the bedrooms by the moon. There is complete freedom—no overseeing—and anyone seems able to disappear in a gutter for days with no reproach. I have a pint of rye on hand for medicinal reasons. You learn to be very stingy very soon and drink alone in the dark, so I am told—not for moral reasons but to keep the thirsty pack from snatching it.

I hope to get some work out of here when my bones recover. Otherwise I may leave a week early as a month is too long to waste. Very likely I will get so

---

*The MacDowell Colony is a prestigious retreat for artists. It was founded by the widow of the composer Edward MacDowell and continues to this day.

charged up by then I can write anyplace even with Louise on my lap and Fagin in my hair.

Do get him some Alpo at Reuben's as a treat.

Jojo sounded fine. . . . Also why not come up here for the weekend—you take fast train to Worcester, then local to Peterborough (two hours) and stay at rather revolutionary Peterborough Tavern. Whether it would be worth the trouble I don't know as it does not have the invigorating effect of just one day at the shore. Indeed I feel tired constantly in spite of long hours asleep. Spiritually and mentally the joint has nothing to offer me but it seems to do well by others. Everyone talks about how broke they are and evidently they are but it makes for a dispiriting atmosphere of failure and frustration rather than for work. I will give it a week or so more before I cave in, however. P.S. The walking does not make anybody thin here. It seems they all gain 10–20 pounds a month from it. Is that fair?

Love,

Dawn

(COLLECTION TIM PAGE)

TO MARGARET DE SILVER

[MacDowell Colony
Peterborough, N.H]
Monday [summer 1949]

Dear Maggie—

I have been carrying many postcards to you and others around but cannot entrust them to others nor put them in the school mailbox so I guess I'll have to pretend they're my own ever-ready mail from fond admirers.

I don't wonder you feel poorly as that jaunt of ours was extraordinarily unrewarding, which shows the disadvantages of sober expeditions. I don't see what is supposed to be so dreamily beautiful about this place as the country isn't as mountainous or as lovely as [that] around Sherman and Brewster [New York].

The place is curiously like my imagination of it but much better run. My woodland studio is better built and fitted than any summer home I ever had and the whole place has all sorts of little touches thought up by loving heads—cups beside woodsy springs and taps, matches, sternos, cords of wood and kindling, sugar, tea, ink, etc. in the cabin—carefully laid fires in the enormous stone fireplace etc. However I am still under the strain of breakfast bells (7:15 to 8:30), dress & pack notes etc. to walk over a mile to my studio—a pleasant

walk but I don't like to HAVE to get up and walk to my occupation. I keep a
snort of rye to wake me up when I get there but it puts me back to sleep. I
march back to dormitory, walk mile and half to town for no purpose but tooth-
brush or two-penny nails, taxi back for dinner. Last night I was entangled in a
croquet foursome and later a mad ride to town for beer or cola so I was too
excited to sleep. However I have spent a profitable morning making a toaster
(or trying to) out of paper clips. I could not make the toaster, it turned out,
only a lousy old electric razor. . . .

There is a preponderance of writers and composers—my favorite is a brash,
loudmouthed blue-jowled swaggering Chicago brat about 25 named Bazelon[*]
who looks like a Polish truckdriver and fullback with beetling black brows,
bullneck and fierce purple eyes usually to be heard sounding off at different
tables on Young Composers Have No Chance—or else showing off for the lady
writers with his memories of 8th-grade English Lit. "By the way, have you ever
read the works of Samuel Johnson?" Or else "Any time I get depressed I just
take a look in the mirror and I say, Bazelon, you ain't so bad looking, you're all
right, boy, and then my day is made." He is proud and gratified that I laugh
hilariously at everything he says. "I can't seem to make a living at my music,"
he says morosely, "I guess the only thing for me to do is sell a piece to the *Readers Digest*."

"Boy, I miss my women," he says, and adds courteously for the benefit
of the older ladies, "Not that I could carry on an interesting conversation
with them such as I can with you ladies here. The only girls accustomed to
being crazy about me have always been socialites or members of the social
scale."

He has a couple of music degrees I daresay from Noter Dame. Anyway he
is all fired up with artistic integrity and Mozart.

Or maybe Chopin. "I am exclusively a piano composer," he says haughtily.

I have been here ten years now I guess and still in a daze of muted dol-
drums. I well understand how a former colonist named Frances Frost found
herself ossified constantly and one night stumbled to be on the august grave of
Mr. MacDowell himself in the sacred park. Mrs. MacDowell was furious at this
seeming tryst beyond the grave and fired her at once as a homewrecker.

I believe it was a bare two months (and one week) ago today I lay on the
cutting table with the smiling surgeon shoulder-deep in my back, so perhaps
my constant ennui is only normal.

The Peterborough Tavern is not bad, I hear, but beginning to be jammed

[*]The Chicago-born Irwin "Buddy" Bazelon (1922–1995) was a gifted and uncompromising American
composer.

with high-voiced retired dilettantes from Boston fairylands. Mail gets here very fast—your letter mailed at 1 a.m. last night arrived this a.m. which astonishes me, used to Long Island and intercity postal delays. People fly off to rendezvous in N.Y. by bussing to Keene (20 miles away, where I hear there is a good hotel with bar and privileges very different from Peterborough) and take a plane from there to New York in one hour.

I have made a garter belt of oilcloth with no garters in addition to my paper-clip bendix.

I doubt not that I will glue myself to 35 E. 9 on my return. The air is good and the sun lovely but I am sunk and paralyzed by the meager mental inspiration and claustrophobic hazards. I am accustomed to concentrated work then leaping out to extremes. Also I am a sea type. However all is better than the frantic life of dodging the summer's idle women and children at Sailor's snug.

much love—
Dawn

P.S. Not sorry I came.

(COLLECTION JACQUELINE MILLER RICE)

TO JOSEPH GOUSHA

*[MacDowell Colony
Peterborough, N.H.
ca. June 29, 1949]*

Dear Joe—

I thought this was pretty cheap at $20 per week and the mountain air making a pint of rye last a week. However, I can see where sheer boredom could make it mount up. Chip in for cocktail party, tax and the inevitable Italian restaurant downtown (the only dissipation). Also I find one leaves check for servants—say $10—for distribution. Whether anybody but Mrs. MacDowell sees this I don't know. I do not think—now that I am really well, as I seem to be—that I could endure this weird setup of rubbing your nose in whatever you're doing day and night with no change of scene or pace or face. It is a definite strain for so lax a person as myself to keep rigid 6 p.m. dinner hours—7:30–8:30 breakfast—and the politely veiled law of appearing at whatever reading or concert some egotistical colonist announces for the evening.

I was told one did exactly as one pleased about these matters and God knows how any normal person could stand the pace. Rap on tumbler at dinner and composer says, "I wish to announce I will play my concerto in the library tonight or my chorale for mixed bar and grill and all are welcome." At this point, Charles Norman* inevitably springs to his feet, writhing with wounded ego, and says, "The following night *I* will read my poetry in the Watson Studio and all are welcome." "Welcome" simply means By God any colonist not showing is in the doghouse. Last night I discovered this when George Milburne and I innocently skipped the second rendering of an operetta about nymphs and shepherds by Lydia Pinkham's grandson† and were found in Gatto's Italian Restaurant drinking beer and playing the jukebox. You would have thought we had defiled the reservoir—not for beer-drinking for they were all there doing that, but *they* had attended the concert. Now I see why they asked me three times if there was a mistake in my name's not being on list for going to see the Peterborough Players play *Blithe Spirit* Wednesday. By God, the colonists *always* attend that summer theater opening. No compulsion, naturally, but in case you change your mind, Miss Powell—

Also I talked to town people. No fraternizing, please.

Did you know MacDowell was off his rocker up here the last few years? I know why. There is a bird all over the place supposed to have inspired "To a Wild Rose" as it sings [its] first four notes. (I *would* say it was "From the Halls of Montezuma"—until frowned on and told it was the Wild Rose bird.) Well, this bird shrieks this from every tree and bush and after MacDowell had written the song (and very likely taught the bird to plug it) he wanted to do more profound work but the damn bird kept dinging away at his old popular hit till the poor man cracked. My theory is that Mrs. MacDowell started this place after his death to see how many other artists would be driven nuts by it, too.

I am sending square trunk Railway Express Collect so leave two or three bucks with Louise. Ought to get there Thursday or Friday. I have plane from Keene reservations for Friday but may switch to train instead.

Love,
Dawn

(COLLECTION TIM PAGE)

---

*The author and biographer Charles Norman (1904–1996) was one of Powell's first friends in New York. He left a charming portrait of the Goushas in his memoir *Poets and People* (1972).
†Daniel Pinkham (born 1923) is an American composer and organist.

TO EDMUND WILSON

*MEMO FOR HAITI**

[Late 1949]

Do not depend on getting any daily necessities in Port-au-Prince. . . .

Take Barbasol or similar stuff as basic conveniences and antiseptic, also ordinary small medicines, penicillin lozenges, aspirin, Empirin, iodine, tooth powder, razor blades, pins, needles, threads, witch hazels, cosmetics, Kleenex, cotton, etc. Most stuff like that stale, expensive, difficult to find. Days can be spent and taxi fortunes in tracking down a package of Gillette razor blades or a darning needle (usually 40 cents to $75 with barter).

Useful gadgets such as needle threader, roller knife sharpener, etc.—usually $1 or so at Abercrombie's—more desirable than dough as tips since shops have nothing or else too expensive for natives.

Best stay in hotel to avoid being in complete blind custody of one group.

Streets like Pompeii with gutters sidewise and lengthwise so watch step walking in town. Falls customary.

Don't eat mancoti or breadfruit bread—certain dysentery.

Drink native rum—like a good rye—with no hangover. Whiskeys not as good. Even the new rum "Clorin" is good.

If time for Cap Hatien, take plane and stay in the town hotel there—very bizarre (by report). Moroccan effect, fine service, fifty styles of uniforms, hospitable and more gay than Port-au-Prince.

THE REFUGE (a probably Nazi German nest on top of Kenscoff Mt.)—fine food, quiet rooms for six or seven, small horses for riding, fine meals, marvelous view of the world. Strange sense of Haitian doom up there. Birds—mal fini ("gris-gris" or "gri-gri") and trees—"Palma Christi" (from Chalet des Fleurs to the Refuge). Benedictine (I think) monastery on road. Note wild, 8th-century ferocity of monk faces on road—wearing their black robes like bat wings.

Safe to address all boy babies as Christophe. (Girl babies will address *you*.)

In Creole words have different meanings according to key of voice (usually subtle insult to White Man is indicated in treble mocking tone). "Bam nouvelle" means *what's new*. ("Bam" is *give me*.)

Hotel Excelsior looks very charming, said to be very cheap with only hot water in town (then). American embassy and French visiting professors seem to stay there. Conveniently located on Champs de Mars within walking distance of town centers. Next to American embassy.

*Wilson went to Haiti in late 1949 to write a series of articles for the *Reporter*. Since Powell had been there the previous year, she wrote out some advice for him.

Hotel Oloffson good if you get Dos's big room there or, best of all, my balcony room in the hotel overlooking Haitian bay. ALSO good as Maurice De
Young, owner—white and knowing Creole as well as mulatto French (also
knows N.Y.)—can give general useful practical information. Also knows all
gossip. Depends on whether you like each other—can be more useful and
more fun than anyone as he mixes in all circles. Might be more fascinating to us
ladies, however, than to gent. . . .

(YALE COLLECTION OF AMERICAN LITERATURE, BEINECKE RARE BOOK
AND MANUSCRIPT LIBRARY, YALE UNIVERSITY)

POSTCARD TO PHYLLIS POWELL COOK*

November 7, 1949

Fortunately you paid my flower bill or I would have had to get out at
Croton-on-Hudson and swim, as train was more than I expected. Auntie May
was so nimble that I was just unpacking for a long winter lying in her bed when
I found myself in a wonderful little roomette on my way home with a jug of
homemade wine for my husband. I forgot how to work the roomette and hated
to throw the bed back into the engine and back out into the hall every time I
wanted the Ladies' Convenience. I finally worked out a scheme with Lily cups
and the ice water compartment very similar to your aviation tricks. I had to see
if the wine had turned every once in a while as I knew you'd hate that sort
of thing and I made sure it was all right every hour or two what with changing
climate. When I got home I rushed into Joe's room shouting "Look what a
pretty bottle Phyllis sent you!" (No, I did leave enough for a growing boy
and he was as pleased as he was surprised.) The trip seems like a bad dream.
Love, Dawn.

(COLLECTION TIM PAGE)

TO SARA MURPHY

[35 East Ninth Street]
December 14, 1949

Dearest Sara—

I did not feel neglected at all—and I think I am just about as insensitive as
the next one.† Anyway I would rather be neglected by Bessie than anybody in

---

*Powell wrote this charming but curiously beside-the-point postcard to her younger sister, Phyllis, dur-
ing the train ride home from the funeral of their older sister, Mabel Powell Pocock. Mabel had died on
October 26, 1949, of metastasized uterine cancer; she was fifty-four years old.
†Exactly what Powell is referring to here is unclear.

the whole (wide) world. I did feel a trifle hurt that my bedmaking fell short of triumph. I should be accustomed to this lack of appreciation, however, since jealous friends have consistently refused to admit this uncanny gift of mine.

Drifting down Memory's sewer I can recall the time I was giving a woman's touch to the apartment of an edible bachelor. I suppose I was setting my cap for him and wanted to show that two could live longer than one. Anyway I slipped unobtrusively into the bedroom and deftly unplumped the pillows, beat up the mattress, tied the pepperells into an attractive four-in-hand, lightly sprinkled fresh plucked duck over the ensemble and was back with the others in a trice. Obviously I was the girl to marry but this oaf, this lout, on blithely setting foot in bedroom door stood stock-still and cried, "Jesus, what's happened to my bed, it looks like six jumping whores have been at it." Blowing my nose to hide my tears, I saw I was licked and went home and drowned myself in a French novel. Since then I don't make beds, I break 'em.

I had a lovely time and am now discontented with any bed that isn't plumped.

Love,
Dawn

(COLLECTION HONORIA MURPHY DONNELLY)

TO GERALD AND SARA MURPHY

35 East Ninth Street
April 5, 1950

Dear Sara and Gerald—

Yesterday was the anniversary of my grapefruit suction via [Drs.] Solley and Ada so I celebrated quietly with a racking cough and a rheumatic hip induced by sitting through *The Consul.** There seem to be two schools of thought on that subject and I belong to both. I do think Menotti's chief genius is in the performances he gets out of people and in the extraordinary coordination of material for theatrical effect but I still feel completely beaten up by the subject. I have never felt that I did a worthy cause any good by bravely sitting through a movie or play about it. . . .

My dumb brother-in-law, age 58, in an excess of emotion over my sister's death from cancer last October, is about to marry a 25-year-old elevator operator with two babies. This seems to be the tidings now rocking northern Ohio.†

The Consul, an opera with words and music by Gian Carlo Menotti (born 1911), had just opened on Broadway.
†This marriage never actually took place. Instead, Edgar Pocock would marry Helen Turner several years later, and the two would live happily together until his death, in 1986.

I am struggling over an article for *Flair* to fit some already purchased [Saul] Steinberg illustrations and to make me a really venal journalist I am also writing a piece about *Flair* for *Furioso*. Later I will answer myself back.

Fondly,
Dawn

P.S. Did you see the reference to *The Wisteria Trees* as "Southern Fried Chekhov"?*

(COLLECTION HONORIA MURPHY DONNELLY)

TO EDMUND WILSON

[35 East Ninth Street]
June 5 [1950]—or Has
That Check Got Back to
the Bank Yet?

Dear Wig—

Somebody anonymous sent me this clipping which I suppose you saw. I don't know why they haven't sent me more Wilsonia if they think I'm the librarian.

Socially, the past week has been a dilly. Mr. Dos Passos dropped in Monday, having gotten his figure back and seeming very happy. Wanted to read [Wilson's play *The Little*] *Blue Light* but his changing addresses had the mail confused. Expected to find it at Spence Point. The Chamberses arrived from Key West with reports that the Key West–Havana sage, Ernest Hemingway, is stated (by near and dear) to work two hours early each day, then spend rest of day talking steadily to Anybody on art, literature, life. His younger sons—very intelligent, nice, modest boys—say, "Father is in touch with reality almost 20 percent of the time."

Jack Lawson's wife, Sue, appeared unexpectedly at Margaret's on Wednesday night to sentimental delight of her old friends but evidently strain of standing by while her husband is a martyr† has filled her with an understandable hatred of everybody else in the world. Suddenly she hauled off and started beating up Canby (in midst of sentimental old-times talk) then Margaret took her down in elevator and both came back with Margaret moaning for help and Sue choking her. I pulled her off and got a sock in the face. (I gave her a good

---

*Producer and director Joshua Logan had mounted his own rendition of *The Cherry Orchard*, setting it in the American South.
†John Howard Lawson had recently been jailed for contempt of Congress for his hostile appearance as one of ten "unfriendly" witnesses called by the House Committee on Un-American Activities.

kick personally and pushed her in a chair where she sat with insane blazing eyes, face distorted with hate.) Moral: Never get the idea that you're not interested in politics because you may take a political beating anyway. Every political hero probably has to tax some feebleminded loyal wife's brains to the cracking point. . . .

I went to a Dylan Thomas farewell party. He looks like a blowsy Shelley or maybe a beery Byron—warm, hearty and radiant. The hostess—one of those dumb-intellectual Jewish girls of the twenties—had a large photo on the wall with an earring on it. "Dylan at twenty," she stated to me proudly. "Wasn't he gorgeous? And that's the earring I lost when I lost my honor." Another lady guest was turned away by her and later fetched back and rushed into a bedroom by Dylan. This, according to John Brennan, was the lady who had telephoned Dylan earlier, weeping that she couldn't come because her husband had locked her in a closet. Evidently love had found a way. As the Frankenburgs, Brennan and Marion Morehouse and I left, Mr. Thomas had dropped the totally different two ladies he had had on his lap (a hand here, a hand there) and had pulled his shirttail out to do a perfectly dandy dance. It is rare indeed for us to see an English poet have such a wonderful time—probably the Welsh coal-miner's Saturday night. Other reports are that he loves America madly (what kind of Britisher is this?) and at the Pleasure Club (Surrealists' party place near here) he started to take a swan dive out the window in a peak of exultation. Everybody loves him and perhaps this is partly due to his being the personification of the now-glamorized spontaneity of the twenties. . . .

Whitney Darrow* offered to send me my old plates for $75 f.o.b. New York for melting at a profit. I countered with an offer to melt my typewriter and half-finished novel and send to him for $75 f.o.b. Scribner's.

Selah. I have Said.

Humph

(YALE COLLECTION OF AMERICAN LITERATURE, BEINECKE RARE BOOK
AND MANUSCRIPT LIBRARY, YALE UNIVERSITY)

TO MARGARET DE SILVER

35 East Ninth Street
[July 1950]

Dearest Maggie—

I have been bulging with tidbits for you but decided I would have to get a Guggenheim year to write them and would telephone instead. Then I recalled

---

*Whitney Darrow was the longtime sales director of Scribner's. The printing plates would likely have comprised all of Powell's work for the company to date—*Angels on Toast, A Time to Be Born, My Home Is Far Away,* and *The Locusts Have No King.*

that all long-distance calls are made with either the phoner or the phonee plastered and all must be later confirmed by letter anyway as nothing has registered, or else the phonee is surrounded by the subject of the conversation and cannot communicate freely.

So I arose with the riveter this a.m. (7) and am now down here, the typewriter under my chin, Fagin on the keys, and your letter just arrived. . . .

Bunny and I had a very amusing lunch and he looked fine. Elena's prime achievement (apart from Henry and Helen)* seems to me to have been in deirascibilitizing as well as rejuvenating the Bard.

The town has been heavenly and I have not had to visit anybody in the hot nasty country where you get no fresh air or peace or sunshine and have to knock yourself out talking fiddle faddle with drearies whose names you didn't quite catch or their children. However here is the catch. I have taken over your desperate device of having to put hats and opera-length gloves on and rushing out to mythical engagements in order to get cocktail callers out of the house. I refer naturally to young [Thomas] Wanning[†] (he really was shoved out by Joe and me at merely eight but the push had begun at seven and I got sort of hysterical for fear it would be forever, what with his saying, "I know I'm being difficult and you have a dinner engagement but I am going to finish this gin I brought"). . . .

Lunched with Dos who looked fine and was sorry to hear you weren't in town. Baby[‡] weighs 12 pounds and yells some and Dos was buying an 11-foot boat in Baltimore to drive back to Spence Point on his truck. He *had* visited Bill Rollins that day he came to your house and was quite shattered, he said, at the sight of this living Death in the Throat.[§] Wasn't that wonderful of him really? I don't know of any other great man who would do such a thing on his one day in New York on business unless of course photographers and publicity men were present. Bill had showed him part of a novel he was doing and Dos said it seemed fine but he was so upset by the conditions under which he was reading it that he didn't know what he was doing.

Louise's two weeks' absence permitted me to sleep late, tinker with futile carpentry, sewing, cooking and other domesticanities with company in the parlor anytime I liked (my own, too, instead of hers in the kitchen) but fortunately she came back and so now the beds are made, the bathtub cleaned, and Joe's

---

*Elena Mumm Thornton Wilson (1906–1979) was Edmund Wilson's fourth and last wife. They had one daughter, Helen Miranda (born 1948). Henry Thornton was Elena Wilson's son from a previous marriage.

†Thomas Wanning was a young friend of independent means. He would become one of Powell's favorite drinking companions.

‡Dos Passos, who remarried, had recently become a father for the first time. Lucy Hamlin Dos Passos, later Coggin, had been born on May 15, 1950.

§Dos Passos had visited William Rollins, a friend and would-be writer, on his deathbed.

balcony hung daily with banners of old rags, pillows, her own underwear and other signals to the outside world that Here Is Where Good Housekeeping Is Going On, though it looks like an East Side tenement from the street and has always driven me crazy. Louise has always been a defender of the right of Old Rags to Get the Sun. We used to go mad in Mt. Sinai, where there was no stopping her from hanging a clothesline full of valuable old ravelings between the veranda and the lovely sea so that no matter where you turned you could only see the sunset through a hole in some flying gray crotch.

Jacques LeClercq is a new man since he got his wife and kiddy off to Europe.[*] This permits him to boast freely and happily of Tanny's sensational success in London with the ballet, at the same time having the apartment to himself. He seems to have picked up his life just where it was in 1929 (when he married) and it would be boring if it weren't sad to hear him have get-togethers with characters none of the rest of us care to remember. Like Canby, I mean—as if life had stood completely still for 20 years. He got Katherine Brush, Putnam, Coby and me in last Saturday for warm cocktails and then we three went to dinner at Carlo's (61st and Lex) and were at the bar when in breezed Mary Grand[†] berating in a shrewish wifeish way a young man I had met before named Rosenthal whom she loudly described as "terribly rich."

I was anxious to provide Jacques with some summer tail so I got her to join us (what do I mean, GOT?—she flung herself and all 200 pounds at tiny Jacques and said WHO is this Adorable Man? Whereupon her escort said gallantly, "Watch out, old man, that big behind of hers will crush you the way she's throwing it around!"). She looked to me handsomer and more Diamond Jim Brady than I ever saw her. It seemed Jacques had heard her telling anecdotes of her daughter all evening in the same restaurant the night before and SHE had seen him and wondered if she could ever meet him.

She joined us at dinner—escort saying, "I feel like a louse dumping Mary on you people." In fact I still can't get over the amount of insults the professional tart takes in order to get a free martini (I understand it in wives, of course, but they HAVE to or else set up in business for themselves) but maybe this was more than a casual affair. Maybe these were not transient insults. Maybe this was LOVE. Anyway, this was an ideal mating—LeClercq and Mary for she had Todd Bolender's apartment and he was the ballet papa— so I left them with tiny Jacques supporting weaving big blonde down the

---

[*]Jacques LeClercq (1898–1972) was a poet, writer, and translator, and a longtime friend of Powell's. His daughter was the celebrated ballerina Tanaquil LeClercq, whom Powell had known since she was an infant.

[†]Mary Grand (1910–1977) was a sometime friend of independent means and a fellow Greenwich Villager.

street. This may work into something unless rival parentry of glamour children
sets in. . . .

Love,
Clarissa Harlowe*

P.S. I forgot to say Mary Grand said, "Dawn is so wonderful—everyone says
she's just *everybody's* mother." Stepmother, I would say if she only knew it.

(COLLECTION JACQUELINE MILLER RICE)

TO MARGARET DE SILVER

[35 East Ninth Street
Summer 1950]

Dearest Maggie—

Jojo is okay again due to telephone call and Joe went over but most heart-
ening thing is woman in charge there, Mrs. Roberts, whom he adores and who
simply says, "Listen, you people get the hell over here and visit him and he'll be
all right and don't you dare disappoint him." I mean you realize he has a champion more loyal than yourself even.

Glad to hear success of Bunny's play, particularly glad because it shows
how right I was.[†] I said that audiences are crazy to feel DEEP and producers
have given them nothing but *shows* and very simple stories about simple people
whereas everybody is now so complicated that The Salesman is as remote from
our day as the Monkey from our family. When they try to conjure up satisfy-
ingly deep intellectual problems from a simple superficial comedy of manners
like [T. S. Eliot's] *The Cocktail Party*—which is merely watered Maugham—it
shows the need for a vaudeville of Intellect, which only Shaw has ever given. It
is a cold age, after all, a Birdseye Frozen Heart age so we do not want the usual
fare of the stage—i.e., emotions—we want calculated play of mind so we can
rest our broken hearts on some beaten-up icebergs.

I have a great deal to thank you for—immeasurable, in fact.[‡] In the first
place it is so rare that gifts of money are tied up with those fabulosities—the
gift to the soul. You did it in sending me to Haiti at the right time. I can't imagine going there again or ever being able to like it again. Right now I am so fed
up with years of middle-class domesticated conversations and their rewards that
Haiti—striving as it is to become babbittized—seems worse than Forest Hills.

*Powell often signed her letters with such pseudonyms.
†Edmund Wilson had just published his play *The Little Blue Light*; it would be performed by the
Provincetown Players the following summer.
‡The wealthy De Silver had just promised to support Powell for a season in Paris.

Anyway your major step in shooing me to Paris—the mere idea—has already been a godsend so far as my work is concerned. I am suddenly emboldened to telephone editors, producers, etc., who are delighted to have me go away, buy me fat lunches, beg me to do pieces for them (none of course certain, but still it is a pleasant feeling), and I feel that I am really doing something people want me to do. I also realize how completely a few weeks here and there of impotence (hospitals, etc.) permit the terrible rot of domesticity to weigh you down—until nobody thinks of you as anything but the lady of the house who fiddle-faddles with typewriters instead of crewelwork. So these are the depths you rescued me from, madame, and for this much thanks.

I have in the back of my mind my childish dream of London which has been to me what Paris has been to other people. I know a great many amusing and gifted people there as well as several publishers, editors, etc.—who usually look me up when they are in New York and so I have that as an out in case Paris is too full of French people all saying "Comment?" I have a tourist ticket on *Ile* for Oct. 14 and am saying (as you heard) that I am going over on assignment, since all my physicians and debtors are going to raise hell with both Joe and me, saying, If she can cruise around Europe she can damn well pay her bills here.

Mr. Thomas Wanning is coming in later. He has come in twice, both times bearing large bottles and being very decent which makes me pleased that I don't have to act so awful myself. He says Annetta Hart who had to live very cheaply stayed at the Pas de Calais, near St. Germaine de Pres—and he was pretty sure it was less than $2.50 a day (that seems a lot but he says it might have been much, much less), but it sounds pretty good, because he said the management was reliable and she left her trunks and stuff there safely whenever she traveled around.

I am dining at Sardi's with Bobby Lewis* and going to his show—*The Happy Time*—with him (he directed it) and Oscar Hammerstein is having a party for the cast afterward but this I may skip. Anyway he is bringing his little book of where to get what in Paris. Also I am lunching later on in the month with Leo Lerman, who has George Davis's former job on *Mademoiselle*, and wants me to do something for them. I have yet to see the *Bazaar*.

My darling John Faulk† (the radio boy from Texas) and wife came in with a Texas guitar pal and the Lucas‡ came in and they got on very well—all four being pretty and the Faulks' staying at Mrs. F's folks' handsome apartment just

---

*The actor, producer, director, and all-around theatrical guru Robert "Bobby" Lewis (1909–1997) had been a good friend of Powell's since the debacle of the Group Theatre's production of *Big Night* in 1932–33.
†The American journalist and telecaster John Howard Faulk (1913–1990) would later become a famous victim of media "blacklisting."
‡Russia Luca (born 1920), an American educator who was long a research assistant to Dr. Kenneth Clark, would later marry William Hughes. She is the mother of Neill Hughes (born 1954), an artist, and Morgan Hughes (born 1957), a writer.

above Elsie Maxwell's at the Park Sheraton (used to be Central) across the street from where the Lucas will live.

I am sorry to say I am at last devoted to young people—I guess I like them when they are ambitious and busy and adult. Most of my older pals have been so goddam sunker than me and also really older—the Murphys for instance—that their respectability and the senile veneration for three squares a day and proper elimination bore and depress me.

Anyway the Lucas are really about the best people of any age I've met in years. Mark is not at all the naive broker type—but amusing, and delightful—and Russia is a darling—though I wonder if she doesn't give up too much of her own ambitions to his. Hell's pecker, anybody who does that isn't ambitious enough, then, what am I talking about.

Anyway they are amusing, and oddly enough considerate besides—a rare combination—and they are extremely à le page—they see plays, read books, know the talk and that is very rare, too. They are more New Yorkers than old-timers.

Does "substantially" on Sept. 4 mean you will be here in Ze Flash?

Oh yas.

love,
Dawn

P.S. I ate into my Paris lunches by getting a beautiful dark-green suit with black velvet collar. My.

I laughed ha ha at Mary Grand's anecdote of LeClercq's grand passion. Since he has been after me to telephone his charming young lady friend (now age 29 I believe) of 6 or 7 years—to make her come back to him and weeping over her late coolness—I was glad of the Mary Grand interlude. However he called me up before he went to Dennis [on Cape Cod] and said, "Jesus Christ, why didn't you tell me this woman is the bloodiest bore in the world? I have to listen to more ignorant psychoanalytic crap than I ever heard and I have listened to titans. Thank God she's gone off someplace but Christ, Dawn, be a friend next time and give me warning."

I know he is jealous because he is frightfully jealous of everybody, and maybe he's mad that she has horned in on his friend Oscar.

Did I tell you Niles [Spencer]'s funny crack when he heard about Mary's being in Dennis or Barnstable with a beau, he said very beaming, "That's great! Mary has worked her way through everybody down the Cape all the way to Barnstable and from Key West all the way up to Sarasota. I'll be darned."

Dawn

[35 East Ninth Street]
Aug. 8 [1950]

Dearest Margaret!! Whee! M. Harold Hoag of the Male Clinic has outside tourist berth D610 for *Ile de France* October 14 and I insisted on paying all at once lest family mice gnaw into the stub. Dumbfounded and rescued by your fast generosity, in fact scared. Am being reasonably secretive until moment to spring as I don't want to spend next month answering people's angry queries: "But I thought you were going to Paris!" Esther [Andrews] more elated than I am even and called to suggest Hôtel Quai Voltaire on same quai as very marvelous for window on barges, etc., and balconies and near Hôtel Université. Do I write direct to hotel or have Male Men do so? Mr. Hoag feels tourist is very rugged except for college students so I gather he does not take me for a prom queen in the pink, but a faded flower apt to require nurses and strong young arms. I will change to cabin, I assured him, if the other inmates are too gross for my elegant sensibilites.

Jojo home—also Joe and Louise and three meals a day housekeeping roaring around with me marketing most of the day and making lists the rest, and surprising myself by yelling and shouting and fishwifing out of housewife's nerves—forgetting words, names, etc.—in general tension of remembering to get salt and soap and baking powder. Understand Esther perfectly now. Have screaming headaches due to sudden family noises ripping me from stupefied sleep. So Paris looks divine from this overwroughty. Miss you fondly and ecstatic with gratitude.

Love,
Dawn

(COLLECTION JACQUELINE MILLER RICE)

35 East Ninth Street
September 18, 1950

Dear Jack:

I thought I would confirm the conversation we will or will not have tomorrow at luncheon when I will very likely get on the subject of how to make grape conserve and we will quarrel so bitterly the subject of my future will never come up.

*John Hall Wheelock (1886–1978), American poet and editor, was associated with Scribner's for half a century. He eventually rose to become editor in chief.

On October 14 I sail for Paris on the *Ile de France* and expect to have the new novel done by January hoping for spring publication.*

The sequel to *My Home Is Far Away*, which you saw in part, has undergone considerable revision and may get done first. As I told you, the death of my sister last year paralyzed that background for me in a curious way, and it only became workable a short while ago, but the novel will be a very good one and may detach itself from my personal feelings at an ocean's distance.

The new novel in the manner of *A Time to Be Born* is also about half done. So far I have called it *The Wicked Pavillion* (sp.?) for a reason that will seem logical only to a wondrously illogical person. Here is its base, or rather source of inspiration.

Reading the gossipy letters of French ladies and all the letters in the *Creevy Papers*, it struck me how sad it was that the vivid realness of the life as described by these ordinary letter-writers—the customs, the town talk, the scandal, the financial and personal problems of a Londoner or Parisian—was never really done in a novel. Not that that should be the novel's function but still it is a valuable kind of novel. I daresay *The Tale of Genji* does it—combining in a forever living way the time, the place, the manners, the people.

I felt compelled to do my own favorite city the service the old letter-writers did for their times. I know New York very well and am still exploring it—walking around the water's edge from Battery to Throgs Neck, under its bridges and God knows in and out of dozens of levels of society. Naturally my angle is not "O City of Stone and Steel" or anything like that. My angle is—remind me never to use that awful word *angle* again—New York as it is since 1947, the kind of Only-One-More-Minute-to-Live panic that seems to exist in people's lives, and I don't mean War, I mean TAXES. In other ages people lived in fear of death and retribution; now this city lives under the shadow of a guillotine called Income Tax. Nobody can ever make enough money to satisfy this Gestapo lurking outside every door, the finest business minds are bent to the problem of evasion, the desperate aim at underground profits, the Friendly Loan man, the Smiling Long-Term Payment man, the Laughing Banker, all infiltrating the honest citizenry and terrorizing them with their last laughs as they wrench the arm off in the jolly greeting.

The focal point is an historic old café (soon to be torn down) because I am dealing with people who are chronic café-people. I do not mean drinkers, I mean people waiting for something to happen or for somebody. Unable to solve their own frenzies, they wait for miracles; better to wait than to make a

---

*It would take Powell almost four years to finish *The Wicked Pavilion*. She would never manage to do more than some cursory work on the sequel to *My Home Is Far Away*, provisionally entitled *Marcia*.

decision that might be wrong. I regard the city as a kind of café (not the convivial kind) where you read the French papers, play checkers if with someone, mark time till the Answer. In the *Creevy Papers* Mrs. Creevy often deplored the way everybody sat around the Brighton Pavilion clareting, just waiting to see if the Prince would or would not come out of the dining room and join them. ("Oh, that wicked pavilion. Last night I clareted there till one waiting for the Prince to come out and this day I could not get up till afternoon"—she says, or something like that, poor dear.)

I mention this to show you how irrational the title is but it seemed, at the time, to illuminate the entire novel. I recall that when [Max] Perkins asked me what the plot/general idea would be of *A Time to Be Born* and I said, "It's about that man on the ledge of the Gotham about to jump off, only that has nothing to do with it," he nodded as if it were all clear as a bell to him and away we went.

The things that make people and the times so vivid to you in the old letters are the same things that make you *know* your friends and when you make new friends (as you will in this novel) the acquaintance is formed slowly or speedily once these basic facts are made known:

How much money does he make?

Did his family have money and will he get it or has he got it and will he spend it or will he save it?

Does his wife have money and will she inherit any in which case will he get it or will she waste it fixing up the old home?

How much rent do they pay? Is it too much?

Once this is cleared up, the behavior of the friend becomes understandable, his tastes, his vices, his virtues are either following or rebelling against the financial dictation. After that is cleared we want to know his geography, his genealogy (not so much), his aspirations and his gifts.

You see that this is a shorthand to character and as good as any other. You spend an afternoon with a very intelligent, interesting man in an art museum where he tells you many fascinating, intimate details of his life, but you form your really basic opinion of him when he carefully doles out a five-cent tip to the taxi driver. More so than if he made an overture to a passing one-eyed goat.

There are three pursuits in the book and many kinds of people—common New York types that are so taken for granted that no one bothers to write about them. I will show you a section before I leave to give you a general idea.

Best,

Dawn Powell

P.S. This novel is part of the New York series I started with *Turn, Magic Wheel* and some of the same characters wander through as they did through *Happy Island*, *A Time to Be Born*, and *Locusts Have No King*, though no one has ever noticed this, oddly enough. It gives me innocent fun to ship off to war or fame or motherhood stars of former novels. Denny, hero of *Turn, Magic Wheel*, met the heroine of *A Time to Be Born* and they both marched off to war, though in *The Locusts Have No King* I believe Denny was drinking much too much. In the present book it seems he's too drunk to even get into it, what a pity.

(RARE BOOKS AND MANUSCRIPTS, PRINCETON UNIVERSITY LIBRARY)

PARIS

1950-1951

Powell set sail for Paris on October 14, 1950.

TO JOSEPH GOUSHA

French Line
Ile de France
October 15, 1950
[en route to France,
apparently not sent]

Dearest Joe—

Stayed in bed with Dramamine pills. Not sick but ominous whirls in head. Not bad. Very quiet aboard. Miss Davis or Daly, the Boston spinster roommate, is sorry for the ship because she fears there are not enough aboard to pay the company. She is a road-company version of your mother in many ways—full of beans and adventure and not wanting to miss anything. Travels all over by herself—Guatemala, Cuba, etc. Shocked at immorality everywhere but crazy to find it. Very considerate and interesting up to point where the Pope or the Capitalists come in—regarding everybody against these as Communists. Boat full of nuns and priests and since Miss D. is planning to end up bussing the Papal Ring, she has a good time picking up young priests here and there. I notice she doesn't bother with the nuns. Rather serious boatload.

Luxurious meals—bottles of red (Beaujolais) and white (Bourgogne) wines on table with splendid filet mignons and a specially good cheese between Port de Salut and Provolone called Rebouchon? (forgot it already). Passport case did not arrive so guess it hit boat too late as did Margaret, etc., who sent cable. Seems it would cost $9 to telephone New York from here but of no value to anyone.

[Gertrude] Flynn's* and [Lloyd and Loren MacIver] Frankenberg's[†] brandy got me out of bed at 1 today after Dramamine had doped me for about 18 hours. Doubt if I mingle. Hate to open trunk to find belts, etc. Purser gives only 345 francs to dollar so I got only a little for messenger tips. 50 francs— seems more respectable tip for minor messages than 15 cents and I am money-mad.

Monday night—The joint is jumping but not high. Boat emptyish. A New Brunswick Sacred Heart nun just took me walking on the deck—very fine type girl but I was on way to bar and the devil. The cheese's name is Roblochon and is like cheesecake. Bought ticket from Havre to Paris—$2.45, I believe. Trunk checked and delivered to [Hôtel] Lutetia for $4 (I hope) but warned to remove bottles, nylons, cigarettes and dutiables. Tell Flynns and Frankenbergs that brandy was godsend (Miss D. nips it for her chills). Very subdued crowd and do not believe they have roused anyone to dancing by night. Is this war?

Tuesday—Very rough. Seasick as result of Mère Josepha's walking me briskly up and down deck to shake down her dinner. Dramamine pills keep me asleep 23 hours daily except when Miss Daly of Boston has my ear. This little lady is all over the place every minute, bustling about always in her little blue hat (for purposes of going to Mass any moment when her audience gets away). Stormy seas make her say fretfully, "This wasn't what the Monsignor told me. He said it would be smooth after we passed the Newfoundland banks. What have they done?" Rather greenish but still game, she lay down as boat rocked in storm and said, "I suppose the Captain's up on the bridge. My, wouldn't I like to be up there." I expected her to jump up and go but then she said, "It seems awfully dangerous but I guess all our Annapolis men are up there taking charge."

There is a different movie every day—previews—and I saw her bustling out before it was over. "It's Clark Gable and he's an auto racer but my goodness it's so dangerous I just walked out but I suppose a regular he-man like Clark loves it. I do think he ought to be more careful or he'll get killed." She slipped out last night to go up to 1st Class and watch the dancing and is irritated that I won't do the same. . . .

We stop at Plymouth Friday morning.

Gerald's passport case lost—it came to boat and they have the card but

---

*Gertrude Flynn was an actress friend; she had played the role of Julie in *Big Night*.
[†]The artist Loren MacIver (1909–1998) and her husband, Lloyd Frankenberg (1907–1975), were among Powell's friends.

case stolen or lost I found on tracing, which will make him madder even than me. Was in bar once for couple drinks but so dull.

Wednesday a.m.—Everything roped and nailed down and shuttered for last two days but calmer today and I seem to have finished sleeping and sea-sickness. Found fine privacy here in sunny red-furnished bar balcony which you and Louise and I went through. Don't have to order . . . [letter breaks off]

(COLLECTION TIM PAGE)

TO JOSEPH GOUSHA

[Paris]
Tuesday, October 24 [1950], 5 p.m.
or 17 hrs. or 12 o'clock high
in your money

Cher maître (must remember not to say *cher merde* unless it's a very dear very old friend)—

I am overlooking the *toits* of Paris at the same time eating the remains of a 500-franc breakfast (a cold *jambon* enough for three, brioche and soluble Nestlé tea and soluble Zeeman's rye in same). I had the breakfast in bed so I would be able to work which was very successful though expensive. I usually wander around for break around 11 after an early instant coffee, but my stomach is still queasy from *mal de mer* and cannot endure any more wine for breakfast which is rather necessary in these very cheap places where the whole thing is only about 150 francs anyway. Besides, as soon as I get out I can't stop walking. This is distinctly your city as an old waterfront man and I try to lay it out for your future visit.

Everything is working out as I planned so far. I have seen nobody and have not tried to. I celebrate my loneliness and this is a wonderful city to be alone in and I trust you will have that privilege. I mean it is so overwhelming that to have somebody with you trying to talk about how Elsie has her hair fixed now or what kind of car your wife likes best would be just like an interruption while reading the most galloping mystery. However, in a few days I will probably be wishing for an evening of sensationally silly conversation with remarkably silly people or even relations.

The maid pleaded for the room about 2:30 so I dressed and took my first Autobus (No. 68—20 francs) across the same bridge I covered yesterday past the rue de l'Université, Louvre and on to the Avenue de l'Opera whence I trickled over to the rue Scribe to the American Express Company which was very empty indicating lack of Americans in Paris, I guess, at present, as I had been warned you had to stand in line for hours. Then I spotted the Galeries aux Lafayettes next to the Café de l'Opera (all these familiar outdoor cafés including Floré look rather seedy and Coney boardwalk-ish right now, though in the Floré neighborhood my eye was taken by one Café Royal because it had an enormous round bar inside). I found the people outside these places looked sort of pathetic and certainly chilly though I daresay after being here long enough there is always the hope of seeing somebody from Duluth ambling along with a wad in their hands. . . .

The room is pleasant and light, very quiet except for the dining-room orchestra, which stops before 10:30 and is not at all tempting as it only has eight pieces and a strictly metronomic beat, inspiring an old soldier to the march, perhaps, but no mad lust to the ballroom. The chambermaid, waiter and *valet du chambre* are lovely and thoughtful and helpful and jolly, but everywhere else the conduct of business is no smiling matter. Even a mere cashing of checks is an exchange of military insults, grim and solemn. You laugh when you are on the picnic, in the theater, playing with the *bébés*, but not when money is being exchanged, I gather. Courtesy and respect, yes, but let's not horse around with Our Lady of the Bourse.

There are three little buttons on the wall phone, one each for *valet du chambre*, *femme du chambre* and *maître d'hôtel*. Whichever one you ring, an old Edison Record cracked voice wheezes, "*Vous faites mepris,* go crochet yourself." So you crochet yourself and presently someone knocks on the door and all is well. The cutest thing is the little glass mail chute which suddenly has a sound like chimney swifts fluttering around in the chimney and there is a letter in it for you, blown in from goodness knows where, but it's very clever and Fagin would love it. The bidet is a fine thing, too, but your feet hang out (us big California girls). I don't know where you Americans get the idea we have no toilet paper in France, we have plenty of it and nothing ordinary either, it's made of the finest isinglass, in fact a Dupont product I think. I'm making some lackluster contact lenses out of it.

The loveliest place I have seen is the Hôtel Voltaire on the Quai Voltaire which both Esther and Dos recommended. Opposite the Louvre on the Seine and small. When Jack's young friend Marcel Clarin* wrote me, he found it full up for four months. I daresay it is without these Hotel Taft conveniences but in another week I may not be able to stand this busy place. The Voltaire is very convenient because it is the last stand before going over the Seine but you can get the Boulevard Raspail bus going back to Montparnasse, etc.

This break indicates a telephone call and who was it but Monsieur [Eugene] Jolas downstairs. He just came up for a few minutes, looking very

---

*Marcel Clarin (1920–1992) was a French businessman who had become close to Powell's cousin Jack Sherman during the war. Sherman witnessed Clarin's marriage to Jacqueline Fenet in 1945 and was godfather to one of their sons.

distinguished and faunish (stout faunish) and much gray hair. This is my first human contact and I was very pleased. I will dine with him and Maria* tomorrow night, if I can remember how to act after my last social life with Miss Daly of Boston. He wished you were here. Said he was just back from Germany two months and had turned down a big job at big money (this is his 6th year with OWI or whatever it is) but he wanted to do his own writing. Said he was doing so very well and Maria had bought an apartment on the black market for $2000 not far from here (the rue Bonaparte) and both daughters were married, one with baby and another one coming up. I still had an untouched bottle of the Frankenberg-Flynn brandy and Wheelock's Bonded Beam and some Carstairs but he said he did not indulge in those Americanisms which was just as well as we would probably both end up in the St. James jail. . . .

I may move to a cheaper place if I find any next week, as Gene says this is a bad, cooperationist hangout, though he and Maria have often lived here.[†] I think there will be strange mystery taxes on the regular bill since no one charges or presents bills at the time.

Much love and take care of Fagin and Louise and write me about your mother. Have dinner for the boys.

Dawn

(COLLECTION TIM PAGE)

TO MARGARET DE SILVER

[Paris]
Oct. 30, 1950

Dearest Maggie—

I am as isolated from everyone as I planned to be, though occasionally I get a furtive qualm wondering what would happen if I got a simple chill, let alone anything else. I don't think even the hotel knows anything about me. I walked my head off today all over the Right Bank, ready to be tempted into buying a hat, but fortunately nothing visible looked tempting. The department stores seem extraordinarily and sublimely Gimbelish but more expensive. I don't know what I would wear for any royal command dinner as I haven't taken off my coat since I've been here and certainly don't wish to. In fact I dread the little dinner with my cousin's French couple tomorrow night as I look like the

---

*Maria Jolas (1893–1987) was a translator and founder of *transition*, the French literary magazine.
†Powell was staying at the Hôtel Lutetia, an establishment on the Left Bank that had indeed been a center of Nazi and Petainist activity during World War II.

devil. This hard water has dried my skin into scales that resist all creams, and my hair has dried into hopeless strange-looking hay.

I spend some time thinking up ways to dodge the goddam wine shoved at you for breakfast and now have some buns and marmalade in my room just to keep from fermenting right in the Louvre. I went to a fine German prize movie—*Berlin Ballad*—with French titles and it was fine to see something comic. I also heard someone laugh day before yesterday—first time that's happened—and it was right outside. Germans, it turned out. Maybe in Germany the French crack a tiny smile. Naturally I see them only transacting business so that is so sacred they would not want to lose any of its holiness.

I run into the Deux Magots, Dome, etc., from whatever street I walk—all looming up like manholes and I flee in the other direction madly. I can almost smell the characters I would meet there, but unless I move from here to a monastery in a complete renunciatory mood I may plunge into them with a terrific whoop some chilly day. This is really a wonderful city to work in because the people you would be social with if you were social are so much drearier than anyone in the Cedar.* It is splendid to find such an ideal place. God, what terrifying women—vultures behind cash registers wherever you turn, bleak, veiled avarice and hate. However in the world did they get those good-for-nothing men to marry them in the first place? Evidently they can't get to making money unless they've got a respectable married name, so they drag some poor bastard to the altar, and it's like a working license—then they are in business.

Joe wrote me that he and the Boys had a good time at Madame Julien's (their 40 W. 55th French place) the other night because Gaston (of the old La Bonne Soupe place next door) was in getting drunk with them and talking about old days at the Café Martin. After he closed the Bonne Soupe he opened another restaurant opposite Mecca Temple there in the Hotel Gorham named after his wife—Chez Georgette, I guess its name is—and what a hard little number SHE was, too. Anyway Joe said Gaston finally went home and found Madame Chez Georgette had locked him out so he had to come back to his old rival's and stay all night.

I hope to goodness my agent doesn't simply file me away now that I'm out of sight, as this town is expensive in odd ways, though immeasurably cheaper than New York, largely because I have no bar bill, being afraid to drink in these bistros for fear I might smile at the busboy or laugh out loud and get arrested as this town is not one to encourage democratic good nature. So I sit grimly at my table in a different restaurant every night and glower and try to get out

---

*Powell had already begun to frequent the Cedar Bar on Eighth Street in New York, later a legendary hangout for the Abstract Expressionist artists.

without having more of the goddam swill of wine shoved at me. I think this country needs a good shot of rye to make it a little merrier—an American Legion convention, let's say. I am very depressed at the thought of having to go through a social evening tomorrow night with a pair of wine-drinkers and frog-talkers. I have a fine time with the Paris papers, which I love. Today I extravagantly bought a *New Yorker* for 130 francs, then lost it on the bus. Never mind. I can always read myself to sleep with *Les Temps Modernes*. . . .

much, much love,
Dawn

(COLLECTION TIM PAGE)

TO MARGARET DE SILVER

[Paris]
November 11 [1950]

Dear *cherie—cheries* are ripe? No?

Libby Holman is having a concert here Monday but I am in such a genuine Parisian mood that I don't want to spend the money for taking somebody and don't like anybody well enough to take them or ask them even.

I am doing considerable work and everything is exactly as I expected and wished, though there are many times when I feel I have my wish on the end of my nose. There is no chance of my ever having any good time until I get my work in order (and get some editors in order, too). I must say I was depressed by the rather unnecessary jinx that made the *New Yorker* almost buy my first story from here but then decide it would take too much time discussing necessary revisions across the ocean in time for publication before its subject was dated. Do you have any money in your pocket? I told Joe to send me whatever was left jingling in my bank after Louise cashed my last check and maybe there isn't any, just as I anticipated.

It is rather scary being in a town alone and finding yourself in the curious position of paying for everything—no icebox with leftovers, no newspaper at the door, no cocktails or dinners at any expense but your own, no charge account at the drugstore, no doctor or dentist bill to add onto at will (a tooth cracked up due to this goddam sugar and chocolate and croissant country). I am now rather inclined to stick to the Waldorf cafeteria downstairs rather than risk a sudden extra charge in a nice little backstreet restaurant. I had a choc. and ham on a dried biscuit in a drab café in my rounds yesterday and the man threw quite a fit when I asked for mustard. It was near a spot where François

Coppée died. Also Paul Bourget. Also Chateaubriand, maybe, and Mme. Recamier. They all died and all Paris ever did for them was to give them a plaque in the pavement. No wonder they died.

Consequently I immediately went in a store and bought a beautiful crystal-purple necklace for 900 fr. and proud and happy went into the Waldorf cafeteria or oyster room and ordered Mashed Potatoes (puree) by God instead of their fucking allumettes, soufflées, French frieds. People were busy feeding their poodles and I was very pleased to see some of them drinking a nice white wine out of goblets from Papa's or Mama's hand. I think the reason the French lavish so much love on their animals is that they've given up all hope of having the animals buy them a meal, and they are frustrated elsewhere by the fear they might be giving away a kiss or hug that could be sold for two centimes if they held tight. Furthermore the poodles *seem* (I'm quite sure they suspected them for centuries) to be incapable of slipping any fast deal over on them.

I have figured out the way Paris is laid out, now—and "laid out" is right. After Max* said he thought Paris lay down and spread her legs out before any invader, I realized that the reason you keep meeting yourself coming back on the streets is that all the streets spread their legs out, too, and other streets get in there and spread theirs out, so you have pi squared, pardon my mathematics. I can cross the rue de Bac somewhere if I walk east, west, or north. Haven't tried it on south.

Monday. Just had your letter. Saturday I went over to see Sheba who was waiting for another doctor's say before going to hospital, though she is pretty sure of going and doesn't seem to think it will be much, and we had a very jolly little dinner, and even laughed, something I have found does not exist so far as I'm concerned anymore. They live in a very pleasant section and Bus 68 passes here and passes their apartment also. Max has the most marvelous radio and record machine I ever heard—a Schneider—beautiful tone, slightly larger than yours and getting all stations and throwing its sound out of the walls, and due to the Schneider salesman's being a cigarette (American) fancier he got it for 32 cartons of Chesterfields (which he himself gets at the Embassy store at a discount). Mr. Goodman has promised on Sheba's recovery to take us to a Bad Place where he will dance the can't-can't. I did have Bunny's note with Mrs. [Arthur] Koestler's address, which Koestler had given me, as you know, saying modestly, "You might like her, you know, she isn't a bad sort." I am very lugubrious most of the time but that's the only way I get any work done and I am in no mood to thrash around new

*Powell's Paris friends Max and Sheba have yet to be identified.

acquaintances, it's too expensive and too much work. From here I go into my Lady Trappistry.

> love (unless I can sell it),
> Dawn

TO EDMUND WILSON

> *[Paris
> ca. November 17, 1950]*

Dear Wig . . .

I just cashed my last ten dollars and was economizing on lunch at the same time disposing of—*alors,* let us say I am the Count of Monte Cristo and the world is mine, at least it feels as if somebody had bashed it over my ears like an old silk hat. Anyway, it would be a hangover in any other country, though in any other country what I drank would be regarded as mere civilized drinking and I wouldn't be *having* a hangover—so the waiter shortchanged me a hundred francs. With that hundred francs I could have lived like a prince for as long as I cared to in my present mood.

The mood is due to three *amer picons* with M. Jolas (who cleverly was having martinis), an Alsatian *beaucoup* wine dinner at a brasserie on Champs-Elysées with both Jolases, myself longing for less raw French meat and eternal French fried, souffléed, allumetted *pommes*—who would have dreamed that they really did have French fried potatoes in France?—and finally a delicate grog with Maria [Jolas] at Deux Maggots* (I never dreamed decent people went there anymore, either), Gene having left. The reason he left was my remark that Sartre was the Hopalong Cassidy of France, and he said I should be more humble before French letters, though he himself is not a Sartre admirer. I returned that this view was not—as he held—the stupid view of America toward France, but my own and based not on my brief but not brief enough stay in Paris but on Sartre as a commercial enterprise like cornflakes or Shirley Temple—that is (and he does make the trains run on time) restaurants, hotels, magazines, theaters, real estate thrive on his okay, just as our Hopalong Cassidy boots, breakfast foods, etc. Furthermore, he might be the big frog in Boston but Elyria would still believe Louis Bromfield was the country's leading mind, Carolina would be astounded to learn that there was anybody but Paul Green, New Orleans would have or have had Roark Beadford, and of course

---

*Powell had much sport with the name of the famous café Les Deux Magots.

there is a group that calls Ben Hecht Ben. Anyway you can see those Uncle Sam pants getting too long. . . .

Margaret probably told you Koestler came with Jim Putnam to my deportation party and gave me his wife's address then as he thought I should look her up. Maria says she's been very sick with asthma. I cannot look up anybody till my finances get more financial. I knew exactly what this would be like but rather fancied my fortunes might change with an ocean voyage.

I would like Paris better if I had any deep feeling for what they like, but I really dislike the pallid, watery-eyed churchly old-whore sentimentality of their limpid pastoral novels—Maurois, Hemon and that school. I find Sartre's work (novels) cutouts from Colette, Aragon, Roger-the-Thibaults'-man, and every other leading novelist, and I hate the rather insanitary tidiness of the people—the newspapers folded just so, their enjoyment in all their little chores, their fixed ideas—the way the newsman is horrified that I want different newspapers every day, and more than one. "But Madame took *Le Figaro* yesterday and so she is a *Figaro* reader, how can she take *Humanité* and *Paris-Presse* too?" Also, I cannot get anyone to admit that rue Jacob is a continuation of rue de l'Université or Boulevard des Italiens is a continuation of Boulevard des Capucines. No. These streets have nothing to do with each other. No, Madame, it is not the same street under a different name, it is an entirely different street. And Fourth Avenue is *not* the lower end of Park Avenue. It is, on the contrary, completely different, in fact it leaves off at 34th Street, whereas, you must admit, Park Avenue only *begins* at 34th Street. Good God, Madame has put her stamps on the letter upside down. The Post Office will not accept. Madame must buy fresh stamps and put the blue one here, so, the red one there, so, and the other one here. This is the order in which it is done.

I do love the tiny little noises in the morning, the autos squeaking *oui oui*, the birds peeping *oui oui* and the whole hotel *oui oui*. The radios go on and I have such a good ear for language that I have picked up one favorite song I hear. It goes:

> LAUNDREE—*come you to me once more*
> *Laundree—what did I pay you for*
> (*parlando*)   *You went away*
> (*sing*)   *one summer day*
> *Occur this way, s'il vous plaît*
> *Laundree, come sleep with me ce soir.*

Maria says Joyce's son comes in from Zurich only to get Pop's checks to drink up. She also states that many Americans who entertained Sartre and Beauvoir lavishly in America and rather expected some return favors here have been surprised to find them rather grudgingly given one cassis at de Floré café and briskly shoved off. Maria said that the French were really very hospitable, only their hospitality consisted in allowing people to have as many men in their hotel as they liked or allowing them to bring their pets into restaurants.

Most people here seem irritated and surprised that America has so much war talk. However, Gene, who has been on the Frankfurt *Zeitung* for some years (now through with it) says a new war seems certain. . . .

The New Yorker almost bought a story of mine but unluckily decided it would be dated by the time I had made some changes they wanted. I enjoy walking from one end of the Right Bank over bridges and under and over the Left Bank and I like the newspapers and little bakeries. I don't like the cafés because a gentlewoman can't go prancing around alone in them unless she's expecting her group, and the stores have an enormous amount of junk at high price, and in the main I think this is a good place to study to be a dope fiend. I haven't been so abysmally sunk (though I did expect it) since I was making $1000 a week in Hollywood. I have found that money does not bring happiness but neither does the lack of it. (Doesn't that have the old Gallic touch, though, my brave?)

My best (which hardly seems good enough) to Elena and Rosalind and tell the Givenses to get over here for Halloween. Tell everybody and I will meet them at the boat with my hat in my hand. (French courtesy.)

Fondly,

Dawn

(YALE COLLECTION OF AMERICAN LITERATURE, BEINECKE RARE BOOK
AND MANUSCRIPT LIBRARY, YALE UNIVERSITY)

TO JOSEPH GOUSHA

[Paris]
Friday evening
November 17 [1950]

Dearfriend—

My boat roommate just called up, having "been ALL over Italy and ALL over England and all over the cathedrals here" and feeling perfectly wonderful and a lesson to me. I rather gloomily invited her to tea Monday, if any. . . .

Last night Gene decided to show me Paris at 5:30. We went to the section around the Odéon, walked through the bookstalls of that theater—now the Comedie Française with very conventional operas appealing to concierges' tastes, I gathered—then walked down Monsieur Street (named after Louis XIV, I need hardly tell you, who was a fairy so his court mocked him as Monsieur le Prince) past the Shakespeare Hotel formerly housing Sylvia Beach's bookstore and above which she still lives and out of which emerged a nice-looking

Englishman named Stuart Gilbert (pal of Gene's) who wrote a fine book on Joyce.

We passed the Café Voltaire before that, where Verlaine used to be carried out drunk nightly, and walked over to the Café Balzar, a favorite of Gene's, where we sat outside and he had martinis and I *amer picons*. The place is near the Sorbonne and full of students and Gene watched with journalistic interest as a young girl fell in the street with her skirts up. Old Nose for News Jolas, I said, as he blushed. Here we met an Irish writer named Sam Beckett (celebrated as one of Peggy Guggenheim's lovers) who now writes in French, and he recommended a new group called Les Noctambules, night performers in a café nearby—*chansonniers,* I should say. Then he took me to the rue Maguet and the disreputable little hotel where Elliot Paul* stayed (with Gene bailing him out periodically) and this was most jolly, then we picked up Maria and went over on the Champs-Elysées to a vast brasserie Alsatian (like a Brass Rail, only waitresses in Alsatian dress and hats) and had delicious wine, of course, and *choucroute garni*—wonderful after too much French—large sauer-krauts, potatoes, frankfurters (these are fine here), ham and delicate, ungreasy sausages. About this time we got on Sartre and Gene got his neurosis so maybe they'll decide to let me rest for fear it will rouse him too much. Maria and I went to Deux Maggots for a *fin* and Gene went to Lipp's, which he continues to patronize. He was writing a piece in French on some German poet. In the main he seems fine here and only blows his top about hating Paris or hating New York once a day. . . .

> Just got your last letter—love,
> Dawn

(COLLECTION TIM PAGE)

TO JOSEPH GOUSHA

> *[Paris]*
> *Wednesday a.m.*
> *November 22 [1950]*

Dearest Joe—

It was fine hearing you, particularly since it was practically the first day I rose above the lower basin blues (street I mean). This may have been due to contact with home, or the fact that I had a note from Libby Holman who has been giving a couple of folksong concerts here at the Comédie Champs-

---

*Elliot Paul (1891–1958) was an American novelist and autobiographer, probably best known for his book *The Life and Death of a Spanish Town* (1937).

Elysées, asking me to come and come backstage. She has a chateau in Louvciennes. Anyway I went to the theatre the night before and could get nowhere about tickets, and having carefully looked up that they closed at 6, I went at 5:30, waited as a porter instructed me till the immediate sales were over for advance tickets, then ticket window banged shut, nobody ever heard of Holman, no concert, nothing—Monday, madame, the theatre is always closed.

I showed the ad (on Mondays they're always closed so concerts are given then) but only Lady Vanishes sort of Never Heard Of. This is that rare old French *politesse* that crushes you. Next day decided to put it in hands of the ticket agency of the hotel, thinking it would cost a fortune, but I had already invited Max and Sheba as bodyguards. So the expert himself calls up the theater for three tickets, informs me theater says no such person, also closed on Monday—in fact same runaround in spite of ads' being displayed. Trembling, he calls up again. No. There are no performances on Monday. This time he calls a third time and is calmly given three tickets as I requested and he seems not at all surprised (500 francs apiece or $1.40 with a big rake-off of 100 francs for the agency). Anyway I realized it was an accepted form of business deals and not a personal Marshall plan insult, and when the Frog expert himself gets the runaround, okay.

Then Libby had a crowded house of very good-looking Americans largely. She looked terrific, though refusing as usual to sing "Moanin' Low" (like Dwight's Ida), but sang a baffling amount of folksongs to do with lost babies, etc., but enough, "I'm a Bad Woman and How I Love It" to get bravos. Backstage, she was surrounded but gave a yell to see my Voice of America and some gents said they only knew me by record (these are the drunken records of Romeo that Bobby Lewis and I made at her place)* and insisted she come in and get me out to her chateau. First human gesture outside Maria (Gene is fine but so neuro, thinking everything I say represents American lack of reverence for Racine).

Ivan[†] gave me a very thorough statement about my stories—seven or eight there, all *almost* selling, but I saw they were really very active and thorough which was encouraging. Here is what I want you to do.

I am having a fine time with a part of my novel dealing with some poverty-stricken artist holing in either College Point district or Steinway—anyway, you recall you spoke yourself of fine chance for hideout, the broken-down old houses, etc. I am describing, with variations, one of these sections and want you on some Saturday or Sunday to recheck. I like it as a place where artist of note, broke, pretending to be in Paris, finds same kind of rotten old broken-

---

*It would be fascinating to hear these records, of which several copies seem to have been made. To date, however, not one has turned up.
[†]Ivan van Auw was Powell's new literary agent, at Harold Ober Associates.

down building, smell of rats and old sewers and cemeteries, never disturbed by Board of Health. I think perhaps around Flushing might be too well kept and Staten Island (I prefer the Astorian jungles). Anyway wouldn't it be possible— as it seems to me—for a warehouse or house (I've seen both with Jojo and with you) where no one ever fixes it up and certain characters can use every few years—never being sure whether it's there or torn down? Find out whether I'm thinking of the rat joints around Steinway (I wandered through some when I was trying to show Hassoldt* the charms of the place) or Williamsburg or College Point, which looks respectable on its main ends but did have some battered fringes I could use.

I am also cheered by your American Express draft (better tell Louise not to cash any till I get some more) and my darling restaurant Maison Barraud. I walked for miles and found it out of hunger—Daumier proprietor genially pouring himself snorts, Madame and girls busy in kitchen, genial waiter, marvelous stews, ragouts, soups, cheese and everybody understands my French, due to its being as ignorant as the overhauled streetcleaners, pushcart ladies in shawls and aprons having a real snort (none of this crappy wine stuff) at the bar, and never more than 200 francs (with wine, soup, main dish, cheese, coffee and maybe a *fin*). Anyway it's jolly. It turned out, of course, to be just about behind this hotel, by 100 yards or less, one of those things that make walking in Paris a puzzle. Walk away from Boulevard Raspail and after an hour's walk straight away you come to Boulevard Raspail which mysteriously has hooked on to Boulevard Montparnasse near Le Dome.

I have the conviction that something is to be gotten from this expedition if I can stick it out (and you too). I am convinced it will retrieve our fortunes, difficult as the immediate thing is. I would like to make some money to assure my home ticket, natch, but otherwise my entire expenses (when I can pay them) per week are about two dinners at Tony's. . . .†

Love,
Dawn

Will make fortune very soon. Just got *Oliver Twist* in French for Jojo—will send with *David Copperfield* when I figure out how to do so.

(COLLECTION TIM PAGE)

---

*Hassoldt Davis (1907–1959) was an American explorer and writer who became a close friend of Powell's.
†Tony's, on West 46th Street, was one of Joseph Gousha's favorite restaurants and bars for more than thirty years.

Paris
December 11, 1950

Dearest Joe—

Hooray for American Express! As Margaret sent me an amalgamated check which covers rent for another week (and Maria gave me a little man who cashed it with no questions for 360 francs per $1 instead of 345 as Express and banks give) I am planning departure for January, tourist ticket.

Guess who turned up? Chester McKee—the father, really, of our whole social life.* (Chester to Gene to Cheyneys to Chambers to Dos to etc.) He got here Tuesday, stays at Hôtel Cayre down the street here, plans to stay a year. Came to see me, decided my room and bath were best bargain and warmest in Paris and may move here. Anyway, he went down to the café here with me for dinner, thought the orchestra was wonderful—playing "Fortunio," he said, by [André] Messager, soothing after French orchestras' usual attempt at unrhythmic jazz. He is full of beans, seemed the same, proposes to finish his work and stay here a year. Really very nice.

Had very sweet card from Jojo dated November 24. Did his books come yet? I note all boat first-class mail—let alone second-class—is four to six weeks coming. I did a short article yesterday for, I think, *Promenade* to make sure, but may decide to let Ivan try it somewhere else. . . .

Several Embassy and news people there. (By the way, telephone has new service here—you call up for weather and get the latest news.) General inside talk was: French elated at our Korean defeats, but on second thoughts said their gratification was not meanness but merely thought that now they would have a voice in the world planning. Personal office gossip had it that French richer nations now instructing their help to start being nice to Russians as they would soon be living with them. If direct war, word is that Russians would be in Paris overnight and Americans had to beware them. They did not seem frightened though.

People have asked me where I intend to go when the big putsch comes— Majorca being once again *the* place, or Spain, where black market gets you 56 pesos to $1 (legally 25). Majorca has luxury for $2 a day—Whee, they cry, off we go! I do not know whether the idea of returning to U.S. seems impossible to them or merely unpleasant. Gene getting neuro as Maria says—Stupid Americans! Stupid Germans! Stupid! They have tiny kitten of Fagin's rare breed, but this one is a female heller with only two rooms to wreck. Both Gene and Maria

---

*I have been able to find little information on Chester McKee, but the social genealogy Powell traces here includes Jolas; the poet and lecturer E. Ralph Cheyney (1897–1941), who published Powell in the *Independent Poetry Anthology 1925*; Canby Chambers (and, by extension, Esther Andrews); and finally John Dos Passos.

very devoted—usually all lamps on floor, typewriter ribbon wrecked, and sharp little fangs ready to take on any human flesh.

Big toy display in window of Au Printemps—department store like Lord & Taylor. Blast of record playing and singing "Dear folks and gentle people, the folks that live in my hometown, etc., etc." in English. Window labeled "Le Texas" and five electronically operated figures of wild Indians on horses; cowboys, all shooting, and figures dropping dead; a bar with can-can ladies in satins and lace embracing and having tug-of-war with bartender and his towel, trying to pull him over bar; dead man on floor; Mexican jumping out window onto moving covered wagon below; Bad Man shooting [while] being kicked out of Epiceria, bang bang—and song continuing for kiddies, "These dear friends and gentle people, they never let you down!"

Thanks so much and love,
Dawn

P.S. Friend of Lewis Gannett's and old League of American Writers speaker Louis Fischer here for some French American Congress. Met him at Sheba's, then ran into him on street with his niece. . . . Asked me to come to reception for him and Sartre and probably speeches so I took Maria last night. Seemed half black as Sartre loves them and Richard Wright *(Native Son)* was there whom I remembered—he lived in George Davis's house in Brooklyn with his white wife—a nice fellow (we were on same committees). Wright was M.C. and Sartre's bosom friend. Mme. Beauvoir a Carol Hill [Brandt] type only with a French mean look. Sartre looked like Harry Gousha a little, only a very tiny, sandy, little jockey type who seems very keen, interested and much nicer than I thought. However, I did not think it opportune to give him Bunny's and Dos's messages ("hello" was the message). Doubt if this new organization for Mutual Relations comes to much as all white Americans are afraid to sponsor any organization with the words *American* or *International* in it for fear they'll lose their passports, those words now meaning communism to our State Department.

TO JOSEPH GOUSHA

Friday Paris a.m. Rain.
In Lutetia brasserie
waiting for omelette
jambon brunch having
had tea and stale
delicious bun in room.
[ca. December 15, 1950]

Dear American friend—

Behold a wreck. . . . Thought to soothe interim with view of Paris rain from gargoyles of Notre Dame. Interior is like walking into a sapphire—incredibly breathtaking. Go outside church to spiral up (30 francs) an ancient dungeonlike stone stairs lit by wedges of light and narrow and when you give up you can't go down or up so you have to continue gasping and spiraling while schoolboys and a pair of girls pass you. On last (I thought) roof I was only afraid I would drop into the gargoyles from spiraling and puff, but smell of cooking cabbage drew me on, emerging evidently from tiny cell atop Notre Dame (probably true of Eiffel Tower too) and a bright-eyed and beaming little woman materialized—scarf over head, leather oilskins, mittens, boots—and beckoned me.

I gasped, "No more, please!" but she beamishly insisted and we crossed a gargoyle ledge to the awful horror of God's own garden—saints and monsters all perched on air or dangling vertigo-making sidewise—and suddenly no church underneath. Two French girls cheered me on to follow this merry witch who refused my "Non, j'y reste" with a "Montez, madame, montez!" and I pitched behind her on up dark wooden stairs of an atticlike unsafety where the Bell itself sat. She bonged it to show it was 2nd finest in Paris—then came the Descent!!! The dungeon chill, the sense of stepping into infinity of B.C. and Ad Infinitum—left me chilled and in a sweat. The witch stayed aloft. I had already seen her black cat asleep among the lower Chimeres with Gene one dusky walk.

After that the young du Bois couple [William and Jane] restored me.* He has $100 a week from Viking to do (illustrate and write) children's books. . . . My great need is simply music (and I don't mean *good*, in fact *any*) and Jane's passion is Maurice Chevalier, who, she said, stares straight at her if she sits down front. We went to theater where he packs them in nightly—got usual seats, which they immediately changed to front row through 100-franc tip to usher, and Maurice appeared. They know it all by heart and I don't care much and I was largely concerned with desire to pee—due to frozen theaters, no dinner yet. Then we went to wonderful joint Chez Inez on rue Champollon (near

---

*William Pene du Bois (1918–1993) was an American artist and illustrator. His wife, Jane Bouché, later Strong (born 1922), had known Powell since her childhood.

Sorbonne), Inez being a handsome colored character with an Indo-Chinese gent, both singers and black. . . . Her songs are splendid—super-Fiske as no holds are barred. One song "Everybody's Pissing in the Bidet 'Cause It's Cold Down There in the Hall." Another one "Who Took Me Home Last Night?" with a guess in it that it was a guy who was French from the top of his head to the toes of her feet. . . .

Maria tells me Faulkner is in Lutetia as ideal place for celebrated anonymity. She also said the newsmen of *Le Monde* got him out at Floré and he got off some remarks on the negro that (says Maria) Finishes Him with France. This is bushwa—as I can well understand anybody's reaction to that superignorant sentimentality Europe and England have about the negro. You don't see the people who scold about it having any permanent black connections—they love them in the slumming way as Entertainers. Billy du Bois said sports announcers on radio described Ray Sugar* (as they say here) in his fight with Stouck as a fashion show and the announcers and reporters cried "Voilà! Ray Sugar appears in tres bean white—but beautiful—robe, his hair perfect, the crowd is going wild, now the beautiful robe white goes and—Mon Dieu!—the beautiful blue satin trunks—the crowd already accepts him as victor! Now Stouck in a dirty old brown robe—hair disheveled—he removes unfortunate robe and *dommage*! Dirty brown trunks. What kind of fighter is it?" Theory is that Ray Sugar killed him with embarrassment.

Love and again thank you!

(COLLECTION TIM PAGE)

TO JOSEPH GOUSHA

Paris
December 21 [1950]

Dearest Joe—

Am mailing my 1000-franc portrait done by itinerant painter at Deux Magots. I'm the one in the middle—almost looks like me but very flattering, too. Walked in on Jolases last night and had dinner with them and their ferocious tom kitten (Gene's special joy) Blitzy, a young hellcat of Fagin's breed. "Do Not Reproach Him, Maria, Please," Gene shouts at Maria as cat jumps on table. "Let him have my cheese if he wants but do *not* raise your voice to him!" Maria flabbergasted by sudden sentimentality in otherwise non–cat man. . . .

I wired Scribner's to send dough for emergency return (on a chance) and willy-nilly am counting on sailing January 12—*Liberté*. Would rather make it sooner but knowing I'm off soon makes delay tolerable. Arriving New York

---

*"Sugar Ray" Robinson (1920–1989) was a popular American boxer.

17th. Will hope for check from Margaret—anyway, why not send me $100 or $200 or in between if possible, which buys tourist ticket ($165) and will clear up hotel with possible Margaret's check or possible Scribner's coming through. Also would like to bring some armagnac ($1.75) to wear for Lincoln's Birthday.

Suggest in case Jojo happy in Philly you go down for weekend—stay at Valley Forge and go pick up each day on Saturday and Sunday New Year's unless a few days home pleases him more. Expect a few days' general rally when I get back to settle and then perhaps either I will go down or have him home for a first week in February or so. Use your judgment if any.

I realize this is expensive outing—especially considering the short (?) stay but the fact is the constant gray weather, rain, solitude, are not helping the novel right now (or is it that old Xmas migraine that travels in spite of one?). . . . As you know, Paris or no Paris, these old expeditions of mine to any Atlantic City for concentrated work run dry sooner or later and the minute it happens I must get home. Next time we'll do this for pleasure and mutual profit together. Oui? . . .

> Love and *dieudon* and see you soon,
> Dawn

(COLLECTION TIM PAGE)

TO JOSEPH R. GOUSHA, JR.*

Paris
Sunday, January 6 [1951]

My dear Jojo:

Here I am, getting more and more anxious to get home. I did not hear about your New Year's and Xmas yet and I hope it was a big success, and that you and Daddy had a comfy time. He wrote that you had just arrived and had been very quietly taking care of your household and personal duties. I had hoped to get a passage on the ship leaving here the 12th but all the fast boats seem filled so I have to wait for a long boat—I mean it takes nine days and will not get me there till the 25th. It seems an awfully long time to wait, and I am going to London to see my British publisher and agent. Everyone says I will not like London as the people are not very friendly but I am tired of foreign countries right now anyway and want my own home and family.

How was your Xmas program at Gladwyne? I received your postcard and

---

*This appears to be the only one of Powell's hundreds of letters to her son that has survived.

am always glad for news of you. We will have a lot to tell each other when we get together for the first time in ages, won't we?

Yesterday I saw young people going around town with little gold paper crowns on. It seems this is an annual holiday (Epiphany) when the bakers put a coin in their cakes and whichever member of the family bites into it is called King (or Queen) for the Day and the others give him or her the paper crown to wear and they go around the street (like our New Year's or Halloween) joining up with other young people who are wearing crowns. I never heard of such a holiday before. Sometimes they call it the Day of Kings. Then last night I saw a young man on stilts in front of the hotel. He had on a white fur coat and white fur boots and I was told he was a shepherd from the southern part of the country, dressed in sheepskin, and that they sometimes go about the fields on stilts to collect their sheep. Everyone has curious customs, and in America we have such a large country we have probably more varieties of customs than other places.

Today I went on a train from the St. Lazare Station (it looks very much like the old Staten Island Station, and the trains look like the St. Island ones). With a friend I went out to a lovely village, St. Germain-en-Laye, which has spacious parks and a view of surrounding countryside. It is the place where Louis the XIV was born. I rather hoped to see some of the French countryside but this was more like a suburban town. It was very crowded, too, as it is a place people go on Sundays to walk around with their families.

I am wondering how you are getting on with your music and painting, knowing how interested you are in them. I am anxious to hear if you have any new friends at Gladwyne. Daddy informed me an Xmas card came for you from either Tom Harvey or Walton, I wasn't sure which. Tom, I guess. If I had his address I would write to him from here.

Hooray—I leave here Wednesday—but I am not sure of my London address. Very likely I will hear from you before I leave or Daddy will forward it from home.

I have met an interesting man here, a Dutch architect from Amsterdam, who planned the Holland department of our old World's Fair in Flushing. He is very nice, quite old, and spent four years in a German prison. He plans Dutch exhibitions for big international fairs. He speaks some French and English, and he says that a Dutchman's language is so difficult that nobody else can ever speak it, so he has to spend half his life learning to speak other languages. He speaks English and French.

How did you come along with your cooking and how did you get on with Fagin?

I think about you and hope you are having a good time and soon we will have a reunion and talk things over. Be good and remember me to your friends. All my love and best wishes for 1951.

[No complimentary close or signature]

TO JOSEPH GOUSHA

[Paris
Undated; early 1951]

Dearest Joe—

Hangover. I experimented with Pernods since nobody here in decent circles drinks same. (Sort of workingman's drink—in fact, in the cognac country I hear they are so bored working in style they drink *hot* Pernod—very cheap and *beaucoup* lift.) So I had my own *berger* (40 percent) blanc, then I had *Ricard* which seemed better than any to me. (I'm the only person I know who likes them.) Also the *berger* and Maxiton (Parisian benzedrine, 20 cents) allowed me to write marvelous piece.

Traveling to London Wednesday—also too many chums here. Going Dutch is more expensive than being host (where you pick your place). Now I can creepy-weepy up on expenses.

Mail. *Promenade* buys charming gourmet article of mine, but only for $100 which saves my life and I'm asking them send me same at Brown's Hotel, Dover Street, London (not sure but wrote for reservation there).

Am writing marvelously due to this imaginary drug Maxiton. Also I no longer even try to speak French because just as I was getting good I realized that they are all Pelham or New Rochelle and I would be able to speak a good wifeish French whereas as a visiting American I can talk news with the men. The only real wits here know English (or Spanish) and love the language of wit—strictly a British invention. Anyway I am glad to report I won't need your finances darling but boy will I be glad to see you all!

Fondily,
Madame

35 EAST NINTH STREET

1951–1958

Back from Europe, Powell decided she needed to make some changes in her professional life and promptly ended her association with her agent, Ivan van Auw, and her publisher, Scribner's. Her friend Rosalind Baker Wilson signed her at Houghton Mifflin, where she would remain until 1958.

TO ROSALIND BAKER WILSON

[*35 East Ninth Street*
ca. July 1951]

Dear Rosalind—

Have you seen my Green Paper?

My situation with Scribner's is as follows, as near as I misunderstand these matters.

Since 1939 I have had one-book contracts with them. After publication of *My Home Is Far Away* in 1944 I signed a contract for a novel continuing the chief character but after about 100 pages gave it up in spite of Max's enthusiasm. I found contemporary life too disturbing and exciting to bury myself again in Ohio of 30 years ago. Instead, I wrote *The Locusts Have No King*, a New York novel in the N.Y. series comprising *Turn, Magic Wheel*, *The Happy Island, A Time to Be Born*. After this was published I signed for another book and again it was to be the Ohio book and after another struggle with it I ran off again to contemporary New York with the novel I am now engaged on, *The Wicked Pavilion*. Mr. Wheelock is very keen on this and would like the other one also. As sickness slowed up my production I wanted to have my short stories published in order to have more time on the novel, but Scribner's felt the novel must come first and later the others. At present I feel that my name has been out of print too long and that my chances of selling occasional short pieces would be greatly improved by publishing the short stories as soon as possible, and personally I need the incentive of a greater show of confidence to enable me to get *The Wicked Pavilion* done. As near as I can recall, I am into Scribner's for somewhere between $2000 and $3000.

The collection has never been offered anywhere as Perkins originally promised to bring it out "at the right time." My position is that a satisfactory publisher bringing out the stories could take over the novel I am now finishing or whatever arrangements normal people make. (Excuse the word.) My agents are Harold Ober, Inc.*

Baffled by title for short stories.† They seem mostly about women which reminds of one story *(Cosmo)* I liked but couldn't find called "Every Day Is Ladies' Day" (Petrillo could sue me for that.)‡ Mr. Gilman says to call it after the one N.Y. story "Such a Pretty Day." I'm rather bored with that as it has appeared in anthologies and somebody is always saying, "Miss Powell, did you write anything besides that *New Yorker* short story 'Such a Pretty Day'?"

> Champagne on ice with gin in the hold,
> Dawn

TO IVAN VAN AUW, HAROLD OBER ASSOCIATES

35 East Ninth Street
New York
July 31, 1951

Dear Ivan:

I find myself involved in several literary negotiations which I have to handle personally, much as I would love to dump them on an agent—any agent. Since most of my dealings these days seem to devolve (is this a word?) on me and I

---

*She would soon return to the Brandt Agency.
†Wilson herself would select the title of the collection *Sunday, Monday and Always*, which Houghton Mifflin would publish the following year. "It was taken from a song lyric," Wilson recalled in 1999. "It was just a spontaneous idea of mine—almost a joke—and I immediately tried to retract it because I thought we could do better. But Dawn had made up her mind and *Sunday, Monday and Always* it was."
‡James G. Petrillo was then the powerful head of the American Federation of Musicians, which had sponsored an unprecedented recording ban. Still, this reference remains unclear.

even have to do my own writing, worse luck, there is no sense in burdening a busy agent with my carbon copies, so the sensible thing is to part. I realize this will create a terrible financial hardship for your firm, but I'll make it up in other ways, little ways. You've really been wonderful and generous with so little to work on. When I have something to really drive an agent crazy with percentages I will hope to find you once again. Meantime let's both give up our business life and go back to bed where we were so happy.

Thank you for everything—especially your wasted time.

Love,
Dawn Powell

(COLLECTION TIM PAGE—CARBON COPY)

TO JOHN HALL WHEELOCK

35 East Ninth Street
New York
September 2, 1951

Dear Jack:

This is going to be a sorrowful letter so we must be very brave and not rustle our Kleenexes.

When I promised to have my novel ready by September for spring publication I did not know it was going to get bigger and bigger while I got littler and littler. About six weeks ago I got apprehensive but decided to make a last-minute rush for it. That was the moment my son was sent home for Home Influence and simultaneously a business associate of my husband decided it wise to drive his car through a Connecticut stone wall, smashing car, battering husband's leg and sending him home in a wheelchair. Naturally, the maid was on vacation and could come in only part-time.

I was the one who got the Home Influence. The ham in me was naturally gratified to find I was equal to these horrendous demands, but it kicked the novel out completely. It also made it necessary to cuddle my own nose to grindstone to pay bills. The suggestion again came up to publish my short stories as a means of keeping my name going and making it easier to sell new stories. You recall when this has happened before I weighed the situation and decided if my own publisher did not want to take such a step I would forgo the opportunity, since it would mean giving over the novels too, and losing the Wheelock guidance. (Or should I put you in this package deal?) However I am now obliged to take every step possible to increase my earnings and reputation, so I am herewith asking for release from Scribner's.

Would you please let me know how our finances stand and what adjustments we must make, and would you find out if Mr. Darrow has already boiled up the plates I could not buy at the time but could use now for the wedding? Or did they transform into Spellmania?

Friday the 7th lunch, as I said, is taken but the rest of my year is free. I could come in the office if you like or meet you in the zoo. I do feel badly about this and I don't want you to go around saying I'm leaving a sinking ship.

Let me know soon and here is my love and fondest gratitude for your and Scribner's past protection.

Dawn

(RARE BOOKS AND MANUSCRIPTS, PRINCETON UNIVERSITY LIBRARY)

TO JOHN HALL WHEELOCK

35 East Ninth Street
New York City
September 12, 1951

Dear Jack:

Thank you and Mr. Scribner for being so considerate in this parting. I have relayed the figure you have given me as my price of freedom and hope to make something of myself up north,* maybe another Pearl Bailey or Lena Horne if I had a touch more white blood.

I will know in a day or two just when and how this arrangement will be made. These financial partings sure do tug at the old heartstrings, don't they? At the moment all either of us can think of is money, money, money, but maybe later on in our mellower years the sight of a frayed old peacock fan on the office floor, a withered chrysanthemum (do you remember that game?) or a battered wimpus in the file cabinet will bring a little moisture to the old beadies.

More figures when I get into my other head.

Love,
Dawn

(RARE BOOKS AND MANUSCRIPTS, PRINCETON UNIVERSITY LIBRARY)

---

*I.e., at Houghton Mifflin, in Boston.

35 East Ninth Street
June 7, 1952

Dear Maria—

I can't tell you how shocked we were to hear of Gene in the *Times* last week. [Jacques] LeClercq had told me that Edith had written he was very sick but somehow with all the experience with death we are staggered when it happens. Several times I have passed the Winslow and suddenly wondered if by chance Gene had arrived, and have asked at the desk, thinking maybe I was psychic and would hit it on the button. But it never worked out and I thought he must have liked Ireland and stayed there, as he had planned to go there.

Now Dwight [Fiske] is here and he telephoned last night. He had been traveling and only heard of Gene from this week's *Time*. He said he had been shocked by his appearance. We had such a fine time on our expeditions when I was there and it seemed to me then he was happier and better than I'd ever known him. I attributed it then to being with you where he feels secure and happier. I am disappointed that he did not get here for so many people wanted to see him. What about his newspaper autobiography and could I be of any use here showing any of his mss. to publishers for you? I would be very happy to help. I wish you would come over here yourself for a reconnoiter. Poet Charles Norman, writer John Hyde Preston and many others back to early newspaper days have asked for details and expressed grief. He would be, I think, pleased and perhaps ironically amused at the belated hosannas he received for *transition*'s spadework in American letters.

We cannot believe it. How hard it must have been for you but how good that he did have you there. You have probably heard from Bunny who has been back at Wellfleet for several weeks, but must have heard by now.

My best to the girls, and wherever Blitzy is I'm sure he remembers how many times Gene had to scold you for Raising Your Voice to Blitzy.

"But, Gene, he was eating the cheese off your plate!"

"Never mind, he is welcome to my cheese, but please, Maria, never, never address Blitzy in that tone of voice!"

Love,
Dawn

(YALE COLLECTION OF AMERICAN LITERATURE, BEINECKE RARE BOOK
AND MANUSCRIPT LIBRARY, YALE UNIVERSITY)

TO JOHN HALL WHEELOCK

35 East Ninth Street
New York
March 6, 1953

Dear Jack:

Since I do not have the money to pay off the remains of my debt to Scribner's and since you remind me so tactfully that it was advanced to bring me back from Paris, I wonder if we couldn't settle the whole thing by your sending me back to Paris.

I do propose to pay this, dear Jack, if this alternative does not appeal to the Scribner's well-known adventurous side. I would thank you for your good patience in waiting for my fortunes to rise except that I do not feel your patience is as great as mine.

Let us bear with each other a few weeks more until Mercury is in Mars and Venus is in the Mint. I have many works out for sale at the moment and the bottom of the trouble is not really that I don't pay you but that they don't pay me. The gypsies say this state will soon be rectified.

Love and cooperation,
Dawn

(RARE BOOKS AND MANUSCRIPTS, PRINCETON UNIVERSITY LIBRARY)

TO PHYLLIS POWELL COOK

Dune Flat
East Hampton, Long Island
Easter Sunday [April 5], 1953

Dearest Phyllis—

This is a heavenly day on the ocean as I am here at the Murphys' for the weekend. Jojo won't be home till Tuesday as he is singing a solo at the Colony (Gladwyne) services (very loud I'm sure) and leading responsive readings. The Murphys' two small bulldogs are wearing red-jeweled "ranch-owner" dog collars as their Easter bonnets and I am wearing about 20 pounds extra, largely around the bust as my specialty. They are getting this house ready for some summer tenants and will drive back to Snedens Landing tomorrow, dropping me off in the City with a bagful of the large seashells that I never can resist lugging home from everywhere. . . .

I am hoping we can get a place on the beach as whenever I find myself here I realize how wonderful sea air is though the ocean waves here are too damned high for my type of swimming.

I think I tried Ayds once.* A woman I knew got very thin on them and has stayed so for years but advises everybody against them as she's had liver, onions, kidneys and other disorders ever since. What she would have if she had stayed fat I don't know. I have weighed over 160 (by one or two pounds) before but I never looked or felt fatter than now and, as you say, once you go over the hump—140, 150, 160—you get more fatheaded and care less and find it harder to lose. I have to do something as I am short of breath.

Monday a.m.

I am now sitting on log on beach with ocean rolling in on balmy Easter Monday. The oldest dog, Edward Lord Palmerston K.C.B., has just arrived and wants me to throw my glasses so he can retrieve them. The black baby dog (bull miniature) has brought me an empty box of ice cream and would like a bite of human food. I am waiting to be driven back into town. Joe said over phone the *Evening Post* reprinted a story of mine in the magazine section Saturday and I am steaming up rage to know why I wasn't asked and who got paid for it—since I wasn't.

I was fascinated to hear about Sabra [Powell].† I really have come to the conclusion that she never knew she was being and *is* mean any more than we ever knew we were a nuisance to anybody. I sometimes wonder (but try not to) what I would do if a relative or husband deposited three little dolls like us to be cared for (as well as supported).

I told you Charlotte Johnson—my tall, chronic old-maid friend from Lake Erie—got married a few months ago at the age of 58 or 59. He is a retired gent—English—and must be at least self-supporting as she would never be one to forget his share of the bus fare is 8 and ½ cents, payable now. . . . Yes, that was Tanaquil LeClercq. She married her dance idol, George Balanchine (fifth marriage for him, age 60), much to her parents' pride and joy. I think it saves him paying her a salary in his ballet. . . .

Love,

Dawn

---

*This unfortunately named product was a popular weight-loss medication.
†Sabra Stearns Powell, the author's stepmother, was still living in Ohio. These are among the kindest words Powell ever wrote about her.

35 East Ninth Street
Wednesday, August 26, 1953

Dearest Maggie—

Jojo was home all last week with a gay program of swimming, church, movies, Cloisters, etc., all to stave off return of bad spell he'd had before. Friday night he was brooding over what new frustration he could think of when his crush, the Newark hospital lady, Mrs. Roberts (age 59), came for dinner and an Ohio cousin and new husband came in. Louise [Lee] tried to cook, Joe tried to mix drinks and the general hullabaloo seemed to fill Jojo with a rapturous calm for he was only too happy to go back next day. The nurse lady had marched through martinis into highballs, finally said she couldn't get back to Newark, so I gave her my bed and then Joe and I towed her upstairs with a towline, all of us falling down every two steps and ending in a heap on my bed, disentangling later to dispose host and hostess on two boards in the living room which might have had spikes for all we knew. Next day, Mrs. Roberts was fresh as a daisy, being no neurotic-type drinker but a hardy Quaker type from Philly and she said, "Brother, I enjoyed every minute of that wingding." A fine type, with Jojo hugging her on one side and Joe moving in on the other while she talked—as Jojo said politely—all about herself!

The Cape air changed me so that Carl Brandt sold a story to *Esquire* for me on my return—very handy for Jojo's extensive demands. I dined with Gerry Hickey and several fine men, also Annetta [Hart], the other night. I have decided that the "other sex" means men under 40. As soon as they're over that, they might as well be women.

Dwight Fiske is back in town after a long and successful California tour—so successful he has to go into N.Y. Hospital for a double hernia operation. . . .

[Ann] Honeycutt has been under tests at Lenox Hill for the permanent fever she's had for a year or two but they find nothing. I do not think doctors know what ails you till you're dead of it.

Lafayette almost down, alack. . . .*

Dawn

---

*Powell's beloved Hotel Lafayette and its sister establishment, the Hotel Brevoort, were in the process of being demolished to make room for a new apartment building.

TO ROSALIND BAKER WILSON

35 East Ninth Street
September 22, 1953

Dear Rosalind:

This letter is, I'm afraid, going to be a very difficult one for me to write.

This is because 100 workmen are digging up Ninth Street and 100 others are blasting the buildings from Ninth to Eighth all underneath my casement window.

I was glad of your crisp note (?)* as it showed interest and pleasantly indicated that H.M. [Houghton Mifflin] was panting for the work. Furthermore said Work was at a point where I should be reminded that it is old enough now to go to work but I keep curling its hair and putting its finger back in its mouth. With a tear or two, then, I am packing up its store clothes ready to go to town. Pardon my figures of speech even if you can't pardon my figure.

This book has been particularly difficult because I was more excited about the idea to begin with and expected more of myself than anything hitherto, so every time I'd start looking it over I would be disappointed that it was still not *War and Peace*. It has taken longer and used more paper and revisions have been through more Final typings than anything before. Since I stuck myself on a limb by having it as almost immediately contemporary when I started, it began dating faster. Why, when I started that book the hero could get a telephone call for a nickel, and even ride on the subway for the same—at least I think so. I would read over a chapter and think of my vast teenage reading public saying, "What's a nickel, Mommy?"

That's why my next novel is damn well going to be about one woman and she's as fixed in a fixed old past as a fixed cat. (THE FIXED CAT?)

Your note was therefore very tonic in reminding me that the important thing was to wrap the whole thing up before I had to go over and change prices all over again. . . .

Dawn

*Wilson had written Powell a brief letter urging her to finish *The Wicked Pavilion*.

TO ROSALIND BAKER WILSON

35 East Ninth Street
January 2, 1954

Dear Rosaling [*sic*]:

I am still working on the line you suggested which is necessary for the second half [of *The Wicked Pavilion*] and will send you the substitute pages this week re: Ellenore, also Jerry.*

A postcard sketch of myself and a pal at the old Lafayette from Reggie Marsh last week gave me the idea that he might be had for the jacket—the interior of the café which could be completely the Lafayette (later to be denied, of course)—the red velvet curtains, etc.†

I would like the book presented as if it were a gay place to *go*, not a book to read. I dislike any emphasis on a Greenwich Village approach which always conjures up Maxwell Bodenheim, fairies, lesbs. and Bowery types, whereas the "Washington Square" phrase sounds more worldly, intellectual and gayer.‡ You may as well indicate that the original of the Café Julien was the now-defunct Lafayette with touches of the Brevoort, etc. However the three brothers Orteig who ran the Lafayette are still around and should not be given reason to froth. None of them were cooks, as far as I know, and none bachelors, but they may resent the fictionizing more than the truth. Also, as you know, I make the place a restaurant, not a hotel, even though there are cheap lodgings above.

I should like to okay the jacket. As an old Lafayette fancier, Reggie might do it. I would like it to have a shock of recognition (courtesy of E.W.)§ for those who knew the place and a sense of pleasure ahead for those who don't know it. Like standing in the café door looking around to see who's here and what's new tonight.

I think you can indicate that there are characters who may be recognizable to many in the literary and art world (I shall of course deny this and with good reason as some of the people formed their lives to fit the books, it seems to me, instead of vice versa). . . .

Dawn

---

*Jerry and Ellenore are characters in *The Wicked Pavilion*.
†Powell's old friend Reginald Marsh (1898–1954) was, in fact, persuaded to create the book's cover, which bears a close resemblance to Powell's vision of it as described here.
‡*The Wicked Pavilion* would be promoted as Powell requested, as "a novel of Washington Square."
§A reference to Edmund Wilson's anthology of American literature, *The Shock of Recognition*.

TO JOHN F. SHERMAN

35 East Ninth Street
June 24, 1954

Dear Jack—

[. . .] Here is the Indian story.* I must have been with Grandma at the time I first heard it, though I thought it was Auntie May who told me. At a family reunion (probably the summer during college I spent at Grandma's) someone got up and said, "I think we should talk more of our Indian heritage," and somebody else got up and said there were little children present and our family was as good as anybody's and no need to stir things up. This intrigued me and I pried around and Grandma told me a lot—all involving an Indian raid around Bellville in which a white girl was kidnapped and much later was brought back by a rescuing party led by one Captain Kidd or Kyd (not the pirate) and she later had a child (daughter I suppose) who must have been our grandmother's mother for she married a bound boy named George Miller. A Granny Rogers figured in this. The whole story was fresh enough in my mind when I came to New York, for according to Grandma or Aunt Lib it made us (you and me, kid) ¹⁄₁₆ Indian. Mabel knew this and whether she believed it or not she and I started an Indian whoop at Uncle Cline or some uncle at that family reunion Auntie May had there in the park next to you.

Here is what Myrtle [Taylor] told Phyllis and me. Uncle Ide had told it all to Aunt Lib—that Grandma Miller (our grandmother's mother) was a half-breed Indian. She was a fine, noble woman, it seems, an expert on all herb medicines such as the carrot salve Auntie May and Grandma made and other things. She raised all her children on one-pot dishes, was very wise. There was some scandal about her marriage to George Miller as it had been an Indian "marriage" and they had to marry again white style. (Phyllis was careful to get this cleared up but personally I still wonder.) Myrtle said Granny Rogers lived in a cabin somewhere and about this time it dawned on me that Granny Rogers must have been that kidnapped girl who had the Indian boyfriend. About this time, too, Phyllis began remembering something about the Indian's having been very good to her. Good? Hell, he was a wow. Whether Grandma Sherman's Indian Grandpa was alive during her childhood I don't know but I do recall that whoever told me first said the tribe around Bellville would have been the Delaware Indians. I think Phyllis forgot to clear up whether Grandma Rogers had a double-ring ceremony with the real Indian. Anyway I love the whole story.

---

*Most of the people mentioned here are Sherman cousins in the Shelby, Ohio, area, where Jack Sherman was then still living with Orpha May Sherman Steinbrueck near the house in which both he and Powell had grown up. Powell's "Indian heritage" has yet to be either proved or disproved.

If you should visit Myrtle—and you will enjoy her and her antiques— remember this: that she told us Dr. Taylor hates the Indian taint and won't have it mentioned. She said he also deplores his own Irish blood, but you got to take your blood where you find it. He is interesting, and all of them know and love New York so you don't get that claustrophobia some relatives give us. . . .

You were both wonderful to take us around and give up your beds and hand-labor and it is only too bad that we must always concentrate our family reunions so much that we all blow up taking everything in. Next time I'm going to stay in a Cleveland hotel and train out for a day at a time here and there so beware of a dark stranger. I loved seeing June's house and Adelaide and Rita and Burt and Suzy Q. and above all Auntie May and Jack and am most grateful—

Love,
Dawn

(COLLECTION JOHN F. SHERMAN)

OPEN LETTER ABOUT *THE WICKED PAVILION**

[Summer 1954]

I have a peculiar feeling about this *Wicked Pavilion* novel—a feeling I never had about my other novels after they were finished.

I miss it.

As a writer you live the lives of your characters so intently and for such a long time—years, usually—that it's a great relief to get it published and go back to living your own life for a little while, at least till the next novel starts crowding you. But *The Wicked Pavilion* was different—I think because it was so immediately contemporary that every day something more happens that belongs in it. It's too late, of course—it can't go on running like a TV serial. What I wanted to do in this book especially was to make the characters live so that their lives could extend beyond the limits of the book—and I may have succeeded too well for my own peace of mind.

I thought in this book I would let the characters create each other—that is, so you, as the reader, get to know them not by what I tell you so much as by what other characters say about them. They're made up of gossip, you might say. It happens that way in life. There are certain persons you feel you know all about, yet you've never met them and perhaps never will. One mutual friend has told you this, another has told you something totally different, you pick

---

*This letter/memo was evidently provided to Houghton Mifflin as an author's statement, probably intended for use in marketing.

up a bit here and there accidentally and you end up knowing more about this person than his best friends know—more than he himself knows. In fact, if you ever were to meet him, you might burst out with something most indiscreet like "Oh, what a dreadful time you had with that second daughter of yours, and if you only knew what *I* was told you could have saved yourself so much . . ."

What I mean is that the lives of strangers weave through our thoughts through gossip and hearsay and become part of our experience. The people in *The Wicked Pavilion* exchange confidences about each other, gossip about other friends until you—as their unseen guest—know them and have your own opinion about them before they enter. The advantage these fiction friends have over real friends is that if you take a dislike to them you can slam the book shut—and how often you've wished you could do that to even the dearest of friends.

The focal point of this story is a place I call the Café Julien, a French café off Washington Square—I combined the Lafayette and the Brevoort so as not to step on toes. Both of these hotels have been torn down in the last five or six years and with their going a very special way of life went—frankly, I think the way of life was going before the buildings went. For writers, artists and people who work alone all day, this particular café life was almost a necessity. In our work we can't plan a social life too definitely—we never know but what we may get going good just when we're expected at a dinner. We do know that we'll want to see somebody—anybody, sometimes—after being locked up with ourselves all day but we daren't risk tying ourselves down any more than we have to. So we depend on running into friends by chance when we're through work—stay a little while or for hours as we like—feeling that, in spite of the isolation your work demands of you, you are in touch with the world. I do not think this sort of casual life would appeal to young people looking for sheer fun or gaiety, for the pleasure comes from chance conversation and impromptu meetings with a variety of people, some living such different lives that you've never had a chance to become friends. You enjoy each other all the more for knowing the contact is temporary—like cruise acquaintances.

As I say, this special kind of retreat has vanished and that's why I wanted to re-create it in fiction before it was completely forgotten. In my Café Julien sometimes a person got there too early or too late to find whatever they sought. The lives of these characters, you may decide, depend on just what time they got or didn't get to the Café Julien. Dalzell Sloane, for instance, the middle-aged artist, would have had his whole life changed if he'd waited ten minutes longer, because that was when the big advertising tycoon came in looking for him to give him a job. But if he'd waited I wouldn't have had a book. What a difference ten minutes sometimes makes in all our lives.

(COLLECTION TIM PAGE)

TO PHYLLIS POWELL COOK

35 East Ninth Street
August 9, 1954

Dearest Phyllis—

[. . .] Everything has been looping here—Louise is uptown with some friend and I send her a few bucks when I can, largely in gratitude for having her away.* At the moment my chief comfort is a balcony (off the bedroom) full of morning-glory vines which I got started on the roof and then brought down. It has been cool in our place and around here except for two nights. Usually we have at least three weeks of muggy nights—now we use a light blanket or two.

Jojo was remarkably good in most ways applying to mind, helpfulness and adaptability but this time he got slowly worked up over "Will Deesie [Louise Lee] never come back?" and then this worked out into an obsession about wanting to be black, and repeating this over and over with other angles till I had to face the fact that it would get worse and what form would it take—?

Gladwyne seemed certain they wouldn't take him back—partly financial, as he's had very low rates, and then his running away so often, an embarrassment for such an institution. So we aimed at a nearby place, city-owned, named Creedmore, where friends had been, but for the city places (you pay a nominal sum based on salary) he had to have two weeks under observation at Bellevue Hospital. He's been there ten days and first I was favorably impressed and relieved as he was interested and there were more young men there his own age and they had art, music, etc. Then Friday he tried to run away and he was put in a terribly dingy bad ward where I went yesterday and could hardly keep from bawling as he said, "Mother, if you weren't sick when you came in this place you would be when you got out."

Tomorrow we go to the hearings as to his diagnosis by two doctors and find out where he's to go. I know we alone cannot handle the case even if we did nothing else, nor if we had two permanent attendants for him, as his nervous energy is terrific—more or less feeding on others' to nourish itself so everybody around is a wreck by night when he will say innocently, "I enjoyed the sail today and the walk and now let's take a bus ride over New York before playing Parcheesi and reading Mark Twain!" *Every* day! And never knowing when a criticism or sharp word from somebody may set him off into either hysterics, tantrums or blackouts.

I have quite a strain trying to discuss promotion of my new book and the writing of the next one—wondering how I ever did anything—and not wanting anyone to know I had any private worries or they'd tear up the contract and say if she's worried, she won't be able to fulfill the deal.

---

*Louise Lee had in fact suffered a stroke and would never return to the Goushas' employ.

I am terrified the hospital will shoot him off to some upstate place without telling him or us and then he *would* go off or else I would. At least he likes his night nurse who is very good to him, he says, and another patient knows Bobby.* I cheer myself up easily. . . .

This book deals mostly with the characters of Marcia and Almedy living in Cleveland with the Putneys (the Chautauqua man from *My Home Is Far Away*) and doesn't get back to the old family, you'll be relieved to know.†

love,
Dawn

(COLLECTION TIM PAGE)

TO EDMUND WILSON

35 East Ninth Street
August 27, 1954

Dear Wig—
    In the night (watches of) I composed a song—

> *I'm sick and tired of getting drunk*
> *Of gin I'm tired and sick*
> *If wagons took me anywhere*
> *I'd board one good and quick.*

I hope to build this into something fine later. I hear Saroyan's cousin has a new song called "All I Want Is All There Is and More." Will it ever replace "Dearie"?

> *I hate the pals with whom I drink*
> *The drinks that make us pals*
> *I'm tired of chopping ice and mint*
> *To keep up our morales.*

I thought your play reviews were provocative and rather jealous, though the *Times* was good.‡ Henrietta Holland called me to say your house was utterly wonderful.

---

*Bobby Morrison (born circa 1916) was raised by Louise Lee as a son and became Jojo's closest contemporary companion.
†Powell was still working, however temporarily, on the abortive *Marcia*, her long-meditated sequel to *My Home Is Far Away*.
‡Wilson's collection *Five Plays* had recently been published.

Will I join you on the wag, you ask
But then I shake my head.
For I am so conservative and
The wagon is so red.

No, that won't do. I must search the bottle for a more felicitous climax. Things are settling down here in a most constructive way though I still worry about the outcome. It is pleasant having everybody away all summer though soon all will be rushing back to their analysts, heavy with summer guilt and tanned with insecurity. I went to another party of Liz Dunlap's and found her charming and evidently happier. Have I told you I have busied myself inventing a plastic bidet for shut-ins?

Will you and Elena be on hand for Houghton Mifflin's party on Sept. 9 here? I have not invited my closest chums as I want to feel free to fall down personally without dancing drunk-attendance.

Humph

Now I will write the music. Did you know I write the words before composing the air? Isn't that interesting? It all depends on the performer. I think it should be done by Sophie Tucker dressed in a wittle-girl ruffly dress, hair in curls, who comes on with her wittle chair and plops it in midstage and herself on it. She should have a couple of front teeth blacked out and maybe one eye or is that too modern? With her finger in her mouth at the same time stuffing a bean up her nose she sings this haunting little song.

At the end a dozen chorus-men pogo in on retirement pensions dragging little red wagons and throwing her from one to the other and then at the audience of whom I count you a member, leader of the clap section.

(YALE COLLECTION OF AMERICAN LITERATURE, BEINECKE RARE BOOK
AND MANUSCRIPT LIBRARY, YALE UNIVERSITY)

TO PAUL BROOKS*

35 East Ninth Street
October 18, 1954

Dear Paul:

Is it time for a new printing of *Wicked Pavilion*? Julian tells me it is still selling well and is over 6000 with very promising futures. He was pleased that a small highbrow bookshop opposite the New School had grudgingly taken only a few copies as they had no trade in anything less than Kafka or Kierkegaard, but this week reported they had sold over 30 *WP*s, were reordering five more

---

*Paul Brooks (born 1909), an American editor and author, was associated with Houghton Mifflin for more than half a century.

for the Circulating Library alone, and that the library readers came back to buy the book. Let us hope this is indicative of all shops all over the world.

Personally, I find mounting interest wherever I go—letters, phone calls, even flowers from strangers. A young playwright called me to say that during his play's opening last week he had done nothing but hole up in a hotel with gin and oysters and the *WP*. He said it would be of interest to science that it was possible to exist 72 hours on gin and oysters and Powell. He called again last night to say he was reading it all over and that "liquers" on page 306 should have two *u*'s in it. I refrained from saying Brother, I think you have two liqueurs in you too. He was right, however.

In the event of reprinting I enclose a list of errors brought to my surly attention.

Rosalind [Wilson] said it was usually advisable to reprint as soon as it got into the last 1000.

Best,

Dawn

(COLLECTION TIM PAGE—CARBON COPY)

TO GERALD AND SARA MURPHY

35 East Ninth Street
New Year's Day [1955]

Dear Sara and Gerald:

How nice of the *Caronia* to sail again and leave you the mad tourist's house quarters.

I think a fur-lined bathtub is really not a bad idea—maybe foam rubber for fur and a great loofah blanket while natives fanned you to soft music. Speaking of natives, little [Truman] Capote's house of flowers sounds like a house of cards.* The tickets and walls were to be perfumed with a rare tropical incense but the major reviews, alas (I mean hooray), were not. I was sorry to miss the opening for—as at [Capote's] *The Grass Harp*—Men of Affairs flew in from all over the world and up and down the aisles. It seems Pearl Bailey was promoted to Harold Arlen's chaise longue during Philadelphia and this gave her delusions of directing and managing, causing cast dismay and revolts. The pre-opening ad with haughty announcements that tickets would be "available" in March (but only on one or two days) and possible in June must have caused critical disapproval—as if When the Boys Stick Together We Don't *Need* You Bastards! Anyway there were enough surly reviews yesterday for Truman C. to win back many old friends.

---

*Capote's recent play, *A House of Flowers,* had not done well during its short stint on Broadway.

I thought Ernest H.'s use of his Nobel Prize position to defend Ezra Pound was probably the bravest thing he ever did—and in *Time*, too.* Nobody in a new powerful position ever seems to dare use it for anything controversial. I would have expected a ringing defense of motherhood.

Did you hear anything of Jinny [Pfeiffer] out there?

How splendid of Honoria to have a daughter!† I telephoned your secretary, Gerald, for your address and she was very responsive—in fact I was about to ask her to go dancing at Blossom Heath Inn.

I am writing this in Washington Square Park heavily beset by pigeons and drunken children whooping it up for New Year's.

Love and best to Honoria,
Dawn

(COLLECTION HONORIA MURPHY DONNELLY)

TO JOSEPH GOUSHA

[Yaddo, Saratoga Springs, New York]‡
Friday 7:30 a.m.
June 17, 1955

Dearest Joe—

Waiting for breakfast. Good trip up with your bought porter. True that trains have nothing to do anymore with Grand Central information or timetables as this one stops everyplace—running up side roads for new hamlets. Charles [Norman] and friend (with car) met me very politely. 25 patients here—two venerable ones I know, the rest unheard-of, youngish or queer. Females few and carefully chosen, as too young and too pretty might turn some of the boys normal and then what could the manageress do? But pleasant bright lads—sort of from the Ghetto to N.Y.U. or the Little Magazine. Hot and breathless up here at North Pole—cool nights. Mosquitoes take place of riveteers and carry switchblades—the black flies carry extra sets of chompers and slug you with their back feet in roller skates so beauteous walks a hazard. . . .

My room (sleep and work in same) is large and handsome—twin four-posters and chaise longue and two desks, great bath and two closets but distressingly goldfish-bowl as it is next to Ping Pong room in same house as before—on first floor by driveway entrance so have to keep dressed and smil-

*Immediately after winning the Nobel Prize, Hemingway had mounted a spirited defense of his old mentor, then considered a traitor for his Fascist activities during World War II.
†Honoria Murphy Donnelly, Gerald and Sara Murphy's only daughter (and, by this point, their only surviving child), had recently given birth to Laura Sara Donnelly.
‡Powell would spend two extended periods at Yaddo, an arts colony outside Saratoga Springs, New York. She found it much more congenial than the MacDowell Colony.

ing for perpetual window display or else draw shades and cower in dark. Going to bed at 8:30 or before—then waked up till 1 by other inmates' later hours or bedtime Ping Pong. Glad not to be in big house with more or less dormitory publicity though Charles has beautiful room and bath and also has my former work studio and sun porch here for work, damn him.

Food splendid as usual. Soon as I figure out some retreat will be pleased. Take stamped envelopes to Jojo—or perhaps P.O. is open there to buy same. Give Fagin a piece of cheese for me. Get suit.

Love,
Dawn

TO JOSEPH GOUSHA

[Yaddo]
Wednesday, June 21, 1955
Dear Joe—

This is most amazing, this place. Rooms cleaned and fresh sheets and towels twice a week. Iceboxes and kitchen equipment in case you wish to give party or keep wine cold. Superb cooking—fine steaks, creamed spinach with mushroom centers, strawberry shortcake-meringues, field salad, whatever you want for breakfast, all the coffee you want, etc. Music hall with fine library of records anytime anyone feels like it, etc. And a cocktail party (usually only time for two drinks) about every other day before 6:30 dinner.

Yesterday a new couple from St. Louis—writers and editors of a magazine called *Perspectives*—invited everybody to a large party here in the living room you saw. This was strictly Western, with unlimited choice of beverages, caviar (red) in sour cream and after dinner resumed again with the Las Vegas jazz composer (and drummer) Earl Cindars, playing his new composition in pitch darkness and later supernatural stories in dark. Where the hell is this—Grossinger's?

Today Charles [Norman] is taking me to some friends' place near Saratoga for dinner—they will fetch us there in their Jaguar. Up till 5, however, there is nothing but work and after 9 for me nothing but sleep though the night-trotting races attract some of the gifted patients here. . . .

I expect to come back Friday the 1st, as the Boonville trip to Bunny's seems too complicated. His house party is for the Fourth and I don't feel like dragging my wares around for the two days in between my exit here and my invitation there, unless Margaret proposes driving up which I doubt. It is not very far—about 100 miles from here—but sort of like trying to get to Sag Harbor by train from Port Jefferson and probably about a three-hour drive from here. I would prefer to go up this weekend if at all but hate to give up valuable working time.

Mosquitoes terrific. Also bees. We can pick all the flowers we want from all the gardens so I have a window of bouquets. Some very bright nice youngsters here—bright in the head but backward otherwise. "They tell me this town was a sort of resort once"—or "They tell me there are springs around here," etc. Mary Miller (Philip Miller's 70-year-old sister) went to town today to one spring famous for curing eye trouble.

love,

D

TO JOSEPH GOUSHA

[Yaddo]
June 27, 1955

Dear Joe—

I think I have finished a short story and either gotten novel over the hump or into a new one (hump).* Breakfast discussion is likely to take on a Campus English tone and the phrases "The exegesis of that . . . may I exegete . . . the matrix of metaphor . . . the matrices of symbology . . ." in (usually) the "new criticism" or T. S. Eliot's 4th Canto usually suffice to send me flying to my own speller. A playwriting young man complains that Advertising Language has poetry and pith but the New Criticism language is So Boring and Meaningless. The lads do enjoy it, though. Don't see how some of them can get through a whole summer of these deep discussions but they are nice and will outgrow it as they outgrew the Freudian vocabulary, I'm sure.

One group, including Charles Norman, graduates tomorrow and while he has been most kind his persistent anecdotes about Dr. Johnson have rather beaten us all down.

I don't want to fiddle around about leaving Friday but if Bunny does come get me I am told coming back from Utica on Saturday afternoon is no harder than from Albany itself. Am anxious to return to a less barbaric civilization.

Love,
Dawn

Am reduced to riding into town for the great purpose of getting peanuts for the King of Squirrels.

*Powell was then working on what became *A Cage for Lovers* (1957).

TO MARGARET DE SILVER

[New York]
July 31, 1955

Dear Margaret—

I keep carrying this paper around, waiting for the time to write a letter, and I will do so now while Jojo waits for Joe to have breakfast and return him to the fold, as I usually fall into a stupor the minute they leave.*

Did you hear from Esther [Andrews] re: her heart attack? Tommy [Wanning] telephoned her and said she reported she was taking it easy and Canby and maid were doing all housework. (I doubt this!) I suggested she go to Miami or New York to air-conditioned hotel and rest, as there is never any rest in your own home. Besides, the Key West doctors seem (by her admission) to be unfailingly no good. It is miraculously cool—even cold—here today and yesterday but the sun will strike any minute. . . .

I saw *Damn Yankees*, which was marvelously air-conditioned and easy to enter (with tickets!) and very charming—more like *The Golden Apple* than the uproar it sounds like. *The Seven Year Itch* movie was good because of that wonderful man Tom Ewell. Marilyn [Monroe] is slowly turning into Marion Davies.

Incidentally (or not) Miss Jackie Miller† appeared by magic and is the most refreshing, delightful, intelligent and beautiful girl I ever saw—calm, adjusted, and obviously upper strata. Under her worshipful wing, Mr. [Peter] Martin‡ reverts to his best side, so it seems to Wanning, Gilman & Powell, though I've not seen enough to say. She seems able to take part in any group or place without effort. Obviously far higher quality than any of the other young men we know seem to have gotten. Nothing seems urgent about this affair, as she's devoted to her job. However I wouldn't know—it's just pleasant to have somebody nice bring out the nice Martin—but this may be accidental. He had an excellent review in the *Post*.

About your kind invitation for 15th or so: I feel very guilty about pleasuring myself when rest of family is stuck. Besides, you will be full of your own family I'm sure and they would frown on your letting an off-family visitor around. (I'm protecting you from your reckless gestures.) If any easing of my present tight situation appears (four days family & housework—three days

---

*Jojo was now confined to Manhattan State Hospital, where he would live for more than a decade.
†Jacqueline Miller, later Rice (born 1931), would become one of Powell's closest friends in the last decade of her life and would later serve as her executor.
‡Peter Martin (1923–1988) an American writer and editor, was a cofounder of the City Lights Bookstore and one of Powell's favorite drinking buddies. He was the lovechild of Carlo Tresca and Bina Flynn.

writing, then four days writing and three days vice versa) will scream, for your attention.

Tell Esther to go North and air-condition herself.

Love,
Dawn

(COLLECTION JACQUELINE MILLER RICE)

TO THOMAS MONSELL*

35 East Ninth Street
NYCity
December 4, 1955

Dear Thomas Monsell:

I was delighted to hear from you and to know you thought of me. In fact I often wondered why you hadn't written before, but I guess you were busy guarding Xmas trees out at Greenport, holding the Shelter Island gypsies and other sea marauders at bay.

You said you read the Perkins letters.† I was really disappointed in the book for Max's sake because it sounded as if all he did was write kindly Uncle Don letters. I suppose Wheelock selected letters that were general in nature instead of applying them to an author's specific work, but it was the latter ones, of course, that showed his editorial perception. (Max's, I mean.) I used to have lunch or cocktails with him once a week either at the old Ritz ladies' grill or in the Coffee House or Chatham. Like most deaf people, he always selected a hushed spot where he could speak in a low gentlemanly tone and the vis-à-vis would have to shout his or her boyish (stet) dreams and frustrations to a roomful of frowning gentility. Who is that coarse buffoon yelling to that distinguished old gentleman? (Max might have just asked the Plot or the Personal Problem.)

I got around this by asking *him* questions so we never or hardly ever mentioned my work (I merely handed him the latest pages) but talked of Tom Wolfe, Hemingway, Fitzgerald etc. legends. Many authors seemed to think what the Good Editor did was to sort of go over their works with a blue pencil like a freshman theme, and I daresay Max did that too sometimes, especially with Marcia Davenport and Taylor Caldwell—the rather uninspiring talent dregs he was finally left with. Mostly though what excited any intelligent person (you know who I mean) was the glittering show of a noble mind at work

---

*The young Monsell (born 1933), then a student at Cornell University, had written Powell a fan letter and received this warm letter in response. He would later become a writer and educator.
†A collection of Perkins's letters to and from his writers, *Editor to Writer,* edited by John Hall Wheelock, had been published in 1950 by Scribner's.

on all sorts of experience. It had nothing to do with you or your ms.—but you felt inspired that such a person found you worthy of his time.

Another editor (Harrison Smith) said once bitterly, "The reason all authors regard Max Perkins as the greatest editor is that he's deaf and doesn't hear all the tripe the bastards are saying."

You have a wonderfully gifted typewriter—I laughed and laughed. My simple banana mind rejoiced today over such a mere slip in the *Trib* or *Journal* as the news that Marguerite Lhaski finds 85% of British females sleep with their finances before marriage. How I wish everyone was as easily pleased as yours very truly and take care of the trees this Yule—

Dawn Powell

(COLLECTION THOMAS MONSELL)

TO EDMUND WILSON

35 East Ninth Street
May 10, 1956

Dear Wig—

I had it on my mind to ask if you are at this very minute in town with your *Waiting for Godot* tickets in hand as it is so wonderful that you should come from all over the world to see Bert Lahr in it. . . .

The Pewlitzer annozments today remind me that nonproduction is the chief requirement. Imagine Elizabeth Bishop,* author at 45 of about 30 dowdy little constipated poems, rewarded because she—she *what*? Well, because she is the recipient of many other prizes. In fact I believe all literary and artistic prizes are given For Industry in Conning and Copping Guggenheims and other prizes and for genteel restraint in setting foot to paper or canvas, thus relieving the judges of tiring labor. In the same way, publishers and editors and film companies pay rates according to the author's penthouses, stables, etc. How embarrassing for Zanuck to offer $5000 to David Schine,† for instance, for his first novel if any. What kind of Schnuck does that make Zanuck? He has the gentlemanliness to offer not what the literary property is worth but what the real estate is worth—i.e., $300,000.

I wonder if David Schine whoever he is IS writing a novel.

Have not seen Dos for some time. I have, for about two years, been getting

---

*The poet Elizabeth Bishop (1911–1979) and Powell shared some mutual friends, most notably the artist Loren MacIver and her husband, Lloyd Frankenberg. Powell was not always so bitter about Bishop's work.

†David Schine (1927–1996) was then notorious for his close personal association with Senator Joseph McCarthy's chief aide, the lawyer and power broker Roy Cohn. He never published a novel.

Jojo on Fridays from the sanitarium at Ward's Island for weekends to condition him for future home life but last week concluded that it was merely conditioning me for Ward's instead, so I took the weekend off to see reaction all around and find faint rumblings from a beat-up brain, so may come to some decision.

Virgil Thomson's *Mother of Us All** was very delightful. Don't miss *Godot*. It is the great historic triumph of the clown. The great Nordic social worker mind is always horrified that poor people (in literature, that is) laugh or mix their cancers, maggots, hunger and futility with jokes. They SHOULD beat their breasts and say I am Underprivileged and I don't Forget it, thank God. Wipe that smile off my face—

Anyway, Checkhov and Gogol knew better.

Isn't there enough unhappiness in literature without going to real life?

Humph

P.S. Dos just phoned and will appear later. I fear my rude remarks about Pulitzer prizes sound biased by never having gotten any. Is there a better bias?

(YALE COLLECTION OF AMERICAN LITERATURE, BEINECKE RARE BOOK AND MANUSCRIPT LIBRARY, YALE UNIVERSITY)

TO ORPHA MAY STEINBRUECK

35 East Ninth Street
June 1, 1956

Dear Auntie May—

Have been wondering how Jack cleared the ocean.[†] It was so good to see him and everything was okay—we were going to dine in anyway as Jojo was home—so we had a really fine evening with him. I guess he was pretty tired and a little astonished to find himself really off. Did he tell you his fine new bag gave him zipper trouble and he had a time getting things strapped up? He was mad. After Rita [Sherman] had given him this splendid luggage to impress the Queen then he said he'd have to show up with that same old straw suitcase tied up with rope. . . .

A new enormous supermarket is installed across the street in the big apartment house where the Hotel Lafayette used to be. This means I am wandering around in there pushing my cart, snatching canned horse feathers or frozen manure half the time under the impression I'm saving a fortune. Then I have a ball pasting up the stamps and only today looked at the gorgeous fishing rod

---

The Mother of Us All was the second of Virgil Thomson's two operatic collaborations with Gertrude Stein.
†Jack Sherman, a passionate Europhile, had arranged to spend his summer abroad. He still lived with "Auntie May," who was then pushing ninety.

and electric hair dryer I can have free after $450 purchase of groceries. As a matter of fact I could get a complete washcloth with only $75 worth of grocery stamps. Joe is on jury duty this week and I'm catching up on his work by night. I have a fine, uneven tan from sitting on the roof. Hope your arm is healing. Give my love to Rita and the girls and Jimmy. Any minute I may lope out for a fast peek at you.

love,
Dawn

TO JOHN F. SHERMAN

35 East Ninth Street
June 5, 1956

Dear Jack:

By this time you are no doubt wondering what in God's name your cousin ever saw in an old fleabag like the Lutetia—such is progress.* Your notes came from London and the progress there seemed faintly familiar too. That incomparable British charm! It suddenly reminded me of long ago when any smashing gent with a good British accent was regarded by us suspicious natives as a bounder or else a real crook, bound to snare the widow-woman's mite and cheat at cards while getting off a Good One. Same way a female Southern accent meant the dame was after your menfolks unfairly.

Years and years and years of experience finally blast home the fact that lots of nasal Midwest and adenoidal female accents are after the menfolks, too, and millions of impossibly rude, crude, surly, charmless louts can outbounder the charmers. I believe, though, that what we mind most is our innocent surrender to the charm.

Another thing about that theory of yours that Somebody's GOT to be preoccupied with money. It's so true. In Paris, the American beachcombers there sit around the cafés bemoaning that old nasty American money-madness all the while they're ducking the check (to show how honest and European they are) and inviting their fellow bums to join in the free lunch. I think the trouble with you and me (I was always the sucker just because nobody else made a gesture) is that we have never gotten over our surprise at having a ten-dollar bill on us. If we've got that, we say to ourselves, then nobody else has anything at all, so it's really up to us. I can't get over early embarrassments at nobody's being able to make any gesture, so I make them, even though I am warned that the

*Sherman was then staying at the same Hotel Lutetia that Powell had resided in in the fall of 1950.

self-invited "guests" are merely being Worldly when they sit on their wallets and muscle in at tables and wiggle out at checks.

This reminds me of a warning. A large statuesque (heroic) blonde neighbor named Mary Grand ("Mary One Thousand Dollars," as a disillusioned boyfriend calls her) set off with her charming, precocious, eleven-year-old daughter (also a nymphomaniac, I think) for the Grand Tour last week and in the heat of a splendid farewell party for her I told her I had a cousin at the Lutetia. I should be sending nymphomaniacs to Newcastle! . . .

I must have been mad but if she should send word you can still be in Normandy (I'll bet you HAVE to go there) or else throw her in the bar for a drink or a fast anything before you are drawn into a rather cozy bed from which few escape with their shirts. Moreover she is traveling with a group of other N.Y. ladies and their young—a lady architect and others. Good God, maybe they'll all pursue you. Change your name. Mary ran away from Vassar or Smith some 20 years ago with Newton Arvin, her teacher (now a Pulitzer biographer), and presently discovered he was really hunting for Truman Capote, which sent her to psychoanalysis and constant reassurance that she can do it as well as Capote. Her next husband was handsome, rich Southern drunk type, father of child. She can be amusing and attractive in a large, warm, blond Holstein way but if you do get caught (forgive me) have excuses, alibis, Normandy, fiancée, ulcers, etc., all ready in case. She is a friend of Norman Mailer's, and has gay parties here. We are reconciled to sparring.

Is a jolly bar called the Montana still popular with Americans late at night—behind the Café de Floré? I used to eat often at a cheap (then) little place on the rue Recamier opposite the Lutetia. I think it was merely called Chez Recamier.* Do find me the names of all the variations of absinthe—berger, Ricard (I loved it), Pernod, anisette, and another one. . . .

Pull the covers over your head and pretend you're in Normandy.

love,
Dawn

Be sure and buy yourself *objets* you want before sudden friendships snatch all your money for their drinks. Better you should drink it all yourself! Act Rich! Be Stingy.

(COLLECTION JOHN F. SHERMAN)

---

*The restaurant, named Le Recamier, still existed in 1999.

TO BRYAN ROBERTSON*

35 East Ninth St.
July 16, 1956

Dear Bryan—

I laughed ha ha ho ho when I saw your envelope with address 4 Louisburg Square.† I had been wondering if Rosalind was on vacation or if you had found time to look her up and above all if you'd survived a Night at the Cedar with the Talking Men. I hadn't realized they were Black Mountaineers, I only thought they were the strange fruitflies from California who play guitars badly and bend ears. What they think is a book or picture in them is just a couple of beers.

I miss you and everyone speaks of you in the loftiest terms.

Buffalo must have seemed dim after the mysterious East and Brattle Inn.‡

The morning after the directors' meeting here—indeed, the day you left—I was rubbing a light Madeira over my temples when Dos Passos popped in and things began again. I told him your splendid words about him—you did say he was the best-dressed man in Ville Franche, didn't you?—and we stroked each other's brains pretending all the time we weren't really killing a fifth of Mother's Cutty Sark, dividing the cork quite evenly, then going over to Rickey's on all fours and having our dishes on the floor to show we live in a democracy. He regretted not meeting you, but I was slightly relieved as you might have been astounded at hearing what I said you said.

Saturday night about 6, those oil-soaked rags you dropped in Wanamaker's old store down the block here caught fire and Peter Martin and Jackie [Miller] and I studied the fire for a while. I think it's one of your best jobs since the Chicago one. It has been going ever since with fire engines and ambulances and, amazingly enough, thousands of visitors dressed for Mardi Gras or Coney Island wandering around University Place and Ninth Street, their shirts out, their cameras clicking, their children howling as the papa pushes them nearer to the spot where the cave-in or blowup is expected, and ice cream wagons rolling around. The ambulance's bell as ten more firemen collapse is the signal for a round of cheers and more pop.

Will it never end?

You ascribe sentimentality about the young to me. Yes. But then I spent my first 40 years being sentimental about the old. Then they started dropping dead or asleep (much worse) and there was no place for a sentimentalist to go but down. I think I like this better as giving more scope to my sugar-dimmed eyes.

*The English curator and art historian Bryan Robertson (born 1925), then on a British-sponsored tour of art galleries throughout the United States, delighted Powell, and the two became fast friends.
†Four Louisburg Square was then Rosalind Baker Wilson's Boston address.
‡The Brattle Inn was a historic lodging place in Cambridge, Massachusetts.

What dolls they are, I say, how innocent, not guessing what creeps they're going to turn out to be.

Mostly I find the Olders exhausting because they come with a whole mess of their dreary families clustering to them, either visibly or in the form of anecdotes—all sorrowful—and you shout at them through mountains of granite wife or husband or progeny, and you get worn out with kindness because they never got anywhere or lost it or her or him. I spring back in the old cage pretty fast, though, after an hour or two with the Talking Young Man.

I think you are terribly brave opening up new cities, one after another, with so many almost unbearably stupid ones among them. Be sure to carry a cask of 200-proof vodka across the desert as there is a shocking amount of dry art in the Midwest. Moreover, beneath the seemingly understanding gentility of Midwesterners is a brain as big as an olive pit.

If you should see John Latouche flourishing around Colorado where his opera [*The Ballad of*] *Baby Doe* just opened, you must give him my love. Also, Dwight Fiske may be playing in nightclubs in the West or South and whether you like his stuff or not he is a very dear old friend of mine and fun.

Be very careful of drinking water and kissing babies.

I will be at the Tin Angel, rather heavily veiled and reeking of House of Lords Fifth. I may be a little late and dried up.

I want to know Everything—Everything! Meantime I'm off to Brattle Inn with my ms. Your broad assertion that this novel was done inspired me to put back 30 pages I'd torn out.* Thank you, dear.

Fonderly yours,
Dawn

(COLLECTION BRYAN ROBERTSON)

TO MARGARET DE SILVER

35 East Ninth Street
Thursday, August 16, 1956

Dearest Margaret—

[. . .] Latouche's death was a shock and seemed a cruel incredible trick to keep mediocrity safe for mortality.† He will make a tough, indestructible little ghost, though. How time softens minds! For instance for years none of us (he or I or anyone connected) ever mentioned our embarrassing connection with that monster musical *Lady Comes Across*. Certainly never Latouche, me,

---

A Cage for Lovers.
†John Latouche had died unexpectedly, at the age of thirty-eight, of a heart attack.

Gower Champion, Vernon Duke, Mischa Auer, Joe E. Lewis, et cetera. Then in Touche's obit the credit crept in. And today the terrible little producer of it, Georgie Hale, died, and after tyrannizing over all of us, only got ¼ obituary space that Latouche did, but mentioning *Lady Comes Across* as part of his triumphs. Then I have been called to Theatre Guild TV department lately to discuss adapting short stories from *Sunday, Monday and Always* for the Steel Hour, and the director says, "Our lawyer is most insistent that we get you for this as he says you and Latouche did such wonderful work on some musical!" The lawyer was also Georgie Hale's at the time and never protected us from the mess or insults at the time. It was Bill Feitelson, as you may recall, as we afterwards reconciled at Herbert's.

The gist of this is that your successes are forgotten but your failures become successes, so why worry?

It is a heavenly day up here on the roof with cool balmy breezes and the sky as soothing (sour grapes) as the sea, without having to put on my bathing suit and go into it.

Jackie [Miller] is back but haven't seen her. Pete [Martin] missed her and said plaintively that the walls of freedom were too high for him and were closing in.

Difficulties about Jojo which Pete will tell you. He is mentally and nervously conspicuously improved—and a showpiece up there, they say, for the place's treatment—but now has sprained or fractured his ankle due to an attendant. So there is much palaver—discussion, worry—and his birthday next week when he planned to be home. Will know today if he has to be in cast. It means I have to take that trip to visit him two or three times a week. Much easier having him home. Have to go up to keep up protection for him really. However he sometimes enjoys a sickness as a break in the monotony.

Have you seen Rosalind? Esther writes poignantly of fear of dying without seeing New York again. I wish Tommy [Wanning] would go down and bring her up—I daren't trust myself on anything anymore. I'm sure I'd lead her to Montreal. . . .

Love,
Dawn

(COLLECTION JACQUELINE MILLER RICE)

35 East Ninth Street
October 1, 1956

Dearest Phyllis—

Where are you and what's your name and line? I think you will have to come to New York this winter to revive our acquaintance. Do you find the real tragedy of "maturity"—as I like to call it—is the slow process of being buried, not by gravediggers but by your Dear Ones, the Family? I thrash around nobly but there are husbands with buttons or no buttons all around, husbands who hate company, husbands who hate everybody, husbands who are dear little boys again—kicking and screaming and spoiled, God knows by whom. Marie (maid), who works for several families, is always telling me of ladies she has worked for for years who unanimously report that Old Husbands Are Bastards, because they suddenly turn into big Homebodies, only their Homes aren't big enough for them and anybody else.

I am jittery after the most hard intensive working summer. I think Joe thinks my writing is done in a Waring blender and no reason to take time off from house for it.

Did I tell you Theatre Guild bought one story (and is considering others) from my short-story collection and contracted for me to do the script—an hour's show for U.S. Steel Hour on T.V.? So I was up at 5 or 6 every day for weeks as it does require intense concentration and work to make an hour's play out of a five-page plotless story. I finished the first draft. Now I wait for them to go over it with a fine-brushed tooth (or fang) and then proceed all over with the Big Hay always waiting (though I got part of it on the contract-signing). Then the finished product is put in deep freeze till program time months away, if at all.*

Jojo comes home weekends and is very good again, looks fine in Jack Sherman's ex–brown suit. He is happier because he can rake leaves now, he plays basketball, has occasional piano lessons, takes part in plays and dances, and since he knows All the Words, Verse and Chorus, to All the Songs ever written from 1920 on, he entertains at parties up at Ward's. He is less nervous and I am constantly impressed by the special care he gets at a place where one wouldn't expect it. I guess the state hospitals are better, medically, now than private ones.

This neighborhood is much changed since you saw it. Big new beaver-board apartment houses all around us renting at $200 for two rooms and up—and since an ancient brook weaves underground in this neighborhood the

---

*Nothing ever came of this project, though Powell did complete a telescript from her story "You Should Have Brought Your Mink."

buildings have a tendency to get lopsided sooner or later. In one new corner apartment house where a friend of ours has a duplex penthouse at $500 or more a month, he had barely moved in before a mountain rose in the parlor floor and the bathtub started tilting. "Yes, this floor *is* buckling," said the superintendent hopelessly. Their baby doesn't want it fixed as he can slide down the humps. . . .

love,
Dawn

TO BRYAN ROBERTSON

35 East Ninth St.
October 26, 1956

Dear Bryan—

Why don't you get back here at once and get me out of these television coils in which I have been tangled ever since you left? If you had been here I would not be this broken reed I am today, fading in and fading out and jumping up into any friendly lap only to dissolve with little static barks of pain. No sooner did I finish and refinish and rerefinfinishish one script than another giant wished me to present another story of mine for TV. It is not the sordidness of the money involved, it's the difficulty of getting your mitts on it, and for all the tentuplicate contracts signed and vast sums mentioned the enterprise is a gamble. . . .

Your two letters delighted and amazed me. So this is what America looks like. Indians, you say. Sheriffs, bang bang. Posses. Rosalind Wilson and I think you must assemble your notes into an American notebook for publication here, to instruct Americans on America.

I never heard of Durgin Park—what a wonderful name for a fish house—till you mentioned it. Then in Boston a taxi driver taking me to the train said I shouldn't leave Boston without going to America's greatest restaurant (he said), Durgin Park, and I thought we were going there instead of New York for a brief moment. Now I hear of it often. Was it there before you invented it?*

Jacqueline [Miller] and Pete Martin were desolate because you left no traces—say an old letter or fingerprints. There are still the Footsteps on the Roof you heard and no clue. Pete quit his job and Jackie has temporary office jobs but this insecurity does not seem to affect their steaks-Old-Fashioneds-and-Cedar-Tavern life.

---

*Durgin Park remains a popular Boston landmark to this day.

The difference between public communication systems and reality is becoming extraordinary here. It is like the Dark Ages with people writing in Latin and conducting their lives in Italian and never the twain meeting. For instance the papers and radio firmly insist Stevenson has a cold, unappealing personality compared to Eisenblatz, whereas wherever he goes people throw more fits of ecstasy and rapture than they do over Elvis the Pelvis. Nobody ever heard of Eisenhower's having a close friend, except corporations, and when the boss changes Eisenhower changes friendships.

There was such an early election hullabaloo this time that by now a booming apathy has set in, and any new face on either side could get a rousing welcome. Now Mr. Eis. has promised the People of Our Free for All that he is going to have a Physical on Saturday. This electrifying news is supposed to solve all problems and also show what courage he has. A Physical! You don't see ordinary men having the guts to go see a doctor, do you?

And What in the World do you suppose this doctor is going to find? Can't you see the headlines?:

DOC TELLS IKE HE'S IN AWFUL SHAPE

ENLARGED HEART ... CANCER ... LEPROSY ... V.D. .... GALLOPING SENILITY

IKE PROMISES USA HE WILL RUN ANYWAY BUT PROMISES NOT TO DO ANY WORK.

No, I fear we will hear that For a Man His Age—etc.—and he has the liver of a boy of 40.

Separate Tables opened here last night to hurrays for the Best of Rattigan. Grace Kelly, speaking her "Broadway British" with ladylike difficulty, woodens and larks around in a most embarrassing style in *High Society*—proving I don't know what, except that two can play at being Joan Crawford. . . .

I am so glad I found you there at the airport in the basket on 4th of July as it made summer very charming. Curious that you should arrive the day my young cousin [Jack Sherman] was to return from two months in France and England, because your letters of nostalgia for America are like the ones he writes me from his horribly good job (he dassent quit it) in Ohio, in which he longs for everything and everybody and everything in France or England, and finds the touch of cellophane and the whiz of Cadillacs and Waring blenders incredibly repulsively American. However he saves up for two years and makes another luxury trip to make his village life endurable.

Did you find your Kent house still there after the storm?

Do write the book for Houghton Mifflin. I want to take you away from all that dirty art slavery.

Love,
Dawn

(COLLECTION BRYAN ROBERTSON)

TO ROSALIND BAKER WILSON

*[35 East Ninth Street
ca. late 1956]*

Dear Rosalind:

I am stymied on a short selling talk on *Cage for Lovers*. I confess to low state of spirit, or fallout. Euphoria may hit me any day since everything else has. Do you think I should stop blacking up and sticking my head through these curtains?

My impression, on finally being about a foot removed from the work, is that it is a new picture of what happens to the young ambitious individual today, different from any other time in our history. The old pioneer values— sense of adventure, courage, etc.—are useless without real collateral or the will to beg. All a young person can do (once they have taken a peek at the great world) is to Hang On—not go after what they want, but just hang on to what- ever there is: the family, the so-so friends, the lifeline—and the longer they hang on the more frightened they get of letting go the rope because where would they get as good a one to hang themselves with?

In another age, a girl of Christine's* independent nature would have resisted the security of life at Miss Lesley's, or being pushed in any way by affection, loy- alty or fear of failure. It is therefore hard to explain that her break required courage. The story actually describes what happened when a girl said—as so many of us say most of our lives—"What am I doing here?" The longer she woke with this question the more she knew she'd better get out before it was too late. The next query—where was she going?—could not be solved till she had figured out what she HAD been doing there and where she HAD been going. She realizes she can only free herself from her old chains by finding new ones. She has been living other people's lives—first her mother's, and then Miss Les- ley Patterson's—until she can scarcely tell what sort of person she is. It is basi- cally the story of an impulsive, warm young woman, detoured but not corrupted by her quick affections, escaping to find her own special destiny. The search for herself is as suspenseful as if the quarry were her enemy.

*Christine Drummond is the novel's heroine.

Dear Ros—you see I'm trying.* Will try again but have had no outside reactions and am still IN it. At Brandts' the words "subtle, brilliant and intense" have come up but I cannot mince them right now.

Will try another day.

Dawn

(BOSTON PUBLIC LIBRARY)

TO PAUL BROOKS

35 East Ninth Street
February 16, 1957

Dear Paul—

It is such a nice day I was just sitting here wishing you would send me $250. I know you don't care what bauble I crave—handles for spectacles, a gold tooth, a bright new ribbon to bind my raven Royal, a fresh typed ms.—so I won't go into it but it would gloriously facilitate and felicitate the completion of this work.

For two weeks, *Cage for Lovers* has been perfectly wonderful—the longest time anything or anybody has seemed wonderful. I did the last chapter this morning but a spare part is yet to be done before that. I daresay I will have it done by the time the typist with twins has finished copying the rest of it. Two weeks or so, maybe. (I'm thinking in twin terms, her usual effect on me.) The book will not run over 70,000 words, I believe, unless I insert my still dangling TV play in the middle.†

I do have high hopes in a disinterested way for this book, first because the heroine does grow and learn and because it is basically about love. She finds that there is no nourishment in love (of any kind) that is subjugation, surrender and blind loyalty. Part of each person must be preserved, intact, not only as a perpetual challenge to the other, but as a support in the other's weak moments.

There is a good case for the Utter Surrender and Blind Faith school, too, but I'm pleading the other side this time.

This is not merely Love-Love but Friend-Love and Family-Love.

Christine loves people so completely she loses herself, and they gain

---

*Despite the natural strains arising between author and editor during the completion of a manuscript—in this case complicated by what amounted to a near-total rewrite of *A Cage for Lovers*—Wilson and Powell would remain friends until the latter's death. The book would be published in 1957.

†In fact, *A Cage for Lovers* is Powell's shortest book, at fewer than fifty thousand words.

nothing. Like the stage stars who give up the stage for the guy, but he doesn't really want a little doting missus, he wants an actress.

I do hope H.M. can send this by the Boston Bullion Express.

My best to all,
Dawn

(COLLECTION TIM PAGE—CARBON COPY)

TO J. SPIERMAN, MANHATTAN STATE HOSPITAL*

35 East Ninth Street
[Undated; mid-1950s]

Re: Joseph R. Gousha, Jr.
Ident. No. 621 394
Keener Bldg.—Manhattan State Hospital

Dear Sir:

I am enclosing a check for $100 to apply to the above account. In explanation for the delay in paying my husband must have told you at the time we placed our son at Ward's we were under a tremendous burden of debts both for his past care and for serious medical care of my own (including radium treatments for cancer, major operations, etc.). As I am a freelance writer my own contributions are never dependable—either uncollectable in the sense that an ordinary worker can collect, or unpredictable—so Mr. Gousha's salary is taxed for past and present emergencies as well as current costs.

It would be a great help if we could be permitted to adjust our monthly bill to a sum I personally could be assured of making—say $50—allowing Mr. Gousha's salary to apply to past loans and debts instead of facing an amount that can only be paid by chance. This could be readjusted to your original calculation within a few months, as we are permitted breathing space to pay off the arrears and our other debts.

I will be receiving advances on foreign rights to books of mine contracted for recently and sums are now being released to me. It will give me great satisfaction to direct this to you as I collect, particularly since our son has been showing marked improvement under this hospital's care.

Sincerely yours,
Dawn Powell (Mrs. Joseph R. Gousha)

(COLLECTION TIM PAGE—CARBON COPY)

*No further information has been found on J. Spierman, who seems to have been a person of some authority at Manhattan State Hospital.

TO DR. HOWARD ZUCKER*

35 East Ninth Street
February 9, 1957

Memo to Dr. Howard Zucker
Re: Joseph R. Gousha, Jr.

We noticed a new advance in Jojo's control after his stay at Mabon.† The change seemed to have stirred a different area of memories judging by his diary, for one thing, and I noticed, in reading it, that he was much more assured of his own importance. He referred to "*my* apartment," "*my* home," "*my* friend" instead of "the" or "our." The lack of medication (and quiet) seemed to have made him more sensible about commonplace things and aware of personalities around him, too, telling anecdotes about other patients or repeating what they had said. He seemed relaxed and confident of your belief in him.

He has been back at Keener now for about 10 days and is now home for the weekend. Several patients had told him the reason he had his vomiting spells was the manner he smoked—gulping and swallowing—so he informed me he wasn't going to smoke all weekend. I said I didn't have any cigarettes in the house anyway and he said, "I figured you wouldn't have." He has not yipped or rocked or muttered at all, though before his Mabon trip he was getting back in that habit, though he had not showed any other signs of tension.

He seems finally assured that his home is his—he sleeps late, bathes and shaves himself, gets himself coffee or whatever he wants, makes tea and brings it in for both of us when he likes, makes the beds and, without any fuss, adapts himself increasingly to the family habits and routines. He reads for long periods instead of glancing over something, and went to considerable trouble fishing out articles on Manhattan State in some newspapers which he pored over with great interest.

Regarding his nurse "Deesie," she was a big fine-looking woman of 42 when she came to us (he was two)—half American Indian and part white and negro, proud of her New England background but not above occasional hard work. Her attitude toward Jojo, however, was completely Mammy; that is, while we were trying to teach him to do things for himself, she was determinedly trying to make him completely dependent upon her. It was impossible to persuade her that if she loved him, she would not handicap him, since her own security lay in his helplessness. She always felt that anything the family did together without her was bad for him (since it was bad for her) and redoubled

---

*Dr. Howard Zucker (born 1916) was a prominent New York psychiatrist long associated with Mount Sinai Hospital. One of the first American practitioners to take an interest in autism, he saw Jojo regularly at Manhattan State Hospital, and their association would continue for thirty years.
†Mabon and Keener were two buildings at Manhattan State Hospital.

her cosseting. She was really an excellent nurse for a sick or old person, which gave her power and control she couldn't have otherwise.

She refused to be fired when we could not afford her or when Jojo went to Devereux and Gladwyne,* and we were in the position of keeping on a sort of mother-in-law (a colored one at that) who could not be put out like an ordinary employee. Since both Mr. Gousha and I resented the burden, increasingly we were apt to be critical of her baby-talk and baby-treatment of Jojo, which doubtless puzzled him. She was chiefly anxious to have him at her side so that there would not be *three* in a family with a servant. As his personal attendant she was in a position to demand and control.

Outside of her excessive piety and babying, she was a good sensible woman and gave him a great deal of love and devotion, which members of her own family had managed to wriggle out of.

I do think that Jojo's improvement in practical outlook and freedom of reasoning since he went to Ward's, though due largely to the treatment there and your own invaluable patient insight, has been immeasurably helped by Deesie's absence in our home.

[No complimentary close or signature]

(COLLECTION TIM PAGE—CARBON COPY)

TO ROSALIND BAKER WILSON

35 East Ninth Street
March 27, 1957

Dear Ros:

I am sending you under separate comforters three former novels of mine— *Turn Magic Wheel, The Happy Island* and *A Time to Be Born*—which would be ideal for an omnibus volume, as all are out of print and I have many requests for them. The same characters run through them—in fact, they turn up in *The Wicked Pavilion*, too. The man, Dennis Orphen, in the *W.P.*, who is writing in the café, is the hero of *Turn, Magic Wheel*, later popping up in the *H.I.* and in *A.T. to B.B.* No one ever noticed this, by the way. These novels belong to one period, leading to World War II, and might be done under one title— *Magic Wheel.*

For some reason the Midwest English teachers are taking me up at the rate of—one a month at least. Illinois, Minnesota, and last was a Marguerite Young,[†] a poet and writer (I think she did a book once on the Robert Owen

---

*Devereux and Gladwyne were two of the institutions where Jojo lived during his youth.
†The writer Marguerite Young (1909–1996) is probably best known for her massive, poetic novel *Miss Mac-Intosh, My Darling.* Later she would become almost as much of a Greenwich Village fixture as Powell.

colony and writes for little mags) who is enthusiastic about *W.P.* and wants more for her course at University of Iowa for her American novel students. These books seem to give everybody a big nostalgie—very happily, I understand.

A publisher has asked for my autobiography.*

I shudder. . . .

[No complimentary close or signature]

TO PETER MARTIN

[35 East Ninth Street]
April 17, 1957

Dear Peter—

Oh looky, I shouted, see what's in the mailbox—a letter with no window. (Memo to Juvenile Department: "The Little Letter That Didn't Have Any Window.") And a Washington stamp on it. Booker T., too.

I am glad Washington has welcomed you with open tentacles. It is the worst city to be lonesome or even alone in, because there's nothing to see but sights and nothing to do but jostle. Give me Coney Island.

Nobody I see has heard from Jackie—no postcards at the Cedar Chest. Sam said somebody came in who reported having seen her in Paris. Carl De Silver (who will be called Brewster from now on) was surprised at this complete vanishing, according to Margaret. I figure she must be having a ball.

I went to Snedens Landing for the weekend and came back full of furious, in fact indignant, health on Monday morning and proceeded to loop, finding Mr. Gilman freelancing so we both freelanced all day with mutual delusions of grandeur—Longchamps, 68, Cedar, Ticino's, Cedar again (I can see your lip curling—God, how glad I'm not in THAT rat race again). Just to cheer you further, there was the usual difficulty of trying to head off Charles Ingle,† giving it up and sitting around here with a bottle and a can, then forging out again. I find the way to handle Coby's drinking problem is to get drunker faster than he does so he's too embarrassed about you to ever do it himself.

We had a threatened 15% rent raise here which stung the lawyer tenants to call a tenant meeting and whip out a fascinating petition in which they accuse

---

*Next to nothing is known about this project. The only other extant reference is in Powell's diary for March 4, 1957: "If autobiography—horrible idea—begin with 'Out with the Stiffs,' " a mini-memoir she had been working on sporadically for years. Retitled "What Are You Doing in My Dreams?," this autobiographical sketch would be published by Vogue in 1963.
†Charles Ingle (born 1926) was an American novelist whose *Waters of the End* Powell had reviewed with enormous enthusiasm. It seems to have been his only book.

our new landlord of not being our landlord at all, therefore having no Rent Control Law rights. This meeting was held in a double duplex upstairs with crystal chandeliers, majestic bank-presidential gentlemen, Garden Club matrons, liveried maid, etc., and it finally dawned on me that nobody else lives like we do—that THIS is Exurbia, everybody's Cadillac is in the garage down the street, the only difference is that these suburbanites just don't want to have neighbors so they live here.

The printing firm sounds like a fast game of Scrabble but you do seem to have a curious Plan in your jobs—an All Around Publishing Man (Pub-blushing, it said there). Do you own the City Lights name—I mean, if you wanted to start the store or mag in Washington do you have any rights left to the name? . . .

I don't see why you don't write the Bowery Bums piece with all that time on your hands. You can't go on teetering at your teetering printing press ALL the time. Everybody misses you. . . .

Love,
Dawn

(COLLECTION TIM PAGE—CARBON COPY)

TO MARGARET DE SILVER

35 East Ninth Street
July 16, 1957

Dearest Marg.
    SOAP OPERA data!!!
    Cedar informants say Pete [Martin] was in town again a couple of weeks ago. Franz Kline* was in the country and said he didn't see him. I have a hunch Nancy Twin [Ward] did, again, however.† The bartender John said Pete was planning to come back in September to New York.

Then yesterday I had some drinks with Nancy Twin who had just returned from Washington visiting her mother and stepfather and had evidently spent most of the time with Pete. She said he had moved from his first place and was now staying in her mother's large apartment. It developed that Mother and husband were not there, however, but at their mountain spot with the other Twin and baby. Nancy reports that Pete was never better, frowns on all drinks but beer, saw her off on her bus or plane and in general was Great Good Boy.

---

*Powell was especially fond of the painter Franz Kline (1910–1962).
†Twins Nancy and Joan Ward were then art students and well-known habitués of the Cedar Tavern in its original incarnation on Eighth Street. Nancy would be briefly married to Peter Martin, and Joan would become the mother of artist Willem de Kooning's only child (and later his conservator), Lisa de Kooning.

Your guess on this deal is probably the same as mine. Whether the "new girl" is Nancy or the family relative. Nancy also implied that Pete is now cozy with her whole family—enjoys Mother's Bourbon pound cake and Bourbon omelette and delights them all. It sounded like that warm, folksy family that he has often wanted to belong to. Or said so. But Washington itself evidently is too boring.

Now for the Foreign News. That roommate (or something) of Jackie's, Alice somebody up on Sutton Place with the *Esquire* job, telephoned me the other night for news of Jackie or Pete—I was having a small party and couldn't get it quite clear. I gave her Bryan's address. . . .

Well, this a.m. comes a long letter from Bryan, advising me to couch further letters in vague, crafty oblique phrases as, he says, my letters have been so prophetic they frighten him. He says, "Miss Miller has materialized and is now living with me (for a time, in worried parentheses) in all senses of the phrase. You were right, she DOES want to marry me. But I think she's impulsive and she's a little bit away from reality after this summer spent living with some friends (a couple) in a vast, echoing villa in Florence. Lost, beady eyes, amusing and out of it all. I know these trios, I've been in them in my day and they unhinge you for years from reality. Sometimes they work, of course—look at your happy laughing years on East Ninth Street with Jackson Pollock and Dave Brubeck.

"Anyway, I think the dear girl needs time to think it all out of her system. I'm sure she sees me as an English mirage in the middle of a Scotch-on-the-Rocks drought. I think she'll be relieved when she leaves England, though nothing would induce her to think that now. She's a wonderful girl and doesn't sleep with her skates on. What about that nice Peter?"

HOW ABOUT THAT, pal? The above is all direct quote from him. . . .

Rosalind [Wilson] and I discussed this farce on phone and she thinks this would make a good match but I hate to be responsible for the charming lad's being trapped, no matter how winsome the aggressor. Do you note that remark about the "trio"—does that mean she was fixing up her Firenze host and hostess into the triangle shape her cookies always crumble into?

Whose cookies? *Anybody's* cookies.

Went over with [Thomas] Wanning to E—— M——'s one night. Her charming child got curious about my boosom—wanted to know what was in them and could he have one? Kicked his mother for not having some, then made very businesslike prowls around them. Told this was a bust—he yelled he wanted some bunsters. I was lucky to get out alive with my bunsters and he finally bit one. Phone rang and E—— stopped spat with Wanning to get ecstatic—it was Franz Kline! So he came over with another couple and E—— plunged on his lap, while Tom stiffuppered. The apartment is so steaming with sex you'd swear it was Mary Grand's. You come out ready to tear off to a palace of sin. The little child—P—— or this Bunster boy—gives an extra hot guilty sense to the scene.

Should I send Billy Graham to all these candidates?

Love,

Dawn

(COLLECTION JACQUELINE MILLER RICE)

TO J. B. PRIESTLEY*

35 East Ninth Street
August 28, 1957

Dear Mr. Priestley—

How very very kind of you to say those agreeable words about my new book, as Houghton Mifflin has just informed me. How noble of you to look at any galleys you don't have to! I am in the usual state of depression with the book finished and too late to do it all over and good God it's going to be coming out in public and there I'll be without even my Maidenform bra.

So you cheered me enormously. It isn't that I'm so fond of this book—at the moment I hate it—but I was trying to figure out a form of curious bondage that isn't sex but uses up almost all the same emotions. I couldn't do it and it's everybody else's fault—my publisher's, largely, for some reason I can't think of offhand but soon will, with my author's cunning.

I never told you how delighted I was with your Southwest book,[†] recalling with pleasure our meeting at the Davisons' after you and Miss [Jacquetta] Hawkes returned from there. In the first place, printed information about America never is allowed to check with what returned travelers relate, so much was new and fascinating in your records. I was in a rage over the incredible reaction here and was writing apoplectic letters to the *Saturday Review* (a horrible little sheet anyway), then realized I was simply un-American. The simple honest American believes in looking life straight in the TV and no nonsense. There is less and less connection between what he's doing and seeing and being and "Real Life," because what's really happening is the lie.

A nightclub-touring friend of mine[‡] tells me that it took him years to remember not to say a word about any town he was in. If he said there was no

---

*John Boynton Priestley (1894–1984) was one of the most successful British authors of the twentieth century, with dozens of books to his credit. He had admired Powell's works since the 1930s and wrote a public statement about *A Cage for Lovers* for advertising purposes.
†Priestley's *Journey Down a Rainbow* (1956), coauthored by Jacquetta Hawkes had received several negative reviews in the United States for its portrait of life in the American Southwest.
‡This reference was most likely to Dwight Fiske.

French cooking in Red Gap, a posse would be after him. If he said there was a four-month rainy season, there was an angry posse. The only place a visitor could sound off to his heart's content against the city was in New York, and after shouting that he doesn't like the town, he finds the New Yorker merely shrugging complacently and saying, "*You* wouldn't."

Boston resents nothing but remarks made by the British. I don't know whether this is because it's so Irish or so damned deef.

What baffled me about your book was that I saw nothing in it that didn't show deep interest in and appreciation of this country and nothing but a desire to share your findings with others. What puzzled me, too, was that when some indignant natives were asked if they'd read your book they saw nothing funny in saying, "Certainly not."

Ah well, it's all blown over and so will we be. . . .

My best wishes to your wife and much thanks to you—(is there such a word as *much*?)

Sincerely,
Dawn Powell

(HARRY RANSOM HUMANITIES RESEARCH CENTER
AT THE UNIVERSITY OF TEXAS)

TO EDMUND WILSON

[35 East Ninth Street]
September 2, 1957

Dear Wig:

[. . .] I was reminded of your thoughts on the gravediggers who ask for your recollections of somebody for their definitive biography of same or Ph.D. thesis. This was because of a bleak blank young man entrusted by Harold Ober with a fresh book on Scott Fitzgerald. His name is [Andrew] Turnbull, as if I cared, and no doubt he has contacted you.* I understand he wrote some bit in *The New Yorker* on this line, the gift of writing having come to him by having his mother rent a house once to FitzG. in Baltimore or Delaware or someplace. I met him at Alice Richardson's apartment—she was Scott F.'s secretary in Baltimore in his last days and an old or ex-friend of mine.

Anyway this drab stuffy Ivy Leaguish type asked me if I thought Hemingway and FitzG. were really good friends, as he thought from Hemingway's letters to Scott they could not have been, since Hemingway used foul language and Scott's letters were always very gentlemanly. I suggested that perhaps Ernest was not writing to him (Turnbull) but to his friend Scott, and that

*Andrew Turnbull (1921–1970) wrote biographies of F. Scott Fitzgerald and Thomas Wolfe.

perhaps Scott was not writing to Hemingway but to him (Turnbull—i.e., posterity). He said that one nice thing about Scott was that he always kept duplicates of every letter he ever wrote to anybody. He also wished to ask me, as a friend of the Murphys', if *Tender Is the Night* was a real picture of them. I tried to explain that it wasn't anything like them as I knew them, but I only began with them in the late thirties—and at that time nobody was like what they had been in the twenties.

However he had some fixed angle—as they always have—and was not going to be influenced by anything to the contrary. As he was making a number of asinine, polite remarks to the general effect that a gentleman wrote in a gentlemanly way and what more could you ask, I dove into a pitcher of Gibsons and left him being earnestly briefed on old Scott, Dos, Bunny, Gerald by no less an old pal of yours than the Pall of All—Paul Peters.* These two were made for each other—ponderous, judicial detachment in handling their meager treasure of fantastic misinformation.

Where is your Turgenev piece—or was it in *The New Yorker* during my chapel cut? I revived him with extraordinary delight this summer, even forgiving Isabel Hapgood,† then suddenly had enough, as if a shadow of Stephen Leacock's Russian-novel parody had fallen over the page.

I have started a new novel, with no encouragement from Houghton Mifflin. In fact I am discouraged about the one coming out, as their catalog gives an extraordinarily obtuse picture of it.

I wanted to study a kind of human relationship that demands more than sex and is a barrier to sex and feasts on kindness, loyalty, and other handicaps to progress.

My best to Elena and Margaret if you see her—

AND NOW BACK to Ivan the Funlover—
Humph

(YALE COLLECTION OF AMERICAN LITERATURE, BEINECKE RARE BOOK AND MANUSCRIPT LIBRARY, YALE UNIVERSITY)

---

*Powell vigorously disliked Paul Peters, a radical playwright and the author of *Stevedore*, among other works.
†Isabel Hapgood was a well-known translator of Russian novels.

TO MARGARET DE SILVER

[New York]
September 11, 1957

Dearest Maggie—

It occurs to me you may not be getting the telepathic soap-opera news I've been beaming in your direction. Here we go.

BBC THIRD PROGRAM. PEARS SOAP.

Letter from Jackie from Paris, saying she is homesick and is waiting for room on a ship. Evidently NOT wed to Bryan. She said she stayed there 10 days and he was GOOD to her, then she moved in with her friends, the Davidsons, from Firenze, who were in London. She also said she had heard that Pete had found out "which twin had the phony," which was funny.*

THEN—as I was wondering how Bryan had wriggled away from those determined little hands—I was addressed on the street yesterday by an odd girl. Who but Mickey!† She looked quite pretty as a blonde, in the Marilyn Monroe style even as to voice. I burbled some excuse when she said How about a drink?—then along came Coby and we all came to my house for a drink. She quickly telephoned her Friend (they are NOT married, it seems) in Hoboken that she would be late for dinner. As I was cogitating how to make one can of tunafish and a hard-boiled egg serve dinner for all, along came Tom Wanning with some whiskey, so the dinner problem faded before the immediate problem of how to drink up the gin and whiskey before Coby got it all.

Anyway, here is a new twist to this perpetual twisteroo. It seems these Davidsons of Jackie's, being originally Mickey's chums, write Mickey about every move of Jackie's. Poor Jackie, having her secrets blasted to her old rival across the Atlantic. It seems she was "thrown out" of Bryan Robertson's apartment by the landlady. This, I think, may have been because it was gentlemen's lodgings, or else it may have been Mr. R.'s own desperate measure, since Jackie, as we know, has had to be forcibly dislodged almost everyplace she moves in, male or female. Mickey reported that the Robertson affair had been very intense while it lasted and that Jackie had written the folks to get out that old wedding list again. (I'll bet this was the day Bryan bribed his landlady.) Mickey also said her informers wrote her how much Jackie paid for the ballgown to wear to the Ball with Bryan and all other details.

Doesn't that sound too damn mean?—if it weren't funny. Of all the people Jackie would not want to hear of her misses. I simply can't figure out what goes wrong with that beautiful girl. It must be that she simply won't take anybody

---

*"Which twin has the Toni?" was a popular ad campaign for Toni, a hair dye for women.
†Mickey Martin was the first wife of Peter Martin.

who is crazy for her, but HAS to mow down a hostile force. It seems that an ex-girl of Bryan's also gave her a talk.

Mickey seemed calmer and not as anti-Jackie as this sounds on paper. It was a big day for putting feet in, however. I assumed she was in on all the artist set same as when Pete had had his apartment, but it turned out she hadn't even seen him since he came back to New York, but felt very tenderly and sad that he should have both his girls leave him (especially herself, I gathered). When I said didn't she think it was amazing how quietly devoted and polite he was to Nancy [Ward], she said, "Who's Nancy?" I said, "You know the twins, the ones he's always liked, those two little girls—." At this Mickey said, "I know Pete's always been good with children," which sent Wanning into stitches, since Pete usually has fits when little ones are around interrupting. Then I realized Mickey didn't know about the Nancy angle and while I was bumbling out of it she gasped, "You don't mean Nancy, Franz Kline's wife—," and she did know her, but somehow this left her positively pale.

Wanning has never been a twin fancier but he and I compared notes on this astonishing setup. You don't even know Pete's in a bar anymore, Tommy said. He and Nancy just sit holding hands and whenever he raises his voice Nancy pats him and says, "Now, Peter—." He confided to Tom that she was terrific in the hay. This always sounds so athletic, as if she did go at it with a pitchfork à la Soviet womanhood.

I can't tell whether this is love or merely showing their exes how happy they are NOW, you bastards. . . .

A charming letter from [J. B.] Priestley today from Isle of Wight. Don't tell Jackie or she'll move in.

I do hope she has something or other settled by her trip, though it never does settle anything. That poor girl does make life difficult for herself. When you think of all the drab dreary asinine little dames that get their man and sew him up.

Love,
Dawn

(COLLECTION JACQUELINE MILLER RICE)

TO DR. HOWARD ZUCKER

35 East Ninth Street
November 25, 1957

Dear Dr. Zucker:

Jojo was home Thanksgiving time for the first time since he started his upsets. I had rather feared upsets if he should hear that his former nurse (and obsession) was leaving Jersey for a religious home near Boston. [Louise] is very happy over this herself, as it is her home state and so there is no woe in it except longer periods of [Jojo's] not seeing her. In fact if she doesn't like it she may come back, and further I have told Jojo we might visit her sometime or she may visit here. To get him accustomed to the idea I told him (and she did, too) that she is visiting one of the nuns there, Sister Juliana, which is partly true. Furthermore she is partially recovered from her paralysis.*

I thought I would tell you these facts in case he is worried and pessimistic.

On this visit home, his first in a month, we were struck by a marked alertness in response, as if further blocks had been removed. A friend telephoned me to ask where to find the Ten Commandments (I had no idea except I didn't have them) and Jojo called out, "Exodus," then added wearily, "twentieth chapter." Later I was working a crossword puzzle and questioned "scruple" as a unit of measure, but he volunteered the whole apothecary weight table, beginning three scruples to a dram, and baffled his father by the avoirdupois weights, complete with long and short tons, when challenged. Previously it has been hard to judge what he knows or notices as he has no normal exhibitionistic sense or is confused by faster-talking people. Moreover, he surprised me by changing to a warmer sweater under his jacket on his own hook. Usually he is oblivious to personal comforts.

He said he was glad the needle shots stopped as his buttocks had been paining him severely—another indication of increased awareness. I am sure the therapy is opening up new areas.

On the other side he had a tendency to flutter his hands and yip and rock back and forth in the way he used to do in nervous peaks.

> With best wishes, I am
> Dawn Powell Gousha

(COLLECTION TIM PAGE—CARBON COPY)

TO DR. HOWARD ZUCKER

35 East Ninth Street
January 8, 1958

Dear Dr. Zucker:

We were so sorry and disappointed that Jojo had the tantrum to set him back in M5. It was a surprise, for the previous weekend at home he had been absolutely amazing, concentrating for hours at a stretch on his Xmas notes and letters of condolence to old Gladwyne associates (he enjoyed them so much I

*Louise Lee had never recovered from her stroke in 1954.

think he is rather anxious for excuses to write more). He found odd items in *Time* to read aloud, he made his own breakfasts and talked interestingly and happily about the new building.

Even his flinty father was stirred to awe and stated that a miracle was happening and perhaps this would be the year.

Xmas, with church and carols, has always been an emotional hazard for him but we thought he had licked it. I guess it's like a cold that leaves the head only to go in the chest.

When I visited him in M5 on Saturday he was frightfully gaunt, gray-faced and quietly hopeless, the way that ward generally affects him. I can see that finding the right ward now, aside from the red tape of transferring, may keep him even longer there, unless Dr. Davidson has already transferred him. I don't see how to safeguard him against these outbursts, since I detect afterwards a certain pride he takes in them as in a dramatic performance. The disagreeable aftermaths do not seem to connect up to any lesson for him. (I can't say they ever do for anybody else, either.)

I thought you should know that the outburst was not the culmination of any symptoms observable here, but quite the opposite. He had, as I say, never seemed so sensible and controlled. . . .

[No complimentary close or signature]

(COLLECTION TIM PAGE—CARBON COPY)

TO THE LAKE ERIE NOTA BENE

[March 1958]

I arrived at Lake Erie College in September of 1914 with a delirious sensation of having been shot from a cannon into a strange, wonderful planet. All summer long I had been working for this great day. In the little factory town where I had lived I saved every cent, working on the newspaper by day, ushering in a movie house by night, winding and unwinding reels that featured Clara Kimball Young, Carlyle Blackwell, Pola Negri. Everybody in town helped me gather proper equipment for this mighty project, so that my borrowed trunk would scarcely close over the made-over dresses, sheets and towels blotted with my signature, tennis racket with limp strings, and a blue serge bathing suit in four sections, 1900 model, contributed by a fat neighbor on the assumption that going to "Lake Erie" meant I would be spending most of my time in the water. A dear old lady had made me a fluffy yellow boudoir cap, something the factory girls wore for Saturday-night promenades, and just as I started for the train my grandmother handed me a bottle of a patent medicine called Vinol, urging me to take it faithfully to get some color in my cheeks.

Three days later, all settled in my room, tennis racket and boudoir cap jauntily decorating the old pine dresser, I took the trouble to leaf through my rosy little roommate's diary. (I wasn't snooping, I merely wanted to check on her prose style.) It was a shock to see this entry: "My roommate's name is Dawn. I think she is fast because she has a boudoir cap and a bottle of wine."

The world of girls seemed mysterious and infinitely fascinating after my town full of factory men. It is a rich, illuminating experience to discover the thousand different ways girls can be girls and still be nothing like yourself. There were girls who cried from homesickness for a hometown twelve miles away, there were girls who sat up after hours fiercely arguing about the prophet Moses, girls who borrowed each other's Housman or Leacock or Shaw to take on hikes, girls who fitted each other out for fine parties with sublime selfless-ness, a girl who wrote poetry brooding over her childhood memories of the bayous, a beaming happy girl who loved Bach and played the pipe organ in chapel.

"Do you know the marvelous thing that happened to me this morning," she gasped one day, rushing into our room, her eyes like stars. "Miss Small came right up to me and said, 'Sophie, you play the organ most acceptably.' *Most acceptably!* Nobody ever said anything like that before in my whole life!"

There were girls who were slowly becoming conscious that they were not just girls, but part of a great world outside, a world of war and noble deeds waiting to be done. Five of us, linked by a common passion to break through to that outside world, marched down to the new dean's chambers one night imploring an answer to our great question, as burning as it was vague. "Tell us what we can do," we begged her. "Things are happening everywhere and we can't just sit in classrooms. Tell us what to do." The tiny little woman in her blue wool dressing-gown looked at us gravely and then opened her door wider. "Supposing you come in and tell me what *you* think," she said. Whatever was said—we all talked at once—we tiptoed back to our rooms that night with the breathless conviction that we had received a revelation. I cannot remember what Miss Brownfield could have said to us, but I still remember the glorious sense of power she gave us. We were free. All roads were open to us. There was nothing we could not do and we would know the right moment when it came.

Such were the peaks from which we sought to soar.

(LAKE ERIE COLLEGE)

TO EDMUND WILSON

[35 East Ninth Street]
March 24, 1958

Dear Wig—

Did you read Dos's new novel?* I found myself wolfing it down one night with very peculiar sensations. In the first place it seems more nakedly revealing of himself than anything else and for some reason this repels me—possibly the same queasy prissiness that the hero has. However I kept snooping through the pages spotting his safari through Havana with that Cape-and-Key type houri, Helen Parker,† spotting his memories of Katy and getting indignant when I couldn't identify some characters. Look here now, you're MAKING THIS UP and that's not fair!

So I was annoyed with myself for acting like nosy readers I despise who think they know the originals of your creations. The fact is, sometimes they know better than you do.

Anyway there was that same perhaps sexual unpleasantness that there was in *Across the River and into the Bed‡*—the old goat hoping one last fling would bring back his professional career. Only Dos's old goat is such a respectable, embarrassed goat horrified at the idea of saturnalia, planning only a stately dido in a dark room for the purpose of starting a goatee. At least Hemingway's goat seemed to enjoy himself candidly.

The odd thing is that this girl character has a briny vitality that none of his women ever had—one of the most alive bitches I can think of—while his Good Woman, Gracie, adorned with Katy touches, seems real but as repulsive as the poor, baffled, stiff-necked hero. It's all like a dear friend's confession—it makes him feel good to tell all but you can't ever think of him again without this fatal knowledge between you.

So it seems a sad book. I hope my feelings are merely the unfair intimate reactions of a fond old friend and not the public reaction.

That bewilderment of an older man accustomed to success and fame since his teens, doing the same thing he always did and finding it not working anymore—that what-happened-I've-been-a-good-boy-what-went-wrong?

Cage for Lovers came out in England a week ago and I already have more reviews than it got here. [J. B.] Priestley advised readers to pick up any old books by me and declared he would support any move to republish my former works, though he did not like this as well as *Time to Be Born*. If I had been able

---

The Great Days (1958) is counted as one of Dos Passos's gloomiest and most autobiographical novels.
†A character in *The Great Days*.
‡Powell is here parodying the title of Ernest Hemingway's 1954 novel *Over the River and into the Trees*.

to recover from Houghton Mifflin's horrible dismissal and bungling of the book I would feel encouraged. . . .*

Best to Elena—
Humph

(YALE COLLECTION OF AMERICAN LITERATURE, BEINECKE RARE BOOK AND MANUSCRIPT LIBRARY, YALE UNIVERSITY)

TO MARGARET DE SILVER

[35 East Ninth Street]
June 18, 1958

Dearest Margaret—

I thought I should keep you abreast of the news but on second thoughts decided I should keep you a whole row of breasts of news and here they are including Jolly Joke by Bennett Surf in your favorite *Journal-American* and more bewildering talk of our sensational hit "Comic Strip."

Heard a perfectly wonderful radio lecture on Dos last night by an NYU prof. named Theodore Ehrsam who had excerpts read from *U.S.A.* and said it was probably the greatest literary work ever produced in America or elsewhere. Today I am going to read it straight through stopping only for a Bloody Mary break. . . .

I saw Nancy Ward one day and right now, as of this week, would say those little girls are the most nervous, tense little desperate creatures—practically paranoid (what *am* I saying or spelling?) in their impression that the whole world is wrapped up in their tiny upsies and downsies. Allowing for the fact that Monsieur Martin has a signal ability to drive the lady of his choice as near nuts as they will go (is it harder to drive them out of their mind when they haven't got one?)—

Anyway Mary [Grand] invited me to a quiet evening with Charles [Norman] and Coby. It developed later that she had decided to quadruple the quiet by inviting Jackie (who didn't come), Mrs. Gus Peck (who didn't come), Ellen (who didn't come because Mrs. Gus Pecker was invited), Tommy (who wouldn't come because Ellen wouldn't), Peter Martin and Nancy and de Kooning. Andy Wanning appeared and Danny Rosenblatt in Bermuda shorts (no onions showing).

Nancy kept loudly whispering, "Why, that man is a Homosexual! I'm sure he is! Of course he's a Homosexual!" I kept shaking my head not to deny but to quiet her, but evidently she was proud of her expert ability to Spot 'Em and

---

*It was Powell's belief that meddling on the part of the top editors at Houghton Mifflin had ruined her book's chances. She held Rosalind Baker Wilson blameless in the matter.

Spot 'Em Loud. I don't know where she's been all these years to be so excited over it. De Kooning came in with the girl he sometimes has, quite pretty. Things got noisy or petered out—anyway, next day Nancy telephoned to apologize for the "conspicuous" way she and Pete had left. As you know, a departure in our group is never noticed so I mentioned this. She said she had told off de Kooning for bringing a Common Whore around when poor Joanie had to stay home with Baby. She said the Common Whore (not to be confused with Miss Common Cold or Miss Near-Miss of 1956) had slept with Everybody (artists only) in the Cypress Garden otherwise Cedar Pot. I said (I was frying Ham and Eggs for Mr. Gousha at the time and believe it or not did not give a flying fuck whether de Kooning brought One Common Whore or Ten Preferred Ones) that I hadn't realized de Kooning lived with Joan which I fear set poor Nancy off into another Spin. I knew he was The Father but he has stoutly maintained to everyone he has his own place, and even Pete has said he was only at Joan's some of the time. Anyway Nancy said Pete and she greatly feared there might have been a frightful scene after they left. I said I greatly feared not and that others left because it was after midnight and hostess seemed well pleased to say goodnight. Next day I was in Cedar with Don Elder (old pub. friend of Bunny's and Annetta's [Hart] and mine) and Joan was there alone (I do like her better—I think she has some spark anyway) and cried, "Didn't you stand up for me in that big scene at Mary Grand's last night?" I said there hadn't been any scene and returned to Mr. Elder as Nancy came in and the two of them picked ticks out of each other's little heads and tails and chattered over the cocoanuts.

I knew you wanted to hear how Soap was Selling. . . .

Love,
Dawn

(COLLECTION JACQUELINE MILLER RICE)

TO MARGARET DE SILVER

[New York]
July 26, 1958

Dearest Margaret:

Romance then is not dead, what? Marian S.'s* letter delighted Joe and I could see what she meant—in fact, I realize that's what one travels for—some renaissance of that spark we hope will be recognized. What a sexpot, my, my—saying *"knee* to *knee!!"* Please tell her that Joe had an equally good time and said she was a "nice kid." Not kidding, either, about the kid part, as he

---

*Marian S. has not been identified.

thought it was sheer bitchiness on my part to say she was over 40. He does have a harmless indifference to ages—except his own which he always multiplies—but his mother is "well on in her *seventies*," he is likely to say, at the same time *boasting* that he himself is 68.

A letter from Esther here in response to one in which I said we all hoped to come see her next season in Key West if she didn't get here. I told her Dos and wife and child were in Brazil for summer. However, she leaps up to say I should bring Dos ("I don't know about his wife," she says nastily) and seems to expect the visit tomorrow or next day so I anticipate futile explanations. . . .

Coby has been low due to the end of his Research, but I think he starts Social Security—that El Dorado—in a month or so and George pays his rent anyway. I suppose he wants to eat one of these days, too, but that's just a habit.

I saw Twin Joan who said Pete and Nancy were in Washington on vacation before Pete started new job on one of those Jackson Burke sex mags I believe. Joan also said the Martin First Avenue apartment is charming—very open-like—and she seemed to feel everything was fine. She is cute-looking. I saw her in line at the bank—minus her daughter, who, I then perceived, had taken a job or a desk anyway with the vice presidents in the area and was busily typewriting with a look of great satisfied concentration. I was about to approach her for a bank loan (it looked like a good chance) but she was opening up file drawers by that time and one of the secretaries came back and fired her. Does your bank need a 2-and-½-year-old vice president? . . .

I am disrupted and distrait about Jojo's being kept in Disturbed, especially since his special doctor is giving up his visits so he will have no protector. I suspect some dirty work among the staff doctors to deliberately show these visiting experts that they don't know what they're doing.

We are hanging on still by a thread—don't ask me what next. On looking into Bernard Baruch's advice on getting rich I gather that the best way is to buy a building then sell at a profit. This I propose to do as soon as I finish this letter so don't detain me.

It has not been too hot in our apartment so far—I use a blanket by night for the cool western breezies. . . .

Love,
Dawn

(COLLECTION JACQUELINE MILLER RICE)

TO MARGARET DE SILVER

[35 East Ninth Street]
August 13, 1958

Dearest Margaret—

Come down for a preview of your new A&P Super at the gorgeous Mark Twain Apartments.* I made my debut there today and found it infinitely more charming than my own super.

I also met C. Gilman on the corner to pass him a sandwich, tea and sugar as he said he only had an egg yesterday. All he really misses is cigarettes and I get very unreasonable when he won't even buy bread or filling things when he does have money. Also, he wanted me to come up to his three flights of apartment and was hurt that I had to come home and look after other stommicks.

It hasn't been at all bad as to heat here, having many N.Y. past summers to compare with. There are western breezes which are handy in my bedroom and Joe's and so far none of the tossing sweltering nights—in this apartment anyway.

Jojo was transferred to a better but still not open ward and seems okay though not allowed home or out except when we come.

Jackie is coming in this afternoon. She said she had a dreadful eve last night because the San Francisco friend named Alice who introduced her to Pete was visiting her on Jones St. and wanted to see Pete so he came over and was absolutely overwhelmingly charming to Alice (to indicate he was not at fault anywhere, no matter what Jacqueline might have whimpered) and ignored J. almost completely. Also, he took over the Jones St. apt. rather grandly even though Charles and Cheko were there. Talked to Alice of his old apartment on Third Ave.—of his various friends and adventures (J. feeling worse since she'd been along on all of them and the friends were sometimes more hers) and spoke at length of his ex-wife Mickey—so talented a writer now (she is trying to write pulps) and such a wonderful person. So sorry Alice never met her in California (when he met Jacqueline, he was beefing about what a lousy wife he had to this same Alice). He later urged them to the Cedar (I imagine Jackie paid for all) and here he continued to be gay and witty and concentrate on Alice excluding J. completely, except to throw out patronizingly that he rather liked Charles, seemed like a rather nice chap. This burned up J.—that he felt entitled to grade her pals and act as if he were the Jones St. owner besides. . . .

A man I know took me to dinner the other night and asked me how those

---

*De Silver was then living at 130 West Twelfth Street, soon to become part of St. Vincent's Hospital, after which she moved to 70 East Tenth Street, her last home. The A&P near the corner of Sixth Avenue and Twelfth Street remains extant in 1999.

weird little women—twins—ever got their hooks into all those artists. He said they sit on the barstools looking like little bugs, glaring around this fellow Martin, he said—how did they get hold of a bright guy like him? Bill said (not being a member or insider of the Cedar, really) that, oh brother, that one twin married to P. Martin and Pete sure fight. They stage a big fight there every night, he said—looks like they slug each other, too!!!

This I never heard. I haven't been in there at the witching hours so I never run into this.

I thought you needed a little Soap. . . .

Joe has taken to wine *instead* of hard stuff!! This has almost staggered me. He has had at least two martinis for lunch as a law for 35 years and economic necessity alone could never change him. He was being horrible for a week or two so this charming helpful "wino" is a great boon. Don't let this shock upset you. My Plum Tomato is of age but not red yet. I propose a great Tomato Festival on that day.

Love,
Dawn

(COLLECTION TIM PAGE)

TO MARGARET DE SILVER

[130 West Twelfth Street]
Monday—28 Sept. [1958]
which hath you know
what I think no fury I guess
like a 31st.

Dearest Margaret—

[. . .] Joe celebrated news of my fortune* by plastering himself solo then falling down (his knee gives way like yours every once in a while since he cracked it) and breaking his falsies and possibly a rib so he is in pain and mad (it wouldn't have happened if I'd kept my fat mouth shut) and can't get an appointment till Wednesday as he's all gums. I think it was very clever of him to find such an attractive way of disposing of the Fortune before it's even out of the grave.

Nuns in white whisk around every corner and I laugh when I think of Carlo [Tresca] trapped here and lassoed by rosaries at every turn.†

Early this a.m. a lady, rather dressy fashion-type wholesale in elevator

---

*Powell had just been paid her first installment by her new publisher, Viking Press, for *The Golden Spur* (1962).
†The Catholic St. Vincent's Hospital had just bought De Silver's apartment building and was in the midst of incorporating it into its campus. Carlo Tresca had been a proud atheist.

frowned at me and asked how long I'd been in the bldg. I said I was visiting and she said, "Well I've been here for years and never seen you." (She did not know I was you.) Does your friend know we all have to move? I said I believed so. So she forgave me.*

I shan't go into all the apartment ups and downs that occupy me till I have done something definite. One thing about life here on 12th St. which I was never conscious of before—it is Big City Life, impossible to conceive of on Bank St. but somewhat like University Place. Only University Place was like Newark and this area is definitely Big City New York.

I was roaming around lower Village and Square Sunday and the parade of Sunday creeps all over the Village—Coney Islanders, etc.—is enough to send me quietly back uptown again. Beards, slobs, dykes, delinquents, uglies of all kinds—.

Jojo was fine when I took him on picnic Saturday. He had deep interest in situation and said, "It seems to me the best thing for you to do is to get into a Project." I met his new pal, a most attractive, intelligent, witty, engaging lad of 18 named M—— R—— (no sign of what his problem is—maybe sudden seizures) whose pappy is dentist at 10th and Sixth Ave. He said they went to the Vineyard and knew lots of artists and writers—and did I know their old friend Joe Mitchell?

I was so taken with the lad that Jojo excused himself and I realized he was standing in the hall outside looking at us solemnly so I resumed my post as his alone. The boy advised me to get Jojo into another ward as he was much too clever and nice to be there. . . .

I do not know which is worse—to be fastened to someone's coattails or to have them fastened to yours. As you have the biggest coattail riders in the world I suppose you know the answer, and as I hate hanging on and hate equally having cargo of my own, I think I will go sit on a steeple and ponder this. Do you want to join me in buying a cooperative steeple?

Expect to be settled or permanently unsettled by Saturday. Probably on the steeple.

love,

Dawn

(COLLECTION TIM PAGE)

*The building in which Powell and Gousha had been living since 1942 was in the process of being converted into a cooperative apartment house. Under the laws of the time, all tenants who did not buy their apartments would be forced to move.

[35 East Ninth Street]
October 28, 1958

Dear Dos and Betty—

Thought strikes me you might be due in sometime soon unless you are back in your native Brazil. We have to get out of this apartment by November 1— (we *claim* it's because it's changing to cooperative and we do have to buy or leave *sometime*)—but haven't found a place yet within our means, if any. Possibly will have to rent a suite for Fagin, Cat, at a Cat Waldorf and go to hotel, either Fleabag Hotel Irving on Gramercy Park or for same money much finer and privater suite at Carteret next to Chelsea Hotel.† One looks bad downstairs and handsome up, the other vice versa. Salvation Army is marching up to accept our three-legged chairs and half-hipped sofas and old Prince Alberts, thank God, and we will store the rest if no place appears. Will leave address at Brandts' or with Monroe Stearns. . . .‡

Best,
Dawn

(DOS PASSOS COLLECTION, THE UNIVERSITY OF VIRGINIA)

*Dos Passos had married the former Elizabeth Holdridge in 1949.
†The Goushas would in fact move into the Hotel Irving, which would prove unacceptable. Shortly thereafter they would relocate to the Madison Square Hotel at Madison Avenue and Twenty-sixth Street, now demolished.
‡Monroe Stearns (1913–1987) was a teacher, writer, and editor who came to be one of the Goushas' best friends.

THE LAST YEARS

1958–1965

[November 20, 1958]

No hot water for three days has us flipping again, this time up to Hotel Madison Square, Apt. 1043, with real stove, real plumbing, a bay window and cat permit. As of tomorrow Nov. 21 until the next mood.

Gypsy Powell

(COLLECTION MICHAEL STEARNS)

TO GERALD AND SARA MURPHY

Madison Square Hotel
35 Madison Avenue
November 28, 1958

Dearest Gerald and Sara—

I take for granted that when I am in a state of flux everybody else is too so I did not notify you of my strange movements. However, now we are nicely unsettled in a charming impersonal suite at this fashionable hotel where I think of you, Gerald—right across the way with the Murphy family "where Broadway meets Fifth Avenue never to meet again" or *something* like that—and I can't quite figure out where Mark Cross was or the Café Martin but it's always good for an argument with Joe. Out of one window in this bay I see the East River and out of the other I *almost* see Chester Arthur rearing up in bronze or maybe gingerbread in Madison Square Park. Expect Stanford White in for marijuana later on.

35 East Ninth Street was still dickering to be a cooperative apartment and I wanted to clear out of the whole overblown mess so we stored everything at great expense and started this cruise which frankly is very edifying. I am always delighted to find new sides of New York and this is a lot of fun—every two blocks a different city. No responsibility—maid whisking in and out, doing everything that used to take the old retainers all day to do (with conversation and huge pay). Switchboard and messages and queer little restaurants all around and a Wall Street hush on weekends.

The cat was at Tiffany's (practically) at first but we have permission for him here and this is the only remnant of solid family life. By chance I parked him at a wonderful vet from Spanish Morocco—Dr. Jehoram Asedo—at 113 Lexington. He looks like Charles Boyer—has great charm and intelligence and the animals seem very happy, including some African monkeys boarding there. He must have given my cat (13 years old) a potent analysis on the side for he (cat) is now a gentlemanly, sweet, friendly, contented creature—no longer screaming at strangers and shuddering at noises (like Ebenezer). The pet house amused us as it was the building where Joe started in advertising in 1922, formerly the home of Oscar of the Waldorf.

We have a vague sensation of being tourists and really enjoying the town instead of dozing in our old rut. At the moment it seems a restful and practical way to live and enormously economical. We have a kitchen unit so we can cook as we like. Most of our old pals are more inconvenienced by our move—as they enjoyed our old apartment more than I ever did, I guess.

I daresay once I get this present novel* done I will be screaming for the old chains. Already I'm sneaking over to Third Avenue swap shops (they "swap" for cash, it seems) for lamps, extra end tables, stools and all those tidbits I just finished storing.

Today is my birthday and I believe Sara's was last week or so. Joe has ear trouble and won't go see the Man so I shout and he gets mad. Otherwise this looks like a real cozy winter.

I went to some parties for Kenneth Tynan and his wife and saw Lillian Hellman. Am looking for Dos about this time. Is he just coming up your front walk?

I missed you. Hope your summer was good. At least it's *over*—it's nice just having things *over*. Come and see this strange nest.

Love,
Dawn

*The Golden Spur.

TO GERALDINE RHOADS*

35 Madison Square
New York City
December 29, 1958

Dear Jerry:

I have moved to a suburb. Here at 26th and Madison, no drugstores, newsstands, taxis stir from Friday till Monday. I understand Fifth Avenue is a block away but which way? I sit in my bay window (my back to my unmade bed or the maid's activities) and stare at the N.Y. Life building. For a month a team of old masters has been feverishly painting Xmas symbols on the windows—angels, sleds, trees, farms—but there are a million windows and the day before Xmas they whizzed through in a desperate try to get a candy cane painted on the orphan windows. Today another team from another union has begun to rub them all out—the angels first, the trees, and as I exercise my eyes traveling upward I see a piece of the old farm going.

Otherwise there is a river at each end of the bay.

Now that you get the picture, there is living in the bayed apartment a retired advertising executive and his writing wife (also at bay).

I have been observing the Retired Male here and there for some time and have some constructive thoughts that I wish to write an article about. About which.

It isn't the need for little hobbies, or pin money, that makes this such a frightening time for men.

It's the indignity of having to use the family instead of—as he prefers it and considers it proper—having the family use him.

These thoughts apply to men who have been in executive positions of varying grades.

Their chief interest has been their job and they have inevitably reduced their "friends" over the years to business friends. As a rule they are impatient with the social life their wives provide and, if they are able to, chicken out of anything unrelated to the Office. Their best friends are the Vice President of Jones Co., the General Manager of Doe—they form their tastes and pastimes to conform with these men, but actually the friendship goes to the job's successor when one of these dummy figures falls out of place.

"Do I see Jim anymore? Oh, Jim. No, he's not with Jones Bolts anymore. Gus Brown took his place. A great guy, you must lunch with us sometime."

The friends our men *used* to have were based on common interests in perhaps music or sailing or childhood background or merely being neighbors. Neighbors at least share genuine feelings about home and human values.

---

*Geraldine Rhoads was an editor at the *Ladies' Home Journal*.

At retirement time, our man finds himself an orphan. No one is being unkind, no one is surprising him really with coolness, for he knows the picture well enough.

But his table is no longer reserved at the old favorite restaurant—he joins others' tables when he does go for lunch. But he's out of the news and the invisible powerful wall of Ins and Outs has descended. What he forgets is that it IS Ins and Outs, not Old Age. He forgets the times between jobs in his twenties and thirties when it was like this.

Shy of being the square at the insiders' parties, he is obliged to fall in with his family or wife's social life. "These are not my friends," he says to himself bitterly. A businessman out of business has no friends.

But he reluctantly wakes to the pleasure of human contacts that have no company interest as basis. He is drawn into the family's friends—since he has no place else to go—and is inclined to be resentful at the completeness of their life with no vice presidents or managers, just people. Resentful and nursing a suspicion he's been cheated. He doesn't like being the receiver of any values that are noncomputable.

This is not because he's any more ambitious or money-mad than anyone else. It's just the game that has to be played—and now the game has new players.

The lesson of the lonely retired man is that mechanized friendships unwind promptly at retirement age. He should have been saving up personal friendships for 20 years against this day—a real social security.

Curious about the difference between the male and female in middle age. After 50, women seem to enjoy and prefer the friendship of their own sex. No fighting over men, no more rivalry, and their family responsibilities pretty well completed. This is the time when men suddenly are thrown back on the home. It is a stroke of luck if the wife's friends, ignored for years by the master, bear him no ill will.

But shouldn't those great experts—who move their employees' private lives around like chess pieces in other respects—have warned him to keep a part of himself for his personal friends against these wallflower years?

This is a general idea, that's all. Let me know if any angle of it sounds workable.

Too bad we have to go back to the *Times* after getting used to the *Philadelphia Inquirer.* * Oh well.

Apartment-hotel life seems great to me here at the Madison Square Hotel. Every time a gent slips in and washes the windows or shampoos the rugs, I think how free and besides I didn't even have to find him or postpone him or

---

*A long newspaper strike in New York had just come to an end.

pay him. And clean towels I don't have to buy or have laundered every day and a dear Irish maid whizzing through everything every day instead of my old faithful colored Marie at $11 a day including three hours' conversation and lists of supplies for me to buy and orders for her lunch.

Did you ever have a white work for you? They're so grateful!

Merry Xmas from me and N.Y. Life and Met Life and all the other surrounding insurances.

Dawn Powell

(COLLECTION TIM PAGE—CARBON COPY)

TO PHYLLIS POWELL COOK

[Hotel Madison Square]
January 26, 1959

Dearest Phyllis—

First, regarding Dry Hospital Skin, let me share my Egyptian beauty secrets of eternal youth. After years of Endocreme I was squeezed out when it zoomed to $5 a jar and took up a rare product called Pond's Dry Skin Cream (75 cents). I was taken with an ad telling you to heat a spoonful and stuff on your puss after cleaning. Well sir, I think it's great. Even on the hands. Also, it doesn't smell. However, if your antennae are still sensitive you may nauseate at a faint sniff of lanolin. If I had saved the 20 years' worth of Endocreme expenditures I would not be the beauty I am today, perhaps, but I would have had more to put on the horses or gigolos or fine jewels or else enough for a rainy day if I'd saved enough water too.

It is 8 a.m. and I sit here in my bay window looking over at the New York Life skyscraper (midget skyscrapers) waiting for the toilers to get to their desks and start staring back at me. I couldn't sleep because I have an appointment in two hours to see a man about a job—a role I haven't played for some time. Do I come in with a curtsy or with a roar? Does he pay me or do I pay him? I have only a vague idea of what the job is—as the publication doesn't yet exist*—and I'm sure the man who phoned me about it hasn't any idea of what I do. So I don't know whether to go in with a list of girls' phone numbers for an Elks banquet or some samples of my upside-down cake. I did remember to get a haircut and shave and I shined my shoes and wiped the cat hairs off my suit. I am fairly sure I will be baffled right back here by noon.

My operation—hysterectomy due to cancer cells—was in 1946 and was not a complete one as I faded out in the middle and had to be transfused and

---

*Powell made several halfhearted attempts to find full-time employment during this nomadic period.

oxygenated and then went into shock so the doctor stayed in my hospital room all night. (Isn't that flattering?) So, to get the rest out, I had two or three months of daily radium treatments that wore me down and sickened me. I had felt marvelous after the operation so I was mad when I had to go take these treatments. They didn't go fast enough so I had to go to Mt. Sinai Hospital for a week and have a radium kind of operation. All this was particularly mean because Joe and everybody were bored by my being sick by that time. However, I will say it fixed me. The radiological doctor is dead now (of cancer) but here I am, Pond's Creamed up the hilt (where the ovaries used to stand) and ready for employment—so cheers! Be of high heart! Or High Bust or something. Get high.

Love,
Dawn

(COLLECTION TIM PAGE)

TO EDMUND WILSON

35 Madison Avenue
March 19, 1959

Dear Wig . . .

I thought of you yesterday afternoon as I sat in Row C with Gerald and Sara Murphy watching [Archibald MacLeish's play] *J.B.* unfold. If *Hamlet* was your Omelette, this is your Jambalaya. Crowds were jamming the streets throwing away their crutches as if it were the Miracle, but as Gerald pointed out, their faces were all grim and purposeful, as if the least they could do for the under-privileged and Hiroshima was to give themselves a bad two hours in the theater.

It is an incredibly insulting, outrageous medicine show (no, not that good, more of a very phony drawing-room tragedy). There is the set straight from Jack Lawson's *Loudspeaker* and some Lawson Olympic and rough characters (only not with the virtue of cartooning), then comes all the furniture Archie has lifted from all along the line. Gerald was startled to find a great hunk of *Family Reunion* lifted quite baldly, inasmuch as Archie cannot stand T. S. Eliot.

Then come all the woes and the poor actors put through more physical discomfort (perspiration pouring down their faces) than in any sweatshop, and the more they suffer the more you don't believe it and the more you are convinced this is the work of a man incapable of human feelings so he thinks the more you pile it on the more it hurts.

The fact is that it is the most ignorant use of language, more ignorant than the barroom savant who loves those words and thinks if you put enough words together (as if they were neckties and I'm sure Archie thinks of them like that) you've got yourself a thought.

The abundance of Discussion Group ladies were as remote from this obscene condescension to mass "needs" as we were. Nobody seemed moved or more interested than if it were *Look Out For Lulu.* A group of ladies in front of us shrugged and left early in the first act murmuring to one of their group who was sticking it out, "Happy holiday, dear, if you insist." This lady left soon, too. There were some cosmopolitan snickers when words like "piss" and "bullshit" were said to show Archie has his Beat side, I suppose.

One thing was that your emotions were left intact but the lack of meaning and the tasteless lumping of pompous words (I mean by "tasteless" that he piled them up and flung them out as if nobody were bright enough to expect meanings in words) left you bored and disgusted.

Gerald said he feared Archie was now going to be the King of Broadway, and was in fact on the sands of Antigua right this minute with [Elia] Kazan cooking up another big cookie, probably the St. MacLeish's Genesis. I predict that the Kazan-MacLeish marriage gets ruptured on the highly social Antigua shores because all those multimillionaires in the compound will crown their own little attic poet, Archie, and Archie will forget to introduce Kazan, probably forget his name, only that he's that very clever little Jewish-Greek fellow whom Archie trusts with all the boring details, my dear, do give him a drink or something and try to get him out of the way before the Alphands get here.

As for Broadway, the only original thing Archie ever did or will do there is not to be a Jew, and he didn't even figure that out without help.

Incidentally, [Christopher] Plummer as the Devil is such a good actor he tries to make it mean something or tie it up by running around the stage physically. Listen Oakes, or rather Raymond Massey or is it Whit Burnett, holds out a mask of Jove and uses it just about as effectively and as seldom as the cymbalist in the Philharmonic.

I left JOB to go meet Job Gousha at the doctor's office because he was being skinned alive by what seemed to be shingles. He was then skinned by a prescription that cost $18.95 of paste and pills and by God this morning he's almost cured. Not shingles, it seems, but an allergy.

My novel is doing well since I can't afford to do anything else but write. This hotel is really cozy and a nice warm little nest (with my cat as hostess) but the whole place smells like a nest too. Maybe that's the allergy.

Best to Elena and family and any more twins you may see.

Love,
Humph

(YALE COLLECTION OF AMERICAN LITERATURE, BEINECKE RARE BOOK AND MANUSCRIPT LIBRARY, YALE UNIVERSITY)

TO DR. BLOOMFIELD[*]

35 Madison Avenue
New York City
May 3, 1959

Dear Mr. Bloomfield:

I would like to urge you again to look into the case of Joseph Gousha, Jr., my son, now in 11A, where he has been confined for several weeks after breaking a window in 7A. He has been very ill with a serious cold in the chest for some time and when I brought him home Saturday he had been assaulted by a fellow patient and his bruised nose and eye were still painful. His condition was most disturbing to us.

He is a passive, ordinarily gentle person and it seems to me—and many of the attendants who have observed him for years—that it is murderous to imprison him at great risk to his health and safety with dangerously violent cases, since his outbursts are temporary and against property rather than human beings.

It would be appreciated if you could find some way of changing him to a better ward.

Sincerely yours,
Dawn Powell Gousha

P.S. On his Saturday visit we walked around the city, marketed, and he visited with a friend, and he behaved with great calm and intelligence, considering how long he's been out of this normal environment.

(COLLECTION TIM PAGE—CARBON COPY)

TO MONROE STEARNS

23 Bank Street[†]
New York City
July 21, 1959

Dear Monroe:

Curious as it may seem I have been meditating on our Dickens discussion of last evening. . . .

Would BM be interested in my conception?[‡]

The dowdy and soppy aspects of Dickens have been drummed into us for

---

[*]Dr. Bloomfield seems to have been someone in a position of administrative power at Manhattan State Hospital, where Jojo had been confined since 1954.
[†]Powell was then living in a four-room apartment that she sublet from the biographer Katherine Anthony.
[‡]Stearns was then an editor at Bobbs-Merrill.

so long that the sheer wit and brilliance of many passages have been neglected. I don't mean the jolly Pickwickish sort of thing but the kind of wit that later became peculiarly Bright Young Englishman wit—the Nöel Coward school. The reason for the durability of these bubbles is that they are actually not superficial or mere smart fizz but are genuine champagne from the very best grapes and the very best-manured soil.

The form of the collection would be—as I see it—not maxims or epigrams (as suggested offhand by LeClercq and which would involve bungling the original at great cost) but something like Fitzgerald's *The Crack Up* with brief excerpts, paragraphs here and there, comments, descriptions, all adhering to sheer sophisticated comedy as it later was embraced by the smart boys. There would be a page of the Misses Pecksniff, the wonderful description of David Copperfield's hangover (not generally underlined in the nursery) and annihilating sentences that pop through *Dombey* even, especially *Our Mutual Friend* and *Martin Chuzzlewit.*

Firbank, Huxley, Coward, Waugh dove for these diamonds while the rest of the world slurped their beakers of tears and treacle.

I don't think this should be a great oaf of a volume—if necessary the material could be divided into other books. I see it as a rather elegant 300 pages or more, perhaps even illustrated with London (or Chuzzlewit's old New York) scenes.

I could have this ready by mid-October, as I have been underlining and snooping for 25 years—ever since I reluctantly started reading all of Dickens to my son, expecting the worst and finding both of us rewarded in separate ways.

I should enjoy working with you, *cheri.*

love,
Dawn

P.S. I want this between us, without agent, which always holds up or blocks everything. Maybe later on.

(COLLECTION MICHAEL STEARNS)

TO MARGARET DE SILVER

[23 Bank Street]
July 2, 1959

Dearest Margaret—

I am wondering if you are out of this heat or in another kind. It has been quite startling, like Florida rainy-season heat, with sweat raining off of you then chilling into an exquisite sort of rheumatism. It was 102 at 6th Avenue and 8th Street, though the Battery only reported 96—for civic reasons, no doubt.

The icebox doesn't make ice so we buy bags at the corner for 35 cents, then pay the refrigerator repairman $8.50 to fix things so that the icebox melts the ice we've just bought. This is Housemanship, and I am crouching here now waiting for the Iceman's Returneth. Every time I see a repairman take out a box of mystery tools for the piano, radio, fridge, or typewriter I know perfectly well he's only going to pry out the good parts of the machine and put in some plastic stuffing that won't work, as well as carting off the family jewels. Yesterday they took the kitchen pail (it's gone, anyway) and left a box of tools. I guess I'm in business.

I did not wish to seem snooty about your suggestion re: the Ohio book. Unlike Stanley Baron's autobiography, *My Home Is Far Away* had only some superficial similarities to my life—viz: small town, three sisters, dead mother, stepmother, and the grandmother's boardinghouse in Cleveland, about one or two years. We never lived in the rooming house with the lecherous landlady and the pal of Papa's, but curiously enough that section is more real to me—I SEE it—than my own life. Nor did we live in the hotel, nor did I see my stepsister before she was 12 yrs. old, and the majestic Mr. Sweeney was a stranger to me but now very real. The second volume, which is mostly in Cleveland (where I never lived), got an advance from Scribner's in 1945 or so on 100 pages, which I then rewrote and did another book instead, then got an advance from Houghton Mifflin and another rewrite of the same material in 1952 or so. Then got stuck again and did the *Pavilion*, then recast the same ms. and got an advance again from H.M. and was prepared to go on with it after *Cage for Lovers* but had no takers.

You can see that it seems sort of jinxy, and I daresay publishers are aware of it. A genuine autobiography has been suggested by others but it always seems to me to use up your capital—all your source material for novels. If you're through with novels it's a good idea. As far as Viking is concerned, Malcolm [Cowley]* doesn't like my Ohio stuff and any publisher could look up the old reviews and sales of *My Home Is*, etc., and see that the sales were lowest and reviews worst, so I would have to be damn sure I could get on with it to sell the idea once again.†

Is this all sufficiently confusing? . . .

Joe has been working for me. He has been tracking down some stuff at the Public Library that Frances Keene‡ wants and then having it photostatted, so that he feels cheered and enjoys the digging.

Very curious but I do have your key, it seems, with its little white flag on it.

---

*Powell's old friend Cowley (1898–1990) had become her editor for *The Golden Spur*.
†Powell here misrepresents the public response to *My Home Is Far Away*, which received mostly good reviews and sold respectably. She would certainly be surprised to learn that it has become, over the decades since its publication, her biggest-selling book.
‡The editor, author, and educator Frances Keene (1912–1997) was a close friend and occasional drinking buddy of Powell's. Keene wanted to bring out a book of Powell's reviews and essays.

I have not checked on the novels yet as I feared the swelter of the closed apartment, and am not sure whether to have the excerpts typed or what process. I
am to have it assembled with an additional essay next week and I was exceed-
ingly impressed by Frances Keene's suggestions and enthusiasm. It is not her
present firm that is involved. As Joe is tending to the details, I am fairly free to
work on my novel.

Monroe Stearns came in and was full of beans about his Bobbs-Merrill job,
and evidently enjoys being a boss instead of a lively worm. Frances K. said she
did not know whether his salary was great and there had been a slight doubt,
because Prentice-Hall pays minimum wages but sews up its slaves with pensions and fringe benefits and family bait, so it holds on to its starving employees. But Monroe decided to break.

Monroe had had lunch with Carol Brandt (my agent) and when I asked
how he liked her he monroed, "I've always adored Carol. She's always been
one of my favorite women." I lifted a brow and said or rather powelled, "But I
thought you'd never met her, that you dealt with Berenice Baumgarten." "I've
always loved Carol," he said stoutly. I need hardly add that next day Carol
called me and said, "I think your friend Stearns is absolutely delightful. I don't
know why I never clapped eyes on him before."

Isn't this curious and crazy—harmless, though I should think it could boo-
merang embarrassingly for him sometimes. It's bad enough when I say I know
somebody and they don't even remember me. That of course is the story of
everybody's life. . . .

A beauteous little redheaded niece of mine (Miss Canton of 1945 or so) and
her husband and two nice kids suddenly phoned here on vacation at a hotel.
When I asked her to come on down to Bank St. she said sweetly, "I'd just love
to, Aunt Dawn, only we've planned to take a tour of Greenwich Village and
just won't have time to see you."*

I was so startled to think I almost prevented them from seeing mysterious
Greenwich Village that I didn't think to say, as [Thomas] Wanning suggested,
"But dearie, your Auntie Dawn IS Greenwich Village." However they thought
better of it and "dropped in" at 10 a.m., family-style, the next morning and
were obviously shocked at such an old beat-up place. (I thought they would be
impressed.)

As I told you via phone I was delighted to get your charming note. You
write the finest letters!

love,
Dawn

(COLLECTION TIM PAGE)

---

*Carol Cook Warstler, Powell's niece, convincingly disputes this account.

TO MARGARET DE SILVER

[23 Bank Street]
Friday [summer 1959]

Cool today at last!

Dearest Margaret—

The Evelyn [Scott]* Papers arrived this minute and I am nearly hysterical. As Esther would say, Now *Really*!! How she (Evelyn) could be so utterly, sublimely selfish as to not know she might be endangering what little mind Esther has left by pelting her with strange government documents, etc., then pestering her for answers, then saying to you, "I did not forget what you said about her forgetfulness!" Good God, she forgets or ignores absolutely everyone's interest but her own. Isn't it odd that a novelist should lack imagination? I howled at the picture of the U.S. Government getting Evelyn's congratulations on painting again (no doubt this should have been forwarded straight to Eisenhower!). At least Evelyn did admit she had mixed up the letter herself and not been loused up by Khrushchev. She does imply, I see, that you "agreed" to her writing Esther which puts the blame on you pretty squarely, doesn't it? . . .

I think every move anybody makes re: Evelyn is murder so I wouldn't write *anybody*. I'm sure Esther must have had a sharp flicker of memory at Evelyn's letter and thrown it away like an old check for a million. I remember the last time Esther was at your apartment and a special-delivery registered bomb from Evelyn to you arrived. You were going out or had said you were damn well not going to even open the screed. I believe you did leave or were gone anyway because Esther and Pete and I were there alone and getting tight when Esther gaily decided to read it aloud with great expression till she came to this—"How are Esther and Canby? I was always fond of Esther but she is so politically ignorant and shockingly blind to everything but her own idea of liberal—" This floored Esther and stopped the reading. I think I would just tell Evelyn nobody in Key West knows her or her dear father or Scotts (we're coming close to Francis Scott Key West, though) and the letter would be automatically destroyed by the illiterate nurse when Esther got it. Anyway I suppose nothing will head her off in her resolute will to be a nuisance. . . .

The icebox now doesn't make any ice and the man said well, he didn't say the $8.50 charge would make it freeze. It needs a new freezing unit—$64.00— which enraged me so that I can't write Miss Anthony till I calm down. Fortunately there were no orts in the box to speak of except the delicious blintzes which we had with applesauce for breakfast. Now we are freezeless till after the

---

*The poet and novelist Evelyn Scott (1893–1963) had been an acquaintance of Powell's since the 1920s. Both Esther Andrews and Margaret De Silver had given her financial support on occasion. In her later years, she was deeply and suspiciously anti-Communist.

4th unless the cooler weather cures the machinery as the mechanic said might happen. Then I tackle my landlady. Glad it happened now so she can't say we wore it out. The place is still lovely and mostly cool.

Love,
Dawn

(COLLECTION TIM PAGE)

TO MARGARET DE SILVER

[130 West Twelfth Street
September 17, 1959]

Dearest Margaret—

[. . .] My cousin Jack Sherman just phoned this minute to say Auntie May died this a.m. Funeral Saturday. I know I should go but I don't think I could bear it emotionally after the fatigue and nerve-rags of this exhausting summer. I look terrible and fat and blowzy and by the time all of my frank distant relatives gave me their honest opinions and the bright ones asked me why I gave up writing or did I ever?—and why don't I write for *Reader's Digest* and don't we own our own home yet?—anyway, grief would give way to fury and I would shout that they were all a bunch of voyeurs of voyeurs (since that made such a hit). It does worry me though—even after all these years—that this dopey little town will be whispering, "Isn't it shocking that Dawnie didn't even come to the funeral after all May did for her . . . ?"

Well, which worry do I like best—the one where they say, "Don't Dawn look awful?"—barefoot and bearded and wattled—or the one where they don't see me at all?

I'll brood on this till it's too late. That will solve the whole problem. . . .*

Just another problem for my dizzy brain, paralyzed as it is with novelitis.

Love and kisses. Wish I were on your sun deck this minute with my novel done; an apartment all arranged; Joe, Jojo and Fagin all buttoned up; and me thinned down to fit my clothes.

I dreamed about you the other night and I was very jealous because you were thinned down to a seductive Viennese figure and had on a black evening dress with a deep ruffle and gold slippers and were dancing divinely (maybe with Krutchef).†

The Castile laundry man came in and called me Mrs. De Silver as several of your neighbors do and this is a great compliment, because the other day

---

*In the end, Powell did not attend the funeral.
†Soviet Premier Nikita Khrushchev had recently paid a historic visit to the United States.

someone showed me a snapshot of me looking exactly like Elsie Maxwell—fat bare arms and bloated chin wattles wagging.* It shows up more in pictures (my Elsie resemblance) than in person, I think—I mean, I *trust*. This picture was taken at a party where I was having a fine time and thought I looked marvelous.

Haven't seen any Martins.

Let me know about when to scat—I assume before the 1st but maybe the cold weather will fetch you sooner.

I long for the day this book is over and I can get out of this cloud into a new one.

Love,
Dawn

(COLLECTION JACQUELINE MILLER RICE)

TO PHYLLIS POWELL COOK

Snedens Landing
Palisades, N.Y.
Dec. 6, 1959

Dearest Phyllis—

I'm spending the weekend here at the Murphys' which is very quiet and peaceful on the river so I sleep about 20 hours. I will take the bus back to N.Y. groggier than ever. Your birthday present was very very nice and allowed me to lavish some hose and powder on *myself* (an old favorite of mine). . . .

I thought of O.K. [Otto Steinbrueck] the other day at an art show where I ran into Virgil Thomson, the old music critic and composer who has lived for some 30 years at the Hotel Chelsea where Edgar Lee Masters lived. I asked him if he had much trouble with Masters's ghost and he said no, because the Old Boy had not *died* there—he had been taken out to hospital a week before he died. I have forgotten whether O.K. had known him in N.Y. or Chicago or where.

We are cozy but confined in our sunny dowdy rooms at the Irving. As we are both *in* all day it is something of a strain but not so much as if we were *out* all day sitting on the curb. Joe did a good piece of *Current Biography* and is this weekend doing another one on Abram Chasins, the music commentator. These pay practically nothing and are addenda to the H. W. Wilson *Encyclopedia of Biography* (I *think* that's it) but worth millions to Joe because the editors are so pleased and he himself is so delighted to find he can pick up straight journalism

---

*Powell was staying in De Silver's apartment while her hostess was on Cape Cod. Elsa Maxwell (1883–1963) was a famous but not especially physically attractive hostess.

again after all these years in advertising. If our financial structure would get more solid he would really be happier than he's ever been in his life, for this is the work he always preferred and now he finds he is still good at it. Usually when people get their wish, it turns out they're no good. . . .

Thanks again and I wish you had come on but I do agree there is little pleasure in visiting N.Y. without enough money to find bargains etc. and relax— anyhow for people of our advanced ages. It takes me a week to get over the bumps of an hour's bus ride up here!

Much love to family,
Dawn

P.S. What do you do for calluses (on the brain, too)? I remember you told me once but now my feet really are a nuisance—too small to carry my weight so shoes have to be too big or if they're good shoes the leather doesn't give so I am full of plasters and other annoyances. Or did I just inherit Grandma's bunions along with the rest of the estates?

(COLLECTION TIM PAGE)

TO JOHN F. SHERMAN

43 Fifth Ave.
Apt. 2WA
Feb. 21, 1960

Dear Jack—

Suddenly found apartment—block up from old 9 East Tenth. Very convenient in ancient, seedy, palatial old apartment house that looks like Roman Baths. Two rooms and bathroom larger than either—crystal chandelier in kitchen. One of Stanford White's architectural triumphs before Harry Thaw got him. Cheapest we've seen (and we'd almost given up)—this is a wing chopped off from a ten-room apartment. Moving in tomorrow. Telephone not in till 23rd but will let you know.

love
Dawn

(COLLECTION JOHN F. SHERMAN)

TO JOSEPH GOUSHA

Yaddo
Wednesday, March 16, 1960

Dear Joe—

The cute Winnipeg girl, Adele Wiseman,* has just told me about the new girdle called "Orbit"—for women who think their ass is out of this world.

The Endocreme arrived smartly Tuesday morning and I immediately slathered it on my leather, snow-scarred face. There *is* a difference. Pati Hill[†] and I gathered buckets of snow and boiled it on the electric grill to wash our hair (avoiding the dry hard water). The snow was so hard we could have fried it like scrapple.

I enclose check for you to be *sure* and get pants or suit (try for suit) as I received one of *Post* checks. Also do get man to hang pictures for sheer convenience to me when I get back. Maybe the Dehn mantelpiece one can go in bedroom as the big Haitian one is rather boring—too big and not art enough to overwhelm a room. The bathroom ones are all more charming really in case you want to rearrange them below. Don't care really. The shadowboxes *are* dirty but art place next to florist's (is it still there?) charges $11 to fix and clean. If they look all right to you, one on each end of my bed, maybe. The box of my published manuscripts by stove can go under bed (with oilcloth or something to protect it from Fagin's squirreling claws and teeth).

If you are uptown do see some shows—Franz Kline's at Sidney Janis (on East 57th Street or maybe Martha Jackson Gallery). Just out of Cedar loyalty. Jackie writes Eddie and Liz and Siobhan McKenna were Cedar callers. Hedy Lamarr is a Franz Kline worshipper.

I cannot stop terrific sleep binge. I do hope you are able to catch up too as we really have had a long strain of intensive, nervous proximity and work and insecurity and monotony of worry, though God knows we have been lucky to have Margaret. Had charming letter from Jojo—very mature, thought "the place looked nice with our belongings." I sent him Kools. . . .

Skidmore College here has been having Dads' Week and signs on restaurants read "Happy Pappy Week." The Ball for Fathers was a social event. Someone said that years ago when Slater Brown was at Yaddo he was in town during Daddy Week and said, "What's happened to college girls today? These girls seem to be going for men old enough to be their fathers!" (Old gaffers of 39 or 40 at that.) We plan to have a rival Yaddo Daddo week to make the Spa rattle. The town is not worth going to—not even for liquor, as I have not been able to work up a thirst for more than a rum toddy before dinner or snort of rye

---

*Adele Wiseman (1928–1993), then a colonist at Yaddo, was a Canadian novelist and writer.
[†]Pati Hill (born 1921), a former fashion model, novelist, and, most recently, visual artist with a specialty in work created with photocopying machines, was one of Powell's fellow colonists that spring.

at midnight between sleeps. We each drink our own except on special occasions (one so far) when we have two drinks out of our host's or hostess's Scotch. Nothing to *do* with a glow, after all!

Dinner strictly at 6:30 on the dot and hour of rather taxing Required Conversation with Mrs. [Elizabeth] Ames afterward.* Often interesting but like a night required lecture course—almost raising our hands when we have answers or anecdotes. She goes to New York tomorrow so we may all explode. Hope Fagin isn't getting sick on dirty water. Try hot water in his milk and also catnip on paper and get chicken for yourself, too.

Love,
D

TO MARGARET DE SILVER

Yaddo
March 24, 1960

Dear Maggie—

Light snow of crumpled tranquilizers still piling up outside here and snow of sleep piling up in me. Is this the "rapture of the deep"? Hard to think of pulling out on Tuesday for that PEN program I had thought would be a lifesaver. Is this life savable, I say? As a matter of fact, after brief telephone conversation with Joe, I realize I will have a large snowbank of wounded feelings to combat and melt on my dip into town. He sounded absolutely sunk and, instead of my cheering him, I only aggravated him. Oh balls—men are too too too! He hasn't seen anybody, talked to anyone, gone to a movie, gone to the Shack, answered the phone, anything. He wants me there to get on his nerves so it's fun to get out. He wants me to ask people in so he can sizzle with rage (but at least have something to sizzle). He seemed appalled when I said I would stay in town till Sunday and I realize he is lonesome but he wants me there and lonesome too. . . .

Mrs. Ames still away. No drinkers here which saves me the embarrassing confession of feeling too elderly to whoop it up. Jojo writes very encouraging letters—hopes I'll get my work done and so on—rather fatherly. Joe said he (Jojo) gives him all the news of Yaddo (which I write to him).

I see a row of Evelyn [Scott]'s books here and sometimes take a look at them—the earlier poetry was rather bad, really. I was surprised to see, recalling

*Elizabeth Ames (1884–1977) was the first executive director of the Yaddo artists' colony, where Powell spent parts of 1955 and 1960.

how well it was praised, "gilded" and "bronzed" and "silvered" and "jeweled" trees, etc. Once I found an early volume of my friend John Hall Wheelock's verse (he took Max Perkins's place as my editor). His early work was full of grapes. Let us lift the grape—come, a cup of purple enchantment let us drain—and while the grape bubbles in our bowl—etc. I accused him of this some 30 yrs. after the opus and he admitted he had had a mighty thirsty youth and every poem had to have *quaff* or *sip* or *drain* in it. *Slurp* would have been better.

Joe said it cost $17 to have our pictures hung (by janitor) which makes me laugh—as if it were a splendid gallery instead of two closets, but the high ceilings, wire and stepladdering make it the equivalent of a flagpole-decorating. . . .

Our charming Chinaman* has gone to town (New York) and so it's us four ladies—and Harvey Swados, the Yaddo Daddo (he doesn't like this).† He is a nice, healthy smart lad—40-ish. I am always against "Harveys"—and he does look Harveyish but turns out very warm. The ex-model Pati Hill keeps writing short plays for Spoleto and skis and defends all moot characters mentioned as "terribly sweet." This for Mary McCarthy too—as Swados lifted an eye (me too) she was even more defensive. Then Hannah Green‡ said, "I hear she is terribly beautiful and glamorous." Whereupon Pati squealed, "Beautiful! Glamorous! Good Heavens, she's the worst-dressed, most dreadfully dowdy creature I ever saw! I wish you could see her dressed up in what the poor dear thinks is smart. Goodness knows she probably spends *hours* fixing herself up and the transparent tops supposed to be seductive and showing her broken shoulder straps and oh my word no—"

So I was given the always pleasant role of defending Miss M.'s clothes—*very, very* well dressed, I said. How *sweet* I was.

The young ladies are very smart and lively, I must say, and there is none of the usual Little Mag Exegesis-[Leslie]Fiedler-P.R. crapmanship as was here before.

Pati Hill discovered a strange dirty old-style book in Mrs. Katrina Trask's weird library—a naughty-nun-and-hot-lover 1880 tale, *Venetian Lover,* translated by Whittaker Chambers! Full of naked bosoms and flagellations on white nun virgin flesh by older nuns and dark lovers—whee!

Swados knows and likes Alger Hiss very much—says it was Pris [Priscilla Hiss] who wanted the divorce and Alger very low, still much in love with her. I thought it was his doing. He (Swados) says he is mystified, though, whether

---

*Powell is referring here to the Chinese-American composer Chou Wen-Chung (born 1923), a fellow colonist.
†Harvey Swados (1920–1972) was an independent American radical novelist and essayist.
‡The novelist Hannah Green (1926–1996) would become one of Powell's closest friends and would care for her tenderly in the years to come.

Hiss was framed by Nixon or some very powerful setup or whether he was really guilty—and canceled it out of his mind. Did I tell you I saw Pris lunching at Cedar with some other woman once?—I'm sure it was she.

Maybe see you March 29–April 2. Happy April Food.

love,
Dawn

(COLLECTION TIM PAGE)

TO JOSEPH GOUSHA

[Saratoga Hospital
*ca. April 24, 1960]**

Dear Joe—

Better here, I guess, than the scramble in New York. . . . Started with feeling fine (all quiet life caused it, I guess) then sneezing spell two or three days, then Thursday night a start. Stopped. No gusher. Apprehensive, however. (Experience, after all.) Doc again but stopped before he saw me as before so he couldn't figure it out. Wouldn't take my report of other doc's say-so. Returned to Yaddo. Felt fine. Then started typing my review of *The Leopard* for the *Post* (really furious at having to read the complicated thing and assemble thoughts for $25 which should be on winding up novel). Then in midst of typing—whoops— same minute you telephoned this a.m. Got worse (worse than other two times but nothing compared to Christmas gusher). Lore Gorszman (writer) and Polly Hanson (Yaddo secretary) brought me to hospital for Dr. Friedson. I asked to have nose packed but it had stopped again and anyway he still couldn't find any focus in nose for bleeding and refused to cauterize or pack without focal point discovered. Said stay in hospital for 48 hours at least and be examined. As bleeding was stopped and I wanted to finish review, I refused—why *examine* when I wouldn't be here for treatment anyway? Went back to Yaddo. Took medicine. Three hours later was talking through window to [John] Cheever and oops—off again so I thought better hospital here. Cheever and everyone very very fine and all pleased to do something to break monotony I guess. So here in semiprivate room. Doc hasn't showed yet. Cheever most helpful as only man. Call Margaret. Ask if she can spare something or other as now I've gotten down toward rent and have to pay more of course. Endorse check for emergency. Have $165 on check deposit now. Make out rent anyway and [letter unfinished and unmailed]

(COLLECTION TIM PAGE)

---

*Powell, suffering from a torrential nosebleed, had been rushed to the hospital in the middle of the night by the novelist John Cheever and Pati Hill. She would return to New York almost immediately after her release.

43 Fifth Avenue
June 7, 1960

Dear Phyllis:

Have been meaning to give you a large piece of my mind but find not much left of it. Anyway it is good to know Uncle Kent left you his protection so for God's sake don't foul him up by renouncing it.*

Keep everything you have in your name and anything else you find, because nobody will be sorry for you when you whimper that your good mate has given it all to somebody else out of the goodness of his heart or liver. (Least of all will the mate be sorry. He will only be mad at you for not having hid some for HIS protection.)

After a lifetime of juggling this sort of thing my own mate finally INSISTS that I hang on to whatever comes in and shouts DON'T put anything in my account, keep everything in yours and for Godsake don't tell me about it. That's all that has ever saved us.

I hung on to my insurance against pressure as long as I dared, using it for borrowing, etc., then had to clean it out last year. If I'd had a little stamina the endowments would have bloomed last year, thus keeping us off the ragged edge of uncertainty or at least paying in around ninety a month or more.

Anyway I can assure you it is a certain thing that men have no sense about handling money for human protection. They think it is some sort of football game and their side will win. And nothing is more painful for a woman past her Prime (as they call it) than to have to tell her man, after he's broken his scooter, that there isn't anything left to give him. And nothing exceeds his love and admiration if she has outwitted him and is still sitting on a few eggs. Fun for her too.

I know women are the nation's rich but they say it is because the men made it and left it to them. I used to think that but now I think most tycoons have had extremely shrewd women managers who knew how to tie things up and let the boys take the credit. I'm sure they would have bought real estate on other planets or ragweed plantations if they'd had full control.

Joe has had his first operation—colostomy—which relieves the strain on the malignant rectal zone. The X-ray therapy has been so far successful in lessening the area of that zone so that the major operation may not be so drastic as first predicted. The doctor will not make definite statements now—maybe he made too many at first—but we think the plan is to continue the X-ray for some days before the next operation. I hope they will keep it up for longer to

*Phyllis Powell Cook had been left a modest inheritance by a relative.

give more of a chance. He is weak from the many exams and treatments every day and tired but otherwise in no pain and reading constantly and I am so relieved not to have to be cold-compressing and braiding splints and so on (and doing it wrong) and unable to get any work done which will make money.

Louise [Lee] wrote today she is in Boston City Hospital, Harrison Avenue, Boston, Mass., Surgical Ward Five—having breast removed soon.

Everybody's in hospital. Lake Erie is awarding me honorary degree of Doctor of Literature on Monday, July 13, at Commencement and I hope I can get there as that's the only way you get it and it is helpful in getting better deals and consideration in my work. I will fly to Cleveland Sunday if all goes well here—not try to cover anything else as it's too complicated—and fly back Monday night. Will not bring cat. Maybe you can come to Cleveland or to the Commencement 11 a.m. Monday, though it will be a drag.

Love,
Dawn

(COLLECTION TIM PAGE)

TO DR. BLOOMFIELD

43 Fifth Avenue
New York City
October 18, 1960

Dear Dr. Bloomfield:

I am writing you again to ask you to consider changing my son's ward from 11A to a better one. He—(Joseph R. Gousha)—became disturbed several months ago for a fairly plausible reason: his father, who took him on weekly expeditions, was taken to St. Vincent's Hospital with cancer and has been there ever since; his grandmother died; a funeral home sent him notice that his long-time nurse and childhood teacher had died—all this within a month.*

While his upset lasted only briefly he has been confined to 11A for months, showing patience and cooperation in general but greatly taxed by the more violent cases around him.

Fellow patients, hospital employees, and others who should know tell me this is the worst ward and that Joseph's nature and general conduct do not merit such reformatory treatment. He has shown an increasing growth in understanding and poise when at home and it would be a great help to him to have companions of better mentality.

---

*Laura Mathias Gousha and Louise Lee had both just died.

Dr. Unger informed a psychiatrist friend of ours that Joseph had developed remarkably well, and he rises to the occasion here at home when called upon.

Hoping you can find a place for him in a better ward,

> Sincerely,
> Dawn Powell Gousha

(COLLECTION TIM PAGE—CARBON COPY)

TO PHYLLIS POWELL COOK

> *43 Fifth Avenue*
> *December 13, 1960*

Dearest Phyllis—

What are your problems, chum? Would you say offhand that 1960 has been cooked up by enemy operators? . . .

Just as Joe was improving so much after a second skin grafting to heal wound that he was due either home or nursing home in a couple of weeks, 4 a.m. Saturday found me gushing gore once again—à la nose and mouth. Fortunately I was alone so there was no panic and by this time I knew about the Emergency entrance of St. Vincent's Hospital—so I got on my clothes, fed the cat, toweled my nose, and also had cash on hand (a commodity impossible to keep on hand with man or maid or chick in the house)—so I was out on the cold street at 5:30—got taxi—refused his know-how but told him where to go (just 2 ½ blocks but driving into Emergency) and so for 4 hrs. I was needled and rested and packed and treated very efficiently. Always before I thought you went to a doctor. (Never, never, do anything so silly! They don't know how to wipe an ordinary nose and they make you bleed to death first too!)

I had planned a weekend at home for Jojo to write his Xmas cards which Jack had sent him and on Sunday my pretty young friend Jacqueline Miller was to borrow Margaret De Silver's car to take him and me for a country drive. So this rare treat had to be postponed (naturally, turned out Jojo had a flip because nobody notified him and he waited all day!). I didn't dare tell Joe as the thing scares him any time. All okay and I took all the phenobarbs they gave and didn't move till midnight Saturday night when bingo! it all burst out my mouth as my nose was bandaged so I sat here with ice and waiting for some daylight as I knew Greenwich Village Saturday night would be full of roisterers and indeed I heard them. Finally about 4 I was afraid I'd choke so I dressed, then repeated my trip and got a cross female doctor who packed it again—said to come back and stay in hospital if it happened again. So I doddered home.

Jacqueline and Coby Gilman were wonderful next day. She took goodies to

Joe and this is good because at sight of her blond tresses the doctors all take great interest in Joe's case and he has a ball. Then she and Coby took Jojo's cards and clothes and candy up to Ward's and took him out to Westchester for a ride and he was very pleased to have an outing with friends instead of same old parents.

Of course, it turned out another patient (or maybe an attendant) had stolen his beautiful topcoat, which Jack had bequeathed him three or four years ago, but they raised another one for him. It had been swiped before and returned. If it is really gone there are compensations as Social Security has been sending $58 a month to Joe for dependent child and for some time has been raising Cain that this should go to the hospital, though Joe had explained it was for Jojo's clothes, their upkeep, and weekends-at-home expenses—which God knows are more than that.

So I can cite this as an example of necessary expense. From my window yesterday I saw cars buried in drifts on 11th St. Finally they cleared middle of 5th Ave about noon Sunday but the cars are still stalled and iglooed under our window. As they've been there since middle of storm I can only assume that people are really dumber than ever—they have such faith in the machine that they think if they can dig their way through a drift from apartment to apartment, the faithful old machine will fly up over the drift and carry them to Beulahland or wherever they like. . . .

This place would be charming and European with its high ceilings, chandeliers, etc. for two people who worked away from home but I wonder how we'll manage, really. Rooms are about 16 × 14—bath is about 10 × 12.

My mouth is still giving out blood and back of throat feels raked but nose has stopped or is bleeding backwards probably, but nothing to speak of. Will go to doctor when blizzard gives up.

Did I thank you for birthday I hope? Do try to get Morgan [Cook] to sell house before its repairs and upkeep take all your extra.

love to girls,
Dawn

(COLLECTION TIM PAGE)

TO JOHN F. SHERMAN

[43 Fifth Avenue]
December 21, 1960

Dear Jack—

Your letter was terribly exciting—even beyond the delightful enclosure which was wonderful of you.

I think the Ashland College and quit plan* is wonderful and, as you say, the convenience and familiarity with the town and college make it much easier to glide into than bucking such a great change at Harvard as we originally planned, as you recall, when Gramps's will was read.

These community colleges—or community-supported ones—are the only alive campuses left and the break from Home and Maw is not so tough. The teachers today that I know seem to have the best life (I mean in colleges where they don't have to wipe noses, too). In fact, they infuriate me, they're so damn smug. They have their captive audience and can shoot their traps at them and be worshipped as The End (I think so) and get foundation grants, etc., and travel every seven years for free, and lord it over their ignorant pals. This has been a sudden change here (at least as I've seen it) from the old frustrated-writer-or-scientist-obliged-to-teaching-rut to feed baby.

My friend Walter Rumsey Marvin† (classmate of Dos Passos, where I met him) suddenly gave up fairly rich legal or brokerage career here in New York at age of 45 or so and calmly said he had always wanted to teach history. Accustomed to hearing people who always wanted to write or paint, this seemed an odd one but he meant it. His wife (he married after 40) taught English here at a smart girls' school, Spence, and by God they shopped around, sold their charming house and bought the Columbus School for Girls and, so far as I hear, have been happily teaching history ever since. He was also (still may be) head of the Ohioana Library in Columbus and I get letters from him spasmodically regarding my books. If you are in Columbus, call him up and say I sent love and that you would like his words on your plan. They have a charming little girl, Miranda, age 4 (at least she was that in 1946 and I have heard nothing to the contrary). In fact I will send him a Xmas card to alert him. He is lovely and Betsey (wife) is too. They used to buy dozens of my books for Xmas presents and I autographed them feverishly. . . .

If you stay on in the nice payday job just waiting for vacation time and paydays, you have the future made for you—sending nieces and nephews to college who don't want to go, looking after aging and ailing kinfolk, contribut-

*At the age of forty-nine, Sherman had decided to quit his job and return to college to study English. As she makes clear here, Powell was delighted for him, and their closeness redoubled.
†Walter Rumsey Marvin (1900–1987) was a close friend to John Dos Passos and a founder of the Ohioana Literary Association.

ing to everybody's happiness (you think) with a drop in the bucket here and a drop in the bucket there (the catastrophes and needs multiply astronomically with each drop) until finally—bucket bucket who's got the bucket? Not Ole Daddy-o Jackie, or if it is a bucket you know what's in it. Little Eloise you sent to Vassar because you always wanted to go there runs off with her friendly abortionist; Willie, after you sent him to Paris to study nudes (because *you* wanted to), comes back and steals your safe and harpsichord, etc., etc. The money down the drain and the drain might as well be *you*.

I think it would be wonderful to do this thing—as it makes you more valuable anyway not only to yourself but to all the people you love to help. Hell, the White House next. And you'd be a marvelous teacher. Men do seem to enjoy it, and there are, I understand, all sorts of extras that make up for the decreased salaries at first.

I get really amazed at the number of men and women knocking themselves out in jobs they hate—so every day is a dull pain—in order to get plastered every night or noon at great expense to make up to themselves for not being happy in their work.

I am still too basically provincial to quite dig it (phony status reasons of course) when men give up city jobs and go back to being carpenters or wagon-dinner runners on Cape Cod because Cape Codders are only happy on Cape Cod, but that's very cheap of me.

A girl on *The New Yorker* just phoned me to say that in tomorrow's *New Yorker* I get a plug in Frank Sullivan's annual Christmas poem.

Last night I choked to death on a piece of steak (I have Grandma's throat-choking trouble—something goes in windpipe and you can't get it up or down and suffocate). It has happened before with steak always—suddenly my throat clamps shut. Dr. gave me gland pills before for it and I laid off beef. So there I was, gasping and sputtering till 4 and finally calmed myself saying, What about if it was somebody else choking, what to do? Why, bread and butter of course, I said, and stuffed it down and by God it worked.

Moral: treat yourself as if you were your favorite case. . . .

Hurray for Ashland and you and luck and much thanks.

> love to Rita and girls,
> Dawn

P.S. Jacqueline's boyfriend is a married teacher at Eastern college and she wails that he will never get divorce from wife he avowedly hates because he loves his work so much he won't risk losing job.

Tip: Get your divorce before going into teaching.

(COLLECTION JOHN F. SHERMAN)

TO GERALD AND SARA MURPHY

43 Fifth Avenue
New York City
December 22, 1492 [1960]

Dear Gerald and Sara:

By this time we would know each other by our symptoms (as reported by middleman Solley)* even if we'd never met. In that crowded room of song, you would overhear a north-Ohio voice saying, "Parm me, but have I told you about that strangled feeling I get after nosebleeds?" and Sara will nudge you, Gerald, and whisper, "Don't look now but that must be THE Dawn Powell." And I will hear a south-Ohio voice whimper, "Duke, do you ever have a feeling that you have a red-hot balloon in your middle, *mon ami?*" and I will nudge good old Greg or maybe Manny and Syd and say, "That must be Solley's Sara, how exciting."

I always feel better after a glimpse of Solley's naughty-faun mask and this time I saw Dr. Millet too who is a good sight.

Are you freezing?

I was glad to have a showy thing like nosebleeds again which seemed like a personal indulgence of my own after other people's illnesses, and it got me out of many exhausting duties or pleasures as people respect blood (it might get on their Ku Klux bibs) who override your 106-degree fevers and inner pains.

Joe is still in hospital but very jolly, eats, takes baths, walks, but is well enough now to be wistfully impatient at incarceration.

Our charming young Englishman, Bryan Robertson, is writing some art reviews for *New Statesman* which are remarkably perceptive from visual sense—not as writing. Also he is on season's honors list with OBE coming up and says he will clank over soon in sword and plume. I imagine he won this for his amazing energy in finding British art and touting it in New Guinea, Australia, Cambodia, and Upper Tooting with his wild and brilliant enthusiasm.

I have a weekly deaf maid who locks the door against unheard rape and doesn't hear me trying to get back in. However things do look cleaner (from out here in the hall).

Love and hope 1961 does a better job,
Dawn

(COLLECTION HONORIA MURPHY DONNELLY)

---

*Powell and the Murphys were patients of the same Manhattan doctor, Robert Solley.

TO WILLIAM PETERSON[*]

43 Fifth Avenue
March 2, 1961

Dear W.P.—

As we say on Madison Avenue.

Today I sent you a copy of *Jig-Saw*, which turned up, also a reprint of *A Cage for Lovers* which came out in a nice little paperback in England around Xmas.

I looked over the play for the first time in years and found it dated and didn't intend to send it. However, I met Tom Prideaux, a *Life* drama or film editor I'd once known, and was surprised to have him tell me he had read *Jig-Saw* a hundred times as a sample of ideal comedy technique.

I remembered then that I had first started this play as a rather scathing picture of the idle women spending their husbands' money or alimony in New York apartment hotels, shopping one day and taking the stuff back the next, hoping for Something or Other to fill in their days without their expending any energy themselves.

In the midst of this my other comedy *Big Night* was produced and criticized as too brutal, too real, so I thought it would be amusing to cast the new material in very exact French farce form.

As you know, form can deaden your live material but it can also protect it. Audiences can absorb as little meaning as they like so long as the function of comedy—to amuse—is fulfilled.

This does make playwriting a first-rate game and I wish I were more of a gambler to enjoy it, instead of being battered by the fighting and selling aspects of the business.

Anyway I decided to send you the copy for your files.

My husband has been home, apparently and amazingly cured, for two months and I have been looping—Visiting Nurses, proper feeding, etc. Also I have an office now two blocks from home where I am trying to finish my book for Malcolm Cowley's return from Leland Stanford this month (he is my editor at Viking). I review for the *N.Y. Post* when I find time.

This reminds me that Malcolm was so fascinated by my reports of Lake Erie that he might enter there himself, he said!

Sincerely,
Dawn Powell

---

[*]The writer, educator, and director William Peterson (born 1926) had been responsible for Powell's belated recognition by Lake Erie College, where he was then teaching. In 1997, he would direct the first staging of *Jig-Saw* in sixty years, in Southampton, Long Island.

TO EDMUND WILSON

80 East 11th Street—My Office
March 2, 1961
43 Fifth Avenue—My Claustrophob.

Dear Wig—

I wake up in the night laughing about our mutual rush for LIQUORS and snatching at individual bottles with a nipple apiece to take home where we could slurp in what I like to think is Civilized Fashion without any nonsense.

I wish Bessie Smith had been there that night at the Albee play.*

Jesus. It just struck me. Is that little bastard heir to the Albee theater chain? If so I turn Commie again.

It struck me that the reason his use of horror and vivisection (or whatever) seemed to sugar his play instead of shock us was that his straight (almost) treatment of family life was so much more lethal.

How many times producers have told me, "You CAN'T have people talking that way to each other on the stage, my dear girl—yes, yes, of course they do in life but it comes out so much harsher on the stage." If the girl says she hates her husband, you must show that she isn't really nasty, she means she loves children and she doesn't say *hate* seriously. She laughs when she says it and tousles his scalp.

I hate hate hate this demanding goddemanding novel and my head, the imported Swiss-cheese one full of holes. On the other hand isn't it better to be me than to be Sloan Wilson, Robert Ruark or Aaron Copland?† I withdraw Copland who at least isn't smug. I withdraw everything. If I was, say, Sloan Wilson, I would think I was wonderful. I mention him because I still feel a little soiled from having to review a book of his.

I saw Dos at a Houghton Mifflin tiny party for him. I must say he does have to take on a lot. Pompous Pricks (courtesy Gilman Dictionary) from NYU cornering him and asking politely: "Tell me, Mr. Dos Passos, what made you decide to go on writing? What answer are you going to make to that unfavorable review in the *South Bend Sentinel*? Do you mind being called a has-been?"

I haven't read this book but I'm sure it's just the same as he's been doing but the terrifying thing is that it's the wind and the time and the tide that decide your luck.‡

If that *Times* fine review had been on page 10 and had led off with one of

---

*Powell and Wilson had just been to see *An American Dream*, by the dramatist Edward Albee (born 1928). Powell makes reference here to one of his earlier plays, *The Death of Bessie Smith*.
†Sloan Wilson and Robert Ruark were two popular novelists of the day. Aaron Copland (1900–1990) was a distinguished composer of concert music.
‡*Midcentury*, a new novel by Dos Passos, had been published the previous month.

its other paragraphs—"It is a pity there is so much tedious hammering," etc.—
with the fine praising first line lost in the middle—

How frighteningly dependent we are on things beyond our control.

Do I sound like Lin Yutang? . . .

I had a drink at Longchamps with my third-floor neighbors, the Lieblings
(Jean Stafford).* I don't really dig her. I never do get these lady writers who
are Foremost of All Writers, Ladies, and go to bed in their laurels the way I
go to bed in my roller skates. (Not as drunk as they are, though.) She is intelligent (for a lady), good company (for a writer), but she is always in touch with
Olympus, a summons to Pakistan to shed probably antidotal culture to that
just shed by M. McCarthy, a call to the White House, having grown up with the
Kennedy Boys—

Oh well, I suppose we can't all be riffraff.

I just read an old novel of mine, *Turn, Magic Wheel.* It is perfectly wonderful. This, however, does not cheer me.

I would cut my throat but the house is such a mess.

aloha,
Humph

Best to Elena and Ros. Turns out I *am* Sloan Wilson! By George!

(YALE COLLECTION OF AMERICAN LITERATURE, BEINECKE RARE BOOK
AND MANUSCRIPT LIBRARY, YALE UNIVERSITY)

TO JOHN F. SHERMAN

[43 Fifth Avenue]
Wed. March 22, 1961

Dear Jack—

The Easter eggs have hatched (Joe's and mine) and were DELICIOUS. I will
take Jojo's to him on Saturday. He is normalized to such an improved degree
these days that the moment I appear he says, "Don't forget to leave me some
dough." This is all to the good. He has also learned to lie a little, he said
proudly, and when a pal asks him for a quarter he says, "I don't have it." So
he doesn't have to give it to them. I complimented him on this advance and he
said, "Well, I DIDN'T have it, either."

He had won a comb at a bingo party and had sung a solo—"Crying on the
Inside, Laughing on the Outside." He knows the verses and choruses to every
damn popular song of the last 30 years.

---

*The novelist and short-story writer Jean Stafford (1915–1979) was then married to the critic A. J.
Liebling (1904–1963).

I have been hoping for an opportune moment to borrow Margaret De Silver's seldom-used car and have Jackie drive Joe and me up to pick up Jojo and go for a ride, as Joe hasn't seen him for a year and the exhausting business of my first walking five blocks to subway, then up and downstairs (I LOATHE this and pant and puff for days), up to 125th Street, up and down again, then bus to Ward's Island, then walk through mud and cinders to his building, then wait for superintendent to show up for pass, then wait more for Jojo, then back again—to do this TWICE in a day, as I have done when I bring him home, is enough to knock me out for a week. Jackie wants to get her mitts on a car anyway, so we've cooked this up as a sort of Christian favor from Margaret at the right time.

Your college future seems great. I will come out to see you hooded.

This week I am reading a dozen stories by Barnard students for a prize given there every year, and this year I am one of three judges—with Bernard Malamud, a new, rather successful novelist, and somebody else I don't know. We don't get paid for our judgeship, as sometimes happens, but I agreed just to see what young literary college students are writing about now. So far they seem to write fluently—more so than in my day when there were just two or three of us in a class who could put a sentence together. However the influence of Freud and psychoANALYSIS is clear—they write in the first person a lot and remember sexy moments from their childhood and faraway first lays when they were a rather bored ten or eleven. In fact they seem self-absorbed, sex-obsessed, oblivious to all surroundings and people—curious.

This is the Elizabeth Janeway Annual Prize.* She herself (Elizabeth) is a dame I knew when she was at Barnard and won a prize and then she had a couple of best-sellers and immortalized herself by endowing this $500 prize.

Remember to do this at Ashland. The J. F. Sherman Prize. . . .

Joe is very jubilant. He had a checkup at the hospital yesterday and the doctors crowed and sang over him and shunted him from Z to X-ray to all departments and called out nurses and voyeurs to look at his bottom and they all cried, "Beautiful, Beautiful, Beautiful," and all shook hands with each other over his behind and announced that on Monday at 3:30 they would have a Showing and Lecture with him as the Show before a group of medicos.

I'm afraid all the flattery will turn his little ass.

Much love and much thanks,
Dawn

(COLLECTION JOHN F. SHERMAN)

*Elizabeth Janeway (born 1913) is an American novelist and short-story writer.

TO WHIT BURNETT*

43 Fifth Avenue
April 12, 1961

Dear Whit:

Thank you for a really extraordinary experience. You never know how cynical you have become of possible good in our contemporary world until something good happens and practically knocks you out.

The mere fact that there could be found 27 stories by young people in America as fine as these are is astounding. I think the very least good—for none were even bad—would shine in any magazine, only of course they wouldn't let it.

The whole group together was like a bus trip through America and how we Americans *hunger* for America, which we can never know anyway any more than we can know ourselves. The great thing was the excellence of the writing in the pure clear sense. Not in the "literary" sense—no tricks, no faddism— sheer, beautiful storytelling, not CREATIVE WRITING COURSE stuff all in imitation of the current instructor (or if so, at least reabsorbed).

Nothing had that mothball smell of STORIES THE ENGLISH TEACHER HAS TO GET PUBLISHED IN A LITTLE MAGAZINE TO GET A PROMOTION BY THE FACULTY—or Pumping a Dry Well into a small rusty pail left by Salinger or *New Yorker* subsquares.

Not a story was selling the merchandise in the ads.

I found the general air whizzing through this collection was Freedom, and God knows this cannot be found in any recognized short-story collection, as they are already selected from ad-directed magazines or coterie-directed little mags.

This was a sad second thought—that I doubt if one of these stories would be acceptable to a popular magazine. I think the editors would think their lack of huckstering was "un-American."

I thought it seemed like a kind of optimistic angle of the New Wave. These American youngers accept what is wrong with their setups and the whole modern picture—not out of negativism but as they accept the rules in a complex sport: not in blind acceptance or surrender, but with the added excitement of meeting a worthy challenger. God help the little bastards, they think they can lick it and I *believe* them!

There were some excellent stories that I dare not look at again or this eenie-meenie could go on forever.

---

*Whit Burnett (1899–1973) was the founder and editor of *Story* magazine, which helped promote such writers as Truman Capote, J. D. Salinger, and Joseph Heller, among many others. Powell had just served as a judge for a competition sponsored by the magazine.

I hope you rush through a whole book of these fast as many people long for just such an expedition—a sort of summer festival or tour rather than BESTS.

Sincerely,
Dawn

P.S. Funny and *good*—lack of Southern homosex and Eastern Seaboard girls in rut.

(COLLECTION TIM PAGE—CARBON COPY)

Powell sent the following letter to her husband in St. Vincent's Hospital, New York, where he was undergoing radiation therapy to control his rectal cancer.

TO JOSEPH GOUSHA

43 Fifth Avenue
N.Y. City
[ca. April 22, 1961]

Dearest—

I daresay it is too early to go to bed but my eyes are closing firmly. I seem to have stood in wrong lines wherever I was all day, ending up at 12th Street A&P on leaving you with a pallid cart of round steak (very tough), pickles, and vapid tidbits which I have just had. I must say this Iris Murdoch *A Severed Head* is a magnificent piece of work—so good I hesitate to have you read it till you can fully appreciate its quality. I will probably finish it tonight.

Margaret sent a nice gift, you'll be glad to know, before taking off.

This morning, Sam—the elderly, white semi-super—was on the elevator. He always asks about you and is amazed that you are his age, as he is under the impression that he only looks about 40. He is married to a 35-year-old who gets taken to hospital with either T.B. or alcohol. I suddenly asked him if there was a bookie in our house and he said no. He said he had been one at 23rd and First for 20 years but his field was really the folding crap game which he set up all over the city for years. He was rather sad, recalling his former classy profession, and the reason he came down to this job was when he had a bad week with everybody's winning long shots and he had to raise $1100 one day to pay off a guy. So he said (to himself), "Sam, you only got $2000. Get out, Sam." So he obeyed himself.

Manaretta fixed the beds but yours seems about to cave in. I recall that it broke with me two or three times.

I hope you are not aflame or in orbit. I am extremely unradioactivated or very done up so will retire and come over the six-foot bend tomorrow—probably after Jojo.

I know how almost excruciatingly boring this radium thing is—exhausting and forever-ish—but you will emerge with a new Radiance.

Love,
W

TO JOHN F. SHERMAN

[43 Fifth Avenue]
Sunday, April 30, 1961

Dear Jack—

That was brilliant of you to have your man in Paris track down the lost Maria [Jolas]. She was on rue Bonaparte when I was there—possibly the same place, though if her two daughters and their families are now living with her she must have been able to buy the whole floor. One lived near Port d'Orléans I think with a doctor husband, and the other in Montmartre with a poet–Sorbonne teacher husband. Maria (with old Louisville Macdonald money) supported the whole lot as she had done—to some degree—for the James Joyces. She was in early days a sort of temperless, quatre-lingual, educated, Gretchen [Steinbrueck] boss-type, but the years beat her down and I liked her enormously when I last saw her.

It was nice of Marc [Clarin] to do all this.

Things have been jumping here—everything but me, but I have to lie low so they can jump on me.

Joe felt fine—or at least well enough to go around two or three hours a day with naps and nips—then the hospital took check and put him back in the jug for two weeks' radium and sprang him Friday. His behind is sorer than ever where they inserted the radium or maybe rayon so for a while he sits down with great reluctance.

A girl who was at Yaddo with me (she is from Glendale, Ohio, outside Cincinnati) has a car and took us all riding with Jojo a couple of weeks ago, then loaned her car to Jackie last Sunday who took Jojo and me for a fine jaunt through Rockland County along the Hudson and across the new Tappan Zee Bridge which is one of those low-slung ball-bearing things so you're right on the water—like the Key West–to–Homestead causeway. The girl feels indebted to me for getting her a charming (sometimes), totally irresponsible, lying little bastard of a lover who has given her a hell of a time. "He hit me—but that's only because his nasty wife got him into the habit of beating her up—and after borrowing two dollars he disappeared and hasn't shown up for a week or called and I'm so afraid he's *mad* at me. Oh how can I ever thank you for getting him for me, Dawn?"

Ah me, women, women. They've got to have their s.o.b.'s same as a fella has to have his bitches. . . .

Margaret De Silver phoned to tell me she has arranged in her will some trust-fund thing, apart from the insurance, for Jojo's expenses. I don't understand this and can't very well demand an accounting, with me as the manipulator and J. F. Sherman again as standby executioner.

I suppose if she told me how much and when and how, she fears I might poison her martini.

love,
Dawn

P.S. Joe had sunk from over 200 lbs. to 142 in hospital and was about 150 when he got out in December. Now he is 165—eating and sleeping, not to mention those ginnies.

(COLLECTION JOHN F. SHERMAN)

TO PHYLLIS POWELL COOK

[43 Fifth Avenue]
Sunday, April 30, 1961

Dearest Phyllis—

I hope you thought better of offering yourself to keep Mrs. Cook.* I am giving you the benefit of my years of inexperience in these matters. Anyway a few old ladies (some even as old as I am) have confided with bitterness of daughters or granddaughters who insisted on martyring themselves so they (the old ladies) couldn't go to the comfortable old-folks' home where they could feel independent and have a good time gassing with new friends their own age and bragging of their former glories, as you do with strangers on a cruise. The testifiers claimed that the Christian impulse of their relatives was pride—that they (the relatives) felt a stigma attached to having Mother "put away." The odd thing is that the nice ones prefer the dignity of a [nursing] home but the real old devils enjoy being a burden in their young's lives. Anyway, a well-to-do mother of a friend of mine (she was from Toledo) bought herself into a cozy home here on Madison Ave. and everybody is happier all around. She rather planned to be a proud stiff-upper-lip martyr about it as a protest against her son's new wife but instead is having a ball in her regal, genteel way. What I mean is, you can't give them as good a time as strangers can, so if she knows a place and wants it let her go before you take the responsibility and crack up yourself.

---

*Phyllis Cook had briefly considered taking in her elderly mother-in-law, May Morgan Cook. As it happened, Mrs. Cook, who was still hale and hearty, stayed in her own home.

I am already tired of this vicarious martyrdom so I will lie down awhile now and fan myself. . . .

I took to having cramps and numbness and went for a check to Dr. Pleshette, my old gynecologist, who took some tests and is now trying to pop me right in hospital.* I don't think I expected this—I thought he'd tell me I was okay so I'd go on and realize I was just tired. So I told him, frankly, I had too much to do— and Joe can't look after himself (turns out he can, I'm sure) and I was damn well not going to have another operation and be completely helpless myself for months and both of us doddering around here probably murdering each other.

Anyway, he said he'd fix me up at Mt. Sinai Hospital (I hate it but—) absolutely for free and I had to. A few years ago I would do anything a doctor said but now I think there is a choice. After each operation, I did get well but was never as good or as strong as I had been before—even sick. So if I feel tired and a little crampy right now, it doesn't prevent me from doing some writing and going out with friends and enjoying some life—and if I get into these hospital shirts and the men in white see all the wondrous things still left to carve I will emerge a broken reed (if I emerge at all, which I question), unable to do anything but weep and *beg* for months.

And so—confidentially—when he calls me tomorrow I think I will hold out. He says it's urgent to see the extent of the "involvement" (but why make it worse with knifework?). Once a doctor whom I trusted at Jojo's hospital said they had decided to give him a lobotomy. I was so frightened but I had to believe them. But my friend Dos Passos in Baltimore (with close associates at Johns Hopkins) came rushing up and said I must not permit it, that the results were still unsatisfactory, and not to let them make a guinea pig of Jojo.† Result was my undying gratitude to Dos, for a psychoanalyst appeared at that time who did more than anyone for Jojo. Then that first doctor for Joe at St. Vincent's told me he'd have to lose a leg (he was *determined* to amputate "just to make sure") but another surgeon disagreed, thank God.

The only trouble is I will offend dear Norman Pleshette who sends no bill and is so kind (and one of the best doctors besides) so then when I will need him I suppose I can't get him. Well—I haven't told anyone about this because I can't stand all the phonings and explainings, etc., from friends who adore calamities. Will let you know later but will try to put things off so I can finish book. Don't tell anybody who is likely to come and shrive me!

love,
Dawn

(COLLECTION TIM PAGE)

---

*Powell's doctors may well have suspected the presence of the cancer that would end up killing her only four years later. However, she staunchly refused to undergo examination at this time.
†Lobotomies were regularly performed throughout the United States in the years after World War II.

TO PHYLLIS POWELL COOK

[New York]
Friday, November 3, 1961

Dear Phyllis—

I was terribly glad to get your report on Aunt Tute and Aunt Bessie and felt as if I were there.* I have a very ashamed memory or two of them, in both cases because of Auntie May's stronger will. Do you remember when we had that marvelous tour and stopped at Charlie and Effie's old hotel? It was all like reentering a dream somehow and I'm not sure which time it was but our Sherman relatives were very annoyed that we wanted to go see Aunt Bessie and Uncle Will where Aunt Tute was also. So we went and stayed about eight minutes only and they were all fixed for a party and we were so mean about our elegant figures we wouldn't eat the ice cream they had specially gotten for us—let alone the homemade cake. Also we had to rush back so that was the last we saw of any of them.

Another time, going through Crestline, I wanted to stop off to see Aunt Tute but Auntie May would have none of it. Same with Aunt Belle, with whom I had stayed often and who had been especially good to me when young, taking me to lodge parties, teaching me dances and songs and pieces. I realized Auntie May had invested more in the property (me) but not in those earlier days.

Aunt Tute was also very good to me and immensely helpful. When she kept house for us she read us Maeterlinck ("Blue Bird"), *Peter Pan*, *Black Beauty* and others every bedtime, though you may have been asleep then. She gave us a high tea instead of supper, remember, and a fine institution—hot tea and milk, maple syrup and soda biscuits. I think the Welsh tradition was stronger than we realized. The way they (the Powells) all sang or played mandolins or guitars.

However I don't think she was the least fair to Papa. I'll bet she wouldn't have gotten her bridegroom if she hadn't had that house for courting ground and a free hand. She was really very happy that year—gay and cute and sometimes Papa gave her $5. She used to complain a great deal that he had promised her five dollars a week. But he didn't say EVERY week, did he—*a* means *one*, doesn't it? So what's the beef?

How in God's name the poor man managed on his $15 a week anyway I don't know. He was so proud he would rather seem like a stingy bastard than be pitied. I know it infuriates people to have a person who ought to be bleating their troubles swagger around boasting and laughing. At my age I find I prefer the swaggerers. I don't have to help *them*.

I was really off Aunt Tute, though, when Papa told how she had hurt his

---

*The various family members Powell mentions here are all maternal relatives, Millers of Cardington, Ohio.

feelings. At Ed Liben's funeral he said she was going to pieces and he put his arm around her and patted her then she looked up and saw who it was and shrieked as if he were some monster, he said, and she yelled "You!" and wrenched away.

How could he have gotten to be such an evil monster in her life? It doesn't make sense.

Joe goes out once or twice a day, but he does have to make a whole career of changing his bandages, soaking twice a day an hour at a time, and every other day there is blood all over the place and I have to keep soaking and cleaning the stuff—sheets, underwear, etc.—before sending to laundry and frankly the smell makes it impossible to have anyone come in who doesn't know. However the doctor says it's okay and maybe will go away. I am lucky to have this office* or I'd go nuts.

I did finally finish the novel† though it took four years and I had to keep going over it as my mind was so harassed with a dozen piddling things.

I do have to do EVERYTHING. Get up, cook, wash dishes, make beds, rush to get chapter ready and then take off for 2 o'clock appointment uptown, rush back and do book review for *Post*, rush to deliver THAT myself downtown, back to pick up stuff for supper, swig a drink and fall asleep.

Saturday or Sunday I get Jojo—this week have to take him out for suit and new clothes—then try to compose my addled head for an all-day Monday conference over my ms. with my editor, Malcolm Cowley.

Joe could write or answer letters but he tells me to—and he doesn't even fill saltcellars. Boo hoo—

Anyway we are both lucky to be here and I am doubly lucky in friends. He doesn't like anybody or want anybody around but me.

I think he really does enjoy it when somebody comes to see him. He doesn't have anybody to beef about his mean wife to and I don't blame him for being irritable.

Otherwise he is sweet and I discover more and more how extraordinarily intelligent and highly cultivated he is. No mental sag at all. Reads all the time.

Don't know when book will come out—not before spring at least.

love,
Dawn

(COLLECTION TIM PAGE)

---

*Powell had taken a tiny office at 80 East Eleventh Street.
†*The Golden Spur.*

This letter was written at St. Vincent's Hospital on February 14, 1962; Joe died later the same day.

TO GERALD AND SARA MURPHY

[St. Vincent's Hospital]
Valentine Slush Day [1962]

Dear Gerald and Sara:

Am here at hospital on tap for Joe who ambulanced here Thursday with recurrence of trouble and pneumonia besides. Long spell of stubborn resistance to doctor or hospital—but have good spirits as long as endurable. I've thought often of you but was in whirl of nursing—"booking"—keeping your friends from bugging him as he didn't want anybody around—and usual business where you go a little batty in spots—screaming at best-intentioned friends, etc. Hasn't recognized me or opened eyes after second day here—had a tracheomy (??) like Elizabeth Taylor to keep healthy and now lies with transfusions, intravenous and a collar and oxygen bulb around his throat—but at least he's still here today contrary to doctor's expectations. I am still so glad he is here and getting kind and good care—some of the same doctors and friendly nurses he had before. I wasn't able to help because I'd gotten numb and was obeying *his* orders as if I were the patient and he the doctor. I was wondering how long I could do everything—nursing, blood-washing, keeping people away, etc.—both our nerves sizzling away under massive control.

At present I am trying to hold off calling his sisters and brothers as I do not see how *I can stand an onslaught of further responsibilities*—just yakking, etc.—when I would like to just take a hot bath, lock the windows and sleep in my own bed for a few undisturbed hours. Fortunately I am perfectly well due to Bob Solley's rescue of me. Margaret De Silver also is very sick in hospital. Many helpful friends—my young friend Jackie does everything and Joe's and my friend Monroe Stearns very helpful. Will call or write in a few days.

Love,
Dawn

I thought you were probably in a similar whirl of life which does gang up on us.

(COLLECTION HONORIA MURPHY DONNELLY)

TO MONROE STEARNS

[43 *Fifth Avenue*]
February 19, 1962

Dear Monroe—

I wanted to tell you how terrifically I feel indebted to you for your kindness to Joe. Outside of your steady delivery of Stearns Homogenized blood[*] and the Instant Stearns service on all critical occasions I have been especially moved by the things that meant most to Joe's psyche in his lowest moments—the Booth[†] luncheons at the Players and the Thanksgiving dinners with Katrina. Only a wife of long standing can be so oblivious to what is major in the mate's happiness and I had a faint glimmer when Joe, who ignored all kindly gestures toward his family and old pals as a rule, said last Thanksgiving Day, "What are you doing about Monroe?" I didn't even know the connection and he said severely, "I'm surprised at you, Powell. This is the first Thanksgiving in three years we haven't been his guests. If you don't know what to do, I will."

I was so overwhelmed by his concern over you that I knew how deeply he had appreciated your gestures, since he was a gesture man himself and clearly had missed all the holiday rituals his family loved and that I had witlessly ignored. I knew he had missed his business friends painfully after his retirement and enjoyed you all the more as a new, younger, stimulating replacement.

It was lifesaving for you to arrange the final matters, especially since you had suffered through them such a short time before.[‡] I just conferred with Mr. Graham and thank you again for him. I could so easily have been shoved into a needless ceremonial ado in my ignorance.

Frankly I don't think either Joe or I could have gone on much more. We were both putting on a show for each other of Retirement can be Fun and the costumes and scenery were frayed, the stars gasping their lines. I'm glad he came back for the first reprise, anyway. Booth would have approved.

My everlasting thanks to you.

love,
Dawn

(COLLECTION MICHAEL STEARNS)

---

[*]Stearns had visited St. Vincent's Hospital while Joseph Gousha was in the critical ward and had given some of his own blood.
[†]These luncheons were named for the distinguished American actor Edwin Booth (1833–1893).
[‡]Stearns himself had just lost his wife.

TO GERALD AND SARA MURPHY

43 Fifth Avenue
New York City
Monday March 1962
8 a.m.

Dearest Sara and Gerald:

It is always a present to wake up and find you are already at the place you intended to go to today and why I stay over places when you're neither one place nor the other that last night anyway. . . . It was such a lovely weekend and rest and I don't think I've ever seen Cheer Hall* more lovely, becardinalized and becrowed.

I think places deliberately get dazzling when they know they were so close to being on the block.

Jacqueline Miller helped its magic, too, by being in a sustained ecstasy over its beauty. Like Paradise, she said over and over, and Gerald and Sara are the most wonderful greatest people I've ever known.

This you are accustomed to hearing.

I find it a great joy myself to encounter a young person reveling in youngness these days. I suppose you don't really enjoy youth until its edge is gone— Jackie is 30 and much freer and finer than in the first years I knew her, though the Miss Rheingold juicy golden radiance has dusted off into a finer edge. Joe said to her, "Don't wait for New York to get you down, but go right back to Oregon and the apples and roses."

She has a Murphy marvelous trait—she wants to make everybody comfortable, unworried, beautiful, fulfilled, fed, loved and gay. I think this trait has loused her two or three great loves—as Lover Boy doesn't want to share the wealth. Usually he (whoever he is) is alarmed to find himself worshipped, overwhelmed with love and protection—I've had to fend off this gorgeous forest fire of affection, too, but should always have thanked my stars for it.

She spelled me with Joe in the hospital and her daily visits—with jigger of martini or with transfusions of blood extracted from her suitors for Joe—did a great deal more than Joe ever realized to keep him surrounded with dozens of doctors. His ward companions were cheered to see her devoted embraces of Joe (an *"uncle"* for the hospital records so she could always come and go) and it was the same when she visited Jojo or took him riding. Everybody felt better just seeing this radiant sunshine.

Joe insisted it was the "Mueller" in Miller that gives her this opulent Olympian love and heat.

I don't know why I am writing this recommendation except I am so

*Cheer Hall was the name of the Murphy home in Snedens Landing.

delighted when friends I love like and appreciate other friends. Usually they're ready to lock horns.

Coming home she kept crying out it was the greatest time she'd ever had and I think she's already planning to send a surveyors' kit to your leading crow and making chutney-cheese-cuits for the smaller pellegrinos.

We felt so guilty enjoying Margaret's new car without her that we left great forsythia bales for her from YOU—so you may get thanks from Margaret.

Love love love. Will report on Wilsonia.

Dawn

(COLLECTION HONORIA MURPHY DONNELLY)

TO MALCOLM COWLEY

43 Fifth Avenue
April 4, 1962

Dear Malcolm:

The novel went to Carol Brandt, who finds it "witty, vivid and convincing," which is high praise from this very cool candid dame. I did an enormous, back-breaking job after Helen Taylor* finished her English VI marginal gradings—first being interested in and astonished at her suggestions for cuts and changes and queries and following them up to a sudden middle when I realized that she'd cut off all my roots and the fact was what she really didn't like was Powell's turn of mind and morals, and one of her paragraph cuts meant six pages of explanations inserted later on.

She is a nice girl—I knew her in the thirties as a chum of my old party pal Ruth Brown Murray. However we made a lot of unnecessary work for each other, and expense, too, as I then mistrusted all her advice and had everything erased and retyped but in my rage and exhaustion got some very good improvements in so am grateful if I live. I really was beginning to think *Powell* ought to be cut to *Pol* and besides I had too many *w*'s—very repetitious—and was I sure it was *Dawn* and not *Donner Pass*? Also I retyped my own para-graphing instead of the Viking style (she says) as I do not propose retyping it for Scribner's or somebody else.

The hard labor took up my postmortem period.

I just took my cat to the cat man for Aureomycin shots. He caught some-thing at another cathouse where I left him to spend a few days at Snedens Landing with the Murphys. An interesting evening was had before Murphys

---

*Helen Taylor was a senior editor at Viking who worked closely with Powell on *The Golden Spur*. Powell resented her amendments and questions and eventually discarded all of her editorial advice.

and I drove out as Bunny had been in town several days and he and I had been having a theater festival. I timorously suggested combining the two Fitzgeraldines when Elena came to town which was done.

So the five of us dined at the Algonquin and no harm came of anything but possibly Arthur Mizener and Andrew Turnbull,* though to me it is most amazing that Wilsons and Murphys are courteous enough to feed and wine and house every academic oaf that wants to climb above a poor dead writer, using his name like a Diner's Card on a luxury tour. I think they feel differently than I would, but you and Muriel [Cowley] have had a lot of that God knows and managed to survive. Bunny and I went to a brief part of the off-B'way *This Side of Paradise* after a few bourbons but had to leave as Bunny got to laughing so hard at the beauteous hero and his beauteous poetry-reading classmate bicycling by moonlight on the arena stage while black-and-gold-sweatered tight-assed lads leapt about shouting rah-rah-rah and other old college practices that existed only in *Leave It to Jane* (which we had seen play the same theater with probably the same ballet-football boys). The Murphys (or Gerald alone) found the movie *Tender Is the Night* pretty funny though the book certainly had no movie in it anyway. I never could see (nor could they) how the Murphys were Divers except Dick Diver has Gerald's manner, clothes, mannerisms and minor ways.

In fact, authors always claim models but what they mean is that is where they took off from (get H. Taylor on that sentence) and not what they copied.

Bunny said the real fact of the Josephson-Rascoe-etc. was not that he bit Rascoe on the calf at all but that Rascoe bit HIM right across his nose so he had to be removed to docs and have stitches taken (he was overadmirous of Rascoe's wife).† Coby was present at the party when this drama took place, it seems. (Don't tell Matty however as God knows how it would come out next time.)

I hope you are getting plenty of burning ice and devil's punches but don't let Muriel get too inflamed by them this time.

Beautiful days here now and the forsythia I brought back from Snedens is now beating me around the apartment forstooning the windows and me.

Love to both of you,
Dawn

(THE NEWBERRY LIBRARY)

---

*Mizener and Turnbull had both published biographies of F. Scott Fitzgerald, each relying heavily on information provided by Wilson and the Murphys.
†Matthew Josephson (1899–1978) was a critic and biographer who would later write the first posthumous article on Powell's life and career, for the *Southern Review*. Burton Rascoe (1892–1957) was a fellow critic and editor.

TO MALCOLM COWLEY

[43 Fifth Avenue]
April 9, 1962

Dear Malcolm—

Stricken that my sulky letter said things behind my back. No trouble between H. Taylor and me beyond that of any other happy couple after the big party—criticism here and angry self-defense, then the big "We're not suited to each other" and final "But wasn't that why we married?"

Helen hadn't read final ms. when I wrote and since she'd really knocked herself out knocking out what I'd knocked myself out writing I rather suspected she'd resent my rejection of hints. Frankly I was too exhausted by three years of drawing an iron curtain between my personal problems and the acrobatic necessities of a comic novel that I was not ready to be challenged ten to twenty times per page on every quip, every reference, every character's reaction, and frequently on characters' expenditures and reactions showing they needed a good straightening-out by a sensible woman.

Anyway I did not feel that my contract demanded I explain Life to somebody's nice little girl.

However she called up to say she found it a Cute ending and it goes to copy editor today after I go up this afternoon and fix up something that had her almost sobbing at its enormity. Naughty author—sometimes putting four dots . . . . as break sign between sections, sometimes FIVE dots, sometimes (the tears are streaming down my shamed face) THREE asterisks and no dots at all (I have two typists and two typewriters, I tried to explain, and sometimes I have to use # and sometimes $$$) and sometimes FOUR and EVEN FIVE asterisks. Before I am thrown out of the Poetry Society I am rushing up to level this off with a simple American Flag between sections. . . .

Also I evidently must keep my foot out of my mouth until I have learned to dance. I didn't mean Bunny or Murphs agreed with me about Turnbull or Mizener. Both liked Turnbull and liked his book. It's ME who beefs about the buzzards who have no other gifts but buzzardry. . . .

Love to Muriel and the Golden West,*
Dawn

(THE NEWBERRY LIBRARY)

---

*The Cowleys were then in California.

TO C. G. BURKE[*]

43 Fifth Avenue
May 18, 1962

Dear Cornelius—

I seem to have walked into the past night before last which it seems was lurking in a quaint apartment on East 24th Street, where Georgette Carneal (now Scott, now Joyce MacIver, author of *Frog Pond*) was having a splendid party of strangers and many characters out of orbit. . . .[†]

I was sorry to hear about Janet, who seemed a fine companion for the Mad Genius in the Big House. Do you do what I did after Joe's death in February—draw shades firmly on the fact like the shades on Dutch paintings, refuse to admit it, find people looking at you strangely (*they* think it's *true*) but occasionally find IT sneaking up behind you and whamming you?

What I find most amazing in my Anatomy of Bereavement is the revolting mirror of your own selfishness. Marriage seems a competition for survival in the long run and a constant insistence that the Mate is someone it never was or even pretended to be. After this real person goes the false image has no use, and that's the part we miss the most.

I finally finished a novel I started four or five years ago—and, as it was to be completely and classically comic, it required considerable bullish willpower to shut off my life and reconstruct this playhouse every day. Joe was retired and THAT was his real death, as it is for most people—much worse than cancer or other desperations. I finally plunged in and finished it after his death out of sheer rage.

The rage was induced by the Viking literal editor marking up the margins with such doodles as "Better change Nash to Chevrolet as they didn't make Nashes in 1956" and "Change Johnny Walker to simply Scotch" and "How could he stop in and buy suit when on page 85 he had only $1.60 in his pocket?"

Goddam it, I said, this Madison Avenue materialism has gone too far, when an author can't let his characters ride around in an OLD car but has to make him turn it in every year for the new model, and this guy doesn't like Scotch—he only likes Johnny Walker—and how dare you tell MY characters how to budget their money? Do I have to show you his credit cards?

So I threw out all the advice I had been rather weakly lousing myself up with and did it all again my own pigheaded way and it's coming out this

---

*C. G. Burke (1900–1971) had been one of Powell's first friends in the Village, though they had evidently subsequently lost touch. Burke was a poet and record critic, and an early editor of *High Fidelity* magazine. He had recently lost his wife, Janet.

†Georgette Carneal was an American writer whose novel *The Great Day* (1933) Powell had had mixed feelings about. Many years later, she had published *The Frog Pond* (1961), a harrowing study of mental illness, under the pseudonym Joyce MacIver.

fall, I presume, maybe on the moon. I had damn well better find a means of livelihood—such as poetry or something I can do in the lotus position. It is easy for two people to live from day to day but one person has to take the Long View.

The friend—Margaret De Silver—who visited you with me is now drastically sick but occasionally she loans a young lady mutual friend her car and we take Jojo out driving or bring him home. He is amusing and original but too absentminded to go around alone.

Come to New York and we will promenade in the Park with our guitars and espresso jugs.

Love—as always—
Dawn

(COLLECTION TIM PAGE—CARBON COPY)

TO BRYAN ROBERTSON

43 Fifth Avenue
May 22, 1962

Dearest Bryan—

I am sure you will want the forlorn story of Franz Kline's death and the general demoralization of Tosspot Row (University Place to Hudson and over to First Avenue anyhow and Springs, L.I.).*

As I am reading galleys on my novel covering the artflies of the district and the fifties, I was particularly interested as a spectator. The Cedar Tavern closed down for the funeral, which was held at a fashionable uptown church—St. Bartholomew's, I believe—and all Art attended and five hundred bereaved ladies in the manner of Rudy Valentino's. I heard reports from all sides.

People always crowd a public person's funeral but Franz was like Robert Benchley—really loved personally, successful too late to give a damn about it or to change his early-formed poor but hearty tastes. Loved more than Pollock, in fact more than any artist I can remember, partly because he didn't have a working wife to insult people for him, or fend off the duds and watch his purse, so he could pay somebody's studio rent or baby bill or buy the bar drinks all night without fear.

Anyway he'd had a heart spell a few months back and was put in St. Clare's Hospital which then had a run of telephoners trying to get at him after bar-closings every night, and nurses had to fend off the pals who knew he wanted

*Powell had been particularly fond of the artist Franz Kline (1910–1962), who had died on May 13.

to see THEM. The extremely nice dame, Betsy Zogbaum (cultured and controlled but deep-end alcoholic when taxed), gave up, I hear, under the pressure of protecting him and was in hospital herself. Then he got out of hospital for home and there got worse. Ladies he had slept with once or twice KNEW he wanted them near and tore over. His managers, dealers, museum types, the press, gathered round.

Jackie (herself feeling the ONE needed just as Pete did) said the doctor said he was horrified to find the bedroom packed with 18 people all slurping Kline Scotch and trying to find more and cheering him up and pushing pencils in his nerveless fingers. So he had another attack and finally died in New York Hospital in a coma, with all the bars filled with men important with grief.

Jackie has a Kline, a large nympho blonde, Mary has one, and other ladies say, "I slept with Kline, too, but I don't have one." Jackie was emotional and indignant at the others. So were they. "How strange of Jackie to wear a green suit to the funeral!" one said. "Because Franz loved me in green," Jackie wailed. She said she went early and was greeted by two other ladies of Kline's—one, A.Z., an artist steady of his, and Ruth, the girl Pollock was with at his accident, but Jackie hastily avoided them and sat alone but other ladies popped up all around her.

"I hear E—— L—— is home sobbing like a widow," snarled Mary.

"Imagine Nancy [Ward] carrying on so she can't even come to the funeral," was among other nasty cracks about Pete's wife, who after all had lived with Franz for a year or two.

The big surprise was Franz's legal wife, the English girl he married some 25 years ago who went mad and whom he visited in the sanitarium religiously for years and used as a buffer against marriage-insisters. Years later, when he made money, suddenly she recovered and he got her discharged from the sanitarium, set her up in an apartment, and though he continued his own life with Betsy Zogbaum—I believe they had a house in Provincetown—No. 1 was his legal wife. At the funeral, Jackie said she was there being the Star Relict, looking a good deal like Betsy, which is a delicate, Italian, ivory, Madonna-like figurine, if you dig—and of course no one could object to Her. She kept saying, wide-eyed, "I had no idea Franz had so many friends! Of course I was committed in 1953—" (really in the '30s but she lost several years).

The parson who did the funeral said he'd never had so many people in his church before and he's had some big weddings. Couldn't understand it. Jackie said the streets were jammed with sobbing men. I asked her if there was a big showing of beards and sneakers and she said they were all suited up like crazy.

Love,
Dawn

(COLLECTION BRYAN ROBERTSON)

TO EDMUND WILSON

[43 Fifth Avenue]
August 7, 1962

Dear Wig—

I was just thinking that Marilyn Miller's surrendering* shows that today in this welfare state you can't win. I mean there's no losing the boogey-man, whoever he is. Whatever became of those good old Horatio Alger days when hard work and stick-to-itiveness and lofty morals got you over the hump? Now they get you over the hill to the poorhouse or at least the loony bin. Who knows what taxhounds were after Hemingway, too? The idea that anybody has a deep personal romantic or melodramatic cause to commit suicide today is really silly. The Gestapo is chasing all of us.

I think of the years of trying to do a major work like *Gore* (patriotic, not Vidal) and that the only way you can do it is to abort it.

Momentarily I think of my splendid inheritance—which means no money at all as near as I can find out, though Phil Wittenberg (lawyer) is trying to shake some out, while the state has informed me that due to this Trust I must (retroactively yet) pay the state $200 a month for Jojo.† As I spent many interviews and letters getting them down from their Top Price of $100 a month to $58 a month, the Cinderella story of their then making a concession of doubling their own rightful charge is just adorable.

It may be advisable to take a luxurious apartment with housekeeper and keep [Jojo] with me in order to get out of state clutches. Ah well, Wittenberg will cope—also a very fine psychiatrist who knows all.

Did *Show* phone you? I did my review of Anthony Powell's last but not a very good one as I found myself of my usual two minds about him. Is he a burlesque of all the Galsworthyish serial trilogists or is he the Bore's Bore? This comes over me after reading too much of him at once—as in Firbank.

Did you see a movie, *Counterfeit Traitor*? Don't know whether I'm getting to tolerate war movies or whether this one is unusually intelligent and instructive. I thought I had seen all the Frog or wop films I could take, always coming in on the same part (as we did in *Liaisons Dangereuses*)—the big rumpled bed, the skinny little Frog lover with hairy chest and ratface and crucifix slamming about skinny neck, the buck-toothed acned art-movie belle rearing up out of sheets all a-giggle with Latin lust—and whee, watch that bed, fellas. Sure

---

*The actress Marilyn Monroe, who had been married to the playwright Arthur Miller, had just killed herself.
†On her death that June, Margaret De Silver had left Powell a modest trust fund that allowed her a measure of financial independence but threatened Jojo's status as a ward of the state, increasing the monthly payments due for his care.

enough, *Shoot the Piano Player* took off from there, too, the new obligatory scene. After that nothing seems funny. . . .

There are great tinklings about my novel as a movie for some reason and Brandts are busy phoning me after ten years' silence. I have been here before, of course, and this time I'm making use of the hullabaloo to extract money from THEM, so if all goofs off as usual they can suffer, too. N.Y. not bad heatwise.

Do not climb those mountains.

Humph

(YALE COLLECTION OF AMERICAN LITERATURE, BEINECKE RARE BOOK AND MANUSCRIPT LIBRARY, YALE UNIVERSITY)

TO EDMUND WILSON

43 Fifth Avenue
August 15, 1962

Cher cherami bébé Raoul cherie—

Did you see *Jules et Jim*, a wonderful Truffaut film? It is all influenced by Edward Gorey who is going to turn out to be the papa of the nouvellest vague ever. The *Shoot the Piano Player* is just fair . . . but Gorey has had a stately sobering effect on Truffaut. My, it is a wonderful thing. Very much like the Willowdale Handcar. I will go again this afternoon.

Or should I read another of the crop of novels by gifted Sarah Lawrence or Bennington girls, now wives of faculty members at various embarrassed colleges and all about a daring new subject, viz.: Can a cultured, educated college graduate find happiness and beauty as mother and wife on a deserted college campus, and is she being fair to herself—or, say!—to Him when her high marks and beauty and blood should really permit her to be whoring around Paris and Rome with Dick? Howard is so intelligent and self-educated and so loyal that her love has turned to hate. These novels (last one I read was touted by Isherwood) are college-educated Kathleen Norris really but more snobbish and the SEX outdoes Ruark or the Frank Boys the way a smart girl can always overdo it, but it is a shock to find it in the same old *Ladies' Home Journal* story. The difference between the boy and girl sex writers is that the girls are more reckless, and throw themselves naked in some fence-corner near their husband's office or outside the sheriff's home, because they are FREE, see—and no sneakiness about it. Also they talk about their ways of performance and their contraceptives all the time.

REVOLTING. I hate the mixture of GRACIOUS LIVING and Spoken Hot Sex. Let's bring back the gay old hypocrisies and the pleasure of black sin framed in white lies. And I wish nice girls would go back to their ferneries and start blushing behind their fans.

I seem to be fortune-sitting here. Moneys are in the air and I fear it is going to damage my lifetime point of view. How screaming I used to find it when somebody, a richie, would say, "I'd love to send you to college, Dawnie, but I can't get at my bonds and stocks." Ho ho. "I'd love to pay my share of this dinner but our money is all sewn up in land." Hah.

Whatever made me think it was funny?

The Brandts, however, while encouraged by movie bites, have been advancing money of their own accord, and Viking will send some. As they are extraordinarily stingy, this means some encouragement. The review I did of Powell (Anthony) wasn't so good but I wish they'd pay me as I want to waste some money. Did *Show* catch you?

It looks as if the only way I can get my own living insured is by being a Trust Fund Parent—the kind that makes their heir-child do all sorts of traveling or moving to justify their own whims. I daresay I can wade into the principle, with reason, if I buy a mortgaged estate with servants and get Jojo out of hock and tie myself up in knots. I am seriously thinking of something I often discussed with Margaret—a cheap country place, bought or rented, for him with some of my poor relations (me, maybe) sharecropping it. . . .

I note in the French magazine *Elle* ads for powdered milk (suggestion for your cow neighbors)—QUICK LAIT. Aren't they a delightful risqué little people? *"Mama"* (cries the little tot wolfing his quick lait in his high chair), *"J'aime ma Quick Lait!"*

Je soufflé pour vous, Raoul, ah.

Aurore

(YALE COLLECTION OF AMERICAN LITERATURE, BEINECKE RARE BOOK AND MANUSCRIPT LIBRARY, YALE UNIVERSITY)

TO CAROL BRANDT

43 Fifth Avenue
September 27, 1962

Dear Carol:

Thanks so much for the extortion from Viking. It encouraged this mad inheritance to spill some interest, too, as money seems to want to go where money is.

I have been wary of talk about my new novel which has been in the incubator for several months, but I do not feel strong enough to withstand that editorial stone wall by trying to explain the jokes, the contemporary references, etc.

et al., which made the last book so desperately hard. As you know too well, a great many people don't understand my crooked style, and that's okay except I daren't risk having them destroy the early roots. I am usually excited and vulnerable at the start and a literal, unimaginative editor is more destructive than a downright hostile one.

So I am in a quandary. I could reduce the general plan perhaps to a suitably conventional prospectus for you. It will be a short, comic dilemma involving only two figures and some absent menaces, with a New York and surrounding airports backdrop. The name of it is *Summer Rose*, for that is the girl's name. I will do a more explicit plan for you later. . . .*

Best,
Dawn

(COLLECTION TIM PAGE—CARBON COPY)

TO PHYLLIS POWELL COOK

[43 Fifth Avenue]
November 15, 1962

Dearest Phyllis—

Amazing! Hope the good feeling goes on—and your stomach returns to its natural barrel-size (pardon me—reg. size).† I am now signed up to adapt *Golden Spur* for a musical comedy with two very smart boys—[Charles] Strouse and [Lee] Adams, who did the songs for *Bye Bye Birdie*.‡ You will not be surprised to know that one of them—Lee Adams—is an Ohio State graduate from Mansfield. About 34 and very intelligent and quick and talented. Hearing of my Shelby background he was very startled and explained to the producer, "Listen, compared to Dawn's hometown, mine was a metropolis!" He was on magazines before becoming a lyric writer. The producer sent me a present of a portable phonograph yesterday which is bigger than my apartment—anyway it was a lovely idea if I didn't know Jojo would play Xmas carols on it 24 hours. Still he'll love it as we haven't had one for years.

Wish I had a big enough apartment so I could stay home when the cleaning woman comes instead of having no place to retire. Wish I'd get these far-off percentages and bequests and so on into cash on the minute—the only economics I ever understood!

---

*Powell would complete very little of *Summer Rose* before her death in late 1965.
†Phyllis Powell Cook was then mysteriously and gravely ill and believed to be dying. In fact, she would live for another twenty-three years.
‡The lyricist Lee Adams and the composer Charles Strouse, who had terrific hits with *Bye Bye Birdie* and *Golden Boy* would work with Powell on turning *The Golden Spur* into a musical comedy until she became too weak to continue the effort.

I imagine your stomach will tolerate plain noodles or macaroni and butter or cheese if nothing else and cottage cheese in it seems to tone up the digestive system.

Here is important *New Yorker* piece—I mean one that sells books since Wilson is the world's greatest critic.* Thank Alice [Cook Hoover] and Carol [Cook Warstler] for keeping me informed.

love and get well pronto,
Dawn

TO ALICE COOK HOOVER AND
CAROL COOK WARSTLER†

[43 Fifth Avenue]
December 5, 1962

Dear Alice and Carol,

I have wanted to call you but I have vivid memories of being absolutely worn out for two or three years of Joe's sickness, houseworking, nursing, visiting Jojo, finagling finances, appeasing creditors, conferring at hospital, and calling hospital all night to see if Joe was still alive—and *then* having so-called friends wake me up in a stolen nap to demand a complete medical report and to suggest their own doctor or how wrong I was in the case. I finally got to a point where I really thought they *wanted* to kill me, and the only really kind people were those who never telephoned. Just as when I was very sick in hospital and bare acquaintances would stand around blowing cigarette smoke (I can't stand it) over me and discussing their parties when all I wanted was to be alone with a bedpan or asleep. I felt persecuted when they brought in great sheaves of hay-fever flowers because then I couldn't get the nurse for hours because she had to spend hours looking for big vases and other equipment, without attending to me.

I have been worried too because Margaret De Silver had some stomach business that sounded like Phyllis's and last year a radium or X-ray job burned her (they forgot her) and infected itself later. And then she was in some kind of pain and upchuck biz (losing weight, etc.) and all of us thought her doctors and hospitals were killing her—and I still think so. The only reason I'm alive is that I walked out of Mt. Sinai Hospital and refused to let them operate.

*Edmund Wilson had published "Dawn Powell: Greenwich Village in the Fifties" in the November 17, 1962, issue of *The New Yorker*. This was far and away the most sustained and serious critical appreciation to appear during her lifetime.
†Hoover and Warstler were two of Phyllis Cook's three daughters.

Thank God there are some good doctors, however, and your surgeon sounds like a godsend. Mostly they dump everything on a sort of mechanized hospital staff that pays no attention to the individual. I'm so glad Morgan [Cook] was able to stop the dope bit. They always try to stuff you with dope and maybe plan to later on cure you of the dope habit. I did not realize your mother had my reaction to this. I am practically anesthetized by ½ an aspirin and only recently have been sold on their virtue as painkillers—which they really are with me, only I know I'll fall asleep for 24 hours or else buzz. I used to hide the pills in hospitals or spit them out later, knowing what they were doing. In Mt. Sinai last year when I wasn't even sick—merely being checked— they *injected* the stuff, a kind of torture device so you'd fall asleep then they'd make you keep awake to have enemas, cardiograms, etc. You are so right about let's clean up the hospitals, and let patients have prisoner rights at least.

So lucky you girls are near and can feed her. Poor Margaret De Silver had two sons and relatives with troubles so they brought her their latest troubles right up to the end, when I'm sure she could have used a filet of sole *bonne femme* instead.

Am working on the musical industriously with these talented young guys who are more original and also more intelligent than the Broadway pros I've been accustomed to. There is a great deal of publicity about the book—much fan mail—and parties given for me, yesterday a wonderful one given by the Murdock Pembertons, old friends. They had *The Golden Spur* painted on their door and about 50 guests, many old friends and an alarming bevy of *New Yorker* baby editors—they *looked* like babies, anyway, and not like my old hard-bitten editors there.

Lunched with critic Edmund Wilson, who loves magic tricks and took me to Lou Tannen's Magician's Supply Store—a hushed, quiet floor in a 42nd Street building, where professionals come for new tricks and the clerks are old pros who demonstrate gleefully each magic cane or silk hat. We went out in the hall and suddenly Wilson had vanished. I thought it was Lou Tannen's Silk Hat trick, then an elevator door opened and there he was. He'd thought I'd gone in. I still say it's magic.

Much love,
Aunt Dawn

TO ALICE COOK HOOVER

[43 Fifth Avenue]
January 10, 1963

Dear Alice—

It is terribly disheartening I know to wake up every morning hoping the whole deal is a bad dream and that a miracle has happened. The thing is that sometimes the miracle *does* happen and you forget all the bad weeks. Joe was on the critical list so long the first year of hospital—and there were weeks they offered no hope and I would wake up to phone at daybreak to see if he'd lasted the night. But he got better and finally got out, so we had an extra dividend of a year. Not even his death was as terrible as the months of suspense and I am still sort of numb.

I do trust that mysterious thing in our systems that makes us sometimes cure ourselves when the doctors can't—some combination of accidental doses or food. When Jojo was born and unable to take bottle and slowly starving I didn't trust the nurses but got out of bed and stood over him night and day feeding him drop by drop from an eyedropper and finally he gained a few ounces and some stamina and could pull on the bottle by the time we got out of hospital.

Wonder if [Phyllis] could take port like that.

Jojo was home last week and Deesie's godson Bobby [Morrison] (you remember the little colored boy out at Mt. Sinai?) came in with his 22-year-old son who is now a father, too. Jojo was delighted but you can imagine this vast dining room with Jojo, two black gents, Fagin bawling out the intruders, me trying to cook noodles and hamburger with them in one inch of space till I dropped the noodles in the sink of dirty silverware and hastily scooped them back up to serve, hoping they'd go soon. But they kept sitting silently while Jojo nudged me, "Mother, I think they'd like some refreshments now that dinner is over." Somebody else came in and I finally had to tell them guests had to take turns in this joint. Hope I can find a bigger place nearby as it's too hard to keep an office, kitchen, parlor and bowling alley all in one.

We are still reading the *Christian Science Monitor* and Newark and Philadelphia papers during the strike.*

Hope for best—

Love,
Aunt Dawn

(COLLECTION TIM PAGE)

---

*The New York newspapers were then engaged in their longest strike in modern history.

TO ALICE COOK HOOVER

[43 Fifth Avenue]
January 20, 1963

Dear Alice—

My sister is lucky to have such devoted daughters, when both of you are so full of children. I'm glad to have some news of improvement.

The sisters and nurses at St. Vincent's here were certainly wonderful to Joe, too. And Jojo took me into the little Catholic Church on Ward's Island several times to pray for his father and later to light a candle for him and it seemed more soothing than our less romantic faiths. When Jack S. was here and we had dinner with our cousin (from Indianapolis) Beatrice Sherman, we discussed this and she said, too, that when she was despairing she didn't feel prayers got anywhere except when she went into a Catholic church. Something more mystical and more merciful, too. However, before joining up some sisterhood, I visited a friend stuck in another Catholic hospital run by the order of Mother Cabrini and these nurses were all old witches gloating over pain and treating patients like animals. I learned that this order was famous for its meanness (here) and they bawled out visitors and patients alike—sent them out, too, in storms before they were well. Anyway, there were many discussions of the different orders—and it sounded like gourmet arguments over wine.

I am lashing myself to get Act I [of the musical-comedy version of *The Golden Spur*] done by Thursday but everything is popping. I have to say yes to requests to do pieces for magazines because it won't happen when I need it to and so I say yes, I'll have it done by Tuesday. Then I stare into the crystal ball a while and wait for a miracle in my brain. As so many things fall through and don't pay off after you've knocked your brains out you have to do *everything* so that one or the other works out. So I won't have Jojo home till next weekend.

Among other crazy things, Mrs. Vincent Astor asked my publisher if I would come see her as she wanted me to autograph some books of mine she *loved.** So she phoned me and I'm going there this Thursday, which means I have to get a haircut and find some dress that fastens and fix my nails and all these things I haven't time to do. Maybe she thinks I'm a boy. She sent me her autobiography *Patchwork Child* which is quite interesting.

There is so much blah blah about writing a book that you aren't left any time to write. And it's all a gamble anyway.

---

*The philanthropist Brooke Astor (born circa 1906) was an admirer of Powell's work, and a modest, unconventional friendship seems to have developed between the two women.

I hope to have a comfortable apartment by the time your mother is ready to come to New York—which I believe will be sooner than we think.

Love to Carol too and Phyllis,
Aunt Dawn

(COLLECTION TIM PAGE)

TO JACQUELINE MILLER

[43 Fifth Avenue]
March 8, 1963

Dear Jackie:

[. . .] On Friday, March 9—at 8:15 a.m.!—a CBS limousine picks me up (blindfolded, I guess) with a Viking representative for a TV panel on National Book Awards over Channel 2—10 a.m., CBS, with Elizabeth Hardwick, Harry Moore (judges), Barbara Tuchman (*Guns of August*, history) and Alfred Kazin (maybe) for discussion of *Spur* and their works on Harry Reasoner's panel.* It is very mysterious—also they wanted photos of me at my own desk. (I thought of Fagin and said no—*redecorating* going on—hah!) This is a lot of time waste and nuisance for a mere booby prize but I can't believe we are the winners. Hell of a nerve getting us run around instead of the real winners, what? Won't know till then. Hear $1000 prize, I suppose to be divided with publisher bastards. Curious gambit. . . .

I visited Jojo Sunday. Due to some TV news of me (I *think*) the patients now come up to me: "I hear you have great power outside. Will you please have Mrs. Kennan in the 3rd-floor kitchen fired because she wouldn't give me a baked apple this noon?" Another says, "Are you a senator? They tell me you're the only person who can get my brother to get me out of here." No. 1 comes back and says, "Maybe you shouldn't fire Mrs. Kennan. Just have her moved to another building."

Jojo handed me your valentine, all crumpled up from being carried around in his pocket, and said, "Will you please take this home and put it away in my files?" In his diary he had written, "The loss of my father a year ago today has been the greatest burden I have ever had to bear."

My God—how these Retarded Children are ahead of normal ones! . . .

Love to Dan,†
Dawn

(COLLECTION JACQUELINE MILLER RICE)

The Golden Spur was a finalist for the National Book Award for 1963.
†Jacqueline Miller had recently fallen in love with the painter Daniel Rice (born 1926), who would become her husband.

TO PETER MARTIN

> *43 Fifth Avenue*
> *Monday, March 10, 1963*
> *10:45 a.m.*
> *(I am putting this down*
> *to reassure myself of*
> *reality)*

Dear Pete:

I was very pleased to get your interesting report of life on Onassis, especially as I have been sitting here since 7 a.m. trying to muddle through Act II [of the *Golden Spur* musical] for a conference tomorrow and eager for any interruption so I will feel even more guilty. . . .

Fortunately, I am not getting that glamorous National Book Award tomorrow so I don't need to feel guilty about that, either. I do not know whether [Katherine Anne Porter's] *Ship* or *Book of Fools* gets it but have hunch that [J. F.] Powers's *Mort d'Urban* will, as this is Catholic year. My great prize is that I don't have to go to the frigging affair—make a crappy speech, buy a dress, demonstrate my inadequacies as public figure, be gracious to creeps, be insulted by pals, sit on platform for two hours wanting to go to powder room or vomick. Moreover, I could never adjust to the Prizewinner front. I might get mellow and see good in gracious livers. . . .

Do not need to feel guilty for inheritance, either, as it doesn't show as yet. Fearful of all the complications in it but have discovered what you may have discovered—viz.: There is no guilt feeling in inheriting. Amazing! If you made it by your hard toil you'd be justifying it all the time. But *Inheriting* (whether you ever see the loot or not) gives you Respectability AND a fine sense of personal worthiness.

The *Post* (N.Y.) started up again and it was good to read of Sadie Schadenfreudenstein's debut at Grossinger's. . . .

> Love,
> Dawn

(COLLECTION TIM PAGE—CARBON COPY)

TO JOHN DOS PASSOS

> *[43 Fifth Avenue]*
> *March 19, 1963*

Dear Dos—

Due to the fortuitous arrival of *Esquire* in the mail my work is delayed by necessary research into the character of Dos Passos. I am infuriated by that query—"Which side are you on?"—as if there are sides. Either you're a Catholic or else you are a Pope-hater.*

"Naturally," one should answer, "I am always on the side of whatever is fashionable, aren't we all?"

Otherwise the piece didn't seem as hostile as kindly apologies from old pals. When they want a straight Yes or No, what for God's sake is their *question*? They never ask one that can be answered except by a complete idiot. "Are you with us?" Who is US?—*Esquire*? the [Dan] Wakefield tribe?

I have been driven into ulcers I think from my stouthearted old stomach's behavior these days and resultant crotchets. Seeing Solley for posset tomorrow.

Deadlines and demands and appeasements.

Bunny phoned. Is in town. Asked Murphys' number. "I'm finally going to DO SOMETHING about the Murphys," he stated ominously.

Next Gerald phones for my bufferage in lunch at Snedens Friday with Bunny and Elena.

I am apprehensive.

Bunny scolded me for going to *Esquire* literary picture but I had failed them on an assignment and wanted to patch connection for future.† "I told Morley Callaghan not to go," Bunny said, "because all those people are ones Scott and Hemingway hated."

As if the okay of these dead titans were still important.

As if Hemingway hadn't hated some other characters too.

The photograph was in fact a scream. I told them before I was not in Paris— they said this was the literary scene '20s and '30s. So there I am, rosy and overfed, squeezed between Carl Van Vechten and Glenway Wescott, May Ray, Marcel Duchamp (Gertrude and Alice couldn't make it), and a guard of Cowleys, Josephsons, Slater Brown, Virgil Thomson, Caresse Crosby and Kay Boyle.

I well remember how we used to read aloud each other's poems in Lee Chumley's or was it the Gypsy Tearoom? Old pal Ben Hecht and Rider Haggard didn't show up but I was entertained by the idea of how history can be buggered up by these chance booboos.

I will frank-harris myself into a past I never had.

I see Dwight Macdonald's beard wagging accusingly—"You weren't in that group"—and I will say, "Look at the record, man. The camera doesn't lie."

Love to Lucy and Betty,
Dawn

Esquire had recently published an article on Dos Passos, by Dan Wakefield, entitled "Which Side Are You On?" Dos Passos had renounced his earlier radicalism and was now a conservative.
†Powell had agreed to be photographed for a group portrait that ran over two pages in the September 1963 issue of *Esquire*, purporting to show the survivors of the "lost generation."

First royalty statement: owe Viking $604 on $2000 advance! Ah, success! I should have this framed for my jealous friends.

(DOS PASSOS COLLECTION, THE UNIVERSITY OF VIRGINIA)

TO PHYLLIS POWELL COOK

[43 Fifth Avenue]
April 11, 1963

Phyllis—

Yes, I used to have some good times with Dorothy Parker who gets too much credit for witty bitchery and not enough for completely reckless philanthropy—saving many people, really without a thought. (Not me, but many others hanging on to her. As a matter of fact *she* hangs on to *her* rich pals with the same abandon!) Did you get the Ohio Literary Map? The *Ohioana* magazine had a nice review of *Spur* in it. I'm sure getting my nose rubbed in that book—4 years struggling on the novel & now months & months over the show! Everybody I deal with lately is from Ohio—including Ted Peckham (Cleveland) the Escort Service King! Good God! If you don't like whiskey try port with brown sugar in milkshake. Pills take away appetite & keep you depressed. Lay off! love Dawn

(COLLECTION TIM PAGE)

TO PHYLLIS POWELL COOK

43 Fifth Avenue
April 17, 1963

Dearest Phyllis—

I forgot about Auntie May's vinegar but I must say all of her health lore for babies and all was 100 percent modern. It used to shock our other relatives that she advised douches daily—virgin and no—and regular enemas, as well as salt gargles and snuffles and there was always her spray for mouth which really was all sheer cleanliness inside so she was one of the rare cases of no cancer and all her own teeth. Incidentally, I have all mine but they are sort of blue so I can't say it's the beauty part. As for vinegar, my newest gynecologist recommends white vinegar in douches and a friend tells me hers recommends same so it's all back where we came in. A publishing friend has cured himself of Everything (except Homosexuality) with Folk Medicine.

Another thing Auntie May used to believe in was all animal medicines—such as horse liniment for rheumatics, etc. She said Grandpa said Always Take the Medicine a farmer gives his horse and cattle because he's tested that and what he gives his womenfolk is either poison or no good because they can be replaced and a horse costs money. So he had the vet in for them. Our Grandpa. . . .

I notice I am doing the same things I deplored in Joe—doping around half asleep, too blah to get out and looking like hell so I don't see any point in showing myself or getting new clothes even if I could afford them. Margaret De Silver told me to buy myself clothes on her charge and send to her so I got a suit and hat but by that time she was terribly sick in hospital and if the stuff ever was delivered to her apartment the maid doesn't know about it. I am god-dam mad as the hat was lovely. Nothing to wear now or later, probably, but still a pleasure in the store. To thank her, I dedicated this book* to her—a corny, servile sort of thing that all her protégés always do—or the *worst* ones who write the *worst*—but still her daughter-in-law told me she was terribly bucked up to know it. Anyway she saved our lives in the last few years and while I can be ungrateful for myself I can't for my family.

Jojo was home this weekend and said, "What did my father leave me, Mother?"—as if I were holding out on the stocks. He said, "I feel better now that I'm over my sorrow." I have been so afraid he'd have a bad reaction as he loved Joe even when Joe was bawling him out so I was steering a delicate course of having him do and go places Joe never would (and Joe was nervous and testy when he was home). So now he rules the roost, phones people, has baths when he likes, and in general finds himself in Top Spot and knowing that if Joe were alive he wouldn't be having such privileges. This has worked out so he remains sentimental—wants a wall covered with Daddy's pictures (thanks for the snaps) and lights candles for him at the [Ward's] Island's church.

So far Joe has not missed anything he cared about except for a dinner at Charles Norman's (an old poet-biographer friend of ours from the '20s), who always consulted him on his poems and books and was a crime buff like Joe. Charles is now 58 and newly (3rd time) married to a lovely Canadian artist (on *Vogue*) of 25 who looks like Alice in Wonderful and can't get over her luck in catching such a Great Man. (He has told her so and he does write well.) She is a marvelous gourmet cook like all the fashion girls who are eager to show they're homebodies.

Instead of Joe they had a very interesting guy named Thomas McDade, ex-FBI and lawyer who looks like Anthony Eden, about 45, and just was awarded an Edgar by the Mystery Writers of America for his monumental

---

*The Golden Spur.

bibliography of all crime literature (real crimes) at $15 a copy. Joe would have liked their talk of unsolved crimes, FBI practices, etc., and ABCs of crime. *Warning to Wives*: Never eat or drink anything from Husband or Lover (a) when he's in financial jam and you've got it, or (b) when his girlfriend has given him an ultimatum. If the body (of the dead woman) is full of bullets or stab wounds, don't waste time looking for prowler or burglar, just arrest the husband or lover. This is a work strictly of love and marriage.

I disagreed about Lizzie Borden and Dr. Sheppard and think they were both innocent. McDade said he was positive Dr. Sam was guilty and proof was in the very book I read about [the case] by Paul Holmes. Holmes, he said, kept referring in interviews to *"We're* working on this angle—," which meant he (Holmes) was simply doing a public-relations whitewash job for the Sheppard family instead of a detached journalistic appraisal of an injustice.

I still disagree.

I agree it's no fun going anyplace without money but New York is better than most because the art shows are so exciting and the ferry is still only five cents. Seems to me I've never been anywhere except Havana with enough money—enough being Too Much. It does color everything. I am still waiting for a large Social Security refund on Joe and Jojo.

I have a sudden thought. I want to go someplace but I really don't want to see people or try to look good. Maybe when my check gets here, I could fly out to your Johnson City for a day or two. No duties to relatives—just a check on that basement wiring and walk around town.

(I doubt this idea strongly!)

I am taking medicine for excessive short wind and incredible weariness. I don't think you ever dare think of any burdens while you're carrying them but you sure get them eventually. I can hardly go someplace for two hours without almost passing out with fatigue and hanging on to a post. So I'm full of fatigue, fat to worsen things.

Will tell you about novel in next installment.

Love also to girls,
Dawn

TO JOHN F. SHERMAN

43 Fifth Avenue
Mon. a.m. July 25 [1963]

Dear Jack:

Take a letter: Never let your relatives See You OFF or you may not be able to go. . . .*

The bus back was the only bargain—going over the dreary wasteland of Queens like a smooth breeze in little more than half an hour. The taxi going out was a bumpy dreary ride—about 50 minutes. Jackie had been very set on meeting you after reading some of your letters for some time and even when I'm tired of her, the mere sight of that radiant blond happy puss of hers is refreshing. She harries her lovers I think by muscling in on their lives and taking over with passionate devotion until they barricade the door of their last corner and their last personal wart and she grieves and goes hunting again like Diana.

She was going to look up my friend Bryan Robertson in London three years ago and by George she moved right in. He wrote me, "She takes off her skates when she goes to bed."

Before further ado here is an errand of absolutely no importance. The review I enclose is by way of the errand. Our very good longtime friend Eugene Jolas, the *transition* editor, died shortly after I was in Paris in '51. His wife, Maria, a large Louisville rich jolly woman who endowed James Joyce and translates and promotes (or did) avant-garde art and *lettres*, lived at 47 rue Jacob last I heard. She usually ate at the Pres au Clerc restaurant, corner of rue Bonaparte and rue Université. Anyway she introduced me to Mme [Nathalie] Sarraute, a pal of hers, so when this book appeared over here I asked to review it. The *Post* book editor found it too precious—I myself found it marvelous and said so, said the translation was superb also, but editor cut out most of fulsome praise. However Maria probably didn't see it (review) so you might put it in envelope with note and my love and ask address of Mme Jolas at Deux Maggots or bookstore next door or near there, and if you see her tell her about Joe, etc., and tell her I miss her.

Have a fattening *gateau* at le Royal St. Germaine for me and if a newspaper called *L'Opera* still appears or even *Arts Quatres* (???) save one for me.

Give my best to the Clarins—Patrice† must be ten or twenty now. Good God—

Have fun,
Dawn

(COLLECTION JOHN F. SHERMAN)

*Sherman had just left on another European jaunt.
†Patrice Clarin was Sherman's godson.

TO JOHN F. SHERMAN

[43 Fifth Avenue]
Sunday, August 11, 1963

Dearcheriest cheri—

I think of you often slaving away over *ouefs* and *oeils* and eek. . . .

The [*Golden Spur*] musical, which was dormant while the producer was abroad and fixing up other shows, now has started up again with me supposed to be rewriting with all sorts of new angles, but my head is pretty empty.

Esquire phoned me to do a piece on James Stewart, flying out to Hollywood and staying on location while he finished his new picture—*Take Her, She's Mine*. I agreed, even was bright enough to insist on more dough. I thought all that luxury expense account around Palm Springs, etc., would bring the roses to my cheeks. However, Stewart finished location ahead of time—piece is now up in air and I am glad because last Tuesday *Life* called me to do a short piece on the Greenwich Village coffeehouse situation (now a scandal but we're always full of scandals, was my angle). It had to be done, they said, in 48 hours. Okay, I said and started to work, clock on my lap. Then the phone rang; it was *Life* photographer. Would I please take cab to Caffe Rienzi to be photographed in several coffeehouses (where I never go, incidentally). This took up a good two hours and I got back to clock and typewriter. Then doorbell rang. *Life* news editor, handsome young Harvard type, wanted to interview me on my book and Village outlook. Another two hours gone. Back to work. Phone rings. *Newsweek* calls. I don't have a minute, I screamed. Not the Village scandal this time. They were doing a cover piece on Mary McCarthy, and wanted to come and ask me questions about her. This killed me. She hates my guts as I reviewed her savagely years ago, so obviously they wanted me to stick my neck out. I refused, saying, "I hardly know her, seldom read her, but understand she is very industrious and has a large and devoted public, good-bye." This will give you idea of my general confusion. Jojo fine. Phyllis says wound healing and Morgan wants her to go down to Tennessee this week with him. Does he want to finish her off? Honestly I get mad at her for being so doormatty, but maybe that's her kick. . . .

love,
Dawn

TO ALLENE TALLMEY*

95 Christopher Street†
October 26, 1963

Dear Mrs. Tallmey:

I was delighted with the way you presented my piece in the magazine. The new title was an inspiration, I thought.‡

Your welcome to this particular story pleased me more than anything in the world. I was well aware that it was not a commercial hope, but I wanted to see how near I could come to catching the creative process right in the act—i.e., the dream itself, before it was deadened by the cookie-cutter into proper, accepted patterns. The technique of communication seems to get as rigid in stories these days as it is in science and psychiatry, and becomes gibberish.

I believe the irrelevances, the broken rhythms of thought, the free associations, establish the communication so much more directly. I was surprised at the number of readers who were impelled to phone or write to me that they were haunted by the piece as if it were *alive*. They seem disappointed when I have no magic new way of saying, "How good of you to say so . . . etc."

Sincerely,
Dawn Powell

(COLLECTION TIM PAGE)

TO PHYLLIS POWELL COOK

[95 Christopher Street]
January 13, 1964

Dearest Phyllis—

[. . .] I remember my first encounter with Mme [Elinor] Glyn. One of Grandma's fly-by-night roomers had left *Three Weeks* in a night flight to skip his bill and of course I had to read it. My greatest education came from reading books left by Grandma's bill-skippers—*Gil Blas, Count of Monte Cristo, Vanity Fair*, etc. Anyway I wasn't over 12 if that and backward because I sneered over the great love story of *Three Weeks*—the lady with green eyes lying on the

---

*Allene Tallmey (1886–1969) was then an editor at *Vogue* magazine, which had printed Powell's "What Are You Doing in My Dreams?" in its October 1963 issue.
†Powell had just broken her lease at 43 Fifth Avenue and moved to an airy penthouse at 95 Christopher Street.
‡This uncommonly moving vignette was something Powell had been mulling over for the better part of a decade, calling it first "Out with the Stiffs" (a title under which it was decidedly unlikely to sell) and later "A Lesson for Runaways."

leopard rug in her tempting chiffons. Ho ho, I cried, that's too silly. But then I got completely baffled because I thought some pages had been lost. True, the hero was on the fur rug too, but I couldn't figure out how the next chapter had a little child in it when there had been no previous mention of the green-eyed heroine's having a child. I couldn't figure out how it got in the book. I could read like a breeze but I sure didn't understand the facts of life or know what the three weeks were all about. I asked everybody, including Grandma, to keep an eye out for some lost pages that would explain how the heroine got a child in the middle of the silly book. I don't think I had the faintest idea of what they were rolling around the rug about, and I was very sarcastic about it. I recall Grandma's giving me a fishy-eye as if I certainly didn't belong in her family to be baffled by that.

I think this odd lingering malaise is petering out. I notice I am better if I force myself out and I get worse lying around napping etc.—I think the mildew from floods has poisoned the place. It's sure boring, isn't it?

The terrace is piled with snow and I feel as if I were lost on a mountain-top with eagles flapping about. The blood-pressure medicine made my pants longer, thank goodness, and antibiotics and iron sent everything into reverse.

Love,
Dawn

(COLLECTION TIM PAGE)

TO PHYLLIS POWELL COOK

[95 Christopher Street]
February 28, 1964

Dear Phyllis—

February 28 is the anniversary of my first lunch alone with Joe in 1920. It was at the Claremont Inn, an old 19th-century inn at 125th Street and Riverside with porches and lawns, and it was freezing winter with river snows. Joe had called up for a reservation, I recall (it was an expensive speakeasy), and said, "This is Mr. Gousha," and the other end said, "Yes *this* is Mr. Gousha," and it turned out the management's name was that utterly improbable one too only he spelled it Goushee. We used to celebrate Feb. 28 up there and Joe would send me a dozen red roses later for years until Claremont and all of us were torn down.

I was fine the day I got out of hospital,* then the no salt and (worse yet) the salt-substitute diet made me sick so I couldn't eat anything. Then I finally got

---

*Powell had just been hospitalized for anemia.

permish to resume light salt—I didn't mind the no sugar and am slowly improving so I swing around the markets—even went out to dinner and have a review to do for *Tribune* by Tuesday and am negotiating a bank loan, arranging to get all stuff out of storage (this requires strength to sort etc.), and will have help in taking Jojo out for ride and dinner tomorrow, thank God, as he's getting mad at me. I must say it isn't fair that he has to stay locked up just because his poor old mother can't get out and doesn't know how to get substitutes even with money.

It's all such a personal kind of chore. . . .

Coby said you called. He has been a godsend, much to my and everyone's surprise, as he never does anything for anybody that is inconvenient, being a thorough bachelor, always making more work than he does. However, maybe age and loneliness have tenderized him, for he calls up to see what he can bring and he does errands (not to conflict with his morning's sleep) and is a good buffer to people who think they will cheer me up by smoking in my face till bedtime. He even washes dishes, and is a willing cook for TV dinners or baked potatoes. My helpful young women friends have a tendency to bring in their boyfriends and this obliges me to either order stuff—for them—and feed them or starve myself.

Will write more later. Will accept Lake Erie's urging to be writer in residence for a week this spring—maybe in May if I feel increasingly better.

Love,
Dawn

(COLLECTION TIM PAGE)

TO PHYLLIS POWELL COOK

[95 Christopher Street]
March 14, 1964

Dear Phyllis—

My friend Jacqueline Miller—now Rice—offered to drive if I rent Volkswagen for weekend so we can get Jojo today and take him for ride and back tomorrow. In end cheaper than taxi and of course entertains him more and easier on me than the frantic hunt for taxis or bus or anything. My only worry is that she and her artist bridegroom will whoop it up in the car tonight after they bring us home and I'll end up responsible. Heigh ho. Hazards of friendship.

Feel well and have only to pull mind in shape for stories promised to *Saturday Evening Post* and *Ladies' Home Journal*—both of which have changed their policy and are more realistic (meaning they want *my* stuff). Keep falling asleep still, however. I am mad at the balances of nature. For instance, I was mighty pleased to lose 14 lbs. in hospital due to liquids' watering (à la blad-der) off and saltless diet but at the time nurses flattered me about my youth-ful (yes) skin and asked me how come? I gave them freely of my beauty secrets but as I have continued to lose weight I now realize that the big beauty secret was simply *Fat*. Suddenly all those there sebaceous glands and fatty cells are dried up and in about a week I look *at least* 60 yrs. old—also skin dried and rough, neck all wattled up, body skin all puckered up. What happened? I ask. I lost my dear fat coverage, that's all, and since I don't have some elegant size 9s to show off, I just sit here and wonder where the tallow went.

I am really fascinated by the aging process, even if the victim is me. Excit-ing things happen to me but it all seems far away and as if it were somebody else (this is, of course, partly due to having no Joe to share the wealth). Some-body told me humans age like trees. I had said one seems to be about 40 for 8 or 10 yrs. and then almost overnight teeth and hair and all age and you are *50* for about 10 yrs., then with a big clank like a rusty chain you're 60 and so on. Anyway, they tell me trees do this too. The ring of the age cycle on the trunk shows up the same way—suddenly. I am telling you this sad story because I recall your wistful complaints about hair and skin during your much-desired weight loss. Maybe losing it for sickness was not clever of us—thin dames don't come out so good either.

Now I will fix the apartment and get in some cider, ginger ale, Coke, cheese, bananas and other Jojo tidbits and take $50 over to the Auto Rental Santa Claus, who will, I trust, refund at least $25 tomorrow. . . .

love,
Dawn (age 80)

(COLLECTION TIM PAGE)

TO PHYLLIS POWELL COOK

[95 Christopher Street
Spring 1964]

[No salutation]

Yes, I had to have Fagin "gathered" by the great Cat Father about two months ago as he hadn't been really conscious for weeks. No smell—no appetite—no life. Cost $10 at vet's for demise. Catholic funeral. The award will not be announced till May, I believe. It is from National Institute of Arts and Letters, of which American Academy of same is a branch. Never can tell difference as members mostly the same. Have assignment from *Saturday Evening Post*. Improving daily.

love,

Dawn

(COLLECTION TIM PAGE)

TO MALCOLM AND MURIEL COWLEY

95 Christopher Street
April 28, 1964

Dear M & M—

Here is a pretty compliment. Coby read your fine letter and mourned, "Why is it all the great letter-writers are women?". . .

I am still unpacking book boxes from storage with no shelves for them. *A Thousand and One Nights* in about 30 pretty volumes (but not Burton or even Liz), the Works of Gerhardt Hauptmann, God forbid, a set of Cabell! of Walter de la Mare! of many Napoleonic biographers and even a sprinkling of Floyd Dell and a Van Wyck Brooks biography of Symonds.

43 Fifth Avenue is suing me for $1055 all of a sudden, the bastards, for breaking lease, they claim, and a creepy underling in Phil Wittenberg's office, instead of protecting ME, seems determined to make me pay it. "It is true you have not paid the rent there since May 1963," he keeps saying sternly and insists I *legally* never moved. Why did I think a lawyer could ever help you from crooks?

Now I must find another lawyer to fight my own lawyer, I suppose.

Love,

Dawn

(THE NEWBERRY LIBRARY)

TO JOHN F. SHERMAN

[95 Christopher Street]
Tuesday [July 1964]

Dear Jack—

Just went down for mail and mailed you note and clipping and got your themes and letter. The B annoyed me and is the type of thing that made me hate most professional teachers.* God knows in any English class most of the

---

*Sherman was then finishing up his undergraduate education at Ashland College.

students/lugs are utterly unimaginative. In the L.E.C. [Lake Erie College] classes and other short-story contests I have been judge in the kids were at best completely literal-minded—This Is How My Canoe Upset That Summer Afternoon. Any idiot could tell yours was a completely literary and professional touch with implications of unknown backgrounds.

I was very influenced in the early '20s by coming across art lectures by Robert Henri, a famous artist then.* They were so valuable for writers. He said you should describe (or paint rather) a room or rocking chair or view from a window in such a way—a slight detail here and there (like a fan or spool dropped on the floor)—that the spectator should feel *in* the room and touching these objects and without a human figure in it he should feel the kind of person who would live there or had just walked out. This you have done, though you were doing people, too.

Anyway in my 4th of July rooting through old papers I came across old college diaries and papers that usually nauseate me with their whiny teenage woes but now I am old enough to feel no identity with the Young Jerk, but some interest and even sympathy. For instance I complained in my first few months at college that the English teacher (Miss DeMent, then, a very affected, snotty dame who must have felt she shouldn't give good grades to *poor* students)—anyway *why*, I sniveled, did she always read my themes aloud to the class *con brio* (how about that, kid!) then give me C–, when the rich girls got C+ for some piece they could barely spell out? Fortunately second term put me in a young Boston woman's class (Louise Bray was her name) who thought I was a genius and had me send things to magazines and help her write news of college for all the papers (which was her job).

But a teacher can certainly take it out of you—as you said your French teacher did. I recommend that you start planning a novel as God knows you have every facility and the very rare gifts of observation, memory and wit. Short stories are really harder to sell these days than plays or novels and do not allow as much freedom. I think your own family's roving life or your father as light-hearted Jay is juicy but might be painful to reconstruct. I have enjoyed *making* a life for some type I don't know but am curious about so it is a game and often my guesses turn out to be close to the actual thing.

Anyway a novel is a pleasant thing to have waiting for a few lines every day for a year or less or more. Short stories demand more terrific spurts. . . .

Love,
Dr.? Dawn

(COLLECTION JOHN F. SHERMAN)

*Robert Henri (1865–1929) was an American artist (born Robert Henry Cozad, in Cincinnati) who published his lectures in a volume entitled *The Art Spirit* (1925).

TO WILLIAM AND MARY PETERSON

95 Christopher Street
July 22, 1964

Dear William and Mary—

I received the *Lake Erie Bulletin* yesterday and was flattered to see my story and above all to see the deft job you did on me behind my back.* Everyone who reads it—I leave it casually on the table or their lap—says it sounds exactly true to life (if that's good). Your contribution and the appearance of my story this week in *SatEvePost* gave me a false sense of accomplishment since this weather leaves me in a constant doze or daze. I recovered some spark of life by seeing *Tom Jones* this afternoon—a favorite book of mine at one time but I must say I don't know what I was reading or not understanding or skipping at the time as the film story was full of surprises, like so many childhood favorites reread from hoary age.

I was startled to learn that the artist's wife who knew the Village was Marjorie and Nat Howard's child. I remember they were an extremely bohemian couple for the times and Eleanor Farnham used to flaunt them enthusiastically as Cleveland's answer to Greenwich Village. Nat later married Eleanor's business partner Edith Moriarty as you probably know.

I ran into Max Eastman at our mutual bank and told him of you and the McGroths, and his old lecherous eyes glittered—"Ah, you should have seen Vera in the old days! I have a picture of her you must see—with her masses of dark hair, great blue eyes and of course she was very bohemian then," he sighed. "She's gotten much more prim, I'm afraid, but still handsome."

He remembered you two pleasantly (never had his chance with Mary, I guess) and said his wife was well enough to go up to the Vineyard now, after her operation. He kissed me tenderly in front of the second teller and we took our money and parted.

Dos Passos took me to the World's Fair which is very tawdry and tiresome but he has more energy than other people. The same day he was flying out to the Cow Palace to cover the dreary events for *National Review*! What *happens* to people! I wonder if this excessive conservatism is due to his having been illegitimate.

I had a very nice letter from President [Paul] Weaver. The whole Lake Erie Experience was a valuable one for me and I cannot thank you and Mary enough for taking charge of me. I treasure the twilight or night glimpse of the lake and the tower—which your father loved to paint.

---

*Powell had just received an honorary doctorate from Lake Erie College.

Best to all my friends,
Dawn Powell

P.S. What a scary [presidential] campaign we have ahead of us!

(COLLECTION WILLIAM AND MARY PETERSON)

TO GERALD AND SARA MURPHY

[Boonville, New York
Summer 1964]

Dearest Gerald and Sara—

Up here for peaceful weekend with Edmund Wilson. Much fond talk of you and bafflement over movable feasts and Dos's ecstasies over Goldwater in *National Review.* ("Too girlish for words," said E.W.) Think of you always but hate to wake up naps with phone calls.

Love,
Dawn

(COLLECTION HONORIA MUPRHY DONNELLY)

TO GERALD AND SARA MURPHY

95 Christopher Street
September 23, 1964

Dearest Gerald and Sara,

I heard from Dr. Solley that you were "more comfortable" and ripping about some.* What I love about Dr. Solley is that he does believe we should be "more comfortable" instead of forever trying to *discipline* our interiors with sword and barium and weapons worse than the ail. He saved me again from some swordplay—I hope—and life perks up in the sullen old bones. (*Yes,* I do have bones after losing 35 pounds of suet.) . . .

Dawn

(COLLECTION HONORIA MURPHY DONNELLY)

---

*Gerald Murphy was suffering from cancer and would die within a month; Powell herself had just been informed that she was likely mortally ill.

TO PHYLLIS POWELL COOK

[95 Christopher Street]
December 11, 1964

Dearest Phyllis—

I am down to 130 and for the first time in my life have *collarbones* that stick out. Sleeping all the time and no appetite now at any time though a hot dog at a hot-dog stand tastes good (not at home, though) and so does milk and ice cream and good soup. I've been invited out this week several times and I notice I can enjoy Long Island scallops and other restaurant dishes so maybe I am merely nauseated by my own food and my own company.

Today I am lunching with Lee Adams and Charles Strouse (the *Bye Bye Birdie* team that your daughter knew), who want to go back to doing *Golden Spur*. I am so tired and blah and brainwashed these days that I really don't think I'm up to it. I might be if I had a seashore vacation away from myself and the pals who go over the same ruts.

I would like to get a let-out muskrat fur coat but don't think I should waste money on my withering carcass. My stomach bubbles and squeaks but does not say "Mama" yet so I can't get it patented.

Producer sent me tickets for *Golden Boy* musical but I could hardly find anyone interested to go as Sammy Davis, colored Jew nightclub entertainer, repels me. However got Monroe Stearns to go and the luxury of sixth-row aisle seats free at a hit show mellowed us and it really is a terrific theatrical sort of show—a real prizefight—marvelous sets and Strouse and Adams music songs very operatic. Davis, Sammy, is so much like our little black Bobby [Morrison] that I was won over though his voice is very hard and brassy.

It is now 11 a.m.—hope I can stay awake long enough to get dressed and uptown for this big-deal lunch, then back for a four-hour nap before bedtime.

Love,
Dawn

(COLLECTION TIM PAGE)

TO DOROTHY POCOCK CHAPMAN*

95 Christopher Street
January 27, 1965

Dear Tootsie—

I was glad to have word of you at Xmas. It's queer about missing your mother, as you say you do, because I seem to miss her more now than before.

---

*Dorothy Pocock Chapman was Mabel Powell Pocock's elder daughter. Her siblings were Keith Pocock and Dawn Pocock Jarvis, both mentioned in this letter.

Phyllis's family and life in Canton, which I visited for a week last summer, are quite different and less like my own as they all seem more interested in antiques and possessions than in *people*—as Mabel always was. Carol [Warstler] and Phyllis [Poccia] and Alice [Hoover] are wonderful girls and very lucky in their homes and families. I had a good evening at Dawnie [Jarvis]'s, who seems to be the real artist of the family, with a genuine creative gift. She looked fine and gave me a beautiful half-shawl she'd made. I don't think she should try anymore for her driver's license because if her eyes have fouled her up so much thus far, don't see how she can drive with confidence. God knows I wouldn't know which end of the car to drive myself.

Jojo got your Xmas card. He is really very good now—lost his jitters due to drugs and in spite of my fear that he would flip when his father died he reacted differently and became very proud of responsibility and being head of the house. I have a number of young friends (my contemporaries are mostly dead or else fall asleep while they're talking) and they take Jojo on auto trips and in many ways make his life more interesting. He could come out of the hospital and live at home but I can't trust him alone, outside or in, as he's absentminded and still has a strange look sometimes in his eyes which makes people think he's about to rape or run or both. Thank God he's undersexed! We play Scrabble, go to restaurants, and in driving in the country he usually astounds the driver by telling him what roads to take, what exits to take, how to connect with another road or town. Very strange gift and all from his passion for studying maps and following all traffic news in the paper. If he had brothers and sisters around it would be simpler. We do have money enough now—as an old friend died and left enough in trust for us to live nicely if he could get out, but it's a problem. He wants another country place but I can't handle it and him and make out with my writing.

What I miss most about your mother is her sudden bursts of silent laughter and her deep curiosity about everybody and enjoyment of things. I miss Cleveland, too, don't you? I am baffled by hearing that Keith [Pocock] is a nightclub pianist and wonder about little Denny and Helen. Sometimes I think your mother could not have endured the extreme problems of Keith. At least I can put Jojo in a place where *they* can handle it.

Right now I am doing a piece for *Esquire* on Staten Island (Jojo answered all research questions from me as to when the trolleys stopped there, where such and such a lake was, etc.—in fact, he is a walking encyclopedia, knows all the words of all the songs, what year they came out, etc.—such a pity to have it wasted). His address is Manhattan State Hospital, Ward's Island, New York City, Kirby Building 6A. We are supposed to pay $210 a month! But I try to quiet them with less. He comes home twice a month for the weekend. He is very kind and sweet and too childish for ordinary life and too smart for other mental groups, slightly bald now but nice-looking. Little colored Bobby, his pal, is a grandpa now and comes in sometimes. He is an expert research laboratory assistant to a Brooklyn medical unit and is very good company.

I keep promising to get a country place this year where Jojo can "garden," as he says, but I'm afraid to be stuck alone with him and no car in some bosky dell. However, we may get a shore place if I make money enough for a caretaker and maybe you and a selection of your family could come east again. We have a very pleasant apartment with terraces overlooking all New York and the river and Greenwich Village but it's only two rooms and kitchen. . . .

I had anemia and lost 35 pounds I couldn't lose any other way but I hate wizening up.

Love to all of you,
Aunt Dawn

(COLLECTION TIM PAGE)

TO JOHN F. SHERMAN

[95 Christopher Street]
Tuesday, May 4, 1965

Dear Jack—

I don't see how you managed all the teaching and then having to skimp on your own courses.

I am on my new hot sunny terrace wondering how to fix it up as I wonder how to do all simple domestic things now. I think the only way I ever managed them was because Joe was so astonished and appreciative that I had to show off that I could grow grass or paint a chair. Applause! That's what we have to have!

Jackie finally had her baby on Sunday—a girl, only six lbs., five oz., although she had grown enormous during pregnancy so I fear all the fat is on her and will have to be dieted off unless she turns into Mary Grand, the Amazon Queen. I haven't seen baby yet though it's supposed to be named Dawn (a poor name to go with Rice, I have told her).* The baby was due March 22 and Jackie's chic, nasty little stupid mother kept bawling her out for "goofing" and *never* doing anything right, until Jackie stopped answering the phone.

I have a suggestion here, also an invitation. Why not come to N.Y.—maybe with Rita—and be my guests on Jojo's trust fund and go to World's Fair which looks good this year and Coney Island (the aquarium with pink whales is

---

*The baby was named Hilary Dawn Rice. Despite her protestations, Powell was delighted by the tribute.

lovely). I have this Hi-riser in the living room though I can't make the bottom thing come out but maybe you could and this neighborhood is full of jolly places—a fairy's restaurant with $1.45 blue plate, dozens of jolly antique stores, cafés, etc., providing you keep off lower Bleecker Street which is too hot and beatniky.

You can rent cars for as little as $25 a week with free parking from certain companies—all a better deal than trying to park your own, they tell me. I would buy this with my fortune. A good cheap gay (queer really) restaurant is downstairs with a sidewalk café—Aldo's. I took a pal last night—two drinks, carafe of wine, shrimps, roast pork, salad and dessert and coffee for two only $7.80 minus tip, and always a chance of making friends with some well-dressed fags or lesbians, though they are not obvious or noisy about it.

Anyway you could mind your own business—get your own breakfast, I mean—or wander profitably or drive to shore. Hannah [Green] parks free nearby (but with her battered car she has little to lose) on West Street and could show you the deal if you liked. Taxis are almost impossible now but crosstown bus (9th Street) stops at our door every ten minutes and shoots you over to Fifth Avenue for buses uptown. I might even go away for a day or two and leave you in charge of my grapefruit plant.

Everything else dries up in the sooty high altitude. It is cool by night and breezy always. It is possible you may find your hostess in the bathroom 25 hours a day as I cannot seem to straighten out my intestines to make it safe two minutes from the *pot de chambre*, but that is an old family hazard.

I sleep late if not always. Lately I have been accepting all sorts of night invitations and enjoying new people. Remember an actress [named] Anna Sten? She was at a young Russian composer's (Horak) the other night with just six other people—all young and either musical or stage, and I find them more amusing than painters or writers. I may even rent a beach house for our pleasure. Who knows? Maybe A.L. would like to travel and pick up a spade at one of our neighborhood dives. All the girls seem hot for coons but really! Must we?

Jojo is fine. Little Bobby comes to see him and takes him out and we may con Hannah into getting us to World's Fair next Sunday. . . .

Love,

Dawn

[95 Christopher Street]
May 13, 1965

Dear Jack—

I have you on my mind as I Identify, as we say here in Freudian circles, where I spin the top.

One piece of news is that for *four* days I have had an *appetite* (I had finally dried up to 121 lbs. from 165! Only last February I was bloated up forever, I thought). Anyway, I realized I have been plain sick, not just aging, because now I get up, eat, am glad of instead of worn out by social contacts, like new people instead of dreading the effort, and can almost write at my novel.* However it appeals to me today to show my recovery by giving out some free advice to far-off cousins.

A. Get started on novel before you get scared of it. You have all sorts of clues to your cast in your brief character sketches for class. And remember— one advantage of the rough life you had is that it is so damn much more inter-esting and literary than the Dull Happy Childhoods of Well-Brought-Up Squares.

B. Get away (I recommend N.Y.), if only for a few days, when all the inde-cisions you are tangled in will suddenly fall into focus and you can see your setup (back and ahead). *Not* what is convenient or practical or easy without too much change—but what you *dream* of and what you would envy in other people. For instance I envy myself many times and wonder how I kept out of the Happy-in-Falling-into-Step traps. Somebody up there usually kicks me out of them, thank God, but *you* never get kicked out and have to kick yourself out as you have (except when Uncle Sam gave you the first kick).

I know you plan and want to teach but do you still now that you've been stuck with these bright little faces turning blanker with each lesson? How about J. Sherman the caustic yet sentimental observer and personal expresser? Start the novel (or play) and have it on the fireless cooker when you take on the teaching job or the new graduate study. For Xist's sake don't take any teaching courses, which, as you know, keep you from learning anything yourself. The best teachers anyway don't follow methods but are richly informed and widely interested and interesting themselves—the difference between a doctor and a mere druggist who spoons out the advised doses.

How about teaching at Lake Erie? (I wouldn't but then I loathe the idea of teaching unless it would be to avid eager learners like yourself who, as you know, never happen.)

What it boils down to—is—I am wasting this a.m. making up homemade

---

*Powell was then working on the never to be completed *Summer Rose*.

homilies to keep from getting to work on this novel which I confer about in a day or two. Anyway—go away from everybody and everything for a few days or a moon and don't think. Wait for that frozen inspiration in your deep freeze to pop up (mixed metaphors are *good* for you) all ready to go. You are an unusual and creative man and by God I *know*—so don't weaken through sheer fatigue and tired blood, and don't let unworthy and quite ordinary little students or causes or duties gnaw away your extraordinariness. Better waste it, honest to God—as Uncle Jay did—than cower in a synthetic bomb shelter.

Say! How about the Metaphor Mix today! Never in better confusion!

The Hotel Earle here (on Washington Square) is only $7 a day—in case you think People Would Talk if you stayed in this seraglio with the Rose of Washington Square. Then you would Get Away—you see—from IT ALL but would get an earful of fertilizer from Auntie Dawn round the clock.

Jackie's beautiful little wild Irish rose of a baby with red gold hair is named Hilary Dawn.

Jackie's maiden name is Miller and I suggested adding *Miller*—viz.:

> *Hilary Millery Dawn*
> *The Rices sing hey nonny non*
> *Of sugar and spice*
> *And everything nice*
> *Oh how nice of the Rices to spawn.*

I'd better get back to my freshman novel course now before the mind totters.

Dawn

(COLLECTION JOHN F. SHERMAN)

TO JOHN DOS PASSOS

[95 Christopher Street]
June 16, 1965

Can't see how I missed you as seems to me I have been cowering in my bathroom for months felled with my stomach. However, as of four days ago when Solley doubled my opium dosage, I think I am utterly well and able to face Portia or life (but hardly my novel!). Outside of that everything has been extraordinarily splendid. Sara phoned me she needed my company Sunday and I went up. She looked as dear and pure as ever but I came out in a sweat. . . .

I spent most of the visit trying to tell her that a California friend told me Jinny [Virginia Pfeiffer] had bought a chateau or ranch on a lake in Mexico, where she now lives with her two adopted children, not far from her old friend Laura, the Italian girl who married Aldous Huxley. Next thing I knew Sara had chuckles thinking how strange for Jinny to marry Elvis Presley!

Not Elvis Presley, I cried out again and again—*Aldous Huxley*—and it was her friend Laura, the one Sara never liked, remember? No, Sara never met any of Jinny's friends. In fact they never knew what became of Jinny. They heard she had gone west to live but she had gotten very strange and was adopting children all the time. Had I heard that she had married Elvis Presley?

Sara then switched to Dr. Solley, who was so *expensive* she never went there and he never called (he has called several times). She thought I must stick to the sugar diet he recommended (where this idea came from, I'll never know!) and insisted on giving me a box of sugar cookies to do what the doctor said. She stayed on a few tracks very sweetly but really it wasn't any worse than it used to be, only Gerald always kidded her back to the fact. When I left she asked me if I ever heard anything of Jinny Pfeiffer and I said No!

She still loves old friends (you) dearly and her forgetfulness does not extend to old grudges, even though they were long ago proved ill founded. I wonder—medically speaking, Dr. Passos—if a person could be cured of this memory shortage by being cued into old animosities, artful queries: "What was that nasty crack Edith Wharton made to you?—What was it that Gladys Saltonstall did to you that time in St. Cloud?" A complete record comes out, alas and alack. How come?

I have a lovely baby named for me—do you recall that lovely blond Oregon girl, Jacqueline, that Pete Martin kicked around for a while? She married a very nice artist named Dan Rice and they just had a baby named Hilary Dawn. I am startled to see this beautiful little golden-haired "Dawnie" which *I* never was.

Jojo is fine and his old little colored pal (Louise's charge) calls on him often.*

I am sick of Civil Rights and well-heeled "underprivileged" types scream- ing for justice when writers are the worst-privileged and [most] underpaid and oppressed of any race.

Read a good book! *Square's Progress* by Wilfrid Sheed, whoever he is. Never see any De Silvers.

> Love to Lucy and Betty,
> Dawn

(DOS PASSOS COLLECTION, THE UNIVERSITY OF VIRGINIA)

---

*Bobby Morrison, whom Louise Lee had raised from childhood, would be at Powell's deathbed that fall.

TO JACQUELINE MILLER RICE

[95 Christopher Street]
10 a.m.
July 4, 1965

Dear Jackie—

I am very fine today and yesterday as result of heavy Luddy yeasting which I like in lemonade. You are quite right about its amazing cheer-up effects. . . .

I ponder on your visit yonder. (Rhyme.) My first visit with baby to country was a nightmare. Slightly cuckoo guy in Joe's office *(Independent Weekly)* had house in Northport and had great idea that while his wife and *their* baby were visiting *her* relatives, Joe and new baby and I should drive out with him for weekend, Jojo's being about six months old and on formula. Turned out wife had left house in a monstrous mess the week before—congealed potties all over, congealed dirty dishes in sinks, unmade beds, sweepings in corners, soured icebox—hellish difficulty for me to sterilize for making formula—and the two gents taking off for downtown leaving me with baby and no milk or any way of getting any for baby, finally wheeling baby—both of us sobbing—for miles downtown to look for Joe and our charming host. Beds were mildewed, I recall, too. Ah, there, happy country outing! . . .

Love to Dan—I do miss you all, especially Dawnie,
Dawn or rather Big Hilary

(COLLECTION JACQUELINE MILLER RICE)

TO JACQUELINE MILLER RICE

[95 Christopher Street]
Thursday
July 8, 1965

Dearest Jackie—

I am getting money for no reason at all—part of the curiosities of life. When for some years I tore open the mail hoping for money *due* me and it never came, now that I don't expect or deserve it, suddenly I get $191.40 from Social Security—in addition to the Widow's Fee and Dependent Child Fee I get as a result of Joe's 40 or so years in harness. If it was for my own earnings—never having paid S.S. but for six months once—I would get about $24 a month, but as a worker's widow and dependent, I'm a millionaire. If I didn't have Margaret's money I probably would have a hell of a time extracting any Social Security at all. Anyway, I queried about the cost of fixing portrait and found it would be at least $100 so I thought I would cheat Dan (being an old pal) of half of it and send him only half. I do not take any pleasure in having work done for free when I am loaded and I'm sure if I were broke, Dan would raise hell till I paid him a whacking sum—if I know the man. Steal from the poor and coddle the rich—the old Rice motto. If you need some for August house advance, let me know as my stomach is in frightful shape and I don't want to conk out with money left to go to Claire so we must work fast. By the time it's gone Dan will be rich and I will demand support.

Rosalind phoned me last night for no reason but to say how wonderful you were (I was astonished at crotchety, belligerent Ros's wild enthusiasm for any new character) and how great and witty Dan was. She confirmed my own conviction that Hilary Dawn is a really remarkable baby—perfectly wonderful, she said—and God knows she's seen a lot of babies and I haven't since I left Ohio.

The pictures were marvelous—ones of Edna especially with H.D.—so I sent them at once to her and I need hardly say that they were back in the mail this a.m. due to my leaving out the name of the town. So I can show them to Madeleine and Peter [Martin], who are coming over tonight. Elliott Hess and pal, Jack Grant, are coming in for delicatessen supper so I thought Elliott's being Harcourt Brace bookstore would be good for Pete's new career. Now I wonder, as both are witty and probably will snarl. However, my stomach retired about an hour ago so I believe I can live through it with Pernod.

Coby finally consented to a housecleaner, which I found in the mail from City Labor Agency—only $1.75 an hour (a man) and after fight with Coby to get soap powder and broom and a sandwich for the man, he did it in part yesterday and then Coby wouldn't let him finish it up and wax floors as it *wasn't necessary*. I could kill him. I gave him $30 and thought it *should* be $100 but it was only $12.50. Coby resented the carfare, too. I did not invite him this eve, as company is chore enough without having to tend my dear old chum.

Jojo was fine over the 4th, happy to watch TV movie of *Yankee Doodle* and we went up to New Yorker to see Groucho and W. C. Fields and the excellent Chinese restaurant across the street, and then to Jack Delaney's next day for lunch, all of which encouraged me about Ipswich* except for the one bathroom and possibilities of owner's sending her own guests back. This town, N.Y., was heavenly quiet over the week. Plants are doing fine in shade of wall.

God, what heaven to have no bellyache this afternoon!

Lloyd Frankenberg has given up *all* doctors now, he says, and is in same testy, nonwork frenzy as I am—just waiting for miracles which occur briefly.

The yeast hopped me up so noticeably that Mr. Gilman demands it now.

---

*Hannah Green had invited Powell and Jojo to visit her at her summer lodgings in Ipswich, Massachusetts.

Thanks, Doc. I have lost a few more pounds and wince as I receive compliments. I give out my rigid diet as a new crash program—four mangoes every two hours, avocado skin and all in tartar sauce for lunch, two pounds of grapes with stems in blender for dinner, with a slice of live eel. Draw four deep breaths twice a week and bend over when you see a dime in the gutter twice.

love,
Dawn

(COLLECTION JACQUELINE MILLER RICE)

TO JACQUELINE MILLER RICE

[95 Christopher Street]
Tuesday, July 13, 1965

Dear Jackie—

[. . .] I am chickening out of Ipswich, largely because of my own stomach and fresh bleeding and the nightmares of struggling through sweltering airports and stations with luggage *plus* Jojo, who might be taken with a spell in a crowd and throw up also on plane. So I just wrote Hannah after another night of personal bleeding and shakes that I will blame it all on her. I will get him out for the last of July and August and we can go to Coney and World's Fair with Bobby [Morrison]'s help and everything will seem easy in comparison based on having the apartment to fall back on. We can go to Aldo's and other spots I can't take him to in ordinary seasons, so I think he will be appeased. I have been in a state of weeps—obviously due to my rigid chin-uppery about the parental responsibility. . . .

I was delighted with S.'s letter which sounded as if the Ayrabs were taking charge of her long-starved nymphomania. Mary G. should try it (Egypt) though she is not the rugged traveler our girl S. is—who can buck fleas and iguanas and native mud in a way I admire but cannot face. In fact, I cringed at dear Margaret's travel fortitude on trips I took with her—always pensions or refined back-street boardinghouses instead of big, vulgar Hotel Commodores (they don't need to be Hiltons for me—just big and luxurious and ungenteel). Joe and I chickened out of a native Havana hotel when we were there with our friend Harry Lissfelt and we took a great suite at the Nacional on the beach and wallowed in American vulgarity. Boy, I can't seem to get enough of it. The hell with native inconveniences and their charm.

I wrote Jack Sherman's sister* for his route as someone (probably Beulah) mislaid it again and I don't know where to write him.

---

*The reference is to Rita Sherman, with whom Jack Sherman lived for more than half a century.

Hannah says she is five miles from ocean and misses the delicious sea breezes of Amagansett—but she has five child bedrooms (one bath) and all sorts of old revolutionary relics.

If the trip back and forth weren't so horrendous (even for me *alone*) it would be fine. Also when I think of the nervous-making of Jojo spillage, breakage, etc., in other people's *friends'* houses—!! No, no—I cawnt. I rally cawnt. Very nice of Hanner to even consider it because she certainly would have to take a large share of the rays.

I am enjoying the basil on Jersey tomatoes. Nasturtiums and other plants growing up in spite of sun. My philodandy on the mantel has really climbed down and around like the beanstalk and seems indestructible. Dan's picture is looking at me—looks like Hilary Dawn. I loved Dan Aaron's* claiming her red hair.

I feel improved having called off Ipswich, I think. I couldn't sleep. Just bought stack of trousers for Jojo too.

Elliott Hess and pal were here and took off for Virgin Islands. Irving Drutman and M. off to London. There are no fairies at my bottom anymore, Mavourneen.

Miss you. Hope Dan is swimming and painting. Madeleine [Martin] peeved at Tommy [Wanning] who characteristically wouldn't let her come in to see if she'd left her glasses at 26 Jones. "Not here," he said, and banged door. Later, of course, admitted they were there. He is pretty impossible.

love,
Dawn

(COLLECTION JACQUELINE MILLER RICE)

TO JACQUELINE MILLER RICE

[95 Christopher Street
July 1965]

Dear Jackie—

[. . .] This is what happens when you leave New York: (a) Your best friends and worst enemies suddenly get together and when you come back you find *you* are the enemy or the Outsider anyway. (b) The organized creeps are all of a sudden the Good Guys and vice versa.

However, there is a certain point like the International Date Line that if you stay away just 48 more hours, everything has shuffled back to the original position and boy, are you appreciated then beyond all reason!

---

*Daniel Aaron (born 1913), who was then close to Jackie Rice, is an American critic and historian probably best known for his book *Writers on the Left*.

Don't be surprised to find me going steady with Joan Ward (no, I guess not! And Nancy has stopped calling me). Madeleine, my new chum, is cooling her Christian devotion to Nancy and says, "I like Nancy but I *wish* she wouldn't sound like a little goat bleating over the phone all the time. But I *do* like her."

The Martins came over, as I told you, one night with Elliott Hess and pal [Jack Grant] and that was fine. Then the other night they came over alone and we went to Aldo's where suddenly Pete switched to Dr. Hyde or the other one and shouted to M., "I hate that bitch there. If you lift that fluty voice again that I hate so much I won't be responsible—shut up, you bitch." I need hardly say that Madeleine had said nothing but agreements, so tears filled her eyes and he shrieked, "Ah yes, now we have tears—cry—go ahead—bitch—just don't let me hear that voice."

I said, "Pete, shut up," and he did. Ten minutes later upstairs here she kissed him tenderly and he said, "This is a *good* marriage, Dawn—don't you think?" I reported the attack to Coby, who was engrossed in [Hubert Selby, Jr.'s] *Last Exit to Brooklyn*, and he said, "Peter sounds like those horrible guys—how'd he get that way?" Who knows? All was calm by 12:30 except every time they started to leave Pete would retire to the bathroom and when he got out ready to go (I was ready for bed myself) Madeleine was rattling dishes in the kitchen until finally I screamed, "Madeleine, *please* leave things alone," and *I* turned into *Last Exit* for she whispered, "But can't I *do* something for you— just scour these pans? I want to *help*"—and I could only gasp, "Please just *go*!" I can't really stay up so late, though in general we were having a fine time. . . .

Today I feel as if I will live, due to doubling my opium, maybe.

Oh yes, [Morris] Philipson,* my editor, phoned and as usual I braced myself with alibis about what I had done. . . . "How is your book going, Irving?" I cried, trying to get him off on his own work. So I praised him some more and he said he was leaving Random House for Basic Books and I said, "But Irving, you're taking me too—" when the hideous thought came that he was *not* named Irving and, what's more, is more paranoiac Jewish-wise than Bob O'Keene— and I could not for the life of me remember the rather classy name, non-Jewish. *Murray,* I settled on, and then, "Murray, when will I *see* you then? How can I *manage*, Murray?" So having assisted his paranoia by Irvinging the hell out of him—at least I didn't call him Izzy or Moe—I have been utterly unable to think of his real name or any excuse for calling him Irving. "Your voice always reminds me of Irving Drutman's." "I know Basic Books is run by Irving Kristol." No, I've done it, I fear, and back he goes to the analyst. Or should *I*?

---

*The novelist and editor Morris Philipson [born 1926] was then working with Powell at Random House, which had contracted for her next book.

(P.S. Name is really Morris, it seems.)

As he has not seen a line of my opus there is no great damage and (don't let this get to [Jason] Epstein or the publishing crowd on Cape) I was beginning to worry that he would find hidden insults in my characters and I would have to keep appeasing him, much as I like and respect him. Do you want my Respect, Mrs. Rice?

My kitchen terrace just escaped a flood again yesterday in our first storm when birds' nests, etc., cluttered the drain and I accidentally looked out and I saw a foot of water piling up so I waded away and plumbed in my efficient way.

Rosalind called from Boston and wants to drive me down [to Cape Cod] from there. She has the [Eben] Givenses' garage due to big family at Bunny's. She thought I'd be happier at Holiday House (more convenient for her, I suppose) but I explained I had no desire to crouch in a room on the highway waiting for meals I can't eat and I wanted to tell you, too: please don't take me to people's houses as I propose to lounge around breathing sea urchins and look after Dawnie and Dawnie* while you cruise around. Maybe a date or two with an old buddy alone on a range and sleep but while you and Dan roam the discotheques I will share my opium with Baby and write my Congressman. I can't eat or drink to speak of and will go to bed when you have the P.T.A. in for a rumble.

Coby is in a shook-up enough state to decide to go on the wagon for a while, as he's quite nerve-racking now.

I am rather looking forward to Jojo's being home, as I feel so much better today, and we can go to Gilbert & Sullivan matinee and other air-conditioned city pleasures to keep me from tackling expeditions. Coney isn't bad, either. . . .

This is Walter Kronkite signing off till doomsday.

love,
Dawn

(COLLECTION JACQUELINE MILLER RICE)

TO HOLLY HOOVER†

[95 Christopher Street
July 1965]

Dear Holly—

I am so sorry to hear about Chessie. I hope she has just eloped and will come back. My old cat Fagin disappeared one day and I hunted the streets and

---

*I.e., the baby Hilary Dawn Rice and Powell herself.
†Holly Hoover, Powell's young grandniece, had lost her pet cat, Chessie, and written to her Aunt Dawn about the disappearance. Powell took a touching interest in the fate of the cat, which never returned.

every nook in the apartment and after three days I called the SPCA for help and just then the crazy cat sat up in the middle of the floor like magic.

Love,
Aunt Dawn

(COLLECTION HOLLY HOOVER)

TO HOLLY HOOVER

[95 Christopher Street
July 1965]

I am the Magic Cat Chessie and my pet Holly Hoover has run away from me. Bad girl! Yow! I must find her before she does mischief.

Dear Holly:

Yes, I love dolls and horses, too. I think horses are the dearest animals, especially the colts with their wobbly legs leaning on their mothers. Have you ever seen a horse race? It is very thrilling. I got a prize for horsemanship once at Camp Caho in Michigan* but I've never ridden since. It is the most pleasure in the world and I hope you can do it.

Love,
Aunt Dawn

(COLLECTION HOLLY HOOVER)

TO JOHN F. SHERMAN†

[95 Christopher Street]
July 17, 1965

Dear Jack—

[. . .] The hospital wants me to pay some $6000 in back bills and I sure wish I had some legal or plain *reasonable* male spokesman but I can't fork out $1000 or $2 again. I shouldn't really complain because they did relieve my mind for a while (for no good cause). Ah, well-a-day. All I really want is my brainpower back as I never had so many demands for my work but I fall asleep and can barely get up. I do feel better if I can down some food—a crab or an egg—

---

*Powell had indeed spent the summer of 1916 as a counselor at this Michigan camp, an interlude documented in some charming photographs.
†Sherman was touring Europe that summer with a favorite nephew, Paul Stover (born 1952), who later became a minister.

but I continue to dry up. "How wonderful you look," people cry. It *is* rather comforting to put on a dress that needs no alteration and gives me a startling good figure which I never had in my youth. One thing about your and my family—we never whimper over the joys of lost youth, do we? Just an occasional prayer that we don't have to go through carefree youth again!

[Adlai] Stevenson's death has been like the opening of Pandora's box, what with everyone's popping out with what he *really* thought of Lyndon [Johnson] and what Lyndon *really* said about that "S.O.B. Kennedy" and it is really funny how that suave, discreet, diplomatic gentleman of all people should have unleashed this holocaust of private dislikes. I enjoyed one crack quoted of his—that since his followers were all called eggheads he was afraid when he lost that everyone would say the yolk was on him. He was the only person who ever got me to contribute $25 to his campaign—and let that be a lesson.

My malaise does permit me to be social around 5 or 6 when the few remaining pals in town come in and drink or eat my simple buffet—paper plates and all. I have no contemporaries anymore—Coby Gilman only—and he is very helpful in companionship but now at 70 has a tendency to be roaring drunk on just two snorts and I have to worry whether he can wobble home. Jackie and baby are on Cape Cod at Wellfleet—and that air is so divinely invigorating and so many old friends are there that I may go there alone (don't tell Jojo) for a few days. I adore the baby Hilary Dawn which surprises me as I am not a baby fancier.

I get Jojo next Friday—July 28, I guess—for a week at home and that will be easier, even though no Hannah or Jackie will be on hand to help entertain. He loves movies now and we can do them. Our old friend Peter Martin—age 40, very brilliant, erratic, bastard son of Carlo Tresca and stepson of M. De Silver—is now married again to a rich Doubleday girl (a girlfriend of Jackie's) and I see them a lot. He started the paperback bookstore gimmick years ago with his City Lights bookstore in San Francisco. His aunt was Elizabeth Gurley Flynn, the Communist chief who died lately—a big jolly woman. Now he is starting a motion-picture and drama bookstore connected with the New Yorker theater—a revival house in my old neighborhood at 88th and Broadway. Jojo and I often go there to see old W. C. Fields and Marx Brothers reruns. He and wife came in last night and we got very excited at the project. He has been messed up in those horrible men's sex mags for some time and I thought he was done for so far as his talent was concerned. He was a pet of mine until he started lousing up a lot of girls I liked and taking to marijuana, etc., as God knows they all seem to do now. I just can't dig that craze!

Glad Paul [Stover] shares our love of London. I guess I told you we have a Liverpool super and now a new English assistant who, when he fixed my window, said, "No, I'm not from Liverpool. I'm from Lancastershire. I have me bit of pride."

Little Holly's cat Chessie is gone—lost or stolen—and she writes me sad notes. If you go to Beirut look up the Stuart Colies at the University of Lebanon—also a wild friend, S——— (her husband recently died and she has been having a ball in Egypt where everyone is lovable and wonderful, she says). Anyway, she is a crack photographer (or a crack anyway) and will be at the St. George Hotel, Beirut, after July 28 if you walk around the waves. I wrote you at Vienna.

Love,
Dawn

(COLLECTION JOHN F. SHERMAN)

TO EDMUND WILSON

95 Christopher Street
July 20, 1965

Dear (*cher*) Raoul—

This is a wonderful pen with cartridges which I found in Canton, Ohio—and then, like all my Ohio discoveries, there it is in the corner store here all the time. . . .

Coby was hopped up over your Pushkin review but I had an allergy to the *New York Review* due to the constipated in-ness of that in-group, so missed it till today and am very happy. It is the best thing you've done since *Anthony Adverse*—absolutely wonderful, and I am now ready to accept the *New York Review* just for that. You explain [Vladimir] Nabokov—whom I met at your house and at Epsteins' and found personally charming but get wildly irritated over his work. His book on Gogol—my earliest literary idol—infuriated me and I threw it across the room after he had wallowed in the grisly ugliness of poor Gogol and jumped up and down over him, then patted him to show Daddy alone loved him. *Pnin* I liked better than *Sebastian* [*Knight*] but, in all, the author seemed motivated by a compulsion to denigrate his heroes and thus strut his own superiority, which he may not have been able to demonstrate in life so must construct these puppets to mortify and humiliate. I disliked his dowdy translations, too—at least Constance Garnett (or was it Isabel Hapgood?) loved the whole and didn't want to stop the horses and the sleighbells just to lecture that a blur of fir trees shadowing the sky (vaguely) was really four half-grown greenish-brown specimens of Max Schling's Spruce Seedlings No. 542. Who knows what the best translation is, anyway—for the scientific exactness can be way off the true feeling. It turns out that there's never been a decent translation of Dumas or Balzac and who cares? "Words do not bring happiness nor grammar good a poem." (Old Persian saying by Omar the Shish-kebab-maker.)

I have a new pen pal—Brigid Brophy,* who admires my work as I do hers. She sent me a novel—*Two Novels*, I mean, that came out last year. These are really dazzling—the kind of writing ladies tried to do in the '20s after Virginia Woolf but they came out pretentious and hollow. Miss Brophy is a Brain, and extraordinarily rich-minded, so her results are dizzying, I find: excited and difficult and, by God, I will say it!—*rewarding!* A special touch I like in this book is her inscription to me "with homage." Now there's a pretty word and to tell the truth I cannot figure out two writers more poles apart. Is that what we admire? *Figurez-vous!*

I am increasingly anemic and stomach-pestered and don't want to eat or drink or nothin'—so lose a pound or two a day and try to think for about an hour. No hope, really, just sleep, though I rouse for a few hours in late afternoon. Is this the way we go, then?—as it's much the same as Margaret and Joe and very boring to see time wasted. I expect to try a few days on the Cape if I live through next week giving Jojo a vacation. I will merely sleep, I guess, at Jacqueline and Dan Rice's—and go nowhere if it can be arranged. Best to Elena.

love,

Aurore

(YALE COLLECTION OF AMERICAN LITERATURE, BEINECKE RARE BOOK AND MANUSCRIPT LIBRARY, YALE UNIVERSITY)

Part of the following letter is missing, and another section has been deleted.

TO JACQUELINE MILLER RICE

[95 Christopher Street]
Tuesday and all is well
[July 25, 1965]

Dear Jackie:

3rd day out of Ward's and doing okay, Jojo fixed tray of melons and coffee to make me get up—very sweet, though a trail of sugar and powdered coffee on kitchen floor, but he is very anxious to help.

We may go to sightsee town today unless it rains, hooray. Fortunately he is happy and I have started him on his own literary project, a book of interesting facts about N.Y. transportation and traffic noise Compiled by Joseph R. Gousha. World's Fair and swimming are the toughies for me to tackle and the ones he falls back on for demand.

---

*Brigid Brophy (1929–1995) was a witty British author and biographer.

I am enjoying his company, really, if I can get him down to sandwich meals like other moms do instead of four-coursers like he expects. He and Bobby [Morrison] and I had a delicious early supper at Aldo's Sidewalk the other day—I even ate a chop and brought the other home for Junior's lunch. I bought him (how good of me) a handsome summer striped jacket at Lane's for $10—as the other one gets coffee stains oddly enough in five minutes— and a barber shave so he looks very nifty and am sending him out alone for newspapers or ice cream now that the locals have gotten the idea so it seems safe.

I have lost another ten pounds and it shows claw-wise. "You look just like Margaret must have looked just before she died," says my little tot at me as I lie prone in bed. . . .

Tot is now napping so I must too.

love,
Dawn

TO PHYLLIS POWELL COOK

[St. Luke's Hospital
ca. September 28, 1965]

Dearest Phyllis—

This is my best day so far but too cool to sit on porch in the hot weather. . . . Surgeon sticks head in and shakes head sadly saying I look much better but won't I be sorry later? Dr. Solley says much improvement and always chance of recovery medically. Eat and drink anything that appeals to me, he says; if it disagrees, no. Trays of roasted and herb dressing potatoes, lime Jell-O, delicious soups always, ice creams, etc. No "supplementary" food necessary as the regular menu is very hearty, even if I only eat a little of it.

I am so excited today as this is day Jack S. starts in University of Chicago.* Talked to him Sunday. I am overwhelmed with admiration for anyone in fifties able to change their life like that: new place, new regime—what willpower and ambition! He spoke of seeing all of you, loved Alice [Hoover]'s kids (especially Ricky), thought Holly should start in modeling at once as such a beauty, admired Carol [Warstler]'s chic and hair and said you looked better than in ages. . . .

Edmund Wilson is calling this afternoon.

*Jack Sherman had just begun studying for a master's degree at the University of Chicago.

Jackie took Bobby and Jojo on ride with her baby and husband and they stopped for snacks and drinks and Jackie said to Baby, "Hilary Dawn, don't you want a martini?" and Jojo spoke up sternly, "I don't think she should have a martini until she's twenty-one years old!"

Newspaper strike left me without crossword puzzles but then when *Trib* came back yesterday I had forgotten crossword puzzle language such as "ort" for leftover and other words that only occur in crosswords, so I was mad.

Esquire calls up—as I told you, I guess—to say they are getting compliments on my piece* and when will I have another?

Maybe as soon as I get crossword language back. . . .

Wonder how my dolls† are doing. Wish you'd taken all of them for custody—next time do.

love,
Dawn

(COLLECTION TIM PAGE)

TO ALICE HOOVER

St. Luke's Hospital
September 29, 1965

Dear Alice—

Glad you liked *Esquire*—they had many calls about the piece so they keep phoning me to get busy on new one. I was flattered at their Back Page plug about me—page 54, I guess. Can't see how brain can get going again but must try.

Have several charming plants here—one that looks like an alligator with a sort of tiger-lily bud burgeoning in it. A very sweet exchange doctor Liebkind (love child?) comes in to see it as it grows in his native Israel and he advises me about it. I think he wants me to give up the bed to it. Also a pepper plant now full of ripe hot crops, a prayer plant, etc. Cut flowers depress me—they die so fast.

Gained weight but now back where I was and up one day and down next. I am to eat whatever I like—roasts, lots of delicious soups, etc.—no salads, that's all. I ate a lot at first but now it bores me so can't see myself cooking or telling some helper where things are when I don't know myself.

Jack S. is crazy about your family—isn't he amazing taking up a new life at

---

*"Staten Island, I Love You!" appeared in the October 1965 issue of *Esquire*. It was the last work by Powell published during her lifetime.
†Powell had a collection of antique doll heads; she had given several of them to Phyllis.

his ripe age? I'm afraid he may get lonesome but he is so interested in people and new things that maybe not. I certainly don't think a life in Shelby could be any reward, either, but then I can't see anything but New York.

Did not mind your mother-in-law's calling but was surprised at someone's calling a stranger in hospital who might be in last throes for all she knew. However was glad to contact the Canton branch even indirectly.

I am up one day and down next—better than when I came in but might as well start home now and work at cure by Jehovah's Witness methods. Snapped at your poor mother for having her own health problems but find myself whimpering and worse than anybody. Can't get well unless I can get mind away from my own unsatisfactory body.

> Love to kids,
> Aunt Dawn

Expect to go home Friday. Sweater not too big as I have big shoulders.

(COLLECTION TIM PAGE)

TO JOHN F. SHERMAN

> *95 Christopher Street*
> *Thursday, Oct. 7, 1965*

Dear Jack:

I was glad to get the word on the U. of C. debut—especially your democratic encounter with the alien scholar. On the other hand I am still very feeble (running a 102 temperature and very blah in spite of major improvements) so I really get tired out thinking of those stiff required courses and so little *fun* allowed in learning—or is it a crossword-puzzle fun sort of putting things together? I know a good professor can make things exciting and I hope so.

I am a great Chaucerian lover (required course in Anglo-Saxon) in spite of hating the course. But I really love the Greek and Latin poets. I wish I had taken more, though maybe it's the translations that give the zest. Right now I am reading my favorite Petronius in a paperback marvelous translation by one William Arrowsmith—but I am bragging, as I last only about half an hour reading these days.

Wonder how long I can peter out in this blah state. Luckily Hannah Green (a block away) comes in every day to make lunch and market or bank (she is trying to finish a novel) and Jackie comes in for a poached-egg supper or vice versa and other errands. Both are such efficient, willing girls and both always broke so it works out. Coby comes in and drinks sherry and manages to get drunk on a pint of Gallo sherry so I have to get cross. Then several fag pals are so infuriated at not having the use of me that nothing will keep them from phoning every day no matter who tells them it disturbs my sleep and please wait till I'm better to call. No sir, by God, it's their civil right to bug sick friends. I scream when they do get me—*No, no,* I don't want to be visited, I don't want to be cheered or consoled, I don't want anything but doctors and sleep. Either they do not get the message or else they do and are being nasty. . . .

I can't tell you how much I admire your courage in such a lonely undertaking. Do you ever think of how Auntie May would really be baffled that anyone could want to leave Shelby or a job in a Shelby firm? You would never have dared do it, kid. I recall that when I thought of college she hastily spoke to Scott ? about a job in the telephone office for me.

> Good luck—love,
> Dawn

(COLLECTION JOHN F. SHERMAN)

TO PHYLLIS POWELL COOK

> *St. Luke's Hosp.*
> *Morningside Heights*
> *Room 1529*
> *Tues.*
> *[September–October 1965]*

Dearest Phyllis—

Colostomy! Good God! Tumor on rectum and in lower intestine—nothing else to do. I said I couldn't stand another one—all morning tending to it and then no good for anything else anyway. Surgeon said okay—my right. Said wasn't sure he could get it all anyway (so probably a series of operations, eh?). Discussed with Dr. Solley—G.P. who is old friend and knows my life. He is also pal of surgeon. Said frankly he didn't think the relief would be enough to justify the general anguish and convalescence etc. and he would keep me here in this luxurious place where I am coddled and fed, and try to regulate the old diarrhea medically. Meantime meals are wonderful—four courses—and I eat— gained back five lbs. after getting down to 105 and weak as cat. However today surgeon called and wants me to reconsider. Says colostomy easier than diarrhea. Another surgeon—nice guy on staff and friend of friend—calls daily. Says those who turn down operation and say "let nature take course" end up begging for it as they get worse—also starve to death and are nuisances to self and everybody as "nature takes course." So am in quandary. Will stay anyway. Feel better than in weeks, really. Maybe mirage. . . .

P.S. Dear Dr. Solley just came in and reported the surgical report and he said I was better and he had many patients who had turned down the colostomy and lived to laugh at their doctors. Thinks getting more food (as I am) makes opium work better and will go back to old regime and if later problems arise tackle them then. So feel much better. Probably be here at least another week.

Love,
Dawn

(COLLECTION TIM PAGE)

TO JOHN F. SHERMAN

[95 Christopher Street]
Friday, Oct. 22, 1965

Dear Jack:

It was good to talk to Rita the other night. Apples seem to be her chief problem and her little Volks her chief joy. I do not see how she manages that big place all alone although how do we know—maybe she has a Mr. Lahm stashed away there?*

I am sorry that you have not so far found a magic professor who can make hard work seem pleasure—you did at Ashland, I believe. Your Jesuit priest sounds comforting and George, too. Will both of you come home Thanksgiving?

For two days I have felt like living and today even like looking into my work, though I haven't been out and I peter out midafternoon and still repel callers. My longtime old friend, the director Robert Lewis, who always takes me to his openings since our old Group Theatre days, called to take me to the big new Alan Lerner musical *On a Clear Day You Can See Forever*, which will be a big hit for weeks even though the reviews were mixed. Anyway it seemed strange to say I couldn't even dodder to the living room without difficulty—let alone nip out into the gay world.

Bobby (the little colored Bobby) is bringing Jojo home for the day Saturday as he is worried, not being home for six weeks or seeing me. Hannah will drive him back. Another patient cut his hand with a spoon because of some rattling of his cup, I believe, and he has had infected gums but he doesn't complain except when he misses church.

Speaking of our old English novelists, Gerald Murphy got entranced by Richardson's *Pamela* and had it by his bedside for night reading for months. I

---

*Charles Lahm, a Cleveland businessman, had a long romantic friendship with Orpha May Steinbrueck.

got that way about Trollope about ten years ago and I was always crazy about Fielding—especially his plays—terribly witty.

Your clipping re [Robert] Ruark seems okay to me as I got disgusted with the big conceited he-man Hemingway imitator some years ago. I think I know the reviewer—Don Robertson—if it is the Cleveland newspaperman (once) who wrote a Civil War novel which our friend Monroe Stearns groomed into a minor success about ten years ago.

Phyllis seems better and Carol sent me a luxurious nightie and a Christian Science editorial. Doesn't she know I'm a Jehovah's Witness?

My doctor's wife (Dr. Solley) died this week and poor man is out in St. Louis with her family and his nine-year-old son so I am on my own for a while which is logical as there seems nothing anybody can do except recommend a change of laxative or something. Hannah cooks me a good plain supper and Jackie shows up when she can—she cleaned out my closets looking for something I could wear and found one closet full of live moths which she rapidly dispatched. I get Coby to spend the night and he makes breakfast very well now if I can keep him from getting tight by hiding bottles (at night) and I feel better knowing someone can open and shut things.

I admire your guts in the midst of strangers.

love,
Dawn

(COLLECTION JOHN F. SHERMAN)

This is the last known letter written by Dawn Powell, who died in St. Luke's Hospital on November 14, 1965. Jack Sherman, Jacqueline Rice, and Bobby Morrison were all by her bedside at the end.

ACKNOWLEDGMENTS

Two warnings are offered regularly to writers in the midst of biographical research. First, we are told that we will inevitably grow to dislike our subjects, whoever they may be. And we are advised never to publish our work while anybody related to that subject is still alive, for fear of hurt feelings and, in some cases, angry reprisals.

Neither of these warnings, however well intentioned, have proven relevant to my work with Dawn Powell. My fondness for this author—with all of her quirks, mood swings, self-destructive tendencies, and occasional crankiness—has only increased during the eight years I've been studying her life. I continue to find her a winning mixture of stoic and epicurean—a stark, no-nonsense pessimist who managed, against overwhelming odds, to keep both a quick, welling sense of humor and an eager appetite for living.

Moreover, I owe an incalculable debt of gratitude to the members of Powell's extended family, for their honesty, courtesy, and spectacular generosity. Once again, my deepest thanks go to John Franklin Sherman—Powell's beloved cousin Jack. He has supported and encouraged my efforts on Powell's behalf from the day we met, in the midst of a central Ohio snowstorm, almost eight years ago. He has sat for countless interviews, copied hundreds of photographs and letters, and corrected many errors of fact and fancy along the way. Anybody who has come to know and love the work of Dawn Powell in the last few years must pay homage to Jack Sherman, for it was he who provided the legal and familial authority to free the author's estate from its long, strange limbo.

Carol Warstler, Powell's niece, has been wonderfully forthcoming through-out my years of work; the letters Powell wrote to Warstler's mother, Phyllis Powell Cook, permit a unique and touching vantage point on the author's familial relations.

I should also like to thank Rita Sherman, Dwaine Warstler, Robin and Debra Warstler, Wendy Silver, Vicki Johnson, Holly Hoover, Dorothy and John Chapman, Phyllis and Nicholas Poccia, and Richard and Judy McLaughlin, all of whom helped flesh out my picture of the extended Powell family.

The late Joseph Gousha, Jr. ("Jojo") was helpful to me on several occasions. In 1993, at the suggestion of his devoted social worker, Michelle Borsack, he assembled a notebook called "Memories of my Mother," a dazzlingly accurate document that has proven invaluable.

It was my mother, Elizabeth Thaxton Page, who permitted her son a deeply appreciated loan that allowed the Powell papers to be brought to the Rare Book and Manuscript Library of Columbia University, located a hundred yards or so from the hospital where Jojo was born and where Dawn Powell died.

Once again, I am grateful to Peter Skolnik, legal representative of the Powell Estate, for his support throughout this whole adventure. My friends Bruce Brubaker, Hilary Dyson, Paula McDonald, and Hester Furman were resourceful in tracking down hundreds of names and dates in libraries and uni-versity archives.

Special thanks to David Kanzeg of WCPN–FM in Cleveland, who has been a great friend and sounding board, as well as a guide to Cleveland and parts Ohioan; to Daniel Rhodebeck, the Mt. Gilead historian, for tracking down archival material about Powell's family and early life; and to William Peterson, for his diligent tracing of Powell's years at Lake Erie College and his important research on *Jig-Saw*.

Hundreds of other people have contributed to this book, with interviews conducted in person, by phone, or through the mail. I apologize in advance to those whose names have been inadvertently left out and will attempt to repair all omissions in a later edition.

And so I am grateful to Lee Adams, Antoinette Akers, Felipe Alfau, the late Leonard Altman, Commander Tom Antenten of the New York City Department of Correction, David C. Barnett, Christopher Bennett, Gary Bennett, John C. Bellamy III, Avis Berman, Nellie Bly, Carl Brandt, David Brezovec, Rachel Brown, Amanda Byers, Margaret Carson, Lucy Dos Passos Coggin, William Cole, John Gregory Connor, Robert Cowley, Hope Hale Davis, Peter Davis, Anna Lou Kapell Dehavenon, Thomas Dobell, the late Maurice Dolbier, Will Lee Doyle, Susan Elliott, Barbara Emch, Olive Ernst, Allan Evans, the late Eleanor Farnham, Johanna Fiedler, the late G. Christopher Fish, Michael Flynn, Gwendolyn Haverstock Freed, Dorothy Gallagher,

Sylviane Gold, Elise and Arnold Goodman, Sunni Gothard, Christopher Gray, the late Hannah Green, Margaret Geissman Gross, Gladys Haddad, Jim Halbe, Anna Strunsky Hamburger, Janice Harayda, Laura Harris, Carol and Patrick Hemingway, Jeffrey Herman, Robert Hethmon, Polly Holliday, Susan Hood, Sharon Hoskins, Carol Houk, Neill Hughes, Russia Hughes, Ben Janney, Karen Johnson, Marjorie Howard Johnson, Betsy Jolas, Fred Kaplan, the late Frances Keene, the late Murray Kempton, Dr. Ben Kightlinger, Susan Koscis, Allan Kozinn, Hildie Kraus, Miles Krueger, Jeffrey Lawson, H. David Leventhal, Sir Michael Levey, the late Bobby Lewis, Hanna Loewy, Gloria Loomis, the late Loren MacIver, James Magruder, Sally Maier, Susan Mann, Andrew Manshel, Ben McCommon, David McDonald, Heather McGahee, Dawn Mendelsohn, Katharine Meyer, Michael Miller, Marguerite Mills, Donald Mineldi, Thomas Monsell, Michael Moore, Claire Lissfelt Myers, the late Charles and Diana Norman, Patrick O'Connor, Dr. Ellis B. Page, Dr. Richard L. Page, Judith Faye Pett, Morris Philipson, Arturo Pilar, Gabriel Pilar, Robert Pound, Eva Resnikova, Jacqueline Miller Rice, Marcelle Smith Rice, Pamela Rice, Frances Richard, Charles Roberts, Bryan Robertson, Cliff Robertson, Molly J. Robinson, Douglas Rose, Dr. Morton Schwimmer, Michael Sexton, Gene Seymour, Charles and Elizabeth Sigman, Phyllis Singer, Alfred Slote, Jeanne Somers, Anita Sparrock, Julieta Stack, Michael Stearns, Mark Steuve, M. George Stevenson, Roger Straus, Jane Bouche Strong, Charles Strouse, Sandy Stuart, Anthony Tommasini, Cia Toscanini, Amanda Vaill, Gore Vidal, Thomas Vinciguerra, Amei Wallach, Robert Wallsten, the late Andrews Wanning, Esther Wanning, Thomas Wanning, Harriet Ward, Alan Weeks, Maggy Wendel, Patricia Bosworth Wilson, Rosalind Baker Wilson, Pamela Wintle, Robert Wyatt, Frances Wyndham, Anne Yarowsky, and Michael Zubal—all of whom either granted inter-views, answered questions, or helped in some significant way in my research.

I am grateful to the Western Reserve Historical Society, the Harry Ransom Humanities Research Center at the University of Texas, Princeton University Library, the Boston Public Library, the Newberry Library in Chicago, the Beinecke Rare Book and Manuscript Library at Yale University, the University of Virginia Library, and Temple University Library, all of whom made copies of their holdings available to me, and to the staff of the Columbia University Rare Books and Manuscripts Library, particularly Jean Ashton and Bernard Crystal. Privately owned letters came from the collections of John F. Sherman, Honoria Murphy Donnelly, Michael Stearns, Claire Lissfelt Myers, Thomas Monsell, and Holly Hoover.

Thanks to my literary agent, Melanie Jackson, who believed in the Powell revival from the start and fought hard to make it happen. Thanks also to Ray Roberts and Elizabeth Stein, my editors at Henry Holt. I am grateful for my ongoing association with Steerforth Press—particularly Michael Moore, Chip Fleischer, Robin Dutcher, Thomas Powers, Alan Lelchuk, Tim Jones, and Helga Schmidt.

I cannot overstress the debt I owe to Vanessa Weeks Page, for her multiple kindnesses and invaluable support over the last 20 years. Thanks also to my sons William Dean, Robert Leonard, and John Sherman Page, whom I love with all my heart.

Finally, I would like to thank my former colleagues Katharine Graham, Donald Graham, Leonard Downie, Jr., Steve Coll, Robert Kaiser, David Von Drehle, Deborah Heard, Eugene Robinson, John Pancake, Judith Weinraub, Lloyd Grove, Joseph McLellan, Gene Weingarten, Paul Richard, Richard Leiby, Pierre Ruhe, and Peter Hayes at the *Washington Post*. It is widely acknowledged that the *Post* is a great newspaper, but I also found it a remarkably stimulating and companionable place to spend four years.

INDEX

Hotel Belleclaire, New York City, 50

Hotel Brevoort, New York City, 88, 90, 142, 210n, 215

Hotel Excelsior, Haiti, 151, 166

Hotel Irving, New York City, 258n

Hotel Lafayette, New York City, xvii, 210, 212, 215

Hôtel Lutetia, Paris, xvii, 183–84, 185n, 227, 228

Hotel Madison Square, New York City, 228n, 259, 261–63

Hotel Oloffson, Haiti, 150, 167

Hôtel Voltaire, Paris, 184

Houghton Mifflin, xvii, 90n, 107n, 129, 203, 204n, 206n, 211, 218, 218n, 235, 243, 245, 252, 268, 286

    see also Wilson, Rosalind Baker

House Committee on Un-American Activities, 169n

House of Flowers, A (Capote), 219

Howard, Marjorie, 57, 327

Howard, Nathaniel Richardson, 56–57, 327

Hughes, Morgan, 174n

Hughes, Neill, 174n

Hughes, Russia Luca, 174–75

Hughes, William, 174n

Humphries, Belle, 56

Huxley, Aldous, 96, 154, 335

Huxley, Laura Archera, 105n, 335

H. W. Wilson, 272

I Am Looking For a Lady (Powell-Johnson), xiv, 17n

Ibarruri, Dolores, 98n

Ile de France, 174, 176, 177, 181

Importance of Being Ernest, The (Wilde), 15

"Impressions of a First Voter," 40

Independent Poetry Anthology (Cheyney), 195n

Independent Weekly, 336

Ingle, Charles, 240

In Old Kaintuck (Ornitz), 89

Interchurch Center, 42n, 43

Isherwood, Christopher, 306

Ivens, Joris, 98

Jack, Peter Monro, 137n

Janeway, Elizabeth, 288

Janis, Sidney, 274

Jarvis, Dawn (née Pocock), 6n, 53, 329n, 330

J.B. (MacLeish), 264

Jeffers, Marie, 263

Jeffers, Marie (maid), 68, 232, 263

Jeritza, Maria, 51

Jig-Saw (Powell), xvi, 91, 109n, 285

John Constable, Ltd., 91n

Johns Hopkins Hospital, 83

Johnson, Charlotte, xiv, 9, 17, 20, 21, 43, 209

    letters to, xi, 24–26, 29–39

Johnson, Frances, 25, 31, 34, 37

Johnson, Lyndon B., 343

Jojo, *see* Gousha, Joseph Roebuck, Jr. (son)

Jolas, Eugene, xv, 147, 184–85, 189, 191, 192, 193, 195–96, 198, 319

    death of, 207

Jolas, Maria, 185, 189, 190–91, 192, 193, 195–96, 198, 291, 319

    letter to, 207

Josephson, Matthew, 300, 315

Journal-American, 252

Journey Down a Rainbow (Priestley and Hawkes), 243n

Joyce, James, 190, 192, 291, 319

Jules et Jim, 306

Kaufman, Bea, 130

Kaufman, George, 130

Kazan, Elia, 265

Kazin, Alfred, 313

Keats, John, 86n

Keene, Frances, 268, 269

Kelly, Grace, 234

Kennedy, John F., 343

Kessel, Helen, *see* Lissfelt, Helen (née Kessel)